Oakdale/Union Hill Cemetery

Oakdale/Union Hill Cemetery

Salisbury, North Carolina

A History and Study of a Twentieth Century
African American Cemetery

Second Edition

Reginald W. Brown

HERITAGE BOOKS
2008

HERITAGE BOOKS
AN IMPRINT OF HERITAGE BOOKS, INC.

Books, CDs, and more—Worldwide

For our listing of thousands of titles see our website
at
www.HeritageBooks.com

Published 2008 by
HERITAGE BOOKS, INC.
Publishing Division
100 Railroad Ave. #104
Westminster, Maryland 21157

Copyright © 2005, 2008 Reginald W. Brown

This book is a reference for historical and genealogical research of a twentieth century African community located in Salisbury, North Carolina. Please note that there are other cemeteries in Rowan County in need of study. The author of this book is only responsible for information relative to the Oakdale/Union Hill Cemetery and claims no knowledge of any other graveyard.

Registered at the Library of Congress

Brown, Reginald W.
Oakdale/Union Hill Cemetery: A Study of a Twentieth Century
African American Cemetery / Reginald W. Brown
Includes bibliographical references, endnotes, index, and maps

ISBN 0-9777389-0-6   First Edition
ISBN 0-9777389-2-2   Second Edition

All rights reserved. No part of this book may be reproduced or transmitted in any form or by any means, electronic or mechanical, including photocopying, recording or by any information storage and retrieval system without written permission from the author, except for the inclusion of brief quotations in a review.

International Standard Book Numbers
Paperbound: 978-0-7884-4760-0
Clothbound: 978-0-7884-7452-1

In Memory of

My Parents

Dr. Frank Reginald Brown
World War II United States Army Chaplain
Dean Emeritus
Hood Theological Seminary

Mrs. Fletcher Jones Brown, Retired Teacher
Salisbury City Schools
Piano Instructor

And

Mentor
Dr. Louise Marie Rountree, Retired Head Librarian
Livingstone College, Salisbury, North Carolina
Local Historian

OAKDALE/UNION HILL CEMETERY
MAIN ENTRANCE

(35° 40' 32" N 80° 29' 26" W)

OPENED OCTOBER 13, 1903
CLOSED OCTOBER 17, 1995

"But I do not want you to be ignorant, brethren, concerning those who have fallen asleep, lest you sorrow as others who have no hope. For if we believe that Jesus died and rose again, even so God will bring with Him those who sleep in Jesus. "For this we say to you by the word of the Lord, that we who are alive and remain until the coming of the Lord will by no means precede those who are asleep. For the Lord Himself will descend from heaven with a shout, with the voice of an archangel, and with the trumpet of God. And the dead in Christ will rise first. Then we who are alive and remain shall be caught up together with them in the clouds to meet the Lord in the air. And thus we shall always be with the Lord. "Therefore, comfort one another with these words." I Thessalonians 4:13-18

TABLE OF CONTENTS

ILLUSTRATIONS, MAPS, AND PHOTOGRAPHS	viii
PREFACE AND ACKNOWLEDGEMENTS	xi
INTRODUCTION	xiii
NOTES	xv

PART ONE
A HISTORY AND STUDY OF OAKDALE/UNION HILL CEMETERY — 1

PURPOSE OF THE STUDY	1
LOCATION AND BOUNDARIES, PAST AND PRESENT	2
HISTORY OF THE HILL	4
THE FIRST BURIALS	6
BURIALS OUTSIDE OAKDALE / UNION HILL CEMETERY	11
PRESIDENT WILLIAM JOHNSON TRENT	
BISHOP RAYMOND LUTHER JONES	
REV. JOSEPH CHARLES PRICE	
OTHER ROWAN COUNTY BLACK CEMETERIES IN ROWAN	12
OBSCURE BLACK CEMETERIES, LISTED BY TOWNSHIP	
KNOWN BLACK CEMETERIES, LISTED BY TOWNSHIP	
FACING THE RISING SUN	14
FEATURES	
REMEMBER AS YOU PASS ME BY	16
PHYSICAL FEATURES OF THE MARKERS	
OAKDALE/UNION HILL CEMETERY – LIVINGSTONE COLLEGE HISTORIC DISTRICT	19
SOME MONROE AND HORAH STREET RESIDENCES OF THOSE BURIED	
IN THE CEMETERY	20
NOTES	23

PART TWO
BURIALS — 27

LOCATING RECORDS AND BURIALS	28
DECEDENTS AND INVENTORY LIST	29
BURIALS	41

APPENDIX

A CAUSES OF DEATH RECORDED IN AVAILABLE RECORDS	246
B ANNUAL OAKDALE / UNION HILL CEMETERY BURIALS 1905 TO 2005 AND	
OAKDALE / UNION HILL CEMETERY BURIALS 1905 TO 2005 BY DECADE	247
C FUNERAL HOMES ACCOUNTABLE FOR BURIALS AND BURIAL SOCIETIES	248
D MAPS FACING THE RISING SUBCEMETERY SECTION AND SUBSECTION MAPS	249

SOURCES — 260

PART ONE INDEX — 265

HIDDEN NAME INDEX, PART TWO — 267

ERRATA: BURIALS — 287

ILLUSTRATIONS, MAPS, AND PHOTOGRAPHS

Main Entrance		Epigraph

PART ONE

Map 1	Early Landowner Map of Frohock Mill Plantation	2
Map 2	Present Boundaries and Sections of Oakdale/Union Hill Cemetery in Relation to Immediate Area	3
Photograph	Murdock Bridge 2007	
Photograph	Main Entrance	
Illustration	Judge Spruce Macay	4
Photograph	Macay's Mill on Top of Stone Foundation of Frohock's Stone Foundation	
Document	Salisbury and Taylorsville Stock Certificate	5
Photograph	Western North Carolina Railroad Bridge at Grants Creek Crossing in 1903	
Map 3	Union Hill, Oakdale and Burton Sections of Livingston Park in 1907	6
Map 4	Land Sold by Stephen F. Lord to the City of Salisbury for Reburials	7
Map 5	West Monroe Street in 1905	
Map 6	Area of Exhumed Bodies and Photos of Three Churches on North Church Street 1 – Soldiers Memorial A. M. E. Zion Church 2 – Church Street Presbyterian Church 3 – Mount Zion Baptist Church	8
Map 7	First Map of Union Hill Cemetery c. 1920	9
Map 8	Union Hill Cemetery c. 1920, Oakdale Circle Section	
Map 9	Union Hill Cemetery, Oakdale Circle Subsection	10
Photograph	Wiseman Curb, Kelsey Plot 1/Moore Plot 96	
Photograph	C. R. Harris and W. H. Goler Plots	
Photograph	Oak Wood Cemetery	11
Photograph	President William Johnson Trent	
Photograph	Bishop Raymond Luther Jones	
Photograph	Joseph Charles Price and Mausoleum	
Map 10	Rowan County Townships	13
Photograph	Moore's Chapel, A. M. E. Zion Church Livingstone College Historic District	15
Photograph	Monument Types, Materials	17
Map 11	Decedent Homes in the Livingstone College Historic District and Surrounding Residential Area	19
Photographs	Some Monroe and Horah Street Residences of Those Buried in the Cemetery 2 - Johnson & Lash 3 - Duncan 5a- Trott 8 – Ferron 9 – Aggrey 10 –Stevenson & Johnson 13 - Harris 14 – Price 15 - Goler 25 – Jones	20 21

ILLUSTRATIONS, MAPS, AND PHOTOGRAPHS

PART TWO BURIALS

Entrance to Union Hill Section		27
Sample Record: Sadie Davis Fair		28

Photographs of Some of the Deceased

James E. Kwegyir Aggrey	[Courtesy of Raemi Lancaster Evans, Granddaughter]	42
Rose Douglass Aggrey		
Rosebud Douglass Aggrey	[Courtesy of Raemi Lancaster Evans, Niece]	
Joe Ballard	[Courtesy of the Rowan Museum]	47
Arthur Brown Bingham	[Courtesy of Arletta Bingham Verley, Daughter]	50
Henrietta Browne Bingham	[Courtesy of Arletta Bingham Verley, Granddaughter]	
Lillington H. Bingham	[Courtesy of Arletta Bingham Verley, Granddaughter]	51
Lucille Bitting Bingham	[Courtesy of Arletta Bingham Verley, Daughter]	
Mabel Myers Bingham	[Courtesy of Arletta Bingham Verley, Niece]	
William Bentley Crittenden	[Cullings from Zion's Poets Hood Seminary]	80
Ida Hauser Duncan	[Courtesy of Livingstone College, 1964 Price High School Year Book]	90
Julia Belle Duncan	[Courtesy of Livingstone College, 1966 Year Book]	91
Lena Belle Jordan Duncan	[Courtesy of Livingstone College]	
John Bonner Duncan	[Satterwhite Papers- Heritage Hall, Livingstone College]	92
Samuel Edward Duncan	[Courtesy of Livingstone College, 1959 Year Book]	
Rev. James C. Fair	[Courtesy of Avis Fair Wilkins Monroe, Daughter]	98
Sadie Davis Fair	[Courtesy of Avis Fair Wilkins Monroe, Daughter]	
William Harvey Goler	[25th Annual Commencement & Quarter Centennial of Livingstone College. 1910 -Heritage Hall]	111
Emma Unthank Goler	[Courtesy Heritage Hall, Livingstone College]	
Mable Harris Graves	[Courtesy of Livingstone College, 1947 Year Book]	114
Louicio Hamilton Hall	[1949 Pricean Yearbook @ Rowan Public Library]	116
Oliver Cleveland Hall	[1949 Pricean Yearbook @ Rowan Public Library]	
Richard E. Hancock	[Courtesy of R. Darrell Hancock, Grandson]	117
Sarah B. Cook Hancock	[Courtesy of R. Darrell Hancock, Grandson]	
William Henry Hannum	[Courtesy of Livingstone College, 1930 Year Book]	
Cicero Richardson Harris	[25th Annual Commencement & Quarter Centennial]	120
Mariah Elizabeth G. Harris	[Source Heritage Hall, Livingstone College]	
Mary Anna Speas Hauser	[Courtesy of Livingstone College]	123
Elizabeth Duncan Koontz	[Courtesy of Livingstone College]	153
Abna Aggrey Lancaster	[Courtesy of Raemi & Fred Evans, Daughter & Son in law]	154
Spencer W. Lancaster	[1962 Pricean Year Book]	
Edward Moore Sr.	[25th Annual Commencement & Quarter Centennial]	178
Jennie Smallwood Price	[Courtesy of Charles Sherrill, Grandson]	194
Mr. & Mrs. Richard Sherrill	[Courtesy of Charles Sherrill, Son]	

ILLUSTRATIONS, MAPS, AND PHOTOGRAPHS

William Dodge Price	[Courtesy of Charles Sherrill – Nephew]	195
Kathleen Jones. Randall	[Brewer, J. Mason. Some Looks and Some Peeps, private collection of R. W. Brown]	196
Thomas Jefferson Randall	[Brewer, J. Mason. Some Looks and Some Peeps, Private collection of R. W. Brown]	
Victoria Richardson	[Courtesy of Heritage Hall, Livingstone College]	198
Josephine Price Sherrill	[Courtesy of Charles Price Sherrill, Son]	205
Richard W. Sherrill	[Courtesy of Charles Price Sherrill, Son]	
Hattie Douglass Whyte	[Courtesy of Raemi Lancaster Evans, Grand Niece]	234

CEMETERY SECTION - SUBSECTION MAPS   249
    Facing the Rising Sun

    SECTION - SUBSECTION MAP   250

Map G:	HORAH SUBSECTION	251
Map H:	LIVINGSTON SUBSECTION	252
Map I - J:	LYERLY / FAIR SUBSECTIONS	253
Map K:	BURTON SECTION / OAKDALE WESTERN SECTION	254
Map L:	PRESIDENT DUNCAN SUBSECTION	255
Map M:	BRENNER NORTH SUBSECTION	256
Map N:	CIRCLE SUBSECTION	257
Map O:	BINGHAM / DUNCAN SR. SUBSECTION	258
Map P:	BRENNER SOUTH SUBSECTION	259

PREFACE AND ACKNOWLEDGEMENTS

This edition of Oakdale/Union Hill Cemetery grew from the need of prerequisite research for another writing project and the encouragement of friends and local historians interested in Salisbury's African American history. Several primary documents needed for citation and people possessing intimate historical knowledge of Livingstone College, Hood Theological Seminary, and the West Ward of Salisbury, North Carolina are no longer available. Custody of needed information is locked within those who walked among the living, fading memories of an aging community, and storage spaces containing historical treasures destined for the trash.

The cemetery is maintained by the City of Salisbury and documented with clues into the lives of those who contributed to our community. This is a fortuitous circumstance because many African American graveyards are disappearing if they have not already done so. There are community members who still maintain an interest in preserving our past. They showed an interest in my study and provided stories, advice, interviews, clues, access to documents and photographs, cemetery tours, and histories of Salisbury and Rowan County, North Carolina. Their interest, help, and encouragement over a 32 month period was the catalyst and motivator that produced this two part burial reference book for the Oakdale/Union Hill Cemetery.

I express my profound gratitude to those who shared many historical facts and clues about Salisbury and Rowan County while pointing me in the right directions for discovery. I am also grateful for their time, patience, and permissions given to one who has much to learn about the place of his childhood.

Fred and Raemi Evans, friends and local historians, extended the courtesy and granted permission to scan and use images of Abna Aggrey Lancaster, Rosebud Douglass Aggrey, Hattie Douglass Whyte, Spencer W. Lancaster, and James E. K. Aggrey. Gratitude is also extended to Raemi Evans a local historian for her assistance in preparing the first manuscript for editing and for advice concerning community history and protocol.

Charles Price Sherrill, the grandson of Joseph Charles Price, extended the courtesy and granted permission to use the images of Joseph C. Price, Jennie Smallwood Price, William Dodge Price, Josephine Price Sherrill, and Richard Wadsworth Sherrill. He shared many stories of his youth that provided avenues of research.

Phyllis Galloway, PhD Heritage Hall, Livingstone College, and Livingstone College of Salisbury, North Carolina extended the courtesy and granted permission to use scanned photographs of Ida Hauser Duncan, Julia Belle Duncan, Lena Belle Jordan Duncan, John Bonner Duncan, Elizabeth Duncan Koontz, Mary Anna Speas Hauser, William Harvey Goler, Emma Unthank Goler, William Bentley Crittenden, Victoria Richardson, Cicero Richardson Harris, Mable Harris Graves, Mariah Elizabeth G. Harris, William Henry Hannum, and Edward Moore Sr. for the first edition. Livingstone College granted permission to use these photographs for this edition.

Arletta Bingham Massey, MD extended the courtesy and granted permission to scan and use images of Henrietta Browne Bingham, Lillington H. Bingham, Lillian Bingham Evans Simpson, Mabel Myers Bingham, and Arthur Browne Bingham who was her father.

Avis Fair Wilkins Monroe and Vietta Fair Roberts extended the courtesy and granted permission to use scanned images of their parents, James C. Fair and Sadie Davis Fair.

Edith M. Clark History Room, Rowan Public Library, Salisbury, N.C. extended the courtesy and gave permission to reproduce a copy of a stock certificate for the Salisbury Taylorsville Plank Road (Public Domain).

Noble and Kelsey Funeral Home extended the courtesy and granted permission to use digital photographs taken of the lobby portraits of Lula Spaulding Kelsey and William Francis Kelsey and of a sheepskin Kelsey map of the original layout of Union Hill Cemetery.

T. H. Hairston Sr., Allen L. Mitchell, and Rosaline Mitchell provided personal tours of the cemetery and made funeral records of Noble and Kelsey Funeral Home and the Mitchell and Fair Funeral Service available for research.

Mary Jane Fowler, Curator of the Rowan Museum and local historian, obtained the F. McCubbins, Clerk of Superior Court document of Minnie Lord Henderson, Executrix of Stephen F. Lord, Deed Statement of Real Property: All in Rowan County

Betty Dan Spencer, local historian, obtained a copy of the deed that certified the sale of four acres of land sold to the City of Salisbury by Steven F. Lord for the burial of remains removed from the Oakes (Freedman) Cemetery in 1903 to make a right-of-way for Liberty Street in down town Salisbury.

Rowan Museum extended the courtesy and granted permission to use scanned photos of MaCay's Mill on the Frohock Mill foundation, the Murdock Bridge with train crossing Grants Creek, and Joe Ballard.

Rowan County Register of Deeds extended the courtesy and granted access to public records over an extended period of time.

INTRODUCTION

Cemeteries are resting places for those who sleep in Christ until the blast of Gabriel's trumpet awakens them for resurrection, while the living are summoned to join the host of the risen and the living God. Some recognize cemeteries as venues of mourning and remembrance that serve as records for family and historians. Others regard them as places of quiet contemplation, removed from the distractions of city life, and sanctuaries for wildlife displaced from natural habitats. Euro-American cemeteries are generally well landscaped with trees and other forms of vegetation. Some of their markers are elaborate with clever inscriptions in park-like settings that contrast dramatically with most African-American graveyards.

To the casual onlooker, some African-American cemeteries appear neglected, haphazardly maintained and disorganized. These conditions are not the result of poor maintenance or bad planning; they are consistent with traditional Africentric attitudes that regard cemeteries as the domains of the dead where place is more important than "owning" a plot of land. Simplicity is a primary characteristic. Plantings, when utilized to mark or honor graves, are native and serve as living memorials that merge Christian religion with the African belief that trees live after death and death is not the end. Formal landscaping is an intrusion that disturbs the dead and violates strongly held traditional African beliefs that forbid grave desecration. African-American cemeteries do not romanticize death. Solitude for the dead supersedes tranquility for the living. Often, gravestones, monuments and indicators of people's former stations in community life were never erected or disappeared over time. God knows their names regardless of missing markers and records, the fading memories of subsequent generations, or the unintentional oversight of researchers. Fortunately, there is a well-maintained, twentieth-century African-American cemetery in Salisbury, Rowan County, North Carolina. This cemetery reflects remnants of Africentric burial customs dominated by Eurocentric mortuary practices while respecting the domain of the dead and honoring our ancestry without romanticizing death.

The City of Salisbury saved the seven-acre historical cemetery from deterioration and oblivion when it acquired and assumed responsibility for its maintenance from Noble and Kelsey Funeral Home in 1995.[1] It was once part of a development called Livingston [2] Park in 1905 and a 700 acre eighteenth and mid-nineteenth century gristmill plantation. A land survey was conducted in 1996 at the request of the funeral home in order to meet one of the City's takeover requirements. A second map titled, "Union Hill Cemetery," and an inventory of visible markers and sunken graves was published one year after the cemetery was closed to unreserved burials.[3] Assistance in locating and identifying some of the unmarked burials was provided by the first map titled, "Union Hill Cemetery," that was drawn and maintained during the early to mid-twentieth century by the Noble and Kelsey Funeral Home. Death certificates recorded and maintained by the Rowan County Register of Deeds verified most of the sites indicated by the Noble and Kelsey Funeral Home map. Obituaries, biographies, wills, funeral service programs, funeral home records, and news articles were used to notate and certify other burial sites. A third map titled "Oakdale/Union Hill Cemetery", with a grave locator, was drawn in 2005.

The City Council of Salisbury named the burial ground "Oakdale/Union Hill Cemetery" over the objections of a few local historians convinced that it should be called, "Union Hill–Oakdale Cemetery." Their perspective is based on firsthand associations with the history of Salisbury and Rowan County. One reason for the conflict is probably due to the many names given to the graveyard. The burial ground was called the Kelsey Cemetery, Oakdale Cemetery, Kelsey-Partee Cemetery, and Union Hill Cemetery according to primary and secondary documents. Tax,[4] survey, and funeral home[5] maps prior to 2006 refer to it as Union Hill Cemetery. Newspaper articles, obituaries advertisements, and death certificates, referred to it by several names. The Salisbury City

Council probably named it "Oakdale/Union Hill Cemetery" because it is impractical and confusing to call it by its many aliases and to recognize it as a burial ground composed of more than one cemetery. Therefore, its official name is "Oakdale/Union Hill Cemetery" meaning Oakdale or Union Hill Cemetery regardless of the existence of more than one graveyard.

The research also unearthed spelling and pronunciation incongruencies between some names and places. Macay, MaCay, McKay, Macoy, and McCoy pronounced, Mac coy, are the surname variations of Judge Spruce Macay and his descendants. Frohock and Frohoch are the surname variations of John and Thomas. Livingston is commonly used among Euro Americans while the African American population of Salisbury uses Livingstone with a heavy emphasis on 'stone'. The differences in the spelling and pronouncing of names and places are sources of amusement among local historians and origins of frustration for the unwary. Therefore, it is recommended that researchers check all possible variations when using this reference.

NOTES

1 Minutes: The City Council of Salisbury, North Carolina, November 21, 1995 4:00 p.m.*OAKDALE/UNION HILL CEMETERY* Page 267 Mr. Kennedy made a motion authorizing the Mayor to execute an agreement with Noble and Kelsey Funeral Home, Inc. to take over maintenance of the Oakdale/Union Hill Cemetery. Mr. Maddox seconded the motion and Messrs. Hancock, Henderlite, Kennedy and Ms. Kluttz voted AYE on roll call vote. The acquisition was officially completed in September 2003 with a quit-claim deed after Noble and Kelsey satisfied the conditions imposed by the City Council.

2 Rowan County Register of Deeds. Deed Book 986: 222.

3 Donald J. Moore. land surveyor. Map. Survey Plat of Union Hill Cemetery, Brenner Avenue, Salisbury Township, Rowan County, North Carolina. File No. 0010RW96. Copies are at the Noble & Kelsey Funeral Home, 223 East Fisher Street and Cemetery Division Office in Chestnut Hill Cemetery, 1143 South Main St., Salisbury, North Carolina

Minutes: City Council of Salisbury, November 21, 1995 Page 267.

4 Hunnicutt & Associates. Tax Map No. 5, City & Township of Salisbury, Rowan County. Petersburg, Florida: 1907. Copy at Rowan County Tax Assessors Office, Salisbury, North Carolina. The map also has a list of parcels and deeds. Some transactions have no deeds according to the list.

5 William F. and Lula S. Kelsey. Unpublished Map. Union Hill Cemetery, Salisbury, North Carolina: Noble and Kelsey Funeral Home.

This is a map drawn on canvas and shows the original circular layout and plot assignments. Some of these assignments were reservations and contained no burials e.g., Bishop Elijah Lovette Madison is buried in Pittsburg, Pennsylvania, according to William J. Walls, *The African Methodist Episcopal Zion Church, Reality Of A Black Church* (Charlotte, North Carolina: A. M. E. Zion Publishing House), 602. The map was useful in locating burials in some of the unmarked graves.

PART ONE
A HISTORY AND STUDY OF OAKDALE/UNION HILL CEMETERY

PURPOSE OF THE STUDY

The purpose of the Oakdale/Union Hill Cemetery study is not to seek the living among the dead. It is to honor those African-Americans who lived and thrived in Salisbury, North Carolina, during the twentieth century, help provide future generations with a certainty of identity, and arouse the curiosity of genealogists and historians to the point where more research is conducted. The cemetery contains the remains of more than two thousand individuals who nurtured our community, social, and spiritual beliefs according to local historians and funeral directors. The markers, monuments, enclosures and epitaphs are commentaries on religious tradition and cultural heritage. The social strategies, ambitions, occupations, triumphs and tragedies of a bygone age can be gleaned from the study of this cemetery while providing some protection from the developer's bulldozer.

The histories of Livingstone College and the African-American community of Salisbury's Union Hill, West Ward neighborhood from the late 1890s to the early twenty-first century are told by grave markers and death certificates. Two college presidents, the first principal of Zion Wesley Institute (subsequently called Livingstone College), some of the ancestors of an African American astronaut, the founder of the Women's Home and Overseas Missionary Society of the A. M. E. Zion Church, as well as many professors and ministers are at rest in the cemetery. All but two faculty members of Zion Wesley Institute's first session in Salisbury are buried in the cemetery. Joseph Charles Price, the only president of the Institute and Livingstone College's first president, rests in a mausoleum located in the Poets and Dreamers Garden on the College's campus.[1] Miss Ellen Dale, a music teacher, rests in a cemetery somewhere in Philadelphia, Pennsylvania.

All stations in life are represented in this common red clay burial ground. Ministers, educators, medical professionals, business people and ordinary citizens were threads of the community's finely woven fabric. They established and maintained churches, schools and businesses during reconstruction, the Jim Crow era and the Civil Rights struggle. Mrs. Rose D. Aggrey, Rev. and Mrs. Fisher R. Mason, Mrs. Adeline C. Jones, Rev. Herclese [sic] Smith and Wiley Dodge, Jr. were educators of black youth from the turn of the twentieth century to the demise of the Jim Crow era. William and Lula Kelsey, Rev. and Mrs. James C. Fair, Mayzonetta Grundy Lash, and Thomas and Kathleen Randall were business people who provided goods and services to the black community well into the twentieth century. Rev. Julius P. Johnson pastor of Trinity Presbyterian Church (once known as Church Street Presbyterian Church), was a leader in the Salisbury and Rowan County interfaith movement. Rev. Wiley Hezekiah Lash Lutheran minister and teacher at St. John's Lutheran School founded three black Lutheran churches in Salisbury and Rowan County.

Some of the graves, including those of deceased members of black Salisbury's elite, are indicated by uneven or indented ground whose written records could not be found. Some individuals have death certificates but have no visible markers to signify that they once walked among the living. Pinkney A. Stevenson, a shoemaker, businessman and instructor at Livingstone College during the late nineteenth and early twentieth century, has no marker. Joe Ballard, a popular Salisbury citizen instrumental in the relocation of Zion Wesley Institute from Concord to

Salisbury, has no visible marker although his death certificate places his burial in the cemetery. More research of the lives of those who preceded us in death is needed for the reconstruction and preservation of the Livingstone College Historic District.

Lula Kelsey maintained Noble and Kelsey Funeral Home's unpublished map of early to mid-twentieth century burial locations. Informal interviews with local historians, as well as with Rosalind and A. L. Mitchell, owners of Mitchell and Fair Funeral Home,[2] provided clues to the locations and contents of many unmarked graves. Mr. Tommy Hairston, of Noble and Kelsey Funeral Home, provided a tour that identified the Oakdale section's original layout and gave clues to burial locations.[3] County death certificates, remaining legible markers, obituaries, biographies, old city directories, informal interviews and old photographs assisted in locating and certifying some of the burial sites that had no visible markers. The burial records listed in Part 2 of this book represent only a fraction of the more than 2,000 burials according to local funeral directors. A deeper level of exploration may be needed to determine the anatomy of the graveyard.

LOCATION AND BOUNDARIES
PAST AND PRESENT

The cemetery is situated on a hill once known as Mount Pleasant in eighteenth century Rowan County, North Carolina. It was part of a gristmill plantation located in a colonial suburb of Salisbury (See Map 1) and was a subdivision of a much larger estate in Piedmont, North Carolina. (See Map 2) Local historians believe that the plantation house once stood somewhere on the prominent hill where the Oakdale/Union Hill Cemetery is today. James S. Brawley, a Rowan County historian, noted in 1956 that the plantation house was *"just to the left of Livingstone College where a line of cedar trees on a nearby hill today mark the site."*[4] He later wrote that it was west of the college and south of the western railroad.

MAP 1
Early Landowners Map of
Frohock Mill Plantation

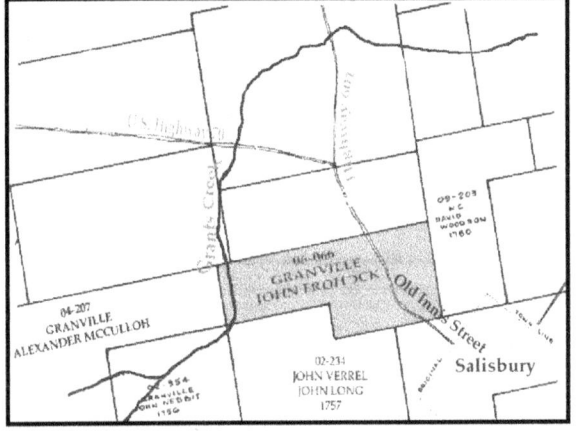

Edited 1994 Early Landowners of Rowan County map sheet 3/6 by R. W. Brown that was drawn by James W. Kluttz ©1995, History Room, Rowan Public Library

The cemetery's current boundaries are Brenner Avenue, Old Wilksboro Road, Burton Ave, West Horah Street and Livingston [sic] Avenue. The main entrance to the cemetery is on Old Wilkesboro Road, near Kelsey Scott Park, Grants Creek, the veterans hospital, and the foundations of the former plantation's gristmill. The part of Kelsey Scott Park that floods when Grants Creek overflows is the remnant of the 300 acre pond used to supply water power for the mill. Today, West Monroe Street terminates on the east side of the cemetery at Brenner Avenue (See Map 3). But, according to a 1907 map (See Map 4) used to identify lots for sale in Livingston [sic] Park, Monroe Street was the southern boundary of the cemetery known by many other names such as Sills Path, and Cathey's Road in the eighteenth century; Salisbury-Taylorsville Plank Road and Statesville Road in the nineteenth century; and Lincolnton, McCoy, and Old Wilksboro Roads in the twentieth.

MAP 2
Present Boundaries and Sections of Oakdale/Union Hill Cemetery in Relation to Immediate Area

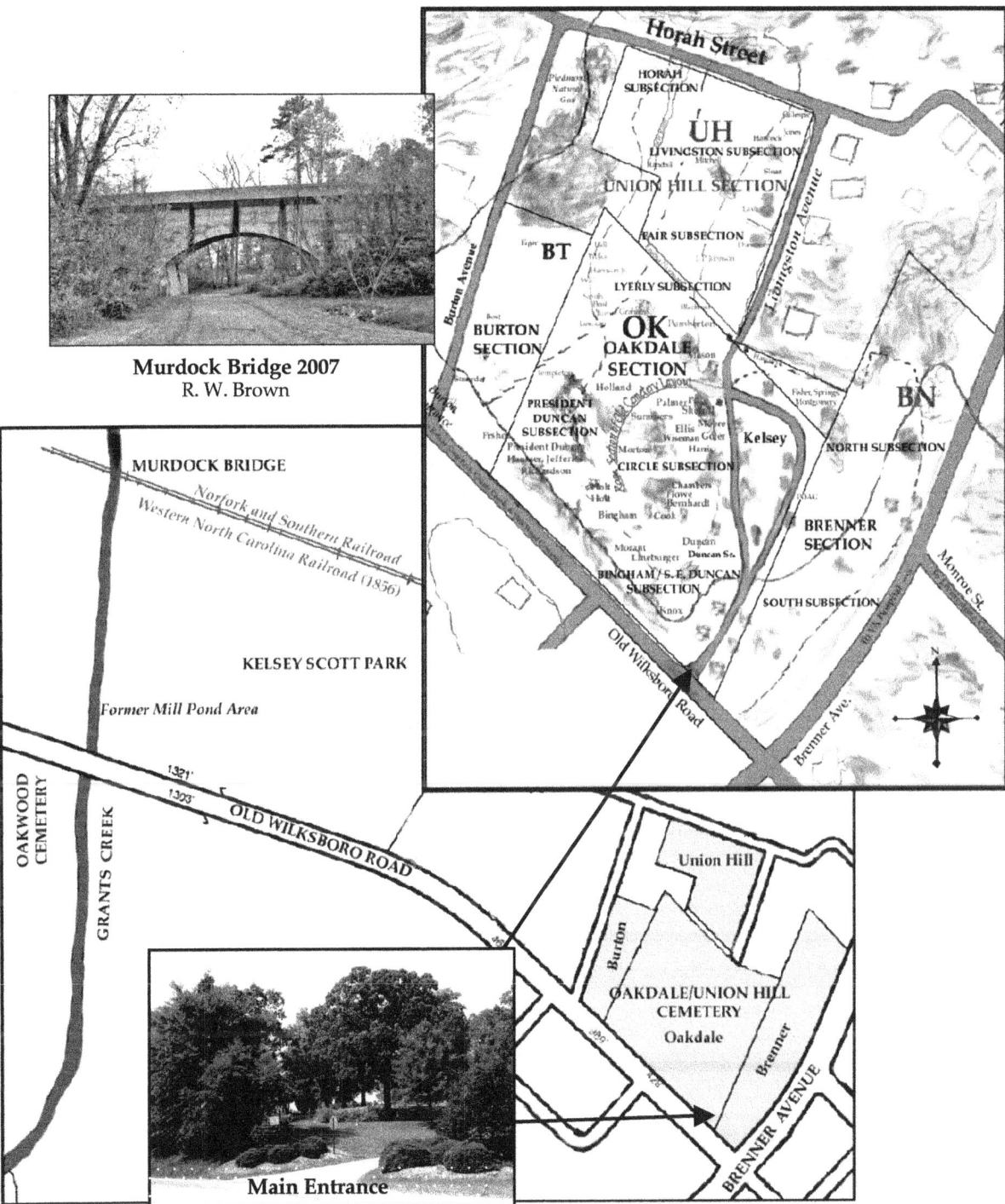

The cemeteries are within 400 yards of the foundations of Frohock's Mill, Grants Creek, Kelsey Scott Park, and the Murdock Bridge, The four sections are Brenner **(BN)**, Oakdale **(OK)**, Burton **(BT)**, and Union Hill **(UH)**

© 2005, 2007 R. W. Brown.

HISTORY OF THE HILL

The cemetery witnessed many events vital to Salisbury and Rowan County History. John Frohock Jr. and his brother Thomas Frohock established Mount Pleasant as a 496-acre gristmill plantation with slaves, a mill, a 300-acre pond, and a mansion known to some as *"the Castle"* one and a half miles north west of Salisbury in 1762.[5] The Frohock brothers were the first to earn a profit from the land that overlooked and included a section of Grants Creek. The parcel was formerly owned by John Long as part of a larger 2,601-acre estate known as the Granville lands.[6] Thomas acquired the plantation and slaves when his bachelor brother, John Jr., died in 1772. Among the 38 slaves shared between Thomas and his other brother, William, were Mary Ann, Bett, Billy, Sharper, Jack, Absolom, George, Dick, Sarah, Till, Poll, Such, Abraham, Pegg, Sam, Darcy, Dinah, Frank, Peter and Sall.[7] John Jr.'s will instructed Thomas and William to give his,

Judge
Spruce Macay

"Trusty and Good Boy Absolom [a waiting man] his liberty or Freedom immediately and that put him to School One Year and let him have his board and clothing with them during the said Term and at the Expiration of the Year give him a good Suit of cloths and Ten Pounds in Money in Testimony for his Honesty and Fidelity to by Interest & Service."[8]

During the Revolutionary War, the mill and its pond was the site where American militia troops were mustered and assigned commands. The troops separated from service at the mill after the war.[9]

In January 1794, twenty-five years after John Jr.'s death and one month before Thomas's death, Superior Court Judge Spruce Macay acquired the Mill Plantation for the sum of 2,500 £.[10] Judge Macay was executor of the Frohock estate, as well as the mentor of both William R. Davie, the tenth governor of North Carolina, and Andrew Jackson, the seventh President of the United States.

Thomas Frohock's last will, dated 26 February 1794, bequeathed the estate to Alexander Frohock, *"except such real and personal property given to his Daughter the wife of Charles Hunt or her children and husband."*[11] Despite confusion over rightful ownership, according to the N. C. McCubbins file in the Rowan Public Library, the plantation was sold to Judge Macay, along with twenty slaves for an additional sum of 1,000 pounds. Among the slaves were: Sarah (age 45), Peg (age 25), Nanse [sic] (approximately age 19), Abram (age 11 months), Grace (approximately age 40), Clary (age 22), Bett (age 19), Patrick (age 11, son of Grace), Bill (age 35), Suck [sic] (age 27), Peter (age 13), Nick (age 10), Vice (age 8), Phil (age 3), Bill Jr. (age 8 months) and Bristo (age 35).[12]

Macay's Mill on Top of Frohock's Stone Foundation in 1903
Source Rowan Museum

Fire destroyed the Mill Plantation mansion and Judge Macay moved to a new house in present-day Milford Hills, another suburb of colonial Salisbury. Judge Macay died in 1808, leaving the Mill Plantation and other real estate holdings to his son, Alfred Macay. By this time, Macay began calling the plantation Milford. William Spruce Macay inherits property and 96 slaves after Alfred's death and improves the mill by installing a new Hotchkiss water wheel in 1827. In 1852, the construction of the Salisbury and Taylorsville Plank Road began at a toll house and slave market that would become the first men's dormitory of Livingstone College on the present-day corner of West Monroe and South Caldwell Streets.[13] The road ran through part of what would become Livingstone College and pass the cemetery towards the Iredell County line. Sections of this road became Statesville Road, Price Memorial Drive on the Livingstone College campus, present-day Old Wilksboro Road, and North Carolina State Highway 1702.

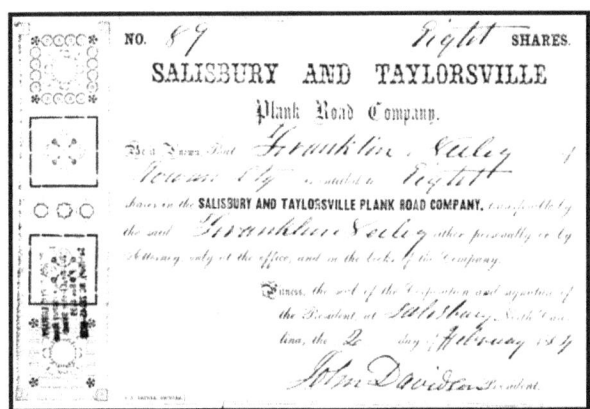

Salisbury and Taylorsville Stock Certificate
Source Rowan Public Library

The first train arrives in Salisbury in 1855 and the first leg of the Western North Carolina Railroad and the Murdock Bridge spanning Grants Creek is completed within sight of the hill. It ran through the Macay property between present-day Kelsey Scott Park and the Veterans Hospital. Railroads proved to be economically more efficient than plank roads due to their relative ease of maintenance and construction. Therefore, plank road construction was suspended in favor of railroads that provided links other than the rough roads between Salisbury and the outside world.

One year after the bridge is built, William Macay's daughter Annie who was named after his second wife Annie Hunt, inherits the property after he dies. Ten years after the bridge is built, the

**Western North Carolina Railroad Bridge
At Grants Creek Crossing in 1903**
Source Rowan Museum

hill witnesses its capture and the plank road by a detachment of General George Stoneman's Union Calvary in April 1865.[14] The hill probably became known as Union Hill because it was on a road used as one of three invasion routes through present-day Livingstone College into the town of Salisbury.[15] Twenty years after the bridge is completed, Annie Cremonia Macay married Stephen Ferrand Lord. She dies in 1879 one year after the death of her son William. Since there were no living Macay blood relatives, widower Stephen F. Lord who would become mayor of Salisbury, assumed title to the Macay property. At that time, the Macay property included the present-day real estate of the Oakwood Cemetery that opened in the early 1960s, the gristmill foundations, the Veterans Hospital, Milford Hills, Kelsey Scott Park, Livingstone College, and the Union Hill/Oakdale Cemetery.

An inventory submitted to the Clerk of the Superior Court of Rowan County, North Carolina, on July 3, 1918, indicates that Stephen F. Lord sold property and kept records but gave no deeds. A four-acre Oakdale section of the Macay estate was acquired by the city of Salisbury in 1903. Part of the Macay estate was sold to William Frank Kelsey and his wife, Lula Spaulding Kelsey, for use as a graveyard. Other parcels in the Union Hill section were held in reserve or sold to individuals and families for family burials. The "reserved" parcels, located in an area once known as Livingston [sic] Park, eventually became a part of the Oakdale/Union Hill Cemetery. The remaining property was subsequently acquired by the City of Salisbury from the Kelsey heirs,[16] Mitchell and Fair Funeral Service and other plot owners.

On July 4, 1907, the Union Hill and Burton sections of the cemetery shown on Map 1 were parts of *"85 lots more or less"* that were designated as Livingston [sic] Park. The sections shown on Map 3 were sold at an auction conducted by J. Edgar Poag, Broker, and B. W. Getsinger, Auctioneer for F. N. McCubbins & Company of Salisbury. The auction occurred after Booker T. Washington's visit to the quarter-centennial celebration of Livingstone College, held in May 1907. According to an advertisement that appeared in the June 27, 1907, edition of the *Salisbury Evening Post*, Washington recommended the sale of affordable "Homes for Colored People" in a suburb of Salisbury. A statement in the advertisement said, *"Booker T. Washington, Richard Carroll and other leaders recommend that the colored people should own their own homes, thereby making better and more substantial citizens."*[17] The homes currently standing on Livingston [sic] Avenue, West Horah Street and Burton Avenue are on land that was part of the sale at auction.

MAP 3
Union Hill, Oakdale, and Burton Sections of Livingston Park in 1907

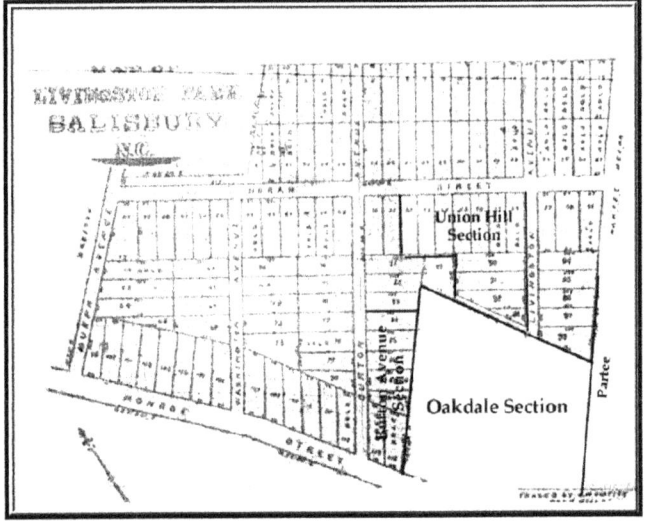

The above edited version of the map in the June 27, 1907, *Salisbury Evening Post* contain outlined sections that are parts of Livingston Park currently in use as sections of Union Hill/Oakdale cemeteries. Brenner Avenue and the Brenner Section of the cemeteries did not exist in 1907.

The Brenner Section on Map 2 is one of two parcels once owned by Frank Partee before Brenner Avenue became a street by eminent domain. William F. Kelsey and his wife Lula purchased the parcels in 1919.[18] Notice the Partee line on Map 3. Frank Partee died in 1923 at the age of 29 and was buried by the Bingham and Carter Funeral Home in the Brenner Avenue section (BN).

THE FIRST BURIALS

Since slaves worked on the Mill Plantation, it is safe to assume that those who were not sold died and were buried where they toiled. According to local tradition, their holder, Thomas Frohock, is also buried within sight of Mount Pleasant in the cemetery.[19] According to some Rowan county historians, the citizens resented the *"greedy ways of the Frohocks,"* who they perceived to be the local version of corrupt Piedmont gentry of the 1700s. George Raynor's article in a *Salisbury Sunday Post* article conjectured that petty graft perpetrated by Piedmont gentry instigated the War of Regulation in 1770 and fed the passion for America's independence from the British.[20]

MAP 4
Land Sold by Stephen F. Lord to the City of Salisbury for Reburials
The shaded region shows the probable location of re-interments.

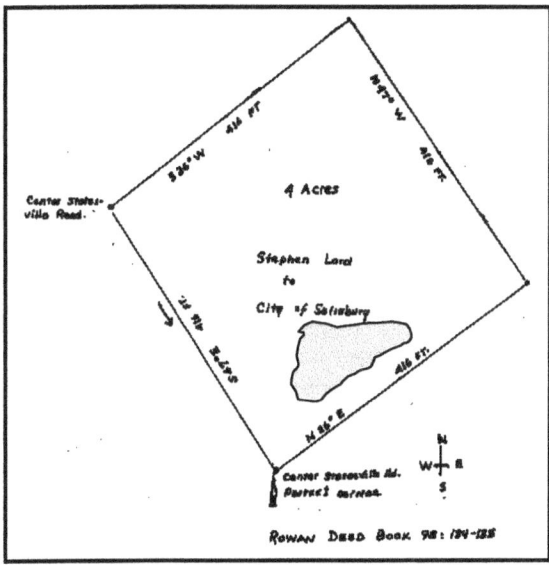

MAP 5
West Monroe Street in 1905

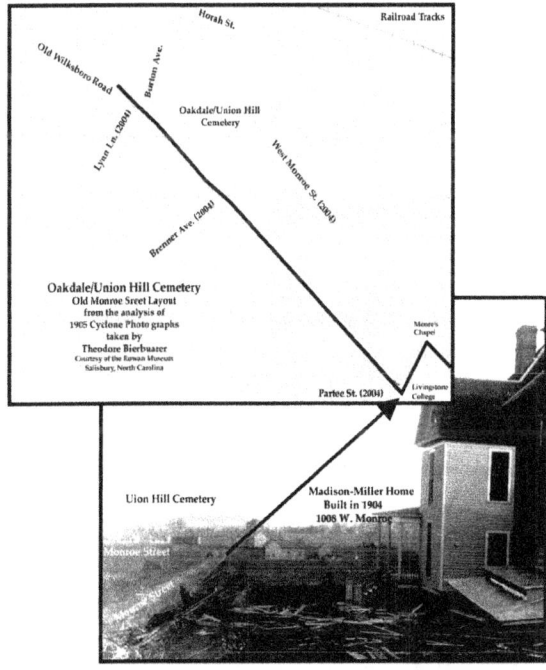

Theodore Buerbaum photograph taken in April 1905 Showing cyclone damage on West Monroe Street with Union Hill Cemetery in the distance.
Source Rowan Museum

Thomas Frohock was disliked for his exploitation of the local citizens, as well as for being on the wrong side of the Revolutionary War. The Frohock name almost faded into obscurity after the Rowan Committee of Safety seized power from the colonial government and recommended to the 1774 Continental Congress the abolishment of slavery. Thomas died in 1794 with no evidence of him leaving the region. Ironically, he donated the land that became the Old English Cemetery located on the northwest corner of Council and Church Streets according to Jethro Rumple.[21] The current Oak Grove Freedman's[22] and Oakdale/Union Hill Cemeteries are connected through Thomas Frohock and re-interments.

Nineteenth and early twentieth century burial records could not be found during the study. Some unmarked graves may contain the remains of those exhumed from the Liberty Street right of way between Jackson and Church Streets from 1907 to 1924. [Maps 4 & 6] A list of those removed, some of whom were probably slaves buried in the segregated section of the Oak Grove Cemetery,[23] could not be found. Some remains were probably those of deceased members of Soldiers Memorial A.M.E. Zion Church, Mount Zion Baptist Church, and Church Street Presbyterian Church (Trinity United Presbyterian Church). The trustees of Soldiers Memorial, including Robert Burton McNeely, buried at Oakdale/Union Hill in April 1920, purchased land from Thomas and Ellen Henderson for the current location of the Church on the present-day corner of Liberty and North Church Streets.[24]

The exhumation, removal, and re-interments would allow the connection of Church and Jackson Streets with a Liberty Street extension. The extension would run through the Shaver property and complete a route from Ellis Street to a passenger train station that would be built in 1908. [See Map 6] The State of North Carolina required the City of Salisbury to purchase land for the re-interments prior to exhumation. Former Mayor Stephen F. Lord sold four acres of land in Union Hill to the city for $200. [Maps 4. & 5] The transaction occurred October 6, 1903, and the deed was executed October 13, 1903.[25] The deed's execution date is considered the official opening date of what was then known as Union Hill Cemetery.

A private act of the North Carolina General Assembly was passed

> *"to authorize the aldermen of the city of Salisbury to open Liberty Street, between Church and Jackson Streets, to disinter and remove the dead bodies in said street to a 'colored cemetery' at the end of Monroe Street beyond Livingstone College. The act was ratified and in force on the 9th day of March, A.D. 1903."*[26]

At the time of exhumation and re-interment, Rowan County was not legally obligated to keep death records. The section of land identified as a cemetery in 1907 on Map 3 was the only part of Livingston [sic] Park certified to receive burials. The bodies from the section of Liberty Street that connected Jackson and Church Streets were re-interred in the eastern part of the cemetery between 1904 and 1910. A wagon path was cut through the Liberty Street right of way in 1909 before beginning work on its connection between Jackson and Church.[27] Additional bodies were exhumed and re-interred at Union Hill/Oakdale in 1922, when Liberty Street was widened.

It is possible to conclude that the first burials in Oakdale/Union Hill Cemetery are mainly of those who were members of three African American churches on North Church Street if the existence of the Dicksonville Cemetery in the south eastern part of Salisbury is ignored. More study is needed to determine the names, occupations, and reasons for the initial burials in the Liberty Street right of way. Is it possible that some of the exhumed and re-interred remains are those of slaves and executed convicts? Could the Oakdale/Union Hill Cemetery be considered an extension of present-day Oak Grove Freedmen's Cemetery that was adjacent to the Old English Cemetery that is land donated by Thomas Frohock?

MAP 6
Area of Exhumed Bodies and Photos of Three Churches on North Church Street

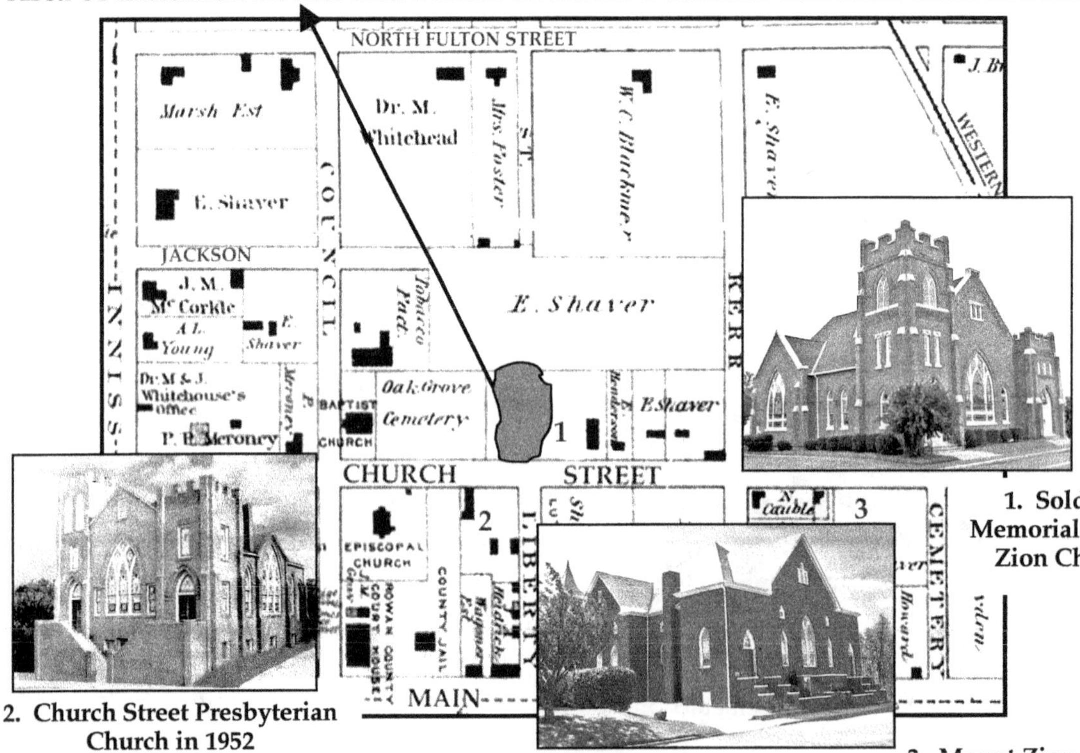

1. Soldiers Memorial A.M.E. Zion Church

2. Church Street Presbyterian Church in 1952
Rowan Library

3. Mount Zion Baptist Church

The two oldest visible cemetery markers are those of Edward Moore Jr., who died March 1905 at age 20, and Alex Kelsey, who died on May 23, 1905, at age 80. Edward Moore's granite fieldstone is located near the granite headstone of his parents, Dr. and Mrs. Edward Moore Sr., in the Circle Section. Alex Kelsey's marble obelisk is located in the Kelsey family plot, across the Circle Section. The Kelsey marker was probably the first one erected.

MAP 7
First Map of Union Hill Cemetery c. 1920
(Maps 8 & 9 Noble and Kelsey Funeral Home)

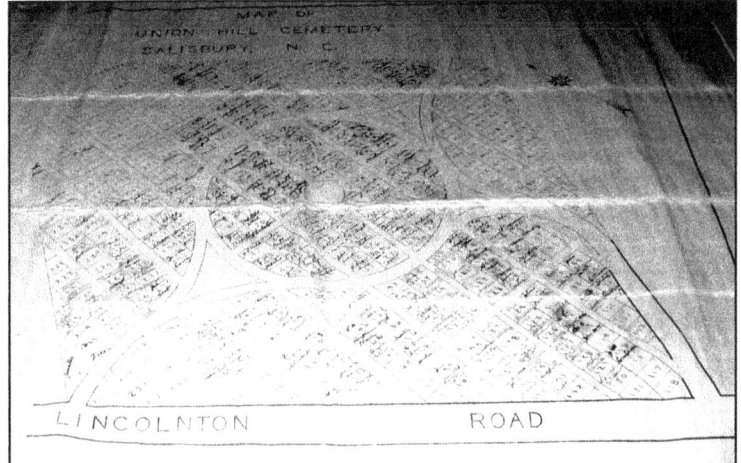

MAP 7 is a photograph of the cemetery map created and maintained by Lula Kelsey until her death in 1947. The original circular layout was totally different from that shown on the 1996 map. The street bordering the cemetery was called Lincolnton Road when Lula drew the map. Lincolnton Road is now Old Wilkesboro Road.

R. W. Brown, September 2004, with the permission of Noble and Kelsey Funeral Home.

MAP 8
Union Hill Cemetery c. 1920
Oakdale Circle Section

MAP 8 is a close-up of the Oakdale Circle section. Some of the burials in this section contain the remains of W. H. Goler, C. R. Harris, Jennie Smallwood Price, James E. K. Aggrey, Rosebud Aggrey, James M. Morton and Edward Moore. Annie and Robert Wiseman, and Mary Propst are buried in a curb without markers. The curb is plot 1 on the Kelsey map and plot 96 on Donald Moore's map.

R. W. Brown, September 2004.

MAP 9
Union Hill Cemetery
Oakdale Circle Subsection

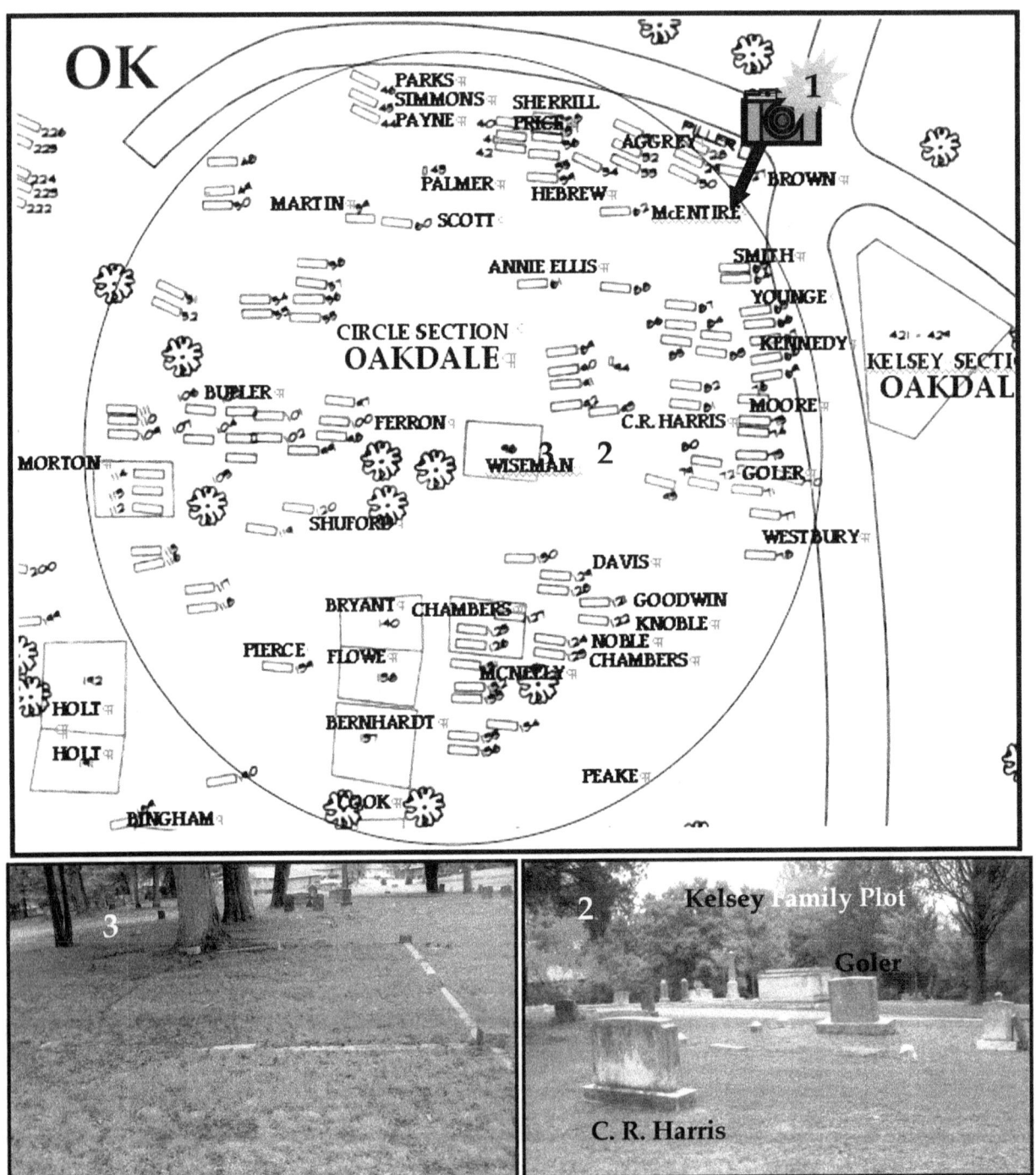

Wiseman curb, Kelsey plot 1 / Moore plot 96   C. R. Harris and W. H. Goler Plots

MAP 9 is an edited version of a 1996 survey plat drawn by Donald J. Moore for Noble and Kelsey Funeral Home. The edited version contains the demarcation of the Kelsey Circle section and identifies some of the graves in this section. Moore plot 96 / Kelsey plot 1 was the initial point of the study. Map edited by R. W. Brown.

BURIALS OUTSIDE OAKDALE / UNION HILL CEMETERY

Three additional burials outside the cemetery warrant consideration. Two are in the Oakwood Cemetery and the other is the Price Mausoleum, in the Poets and Dreamers Garden on the Livingstone College campus. Oakwood Cemetery, located west of the Oakdale/Union Hill Cemetery on Old Wilkesboro Road and 200 feet west of the Grants Creek Bridge, was opened for burial by the early 1960s and currently receives burials. Mitchell and Fair Funeral Services were the first to perform interment in the Oakwood cemetery according to A. L. Mitchell. Oakwood Cemetery was most likely opened due to Oakdale/Union Hill Cemetery's near capacity and inability to accept unreserved burials.

Several of the people buried in Oakwood have close connections to the history of Livingstone College, Soldiers Memorial A. M. E. Zion Church and other churches of black Salisburians. President William Johnson Trent the fourth president of Livingstone College, and Bishop Raymond Luther Jones and his second wife, Mabel Miller Jones, are buried in Oakwood. Isaac H. Miller Sr., a member of Livingstone College's faculty, and other deceased members of Salisbury's African-American community are buried in this active cemetery on grounds that was once part of the old Frohock estate.

President William Johnson Trent
1873 - 1963

Bishop Raymond Luther Jones
1900 - 1972

Joseph Charles Price 1854 - 1893

Joseph Charles Price the first president of Livingstone College is buried on the campus in October 1893. The Price Mausoleum was constructed around the grave in 1923 under the administration of Daniel Cato Suggs, the third president of the College.[28]

"I care not how dark the night, I believe in the coming of the morning." J. C. Price

OTHER ROWAN COUNTY BLACK CEMETERIES

Oakdale/Union Hill Cemetery is but one burial ground in which African-Americans were interred before graveyards were racially integrated. Dr. Kenneth D. Sell while a professor at Catawba College in Salisbury compiled a list and presented photographs of obscure and known cemeteries in Rowan County by townships.[29] He also prepared a guide to Rowan County cemeteries. Both documents are in the Edith M. Clark History Room at the Rowan Public Library in Salisbury. The cemeteries read by the Genealogical Society of Rowan County are underlined and in bold print.

Obscure Black Cemeteries, Listed by Township

Gold Hill Twp.
Concordia
St. John
Zion

Litaker Twp.
Old Mt. Zion

Mt. Ulla Twp.
Oakland

Salisbury City
Dixonville
Horah Family

Scotch-Irish Twp.
Pittsburg

Spencer
New Hope

Known Black Cemeteries, Listed by Township

Township	Cemetery	Established
Atwell Twp.	**Sills Creek A. M. E. Zion Church**	est. 1872
China Grove Twp.	**Covenant United Presbyterian**	
	Sandy Ridge A. M. E. Zion Church	est. 1866
Cleveland Twp.	Baptist	est. 1905
	Mt. Vernon Presbyterian	est. 1886
Cleveland Town	**Allen's Temple United Presbyterian**	est. 1885
	Ambassadors for Christ Baptist Church	est. 1986
	Third Creek A. M. E. Zion	est. 1878
Franklin Twp.	**Ardis Chapel A. M. E. Zion Church**	est. 1869
	Refreshing Springs	est. 1984
	St. Luke's Baptist	est. 1879
	Second Creek A. M. E. Zion	
Gold Hill Twp.	**St. Johns Baptist**	
Granite Quarry	**Antioch Baptist**	est. 1900
Litaker Twp.	**Henderson Grove Baptist**	est. 1912
Locke Twp.	**Miller's Chapel A. M. E. Zion Church**	est. 1885
	Rose of Sharon Holiness	est. 1924
Morgan Twp.	Pleasant Hill	
Mt. Ulla Twp.	Mt. Tabor United Presbyterian	est. 1867
Smith's Chapel Holiness		
Providence Twp.	White Rock A. M. E. Zion	est. 1906
	Yadkin Grove Baptist	est. 1869
Rockwell	**St. Matthew's Baptist**	
Salisbury Twp.	Dorsett Chapel United Church of Christ	est. 1915
	Fairview Heights Baptist	est. 1933

	Jerusalem Baptist	est.1881
	New Hope A. M. E. Zion	est. 1882
	New Zion Baptist	est. 1883
	St. John's Church of God	
	Yadkin Missionary Baptist	est. 1947
Salisbury City	**Dixonville City**	est. 17??
	Moore's Chapel	est. 1909
	Oakwood Mt. Calvary Church	
	Old English – Freedman's City	est. 1770
	Oakdale/Union Hill City	est. 1900?
Scotch Irish Twp.	Church of the Living God Holiness	
	Moore's Chapel A. M. E. Zion	est. 1902
	Rock Hill Church of Christ	
Steele Twp.	**Boyden Quarters /Mt. Zion Baptist**	est. 1867
	New Smith's Chapel Pentecostal	
Unity Twp.	**Cedar Grove A. M. E. Zion**	est. 1879
	Emmanuel Pentecostal	est. 1966
	Erwin's Temple C. M. E.	est. 1928
	St. Paul Mission Pentecostal, formerly New Shepard Baptist	est. 1909

MAP 10
Rowan County Townships

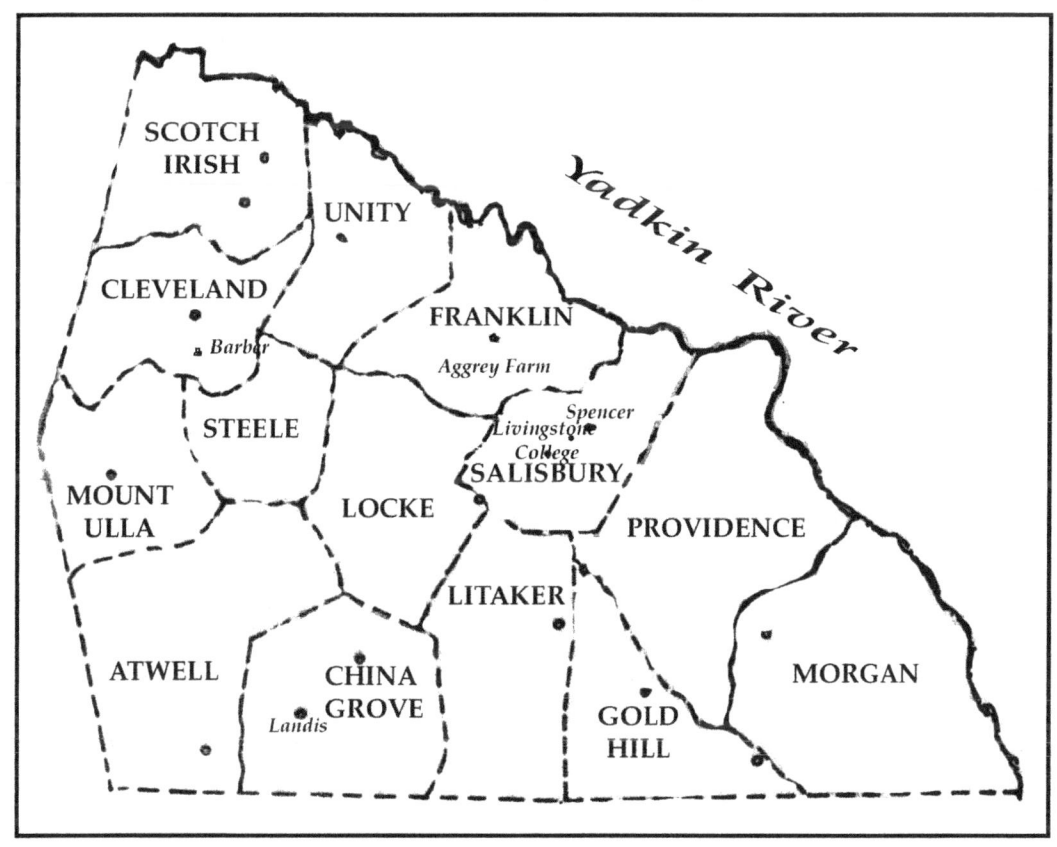

FACING THE RISING SUN

A noticeable feature of the visible graves in African-American cemeteries is their east-west orientation. This orientation is a characteristic of older slave burial grounds, particularly where those interred had more direct ties to Africa. Those burial grounds face east, supposedly because the deceased would then be facing the African homeland across the Atlantic Ocean.[30] A second and more likely explanation for the east-west orientation is the Christian belief that the dead should not be turned around to face Gabriel when he blows his trumpet in the eastern sunrise on Resurrection Day.

Judging from headstone inscriptions and positions, it is clear that the majority of burials are oriented eastward and a few are oriented westward facing Grant's Creek. This does not mean that westward-facing burials were performed without regard for the remnants of traditional beliefs. Another African-American burial custom is to ensure that the deceased is laid to rest either facing a body of water or in prominent view of a body of water. The custom of orienting the body to water is based on the belief that the departed's soul will follow the water to the sea and eventually to Africa. One other possible reason for the westward facing orientation is to indicate that the remains were moved from another burial site. The southward facing Lyerly and Graham plots are some exceptions to the east facing and water facing conventions. It is possible that a different orientation was requested by the deceased The reasons for the exceptions could not be determined during the study. Research is needed to resolve this question.

After grave orientation, the most noticeable aspect of the cemetery is the scarcity of markers relative to the number of known interments. The 1996 land survey shows physical evidence of 889 burials, approximately 88 of which are sunken and 34 are recorded as unmarked. Death certificates for more than 750 additional burials were found,[31] plus an unknown number of 1903 – 1910 re-interments from the Liberty Street right-of-way that have no markers. There are no markers for Thomas Frohock or any of his slaves. Grave markers from the Summersett burials either vanished or never existed. The burials of Wiley Dodge Sr. and Wiley Dodge Jr. are examples of interments recorded by death certificates that have no visible markers.

FEATURES

No evidence could be found of an association between marker presence (or absence) and social status. Wiley Dodge and his son were prominent members of the community during the 1870s to 1920s. They are buried near the marker of Annie B. Dodge Ellis, their daughter and granddaughter. Some relatives of the deceased placed less emphasis on the precise spot of burial than on the whole burial ground. Some probably believed that the spirits of the dead should linger in the general area of the cemetery and not be tied to a specific gravesite. Perhaps permanent grave markers are perceived as unnecessary, because a deceased relative or ancestor could be honored without paying homage to a specific gravesite. Perhaps the fragmented memories of families torn apart by the system of slavery imprinted the fear in subsequent generations that no one would be around to tend to a deceased relative's grave. Perhaps the fear of desecration persuaded some to leave the grave unmarked.

A distinguishing feature of the Oakdale/Union Hill Cemetery is that it officially opened to receive the remains exhumed from the Liberty Street right of way as deeded property and continued to certify its expansion by recorded deeds and other forms of legal documents. Old black cemeteries are typically not deeded or recorded as cemeteries. Most of these cemeteries were probably established during slavery or Reconstruction and were associated with African American communities who felt no need for deeds or maps except for church graveyards. The lack of documentation made community graveyards and cemeteries of abandoned churches more vulnerable to those who wanted to locate a business, build a dream house, or establish a right-of way.

A confounding feature is the presence of Euro-American mortuary practices that tend to mask any physical remnants of African burial customs. The materials and style of the markers are Eurocentric. If there were Africentric markers, they disappeared over time due to their fragile construction or may be hidden in plain sight. If African traditional burials took place in Oakdale/Union Hill, the graves probably had funerary items ranging from bottles to shells that were probably misunderstood as abandoned objects and were removed or left to blend with the ground. Research is needed to determine whether plants and trees were used to mark graves. Is the vegetation in the cemetery indigenous to the region?

There are two unifying features. First is the presence of deceased members of primarily African American Baptist, Methodist, and Presbyterians. Church Street Presbyterian Church (Trinity Presbyterian Church), Soldiers Memorial A.M.E. Zion Church, and Mount Zion Baptist Church are the three churches associated with the largest number of burials in the cemetery. The second was the activities of two burial associations that made funerals and burials affordable to the almost poor. Many members of these churches were able to respectfully bury their departed loved ones because of these associations from the dark days of the Great Depression and World War II to the introduction of whole life insurance. The Florence Progressive Mutual Burial Association of Ellis, Mangum, and Fair and The Kelsey Mutual Burial Association of Noble and Kelsey implemented a strong tradition of mutual aid and cooperation that probably had its roots in ancestral West African customs. Bodies not buried in the Liberty Street right-of-way were not disturbed and remain in the present-day Oak Grove Freedman's Cemetery in historic Salisbury.

Moore's Chapel A. M. E. Zion Church
Photo by R. W. Brown

Livingstone College Historic District

The cemetery also holds the bodies of those who were members of Moore's Chapel A. M. E. Zion Church located in what was once known as the Union Hill section of Salisbury according to city directories. The church is located at the end of the Livingstone College Historic District on the corner of Partee and West Monroe Streets. One of its distinguishing features with respect to the three churches on North Church Street is that it has its own cemetery located on Standish Street. Another feature was its accessibility to Livingstone College faculty, students and others who lived in the surrounding residential area. The student body that walked across town to attend Soldier's Memorial attended Moore's Chapel after it appeared as an offshoot of

Soldiers.[32] Emma Unthank Goler, the wife of William Harvey Goler, Josephine Price Sherrill, the daughter of Joseph Charles Price, and the Herclese Smith family are buried with other church members in the Oakdale/Union Hill Cemetery.

The cemetery is the resting place of many born beyond North Carolina's borders. Approximately one-fourth of the graves belong to those born in South Carolina. President Samuel E., Elizabeth Duncan Koontz, and Julia Belle are three members of the Duncan family, born in Kentucky. Victoria Richardson was born in Ohio and James E. K. Aggrey was born in Ghana, West Africa. Many other occupants of the cemetery were born in Virginia, Tennessee, Georgia and Alabama.

Many burials are of African American professionals and business people who lived in the Livingstone College Historic District on West Monroe Street. West Horah, South Caldwell, and South Craig Streets are also in the general area of the district. Some burials are of those who lived and worked in the eastern sections of Salisbury according to death records.

REMEMBER AS YOU PASS ME BY

Remember as you pass me by
As you are now so was I.
As I am now so you will be
Prepare for death and follow me.

Oakdale/Union Hill Cemetery represents those graveyards established during the transitional period when Euro-American mortuary traditions began to dominate African burial formats. This gradual change paralleled the cultural adjustments imposed upon generations of Americans of African descent who lost direct contact with ancestral West African customs. Their descendents constructed new identities and communities with traces of African traditions hidden in plain sight of southern American society.

The cemetery is relatively new compared to other Rowan County graveyards. Other graveyards were established in the mid 1700s, when Salisbury was founded, and in the mid 1860s, when freedmen started their own communities. Local historians suggest that some household slaves are buried alongside their holders in the Old English Cemetery that is adjacent to the Oak Grove Freedman's Cemetery and the Liberty Street right of way where bodies were exhumed and re-interred in Oakdale/Union Hill. They also suggest that some of the burials in the right of way were those of executed criminals and slaves. Both suggestions are in need of more study in order to be removed from the realm of speculation.

The Oakdale/Union Hill Cemetery is an historically unique site that contains the graves of African Americans who held prominent positions in the area's history. It is an invaluable repository of African-American death and burial culture that underwent a transition. Its layout, native vegetation, inventory of grave markers and style of burials yields testimony to a burial philosophy and belief in an afterlife influenced by African and European mortuary traditions.

PHYSICAL FEATURES OF THE MARKERS

The physical evidence of traditional ancestral West African mortuary practices cannot be seen. There are examples of unreadable weatherworn concrete markers, gravestones carved by amateurs, professionally engraved stones with incorrect information, above ground vaults and elaborate monuments. Materials for the markers include concrete, marble, Salisbury (pink) granite, regular (gray) granite and blue granite. Granite is the dominant material used for monuments that are mainly field stones. The presence of granite is an indicator of the relative newness of the cemetery when compared to older cemeteries where marble and other materials were easier to engrave. Whether granite, marble, cement, or wood, these stones represent an invaluable repository of twentieth century African-American death and burial culture. The cemetery's layout of native vegetation, inventory of grave markers, and burial styles yield testimony to a burial philosophy and belief in an afterlife influenced by remnants of African traditions and dominant Eurocentric mortuary styles.

One measure of a civilization is its reverence for its dead. By honoring and maintaining this heritage, we learn and gain a certainty of our identity that is rooted in our past as we grow to appreciate those who precede us in death. Part of our history is in this cemetery and must be treated as a responsibility instead of a legacy or heritage. We must protect the remaining fragile markers for posterity and preserve them through photographs and records. The oldest and most endangered monuments should be placed in museum collections. Oakdale/Union Hill Cemetery has much to teach about the African-American experience in Salisbury, North Carolina, as it yields testimony to God.

MONUMENT TYPES
MATERIALS

Ledger
Salisbury Granite

Field Stone
Grey Granite

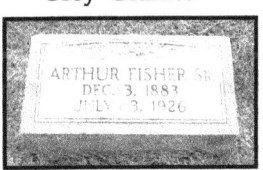

Beveled Headstone
Grey or Pink
Granite

Obelisk
Mable

Cross
Granite

Headstone
Marble

Lamb Headstone
Marble

Funeral Home Marker
Aluminum

Headstone
Concrete Form

Flush
Salisbury, Blue,
or Grey Granite

**Monument Cluster
Salisbury and Grey Granite**

**Vault Mausoleum
Marble**

**Aggrey Family Group in
Curb Salisbury Granite**

**Holt Family
Headstone
Granite**

**Fence and Monument
Marble**

**Vault Mausoleum
Granite**

**Wings
Marble or Granite**

OAKDALE/UNION HILL CEMETERY - LIVINGSTONE COLLEGE HISTORIC DISTRICT

The cemetery is like the Rosetta Stone for studying the Livingstone College Historic District[33] and its surrounding area. It provides clues as to how the puzzle of Livingstone's history and the story of black Salisburians can be assembled. Some of the homes in the Historic District were left for posterity by those who were intimately involved with Livingstone's earliest days. In addition to the original 38 acres purchased by the Board of Trustees of Zion Wesley Institute in the spring of 1882, William H. Goler acquired much of the land on which the college and faculty homes now stand through skillful purchases and land development. Goler built many of the homes in the Historic District.

West Monroe Street once known as College Avenue, College Street, and Maple Avenue before the 1920's is the main thoroughfare of the district. Its homes line the street facing the college campus from the Aggrey home at the intersection of South Craige Street in the east, to Moore's Chapel A. M. E. Zion Church at the intersection of Partee Street in the west. Old Wilksboro Road as it is known today was part of West Monroe Street in 1905 and was a western boundary of present-day Oakdale/Union Hill Cemetery. Today Old Wilksboro Road once a section of Statesville Road in 1853 and West Monroe Street constitutes North Carolina State Road 1702 in Rowan County.

MAP 11

Decedent Homes in the Livingstone College Historic District And Surrounding Residential Area

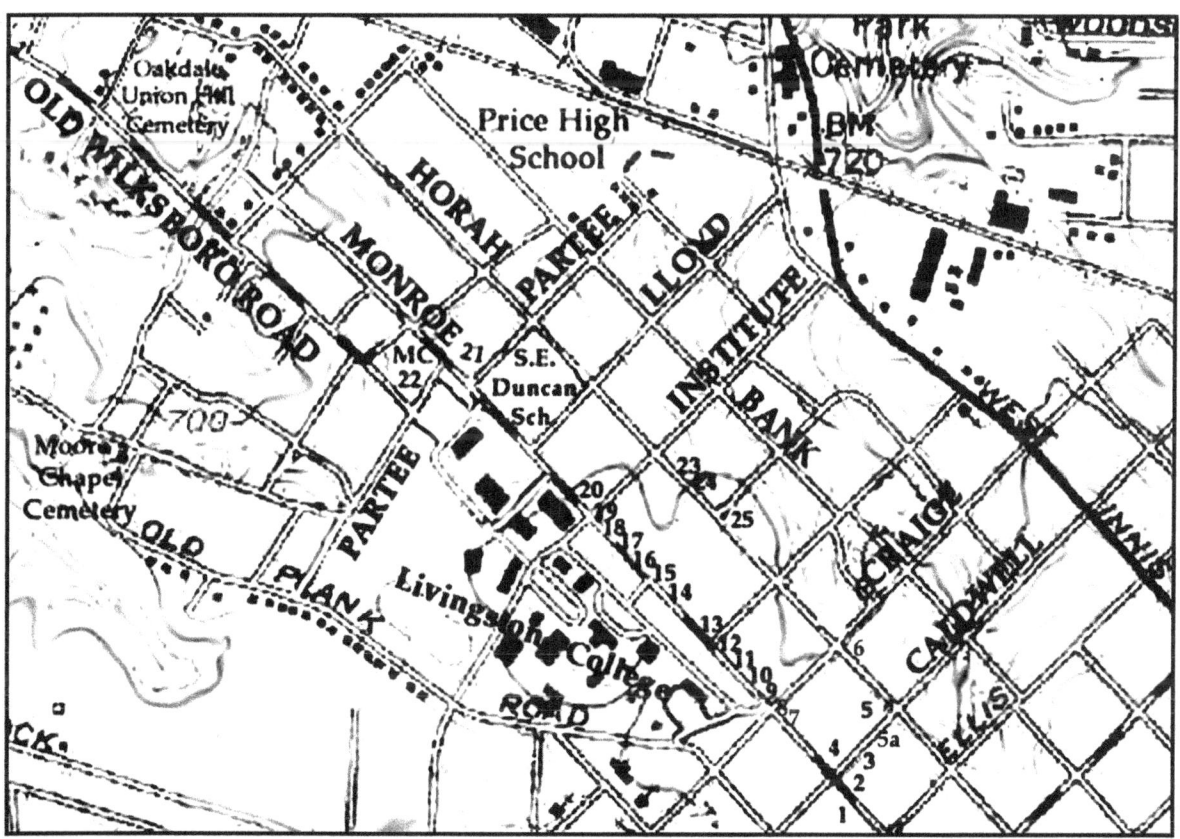

A number indicates the location of each home. Use the following list and MAP 12 to identify the decedents buried in the cemetery who once lived in each home.

SOME
MONROE AND HORAH STREET RESIDENCES OF THOSE BURIED IN THE CEMETERY

1. **Younge**   525 West Monroe Street
James Wells   & Pearl Shines (Wife & Mother)

2. **Johnson & Lash**   530 West Monroe Street
Mayzonetta Grundy Lash Home
James H. Johnson - 1931
Wiley Hezikiah
Mayzonetta Grundy (Wife & Mother)

3. **Duncan**   423 South Caldwell Street
Samuel Edward Sr. (Husband & Father)
Lena Belle Jordan (Wife & Mother)
Samuel Edward, President (Son)
Joseph C. Duncan (Son)
Frederick D. Duncan (Son)
Julia Belle (Daughter)
John Bonner (Son)
Elizabeth (Daughter)

4. **Hall**   420 South Caldwell Street
Oliver Cleveland (Husband) & Edmonia Kent (Wife)

5. **Dodge**   408 South Caldwell Street   [Demolished]
Wiley E. Sr. & Cecelia Giles (Wife & Mother)
Wiley E. Jr. & Mary A. Gray (Wife & Mother)
Grace Marie (Daughter)
Annie B. Dodge Ellis (Daughter) & Charles A. Ellis (Son-In-Law)

5a. **Trott**   419 South Caldwell Street

James Garfield Trott (Husband & Father)
Marguerite Sumner Trott (Wife & Mother)

6. **Fair**   628 Horah Street

James C. Sr. (Husband & Father) & Sadie Davis (Wife & Mother)
Robert W. Fair (Son)
Delbert Sepheria [sic] Fair (Son)

7. **Andrew Whittington**   624 West Monroe Street
                               (Mary Lynch Home)

8. **Ferron**   630 West Monroe Street (Livingstone College President's Home)
William O. Ferron (Husband & Father)
Maria Ferron
William A. Ferron
William J. Trent, President of Livingstone College, 1925 – 1957
     [Buried in Oakwood Cemetery]
Samuel E. Duncan, President of Livingstone College, 1958 - 1968

9 **Aggrey - Lancaster - Evans**   700 West Monroe Street c. 1912

   James Emman K. (Husband & Father)
   Rose Rudolph Douglass (Wife & Mother)
   Rosebud D. Aggrey (Daughter)
   Hattie Douglass Whyte (Sister-In Law)
   Abna Aggrey Lancaster (Daughter)
   Spencer W. Lancaster (Son-In-Law)

10 **Stevenson - Johnson**   714 West Monroe Street   c. 1904
    Pinkney A. Stevenson, 1910 (First Resident)
    Julius P. Johnson, 1935

11 **Noble**   720 West Monroe Street [Destroyed by Fire]
    Frank   (Husband)

12 **Moore**   728 West Monroe Street [Replaced with apartments]
    Edward   (Husband & Father)
    Serena L. (Wife & Mother)
    Edward Jr. (Son)

13 **Harris**   802 West Monroe Street   c. 1889
    Cicero Richardson (Husband & Father)
    Mariah E. Gion (Wife & Mother)
    Victoria Richardson - Niece
    Mabel Harris Graves – Daughter
        (Victoria and Mabel's second residence
            was 1006 West Monroe Street. It was
            demolished circa 1970)

14 **Price**   828 West Monroe Street   c. 1884
            Joseph Charles [Buried on Livingstone College Campus]
    Jennie Smallwood   (Widowed mother)
    Emma Louise (Daughter)
    William Dodge (Son)
    Alma Price Braithwaite (Daughter)
    Louise Moore (Daughter)
    Josephine Price Sherrill (Daughter)
    Richard W. Sherrill (Son-In-Law)
    Jennie Louise Sherrill (Grand Daughter)

15 **Goler**   901 West Monroe Street [Demolished]
    William Harvey   (Husband)
    Emma Unthank   (Wife)
    Johnsie Williams   (Niece)
    Mabel Elaine Williams (Niece)
    Eliza Holms Goler Thomas (Aunt of William)

16 **Hall**   912 West Monroe Street   c. 1915
    Louicio Hamilton (Husband)
    Bessie Corpening (Wife)

17	**Trent**	918 West Monroe Street		c. 1928
	William Johnson, President (1925 – 1958)		[Buried in Oakwood Cemetery]	

18 **Hannum** 924 West Monroe Street c. 1904
    William Henry

19 **Crittenden** 928 West Monroe c. 1928
    William Bentley (Father)
    Lizzie (Daughter)

20 **Richardson** 1006 West Monroe [Demolished]
    Victoria - 1927
    Mabel Harris Graves – 1963

21 **Jackson** 1204 West Monroe Street [Relocated]
    Israel Joseph

22 **Bingham** 502 Partee Street
    Arthur Brown (Husband)
    Lucile Bitting (1st. Wife)

23-24 **Smith** 916 West Horah Street c. 1908
    Hurclese – 1944 (Husband & Father)
    Lula Sujette Harris – 1947 (Wife & Mother)
    Carrie Lena Smith Jones – 1955 (Daughter)
    Lottie Mae Smith Whittington – 1986 (Daughter)
    Andrew Robinson Whittington – 1960 (Son-In-Law)
    Thomas Jefferson Randall (Foster Son)
        Raymond L. Jones (Husband to Carrie Lena)
        [Buried in Oakwood Cemetery]
        Mabel Miller Jones (2nd Wife of R. L. Jones)
        [Buried in Oakwood Cemetery]

25 **Jones** 828 West Horah Street c. 1914
    Julius Jackson (Husband)
    Adline Curry   (Wife)

PART ONE
END NOTES

1 Zion Wesley College. <u>Catalogue of Zion Wesley College 1884-85</u>. Salisbury, North Carolina:

2 Informal interview and tour of the Union Hill section and Lyerly – Fair subsections with Allen L Mitchell (Mitchell & Fair Funeral Services). Personal interview and tour of Oakdale/Union Hill Cemetery, especially the Lyerly – Fair subsections in March 2003. Mr. Mitchell pointed out the locations of burials performed by the Ellis, Mangum and Fair Funeral Home before it became Mitchell and Fair Funeral Service in 1968. Some of the burials without visible markers have death certificates on file. Unmarked burials with no death certificates were identified in the records maintained by Sadie Fair and Marie Dodge Ellis.

Informal interview with Rosalind Mitchell in August 2003. Miss Mitchell, the current manager and daughter of Allen Mitchell, assisted in the identification of recent burials. She also provided access to the burial records of Sadie Fair, the widow of Rev. James C. Fair and previous owner of Ellis, Mangum and Fair, the precursor of Mitchell and Fair Funeral Services. Mrs. Marie Dodge Ellis was the secretary and was probably responsible for maintaining the records. Her second husband, who predeceased her in death, was Charles Ellis, a founder of Ellis, Mangum and Fair Funeral Home, in May 1937.

3 Informal interview and tour of Oakdale Circle Section with Tommy Hairston of Noble & Kelsey Funeral Home at Oakdale/Union Hill Cemetery on April 3, 2003.. The layout of the cemeteries, as indicated by the 1996 map of Union Hill Cemetery by Donald Moore changed. The difference between the actual layout and the old maps caused some confusion. The tour involved a walk-through of the old circular layout of the four-acre section purchased by the City of Salisbury in 1903 for the re-burial of remains from the right-of-way for Liberty Street.

4 James S. Brawley, "The Outpost" Salisbury Evening Post, June 3, 1956, Information on Microfilm, Micro Photo Division Old Mansfield Road, Wooster, Ohio Reel 173, History Room, Rowan Public Library

5 Mamie McCubbins. Collection, Frohock, Deed Book 6: 66, Edith M. Clark History Room, Rowan Public Library and Rowan County Register of Deeds, Salisbury, North Carolina.
On April 4, 1761, Earl Granville (through his agent Esq. Thomas Child) lets John Frohock of Rowan County, North Carolina have 496 acres of vacant land on both sides of Grants Creek …

6 McCubbins, Deed Book 6: 66.

7 McCubbins Collection, Frohock, Deed Book 13: 412 - 413. Edith M. Clark History Room, Rowan Public Library, Salisbury, North Carolina Documents contain the names of Frohock's slaves.

8 John Frohock Jr. Last Will And Testament. Rowan County, North Carolina dated 1768.
http://www.rootsweb.com/~ncrowan/rowan_wills.htm25 (accessed November 25, 2004) Also in Edith M. Clark History Room, Rowan Public Library, Salisbury, North Carolina.

John Frohock (? -1772) was probably born in England, and one of the most influential men in Colonial North Carolina. He came to eastern North Carolina from Pennsylvania after 1751 and settled in Rowan County in 1753. As a surveyor, he was one of the local officials who created Mecklenburg County from the western section of Anson County. As the clerk of court from 1753-1772 for Mecklenburg, Anson, and Rowan counties, he maintained all legal documents. John never married, but his large Mill Plantation was home to 38 slaves.

9 James Brawley, *"The Outpost"* Salisbury Evening Post, June 3, 1956

10 McCubbins Collection, Frohock, Deed Book 13: 412 & 413

11 Dorothy Clarke, Submitter *"Rowan County, North Carolina - Will: Thomas Frohock - 1794 ,"* dated February 26, 1794 US Gen Web Archives http://ftp.rootsweb.com/pub/usgenweb/nc/rowan/wills/f6200002.txt (accessed December 15, 2007)

12 McCubbins Collection, Frohock, Deed Book 13: 412 & 413

13 James S. Brawley, *The Rowan Story, 1753-1953, A Narrative History of Rowan County, North Carolina*, (Salisbury, North Carolina: Rowan Printing Company, 1953), 164.

Toll House, Cardwell Street, Salisbury, Rowan County, NC, Index number NC. 80. SAB, H.A.B.S. Survey No. NC 261. Archie Biggs 1937 in the Historic American Buildings Survey/Historic American Engineering Record, Library of Congress [http://memory.loc.gov] 01/08/08.

14 Ann Brownlee. *"Stoneman's Raid: Salisbury and the Yadkin Bridge",* http://www.tradingford.com/stoneman.html (accessed December 4, 2007), 2.

15 Directory of Salisbury, North Carolina for 1901, Vol. 1. Chicago & New York: Interstate Directory Company.
This directory lists the present-day Freedman's Cemetery as the Oaks. The hypothesis among local historians is that the name Oakdale is derived from Oaks and dale because part of the Oaks Cemetery was moved to a dale in the Union Hill suburb of Salisbury.

16 Rowan County Register of Deeds. Deed Book 986: 222.
Grantor: Noble & Kelsey Funeral Home
Grantee: City of Salisbury
Date: August 26, 2003   Date Registered: September 3, 2003
This is a quick claim deed for ten parcels described on Rowan County Tax Assessor's Map No. 5. These were parcels 208, 209, 211-1, 211-3, 211-2, 212, 213, 214, 218-1 and 216.

17 *"Auction Sale of Homes for Colored People"*. Salisbury Evening Post: Thursday, June 27, 1907

18 J. F. McCubbins. Clerk of Superior Court, Rowan County, North Carolina. Deed Book 156: 271.
Grantor: Frank Partee
Grantee: W. F. Kelsey and wife Lula S. Kelsey
Parcels 208 and 209 on Map 5 Rowan County Tax Assessor.
Present-day Brenner Avenue cuts through parcel 208 by eminent domain.

19 J. M. McCorkle. "Salisbury Yesteryears." Salisbury Post, May 7, 1950

20 George Raynor. *"Milford Hills, Developed as a huge plantation by John and Thomas Frohock, area has a unique and colorful history of power riches."* Salisbury Sunday Post, May 15, 1983

21 Jethro Rumple. *A History of Rowan County North Carolina, Containing Sketches of Prominent Families and Distinguished Men.*, (Baltimore: Regional Publishing Co., 1974): Originally published by J. J. Bruner in Salisbury, N.C. 1881, republished by the Elizabeth Maxwell Steele Chapter Daughters of the American Revolution, Salisbury, North Carolina., 71

22 Murray Edwards, Pastor. *The People of Soldiers: Our Heritage & Our Vision* ., (Salisbury, North Carolina: Auli Printing & Copy Plus, Inc., 2002.), np#

Local historians believe that the name 'Freedman' originated with the history of Soldiers Memorial A. M. E. Zion Church. In 1864, Barry Wilson Davis, George Willis and a Mr. Williams met in a boot shop on the property of Henry H. Bingham in the Henderson Pines Section. The purpose of their meeting was to plan the establishment of a Methodist church for the freedmen of Salisbury. Some time later, Emanuel Jones, Simon Jefferson, William Boyden and others joined them. These men secured the aid of the Freedman's Bureau and organized a group of worshipers in 1865. After a few months, the place of worship was moved to the Freedmen's Building on East Council Street.

On April 4, 1873, Thomas and Ellen Henderson sold the plot of land at the corner of Church and Liberty Streets to the Zion Society (Soldiers Memorial) for $350. The names of the trustees recorded on the deed were Spencer Green, Burton McNeely, William Valentine, John P. Henderson and William Bowden, Chairman (Rowan County Deed Book 47: 368). This deed was enforced after Spencer Green negotiated a bargain and sale deed on April 4, 1873 (Rowan County Deed Book 47: 32). The plot coordinates of both deeds used stones by the 'Colored Cemetery' as orientation points.

Robert Burton McNeely and Barry Wilson Davis are buried in the Union Hill /Oakdale Cemetery. Other members of the board were buried either in the Oak Grove Freedman's Cemetery or subsequently moved to Union Hill/Oakdale or were interred in the Dixonville Cemetery on Concord Road, Salisbury, North Carolina.

23 Arthur Brown Bingham. *"Some Light Shed On Old Cemetery"* Salisbury Post Editorial October 10, 1975.

Mr. Bingham was the historian of Soldiers Memorial A. M.E .Zion Church. He was convinced that there were some slaves buried in the Oak Grove Cemetery's segregated section, known today as the Freedman's Cemetery. Some of the remains in this section were exhumed and re-interred in the Union Hill – Oakdale from 1903 to 1922.

24 Rowan County Register of Deeds, Deed Book 47: 368, Salisbury, North Carolina

25 Rowan County Register of Deeds, Salisbury, North Carolina. Deed book 98:: 184 - 185.
Grantor: Stephen F. Lord
Grantee: The City of Salisbury (four acres from Partee's Corner on Map 5).

The city purchased this land for the re-burial of remains from the Oak Grove Cemetery (Freedman's Cemetery. The four-acre purchase became a section of the Cemetery. Noble and Kelsey Funeral Home performed most of the burials in this section after it was founded in April 1903.
Date: October 6, 1903   Registered October 13, 1903

26 Charter: City of Salisbury. Salisbury, North Carolina, 1903: chap. 366, sec. 1 - 3, 88.
Ratified March 9, 1903, this section discusses the removal and decent burials of bodies from the "Black Cemetery Beside Old English Cemetery" else where. Church and Liberty.

27 *"Liberty Street, Work of Opening Block Commenced This Morning"*. Salisbury Evening Post. July 22, 1910
The right-of-way for the expansion of Liberty Street passed through a former burial ground. A wagon road was cut through the area more than a year prior to the beginning of the work, but the road was rarely traveled. After exhumation of the remaining bodies, Liberty Street connected Jackson and Church Streets with a standard-width road.

28 Rountree, Louise M. Livingstone College, Salisbury, North Carolina 1979-80, Administrative Profiles for the Centennial Celebration. Livingstone College Centennial Publication: Salisbury, North Carolina, 1980.

29 Kenneth D. Sell. Guide to the Cemeteries of Rowan County, North, Carolina. Salisbury, North Carolina: Unpublished, 1988.
_____Obscure Cemeteries of Rowan County, North Carolina. Salisbury, North Carolina: Unpublished, 1988.

30 Hughes, Roberta Wright,   *Lay Down Body: Living History in African-American Cemeteries*   . (Detroit: Visible Ink Press, 1996.)

She gives reasons associated with east-west burials and examines the rise of black benevolent associations. The Florence Progressive Mutual Burial Association of Mitchell and Fair (Ellis, Mangum, and Fair Funeral Home) and the Kelsey Mutual Burial Association provided the means to acquire single and multiple plots that could ensure that spouses and other family members would be interred next to each other. The family plot is a feature of Union Hill/Oakdale that popularized the use of larger, elaborate grave markers, often used to mark an entire family plot.

31 Rowan County Register of Deeds, 402 North Main Street, Salisbury, North Carolina 28144.

32 Dave Brown. Survey and Planning Branch, Archaeology and Historic Preservation, June 1980, North Carolina Division of Archives and History, Item number 8, page 6.

33 National Register of Historic Places, Inventory – Nomination Form: United States Department of the Interior, Heritage Conservation and Recreation Service. Dave Brown, Consultant, Survey and Planning Branch, Archaeology and Historic Preservation June, 1980, North Carolina Division of Archives and History, 109 East Jones Street, Raleigh, NC 27611

PART TWO

BURIALS

ENTRANCE TO UNION HILL SECTION

INSTRUCTIONS FOR LOCATING RECORDS AND GRAVES

Graves, and records of the deceased are located by using the List of Decedents, Burial Records, and the **CEMETERY SECTIONS / SUBSECTION MAPS**. Follow the steps below.

STEP 1   Find the name of the deceased in the List of Decedents, note the page number, and go to STEP 2. If the name is not in the list, the deceased is buried in another cemetery, missed being recorded, buried after October 2004, or died outside Rowan County. Check the North Carolina State Board of Health, Bureau of Vital Statistics for North Carolina deaths or the local funeral homes. If the deceased died outside of North Carolina, contact the state in which the deceased died.

STEP 2   Locate the record of the decedent and note the Section Location, Grave Number, and Map Subsection if one is given.

STEP 3   Use the **Record Key** below to find the subsection map that will identify the place of burial.

Sample of a Complete Record

Sadie Davis Fair   UH-409-I /J   Mitchell & Fair.
    Died 05/24/1981   Age: 92   Retired Teacher: Dunbar High School, East Spencer, N.C.
    0061,0478   Informant: Avis F. Wilkins Monroe, Daughter
    Parents Wilson & Zilpha Davis   Birth Place Rowan County, NC

SADIE DAVIS
FAIR
MAY 24, 1981
AT REST
REST IN PEACE DARLING MOTHER
MAY GOD RICHLY BLESS YOU.

Record Key

Decedent   SECTION LOCATION - Grave # - MAP SUBSECTION   Funeral Home
                      Date of Death   Age at Death   Occupation
Photo if   Rowan County Death Certificate #   Person giving information
available   Parents   decedents place of birth

Marker   *MARKER INSCRIPTION*
Photo

Section Prefix   **Map Subsection Suffix**

    BN   **Brenner Avenue Section**
        Brenner South Subsection   P
        Brenner North Subsection   M
    BT   **Burton and Oakdale Western Section**   K
    OK   **Oakdale Section**
        Bingham / S. E. Duncan Subsection   O
        Circle Subsection   N
        Fair / <u>Lyerly</u> Subsection   I / J
        President Duncan   Subsection   L
    UH   **Union Hill Section**
        Horah Subsection   G
        <u>Fair</u> / Lyerly Subsection   I / J
        Livingston Subsection   H

- The monument for Sadie Davis Fair can be located by using Map I / J

LIST OF DECEDENTS

Name	Page	Name	Page	Name	Page
	41	Baker, Rosa S.			**53**
Acey, Jessie N.			**47**	Blackmore, Clarence	
Acey, Joe collier		Ballard, Joe		Blackwell, Josephine	
Adams, Cora Neely		Banks Jr., James B.		Blackwell, Lillie W.	
Adams, Gloria		Banks, Ida Clement		Blair Sr., Henry	
Adams, Robert		Banks, Mary Etta G.		Blair, Harry	
Adams, Will		Barber, Haskell		Blair, Joe Infant	
Adkins, Mary Alice		Barber, Linnie Infant of		Blair, Raymond	
Adkins, Rosetta		Barber, Mr. Charlie		Bluford, Viola Harris	
	42	Barber, Myrtle		Blunt, Homer	
Aggrey, James E. K.			**48**	Blunt, Katie Parham	
Aggrey, Rose D.		Barber, Nora			**54**
Aggrey. Rosebud D.		Barber, Otis		Boger, Columbus M.	
Agnew, Infant of W. E.		Barker, Harvey		Boger, Dorothy E.	
	43	Barker, John		Boger, May Linda M. T.	
Agnew, Infant of W. E.		Barney, Sallie		Boger, Paul Henry	
Agnew, James		Barret, Henry Howard		Boger, William Byrd	
Agnew, Milford Sloan		Barton, Charlie		Bonepart, Annie	
Agnew, Milton L.		Barton, Henry C.		Booker, Irene Clinton	
Alberta Moore		Bass, Lafayette		Booker, Janie	
Aldrich, Betty		Battle, John Robert		Bookhart, Mr. Marion	
Aldrich, Clara Bell M.		Baum, Daughter		Boozer, Bessie Harris	
Alexander, Alex		Baxter, William		Boozer, Forrest T	
Alexander, Dawn		Beattie, Leona M.			**55**
Alexander, James		Beatty Jr., Donald Ray		Bosley, Maggie W.	
Alexander, James A.			**49**	Bost, Berthia Smith	
	44	Bell, Harrison James		Bost, Ella Odessa	
Alexander, James A.		Belton Sr., Frank		Bost, Francis E.	
Alexander, Laura		Benjamin, Eliza L.		Bost, William C.	
Alexander, Martha J.		Bennett, Tom		Bost. Ephraim	
Alexander, Mary J B.		Bernhard, Sallie		Bost. Mary Elizabeth	
Alexander, N. A.		Bernhardt, Creola		Boyd, Alfred Burley	
Alexander, Norman C.		Bernhardt, Mattie		Boyd, Artie Rose M.	
Alison, Nancy		Berry, Amions			**56**
Allen, James A.		Best, Elizabeth		Boyd, Beulah M.	
Allen, Jennie		Bethea, Charles		Boyd, Effie M.	
Allison, Francis R.			**50**	Boyd, Ida C. Pearson	
	45	Biggers, James Price		Boyd, Maggie	
Anderson, Cicero T.		Bingham, Arthur B.		Boyden, Maggie	
Andrew, Arthur		Bingham, Charles W.		Boyden, Sarah	
Andrews, Lucile		Bingham, Henrietta B.			**57**
Annie A. Glenn		Bingham, Inez		Braithwaite, Alma P.	
Archie, James Allen			**51**	Broadway, Florence	
Ardis, Charles		Bingham, Juanita E.		Brooker, Rosa Mae	
Armstrong, Curley		Bingham, Lillington H.,		Brookhart, Marion	
Armstrong, Infant		Bingham, Lucile B.		Brooks, Tinty	
Armstrong, John Allen		Bingham, Mabel Myers		Brotherton, John A.	
Arnold, Farris G.		Black, Ernestine		Brown, Alford	
Asbery, Blanche Gable		Black, Eula Mae H.		Brown, Alice L.	
	46		**52**		**58**
Ashwood, Florence		Black, Florence L.		Brown, Arthur	
Ashwood, Mrs. P. W.		Black, Julia Rebecca		Brown, Calvin	
Ashwood, Peter A.		Black, Lloyd		Brown, Charles E.	
Austin, Emma		Black, Lloyd		Brown, E. Henry	
Austin, Isabella A.		Black, Lula Holt		Brown, Ella Key	
Baby, Linwood L./M.		Black, Robert		Brown, Fate	
Bailey, Jericho Endigo		Black, Son of Eva		Brown, Goldia	
Bailey, Jewel Archer		Blackmer, Josephine		Brown, Josie	
Bailey, Martha Wooley		Blackmon, Ed			

LIST OF DECEDENTS

Name	Page	Name	Page	Name	Page
		Byers, Tinnie R. Poe	59	Chalk, Henry Leon	
Brown, Kalyn A.		Byrd, Albert L.			72
Brown, Lula Simmons		Byrd, Janice H.		Chambers, Annie Rose	
Brown, Mary		Caldwell, Clara M.		Chambers, Ceola C.	
Brown, Mary Nance			66	Chambers, Essie.	
Brown, Mattie A.		Caldwell, Dr. Edgar L.		Chambers, F. C.	
Brown, Melinda E.		Caldwell, Hazel M.		Chambers, Herbert C.	
Brown, Michael D.		Caldwell, Herman		Chambers, Julia	
Brown, Mildred Louise		Caldwell, James L.		Chambers, Lester	
	60	Caldwell, James R.		Chambers, Lillie	
Brown, Nathaniel A.		Caldwell, John E.		Chambers, Margie L.	
Brown, Nettie I.		Caldwell, Larry E.		Chambers, Moses	
Brown, Savannah			67		73
Brown, Will		Caldwell, Mary V.		Cherry, Ethel M. Miller	
Brown, William		Caldwell, Reatha M.		Cherry, James A.	
Browner, Sallie		Caldwell, Richard Jr.		Cherry, Mary Lee	
Bruce, Charles		Campbell, Annie E.		Cherry, Thomas Lee	
Bruce, Ruben		Campbell, Emma		Cheshire, Bessie Bryant	
Bryant, Carrie Gee		Campbell, Gary		Cheshire, Florence	
	61	Campbell, James		Chesire, Leroy	
Bryant, Roger		Campbell, Lizzie T.		Childress, Mary Ann	
Bryant, Sylvia C.		Campbell, Minnie A.		Chisholm, Alberta M.	
Bryant, William H.		Campbell, Susie			74
Bryant, William Henry		Campbell, Walter J.		Christian, Cicero	
Buford, Arthur Baylis		Cannon, Elem		Christian, Sophronia G.	
Buford, Lula W.			68	Christian, Wiley	
Buford, Mary W.		Carpenter, Dorothy L.		Chun, Lula Osborne B	
	62	Carpenter, Mollie		Clark, Alice	
Buford, Simon Martin		Carr, Dorothy Scott		Clark, Anita Archie	
Bunyon, John Jr.		Carr, John R.		Clark, Charlotte F.	
Bunyon, Willie Belle		Carr, Katie Katherine			75
Burch, Versey		Carr, Lafayette		Clark, Louisa	
Burley, George		Carr, Lula Rice		Clayborn, Annie C.	
Burns, Elijah			69	Clement, Della	
Burns, Henrietta		Carr, Rita		Clement, James A.	
Burns, Neoma		Carr, Scott		Clement, Maggie	
Burton, Emma		Carr, William Scott		Clement, Marshal	
	63	Carrington, William H.		Clement, Otis L.	
Burton, Jim (Baby of)		Carroll, Beulah C.			76
Burton, R. M.		Carroll, Thomas C.		Clement. Martha	
Bush, Gerald		Carson, Annie		Coil, Effie	
Butler, Albert A.		Carson, Charlie		Coleman, Blanche E.	
Butler, Berenza V. H.		Carson, Dovie Staley		Coleman, Caroline	
Butler, Ida Reid			70	Coleman, Eliz	
Butler, Mary Ann		Carson, Ethel M.		Coleman, Ethel W.	
Butler, Usher		Carson, Hattie C.		Coleman, Francis	
	64	Carson, Rachel E.		Coleman, Gerhardt S.	
Butner, Charles Leroy		Carson, William O.		Coleman, John	
Butner, Charles Sandy		Carter, Clare		Coleman, John W.	
Butner, Dulcie Rippy		Carter, Emiline			77
Butner, Fannie		Carter, Evaline B.		Coleman, Vernon H.	
Butner, Lilla M.		Carter, George A.		Collins, John Hillard	
Butner, Sandy A.			71	Collins, Rosie Blair	
Butner, Victoria Huff		Carter, John W.		Colston, John	
	65	Carter, Matthew		Colston, John V.	
Byers, Fannie H.		Carter, Samuel		Coltson, Clyde M.	
Byers, Lorence		Carter, Warren		Connor, Azellee M.	
Byers, Nadine Y.		Caruth, Adam		Connor, Emanuel	
Byers, Silva		Caruth, Mattie B.		Connor, James L.	

LIST OF DECEDENTS

Name	Page	Name	Page	Name	Page
	78	Davis, Edward Luther			90
Cook, Arthur Clinton		Davis, Harrison P.		Duncan, Baby M. Payne	
Cook, Clyde Innis		Davis, Harry James		Duncan, Frederick D.	
Cook, Deshawn Tyrice		Davis, Harvey Lee		Duncan, Ida Hauser	
Cooke, May Troy			84		91
Corpening, Bessie		Davis, Hattie Dunlop		Duncan, John Bonner	
Corpening, Felicia M.		Davis, Hattie Rainy		Duncan, Joseph	
Cowan, Andrew Lee		Davis, Jesse		Duncan, Joseph C.	
Cowan, Annie Milton		Davis, Joe		Duncan, Julia Belle	
Cowan, Annie Ruth		Davis, John M.			92
Cowan, Arthur		Davis, Leon		Duncan, Lena Belle J.	
Cowan, Carrie Neely			85	Duncan, Samuel E.	
Cowan, Carry		Davis, Lillie M. Mason		Duncan, Samuel E. Sr.	
	79	Davis, Margaret			93
Cowan, Launa		Davis, Marie A. Kelly		Duncan, William F.	
Cowan, Roxie		Davis, Mattie Wood		Dunlap, Hope	
Cowen, Annie Mae		Davis, Odessa Francis		Dunlap, Marie H.	
Craige, Frank Charles		Davis, Rashayla Taleea		Dunlap, Walter Cornell	
Craige, John C.		Davis, Richard		Ealy, Amos Willie	
Craige, Kerr		Davis, Rose Douglas		Ealy, Anthony Brown	
Craige, Laura Smith			86		94
Craige, Lula		Davis, Ruth Bonner		Ealy, Florence Brown	
Craige, Willie Hormes		Davis, Sarah		Eddy, Camilla Rogers	
Craige, Willie Mae		Davis, Shawn Demont		Edge, Pearl	
	80	Davis, Sudie C.		Edwards, Will	
Crane, Annie Walker		Davis, Vivian Ray		Eigner, Nancy Beadie	
Craver, Carthia Holt		Davis, William		Elder, James Melton	
Crawford, Caroline J.		Davis, William T. Sr.		Elder, Ruby Lee	
Crawford, John E.		Davis, Wilson		Eller, Irma Alexander	
Crawford, Mable M.			87		95
Crawford, Susie		Davis, Zilphia		Eller, Ulysess S.	
Crittenden, Lizzie		Dawkins, Rudolph		Elliot, Sara C. Holly	
Crittenden, William B.		Dean, Georgia Foust		Ellis, Annie B. Dodge	
Crittinden, Will		Diggs, Louise Holt		Ellis, Edward	
	81	Dodge, Cecelia Giles		Ellis, Emma Lee	
Crosby, Julie		Dodge, Grace M.		Emmason, Catherine	
Crosby, Thomas		Dodge, Mary A. Gray		Ervin, Geneva	
Crosby, Willie		Dodge, Wiley E. Jr.		Eury, Audy	
Crowell, Willie G.		Dodge, Wiley E. Sr.			96
Culbertson, Charles E.			88	Eury, Lillian	
Culp, Clyde C.		Donald, James S. Sr.		Evans, A. L.	
Culp, Lula Ferguson		Donald, Ollie Lee C.		Evans, Carter & Joseph	
Cureton, Mary Burns		Donaldson, James		Evans, Francis Lucille	
Curley, John		Donaldson, James		Evans, Jimmy David	
	82	Donaldson, Nannie S.		Evans, L. M. Hargrave	
Currence, Ella H. G.		Dorsey, Ella Dixon		Evans, Lillie Mae E.	
Daniel, Frank Leonard		Douglas, Dorothy Ann		Evans, Margaret	
Daniel, John III		Douglas, Mary Kitchen		Evans, Margaret Lucille	
Daniels, Fannie Payne		Douglas, William			97
Daniels, Ollie			89	Evans, Mattie	
Davidson, Rev. C. R.		Drafton, Lucille Davie		Evans, Otho	
Davis, Alice Johnson		Draper, Jim		Evans, Robert L.	
Davis, Bessie		Draper, Laura		Evans, Warren	
	83	Dudley, Alice		Everhardt, Bradley	
Davis, Charlotte		Dudley, Connie Infant of		Everhart, Pearl	
Davis, D. F. Wilkerson		Dudley, Laura		Fagatt, Cornelia Mills	
Davis, Delia		Dumas, Mary		Fagatt, Millie Bell	
Davis, Edward		Duncan, Aileene Wade		Faggart, Joseph	
Davis, Edward		Duncan, Annie Ruth E.		Faggart, Lucille	

LIST OF DECEDENTS

Name	Page	Name	Page	Name	Page
Faggart, Rose Lockhart		Fleming. Clarence J.		Gist, Douglas	
	98	Flowe, Ada Graham		Gist, Elsa Winslow	
Faggatt, Bertha		Flowe, Christopher L.		Gist, James	
Fair, Charlie		Flowe, Theodore D.		Gist, Lizzie	
Fair, Delbert Sepheria		Flowers, Adelaide M.		Gist, Nora F.	
Fair, James C.		Floyd, Jim		Glasco, Lula	
Fair, James C. Jr.			105		111
Fair, Mrs. Charles		Floyd, Sarah		Glasco, Rufus G	
Fair, Robert William		Foard, Sarah V.		Glasco, Willie	
Fair, Sadie Davis		Foil, Joe		Gleen, James.	
	99	Ford, Alean Goins		Gleen, Willie M.	
Falls, Bertha Roberts		Ford, Catherine		Glenn, Annie A.	
Falls, James Edwards		Ford, Mollie		Glenn, Isabel	
Feanster, Bishop		Ford, Stokes		Glenn, James	
Feaster, Albert Joel		Fore, Charlie		Glenn, Lambeth C.	
Feaster, Henry		Fortune, Brynda		Glenn, Louise Meeks	
Febby, Walton		Fowler, Edgar Eugene			112
Ferbee, William Coley		Fowler, Sadie		Glenn, Will	
Ferguson, Plumie			106	Glenn, Willie	
Ferribee, Clarence		Fox, Israel Jeremiah		Glover, Maggie K.	
	100	Francis Lyerly, Infant of		Gnatt, Mary Holmes	
Ferron, John M.		Freeman, Robert		Goler, William Harvey	
Ferron, Maria		Frohock, Thomas		Goode, John	
Ferron, Marial or Mollie		Frost, Michael Derick		Goodlett, John Edward	
Ferron, Walter L.		Gaddy, George W.		Goodlett, Modest E.	
Ferron, William A.		Gaines, Annie			113
Ferron, William O.		Gaines, Edward		Goodwin, Nancy	
Field, Henrietta Parker		Gaines, Jerry		Goodwin, Yvonne	
	101		107	Graham, Frank	
Fields, Charles Jr. III		Gaines, Paul		Graham, Hezekiah	
Fisher, Annie Irene G.		Gaines, Willie Lee		Graham, James Banks	
Fisher, Baby of Maggie		Gaither, Geneva		Graham, John Lee Sr.	
Fisher, Carr Harold		Gaither, Infant		Graham, Rayford A.	
Fisher, Catherine M.		Gaither, Laura Sloan		Grasty, Ever	
Fisher, Charles		Galloway, Van			114
Fisher, Clyde Verner		Gantt, Edna Mae		Graves, Mable Harris	
Fisher, Deborah		Gantt, John Henry		Gray, John W.	
Fisher, Dorothy M.			108	Gray, Luther Junior	
	102	Gantt, Mary Holmes		Gray, Sallie	
Fisher, H. Carl		Garner, A.		Green, Infant of John & Ellen	
Fisher, James		Garner, Linda Fay		Greenlee, Jessie	
Fisher, Jessie McCorkle		Garner, Logan		Greenlee, Jessie J. Sr.	
Fisher, John		Garrison, Willie Sr.		Greenlee, Julia Tate	
Fisher, Josie Partee		Garwood, Berry			115
Fisher, Laura		Garwood, Green Berry		Griffin, Mildred E. Ingram	
Fisher, Maggie Rose		Garwood, Lena Lyerly		Griffin, Stanley Jerome	
Fisher, Miss Lovagoos		Garwood, Leola		Guider, Beulah Turner	
	103	Garwood, William		Guy, Ola Harper	
Fisher, Mrs. Rose Sloan			109	Hairston, Adam Forest	
Fisher, Nonie Springs J.		Gee, Harvey Henry		Hairston, Shalene Evon	
Fisher, Samuel		Gibson, Lizzie Poe		Hall, Alice Maria H.	
Fitzgerald, Carl		Gill. Amos		Hall, Bessie Corpening	
Fitzgerald, Fannie Mae		Gill, Ella			116
Fitzgerald, Jeanett		Gill, Nannie Broomfield		Hall, Betty L.	
Flack, Flora Bernhardt		Gill, Romis Morris		Hall, Edmonia Kent	
	104		110	Hall, Florence	
Flack, Neal Roy		Gillespie, Augusta L.		Hall, Henry Buford	
Flack, Rev. E. Rex		Gillespie, John Robert		Hall, Henry D.	
Fleming, Herman K.		Gist, Della		Hall, John Gus	

LIST OF DECEDENTS

Name	Page	Name	Page	Name	Page
Hall, Louicio Hamilton			123	Hickman, Dossie S.	
Hall, Oliver Cleveland		Harris, William		Hickman, Louicio	
	117	Harrison, Emily W.		Hickman, Margie	
Hambrick, Alice		Harrison, James Bell		Hickman, Rosetta	
Hamilton, Lottie Perry		Harrison, Lizzie Mae		Hickman, William Lee	
Hampton, Marie		Harrison, Samuel James		Hickson, William Ray	
Hancock, Richard E.		Hauser, Mary A. Speas		Higgins, Nina	
Hancock, Sarah B. Cook		Hauser, Nancy N.			131
Hannum, Alexander			124	Hill, Amanda Lee	
Hannum, William H.		Hauser, Sanford Henry		Hill, Annie Mae	
Harbison, Bester		Hawkins, Derrick Jr.		Hill, Aron	
	118	Hawkins, Eliza		Hill, Harvest L.	
Hardback, James		Hayes, Pollie		Hill, Walter June	
Hargrave, Clarence		Hayes, Price		Hines, Nolia Smith	
Hargrave, Frank		Headen, Lizzie Mae		Hipps, Eddie Jr.	
Hargrave, Jack		Hearne, Adam Dewitt			132
Hargrave, Jesse Lee		Hearns, Kathleen G. Johnson		Hipps, Georgia Payne	
Hargrave, John		Hebrew, William Henry		Hobson, Beatred	
Hargrave, Lena Brown			125	Hobson, Eugene	
Hargrave, Lizzi		Heilig, Gladys Irene		Hobson, Isabel B.	
	119	Heilig, Raymond L.		Hobson, J. E. Henderson	
Hargrave, Mary L.		Hemphill, Elijah J.		Hobson, Lillie Davis	
Hargrave, Richard		Hemphill, Ella		Hobson, Maggie	
Hargrave, William		Henderson, Abraham.		Hobson, Martha	
Hargrove, Jonathan		Henderson, Alice Ellis		Hobson, Mary	
Harley, Geneva M. Miller		Henderson, Annie Faye		Hobson, Phoebe Carr	
Harley, Lillie May			126		133
Harley, Paul		Henderson, Arthur		Hobson, Rachel	
Harris, Benjamine C.		Henderson, Caroline P		Hoffman, Bernice F.	
Harris, Charles Frank		Henderson, Cecelia H.		Hogan, Carrie	
	120	Henderson, Clanton E.		Hoke, Robert J.	
Harris, Charles Henry		Henderson, Curlee G.		Holce, S. D.	
Harris, Cicero Richardson.		Henderson, Dottie		Holie, Mamie McNair	
Harris, Cleo		Henderson, Douglas		Holland, Johnnie Sr.	
Harris, Eva			127	Holland, Madline C.	
Harris, Florence J.		Henderson, Elizabeth L.		Holmes, Barbara	
Harris, Florence W.		Henderson, Elizabeth P			134
Harris, George		Henderson, Henry		Holmes, Ella Rankins	
	121	Henderson, Isaac		Holt, Addie Gertrude	
Harris, Henry		Henderson, John A.		Holt, Anna Noble	
Harris, Isabella		Henderson, John Lacie		Holt, Baby Edwin Allen	
Harris, James C.		Henderson, Judy B.		Holt, Helen Waugh	
Harris, Infant of John			128	Holt, John Anderson	
Harris, Lee		Henderson, Laura		Holt, John Calvin	
Harris, Lillie		Henderson, Leon Eddie			135
Harris, Lonnie		Henderson, Lula Cook		Holt, Josephine C.	
Harris, Lula		Henderson, Lula D.		Holt, Julia F.	
Harris, Malinda		Henderson, Martin K.		Holt, Kenneth Baby of Holt	
Harris, Margaret Peck		Henderson, Marvin P.		Holt, Nellie	
	122	Henderson, Mary		Holt, Odessa Manuel	
Harris, Mariah E. Gion			129	Hoover, Azree Headen	
Harris, Marjorie		Henderson, William		Hoover, Frank	
Harris, Martha		Henry, George W.		Hoover, Pink Infant of	
Harris, Mattie		Herndon, David W.			136
Harris, Robert		Herndon, James E.		Hopkins, Clara Mitchell	
Harris, Robert plot		Herndon, Mary Jean R.		Horne, Luke	
Harris, So			130	Horton, Alice Harris	
Harris, Steven		Herndon, Polly		Horton, Evelyn Inez	
Harris, Susie Warner		Herndon, Priscilla		House, Henry Robert	

LIST OF DECEDENTS

Name	Page	Name	Page	Name	Page
House, Mary Heilig		Johnson, J. T.		Kelsey, Alex	
Houston, Elmina Bruce		Johnson, James H.		Kelsey, Alexander S.	
Houston, Ida			143	Kelsey, Amanda B.	
Houston, James		Johnson, Jarrie Martin			150
	137	Johnson, Jesse James		Kelsey, Amanda Lucille	
Houze, Andrew R.		Johnson, John		Kelsey, Harvey A.	
Howard, Fannie C.		Johnson, Julius Percival		Kelsey, Lula Spaulding	
Howard, Gerald		Johnson, Lillie		Kelsey, William Francis	
Howard, Henry		Johnson, Lillie		Kendall, Hattie A.	
Howard, Malinda		Johnson, Lizzie Lewis			151
Howard, Rev. William H.		Johnson, Lottie		Kennedy, Annie Letitia	
Howie, Eliza Poe			144	Kennedy, Annie Moore	
Hull, Gordon A.		Johnson, Lucious		Kennedy, Rev. J. E.	
	138	Johnson, Melvin		Kenny, Charise	
Hunt, Francis		Johnson, Mildred J. P.		Kent, Caroline	
Hunt, Fred Robert		Johnson, Nonie Fisher S.		Kent, Pleasant	
Hunt, Julia		Johnson, Thomas W.		Kerns, Brutus	
Hunt, Lizzie Benton		Johnson, Velma Branch		Kerns, Ella Hobson	
Hunter, Charles Wilson		Johnson, Walter Louis		Kerr, James Bernard	
Hunter, Josephine K.		Johnson, Washington			152
Ivey, Bishop Francis R.			145	Key, Sussie	
Ivey, Mattie Abrams		Johnston, John R.		King, Inez Rivers	
Jackson, Arthur James		Jones, Adline Curry		King, Janie Efrium	
Jackson, Israel Joseph		Jones, Alice Nicholson		Kiser, Toleda Elease	
Jackson, Mattie		Jones, Arthur		Knox, Amanda Lucinda	
	139	Jones, Carrie Lena		Knox, Columbus C.	
Jackson, Pearl C.		Jones, Courtney M. H.		Knox, Ella	
James, Ellen		Jones, Daisey		Knox, Emma	
Jamison, Alice B.			146		153
Jamison, Effie Phifer		Jones, Edna Marie		Knox, Henry	
Jamison, Francis S.		Jones, Ellen		Knox, Infant of L. W.	
Jamison, John		Jones, Ernest Maurice		Knox, Julia Butler	
Jefferies, Ambrose L.		Jones, Gabe		Knox, Otis	
Jefferies, Hattie C.		Jones, Henry (Red)		Koontz, Elizabeth D.	
	140	Jones, I.		Koontz, Harry Lee	
Jefferies, Windsor H.		Jones, John Elvester		Koontz, James Eddie	
Jefferson, Hallie			147	Koontz, Lonnie Wilson	
Jeffrey, Ethel Beatrice T.		Jones, Julius Jackson		Krider, F. Pemberton	
Jenkins, Granddaughter of		Jones, L. V.			154
Wesley		Jones, Larisha Elizabeth		Lancaster, A. Aggrey	
Jenkins, Henry		Jones, Lee Clarence		Lancaster, Spencer W.	
Jenkins, Laura		Jones, Mary Heilig		Land, Emma	
Jenkins, Laura		Jones, Minnie C.		Lanear, Dora Hoover	
Jenkins, Lillie		Jones, Mrs. Ida		Laney, E. J. Hancock	
	141	Jones, Robert M.			155
Jenkins, Willie		Judge, George W.		Lash, M. Grundy	
Jenkins, Willie M. C.		Kelley, Arthur C.		Lash, Wiley Hezikiah	
Jennings, Amanda T.			148	Lassiter, Kenderick R. D	
Jennings, Norris T		Kelley, Daisy Lyles		Lawrence, Annie B. S.	
Jeter, Arthur L.		Kelly, Eula		Lawrence, A. Henderson	
Jeter, Florence		Kelly, Grace H.		Leach, Ervin Vinson	
Johnson, Andrew		Kelly, James S.			156
Johnson, Annie		Kelly, Margarine Margi		Leach, Lois I. H. B. A.	
Johnson, Cicero		Kelly, Marie A. Davis		Leach, Samuel	
	142	Kelly, Mary		Leach, Silas Jr.	
Johnson, David Allen Jr.			149	Leach, Virginia	
Johnson, Dock		Kelly, Mr. Savannah		Leak, Pattie	
Johnson, Dupree		Kelly, S. L.		Leazer, Will	
Johnson, Esther Sarah		Kelsey, A. Spaulding		Lee, Betty	

LIST OF DECEDENTS

Name	Page	Name	Page	Name	Page
Lee, Emma	157	Martin, Daisy	163	McKinney, Ms. E. B.	
Lee, John Wesley		Martin, Earl		McLaughlin, Hurbert G.	169
Lee, Livonia Clark		Martin, Eva Barksdale		McLillie, Hattie	
Legree, Lucille Hoke		Martin, Francis Dau of		McMahan, Ben	
Lewis, Ethel		Martin, Jake		McMoris, John J.	
Lewis, Rena		Martin, Lizzie		McNeely, Carrie Logan	
Lillie Ford		Martin, Thomas		McNeely, Charlie	
Lindsay, Julius		Mason, Everette H.		McNeely, Maria Dodge	
Lindsey, Robert		Mason, Fannie B.			170
Lineberger, Calvin H.	158	Mason, Fisher R.		McNeely, Robert Burton	
		Mason, Maggie	164	Medlock, Hester	
Lineberger, Cynthia D				Meeks, Louisa J.	
Lineberger, Hester H.		Massey, Abe		Meisenheimer, Mack	
Lineberger, J. D.		Massey, Freddy		Melba Darrel	
Lineberger, John Henry		Massey, Julia F.		Meller, Demond Dray	
Lineberger, William D.		Massey, Naomi H.		Melton, Vernon	
Litaker, Alta Mills		Massey, Samuel		Meniers, Minnie	
Litaker, Angeline K.		Mathews, Urnette		Merritt, Janie	
Litaker, Angeline W.		Maxwell, David H.		Metz, Melrose	
	159	Maxwell, Elizabeth		Miles, Henry	171
Litaker, Charles Garfield		Maxwell, Minnie		Miller, Allen	
Litaker, Daniel		McCain, Cora Pratt	165	Miller, Alonzo	
Litaker, Elliot				Miller, Arthur Mack	
Litaker, Julia		McCluney, Mack		Miller, Demond D.	
Litaker, Lizzie		McConnaughey, Nettie		Miller, Fannie	
Litaker, Margaret		McCorkle, Gertrude A.		Miller, Francis Pinkston	
Litaker, Mary Jane		McCorkle, Harold J.		Miller, George	
Little, David Eugene		McCorkle, J. Alexander		Miller, George	172
Little, Donald Ray		McCorkle, John			
Lloyd, Black		McCorkle, Johnsie L.		Miller, Hattie Lattimore	
Locke, George		McCorkle, Laura	166	Miller, Helen A.	
Long, Annie C.	160	McCorkle, Miss Alma		Miller, Ida	
		McCorkle, Pinkney A.		Miller, James Henry	
Long, Ben David		McCorkle, Thomas L.		Miller, John	
Long, George W.		McCowan, Richard		Miller, Julia D.	
Long, Lallage Bost		McCoy, Miles		Miller, Lavenia	
Long, Leroy Jones		McCoy, William		Miller, Lee	
Long, Robert		McCoy, Willie Lyerly		Miller, Lonnie B.	173
Lord, Malvina		McCraire, Bettie			
Luckey, Clinton		McCrary, Y. Madison		Miller, Maria	
Luckey, Raymond A.	161	McCubbins, Noah	167	Miller, Marie Jones	
Lyerly, Etta Lee		McCullough, James E.		Miller, Martha	
Lyerly, John Henry		McDowell, Komika D.		Miller, Mildred	
Lyerly, Mary Rosie		McEntire, Rev. W. J.		Miller, Morris	
Lyerly, Mary White		McGill, Minnie		Miller, Norris Jennis	
Lyles, Earnest Edward		McGriff, Booker T.		Miller, William L.	
Lyttle, Adolphus		McGraw, Marion Setzer		Milton, Beatrice	174
Maaks, Louise J.	162	McILwaine, John H.		Mitchell, Andrew T.	
Mack, Elizabeth P.		McIntyre, Dorothy D.	168	Mitchell, Annie Lee	
Mack, Willie		McKennzie, Grace		Mitchell, Anthony B.	
Malone, Lula		McKinne, Bud		Mitchell, Horace Greely	
Manuel, Thenia		McKinney, Charlie		Mitchell, Ira Bell	
March, John Wesley		McKinney, James		Mitchell, John Hamilton	
Marlin, Mary		McKinney, John		Mitchell, Laura Gibson	175
Marsh, George W.		McKinney, Laura		Mitchell, Maggie S.	
Marsh, Stella					

LIST OF DECEDENTS

Name	Page
Mitchell, Mary E. J.ohnson	
Mitchell, William (Bud)	
Mitchell, William W.	
Mitchell, Willie L.	
Mobley, Norma Jene	
Monroe, Mamie P.	
Montgomery, Charles W.	176
Montgomery, George	
Montgomery, Marry C.	
Montgomery, Marry W	
Montgomery, Sandy D.	
Montgomery, Sarah Davis	
Montgomery, Willie	
Moore, Alberta Guest	
Moore, Ed	177
Moore, Edward Jr.	
Moore, Edward Sr.	
Moore, Emma	
Moore, George	
Moore, Harvey	
Moore, Maggie C.	
Moore, Mary	
Moore, Mary C.	178
Moore, Oscar James	
Moore, Serena L.	
Morant, Arminta C.	
Morant, Harvey Alexander	
Morant, Rena Harris	
Morant, Rosa Lee	
Morant, William Fred	179
Morgan, Adam	
Morris, Bessie	
Morris, Edward	
Morris, Mamie	
Morrison, Mike	
Morton, Emma C.	
Morton, Miles Linwood	
Morton, Rev. James M.	180
Moton, Mattie Lucille	
Mowery, Eke (sic)	
Mullen, Rilla	
Murdock, Sallie H.	
Musgrave, Mary J. H.	
Myers, Ellen	
Myers, Maybell	181
Neely, Elizabeth W.	
Neely, Frank Solomon	
Neely, John K.	
Neely, Leonard Albert	
Neely, Margie	
Neely, Milton	182
Neely, Robert	

Name	Page
Nicholson, James J.	
Noble, Angeline	
Noble, Annie	
Noble, Eloise (sic)	
Noble, James	
Noble, Margaret J. W.	
Noble, Minnie Garfield	183
Noble, Stephen	
Norman, Columbus	
Norman, Emma	
Norman, John	
Norman, Rosa Lee	
Norris, Ruby Louise W.	
Norris, Ruby Mae	184
Norris, Theodore R. Sr.	
Oakley, Sarah J.	
Oglesby, Adam Otha	
Ormand, Nelle	
Osborne, Isabella M.	
Osborne, John J.	
Osborne, Walter	
Owens, Ellen	
Pajibu, Johnson Toto	
Palmer, Katherine	
Palmer, Zelpale	185
Parham, Georgia	
Parham, Thomas Lee	
Parker, Hugh Ernest	
Parker, Ruby Lee	
Parker, Sadie Fisher	
Parker, Walter	
Parks, Janie	
Parks, Jasper P.	
Parks, Moses	
Partee, Elsie	186
Partee, Frank	
Partee, Harry Leroy	
Partee, Mariah Bost	
Pate, Odessa Coleman	
Patterson, R; Chisholm	
Patterson, Willie	
Payne, George H.	
Payne, Willie C.	187
Payseur, Nancy	
Peake, Danil	
Peake, Lela Josephine	
Peakes, Lilia	
Pearson, Ida B. Gee	
Pearson, Jesse Edward	
Pearson, Judge	
Pearson, Mary D.	188
Peddrew, Elizabeth	
Peeler, Rosa	

Name	Page
Pemberton, Arnous	
Pemberton, Matthew P.	
Pemberton, Sandy	
Pemberton, Stanly S	
Pemberton, William P.	
Pennington, Lottie	
Pennington, Tom	189
Peoples, Leticia Mae	
Perkins, Howard	
Perkins, Lillian Buford	
Perkins, lla A. Heggins	
Perkins, Roy	
Perry, Edith E. Davis	
Perry, John W.	
Pharr, L. Henderson	190
Pharr, Perreal Conner	
Pharr, Raymond James	
Phifer, Robert Beverly	
Phillips, Alberta	
Phillips, Ed	
Phillips, Edward Luther	
Phillips, Marcus J.	
Phillips, Sallie A.T.	191
Phillips, Willie Mills	
Pierce, Clarence	
Pierce, Cordia P.	
Pierce, Julian	
Pierce, June Brown	
Pierce, Marie Sanford	
Pilgram, Margaret	192
Pinkston, David H.	
Pinkston, John	
Pinkston, Nancy C.	
Pinkston, Thomas A.	
Pitts /Montgomery Inf.	
Pitts, Amie H. Judge	
Pitts, Frank R.	193
Pitts, Jerry Lee	
Pitts, Lewis Frank Jr.	
Pitts, Lewis Frank Sr.	
Pitts, Mae Troy	
Poag, Florence Irene	
Poag, James	
Poe, Rose	
Polk, Baby	
Polk, Hannah	
Pope, Amelia	194
Powell, Mary Frances	
Powell, Oliver P.	
Preasha, Gwendolyn Fair	
Price, Emma Louise	
Price, Jennie Smallwood	
Price, Josephine	

LIST OF DECEDENTS

Name	Page	Name	Page	Name	Page
	195		**201**	Simmons, Glendora	
Price, Louise Moore		Russell, Dan		Simmons, Malissa F.	
Price, Robert M.		Russell, Eva Harris		Simmons, Mary Hall	
Price, William Dodge		Sampson, Lucy		Simmons, Mose	
Propst, Mary		Sanders, Annie Belle		Simmons, Philip	
Pruitt, Carrie M. Barber		Sanders, E. D.		Simon, Ida Fitzgerald	
Quattlebaum Infant.		Sanders, Julia			**.208**
Ramsuer, Alec		Sanders, K. Napoleon		Simpson, Frank Walter	
Randall, Alvah		Sanford, Julia		Simpson, Julius	
	196		**202**	Simpson, Lillian Bingham E.	
Randall, Kathleen Jones		Saunders, Josephine		Singleton, George	
Randall, Thomas J.		Saunders, Mamie L.		Sloan, A. H.	
Rankin, Otto		Saunders, Robert		Sloan, Alphonzo	
Reese, Nathalee B.		Savage. H. H.		Sloan, Frank	
Reeves, Dorothy		Scott, Ardelia		Sloan, Jessie Lowe	
Reid, Bertha Pearl		Scott, Arthur Harry			**209**
Reid, Janie Walker		Scott, Bessie		Sloan, Sallie	
Reid, John C.		Scott, Henryetter		Sloan, Sylvia LaJune	
	197		**203**	Sloan, William	
Reid, Maggie Johnson		Scott, John		Sloan, William Lonnie	
Reid, Nancy Bennett		Scott, Julia Maria		Smith, Alexander	
Reid-Craig, B. M. C.		Scott, Mary Barber		Smith, Alice	
Reliford, LaKendra M.		Scott, Mason		Smith, Amanda	
Reliford, William Leon		Scott, Neal		Smith, Arabella	
Richardson, Frank N.		Scott, Rose Mary		Smith, Brister (sic)	
Richardson, Martha		Scott, Vance			**210**
Richardson, R. Massey		Sellers, Donald		Smith, Elizabeth	
	198	Sellers, Dorothy Ann		Smith, Emma	
Richardson, Victoria			**204**	Smith, Fredrick	
Riggs, Eliza		Setzer, Marion		Smith, Henry	
Rippy, Clarence		Setzer, Maud E. McCain		Smith, Henry D.	
Ritchie, Lela C.		Sharp, Mary Lee		Smith, Henry Lee	
Ritchie, Sarah A. Walker		Sharp, William Alexander		Smith, Hurclese	
Rivers, Elder V. Leak		Sharpe, Christine B.		Smith, Jakia Synquis	
Roberson, Jane		Sharpe, Cleveland			**211**
Roberson, Minnie		Sharpe, Katie Miller		Smith, James E.	
Roberson, William Alex		Shaw, Gus		Smith, James Vickers	
Roberts, Coatny Massey		Shaw, Sarah		Smith, Janie Lucy	
	199		**205**	Smith, John D.	
Roberts, Orr Ulyses M.		Shelton, Annie Cenovia		Smith, John Wiley	
Roberts, Samuel		Shelton, Georgia		Smith, Leonard	
Robertson, Laura Curry		Sherrill, Estella		Smith, Lula Sujette H.	
Robertson, Mary Rose		Sherrill, Jennie Louise			**212**
Robinson, Charlie		Sherrill, Josephine Price		Smith, M. B.	
Robinson, Clarence		Sherrill, Richard W.		Smith, Maria Ellis	
Robinson, Eva M.Twitty		Sherrill, Sutter		Smith, Maugaritte	
Robinson, James Leroy			**206**	Smith, Nora	
	200	Shipp, David		Smith, Patricia	
Robinson, James W.		Shipp, George W.		Smith, Robert Lee	
Robinson, Minnie		Shipp, Mamie Pryor		Smith, Susie C.	
Robinson, R. Kennedy		Shipp, Tryplemia (sic)		Smith, T. C.	
Robinson, Tom		Shuford, Jennie Ann		Snow, Mary	
Rodes, Paul		Sifford, Angle Lovette		Solom, John	
Roseboro, S. Simpson		Siler, Idella Wooly			**213**
Ross, Kiana Lashae		Siler, Shirley Ann		Spaulding, John A.	
Rousseau, Laura		Simes, Samson		Speights, Chris	
Rowe, Nora			**207**	Spencer, Effie	
Rozzell, Amelia Rucker		Simmons, A. T.		Spratt, Nancy Hanks	
		Simmons, George		Spring, Johnie Mae	

LIST OF DECEDENTS

Name	Page	Name	Page	Name	Page
Springs, John E.		Talford, Sharitale Le T.		Turner, Tamer N.	
	214		220	Turner, Thomas P.	
Springs, John Henry		Tate, Ella Louise Harden		Tyson, Mary Bell	
Springs, John W.		Taylor, Berdie Brown		Unthank, Emma A.	
Springs, Leaper		Taylor, Rev. Samuel A.		Vinson, James M.	
Springs, Lemmel		Taylor, Roxie Hairston		Vinson, Lando	
Springs, Lena		Taylor, Willett Irene		Vutner, Sandy A.	
Springs, Lucille		Teaseley, Doc		Wade, Robert W.	
Springs, Robert		Teasley, Helen Marie		Wakefield, S. Monroe Jr.	
Springs, Robert Hope			221		.227
Stafford, Sarah		Teasley, John		Walker, C. Hardin	
Standard, Annie		Teasley, Lula May		Walker, Harold Lee	
Stanley, George I.		Templeton, James		Walker, Jacqueline	
	215	Thirdgill, John McCrori		Walker, Janie Lee	
Stanley, Kevin Eugene		Thirdgill, Mary		Walker, Jesse H.	
Stanley, Lena Griffin		Thomas, Eliza H. Goler		Walker, Lee	
Starr, Gilbert		Thomas, Leroy		Walker, Lizzie Haynes	
Starr, Vina		Thomas, Winifred			228
Steel, William		Thompson, Ada		Walker, Ora	
Steele, Gladys A. R.			222	Walker, Scottie	
Steele, Lisa Crystal A.		Thompson, Annie M. L.		Walker, Winnie	
Steele, Sarah Hogans		Thompson, Cora V. H.		Wallace, Lucy S.	
Steele, Viola		Thompson, N. B. King		Walters, Wakefield	
	216	Thompson, Will		Walton, Febby	
Stephens, Jimmy		Threadgill, M. Talford		Walton, John	
Stephens, Johnie		Tillman, James Robert		Ward, Emiley	
Stevenson, Angie		Tillman, Shirley Ann			229
Stevenson, Pinkey Alexander			223	Ward, Lillie M. Gaddy	
Stewart, Hattie		Timmons, Emma		Ware, Edgar L.	
Stewart, Linda Kay		Tomblin, Willie James Jr.		Warren, Elizabeth Hart	
Stewart, Melvin		Tomblin, Willie James Sr.		Washington, Amie	
Stinson, Jasper		Torrence, Anthony L.		Washington, Frank	
Stoner, Gertrude Boozer		Torrence, Dallas		Washington, Gertrude	
Stoval, B. D. Oglesby		Torrence, James Curtis			230
	217	Torrence, Sha Cole		Washington, Rose	
Strawder, Agustus		Trice, Bessie		Watkins, Ella Youngblood	
Strawder, Robert Jr.		Trott, Benjamine		Watkins, Tom	
Strong, John		Trott, Bessie		Watson, C. Henry Sr.	
Strother, Leon Sunner			224	Watson, Mabel E. Scott	
Strother, Mary Sumner		Trott, Chlora E.		Watts, Lula Johnson	
Strother, Will		Trott, Effalena		Waugh, James Andrew	
Sturdivant, E.ssie Mitchell		Trott, James Garfield		Wayne, Kenneth	
Sturdivant, Teresa M.		Trott, Marguerite S.		Webb, Effie Kelly	
	218	Trueblood, Ella Farmer			231
Summers, Corinthia B.		Trueblood, Ella Mae		Webster, Oscar	
Summers, Destini		Trueblood, Esther B.		Weeks, Wilson	
Summers, Webb		Truesdale, William P.		Welborne, Clark	
Sumner, James D.			225	Welborne, E. Henderson	
Sumner, Jennie Harris		Truesdale, Willie		Welborne, Scott Terry	
Sumner, John		Tucker, Juanita Davis		Wells, Clarence W.	
Sumner, Nancy		Tucker, Lawrence		Westberry, Annie R.	
Sumner, Thelmore		Tucker, Lucille Reese			232
	219	Tugman, Delia Christian		Westberry, John Elliot	
Sumner, Will Charlie		Turner, Joseph James		Wheeler, Edward E. Jr.	
Swift, Earlie		Turner, Lamar C.		Whisonant, Theodore	
Swift, Jessie		Turner, Lelia A.		Whitaker, Daniel M.	
Swift, Rilla		Turner, Nora		Whitaker, Johnnie Mae	
Taggart, Emma C.			226	White, Bessie Clark	
Taggart, Reece Conrad		Turner, Samuel		White, Charlie	

LIST OF DECEDENTS

Name	Page
White, Cora Lee Knox	
White, George W.	
White, Infant of John	233
White, Joe	
White, Lola Bell	
White, Milton	
White, Octavia	
White, Robert	
White, Ruby Smile	
White, Will	
Whitener, Margie	
Whittington, Andrew R.	
Whittington, Lottie Mae	
Whoozer, Bettie E.	234
Whoozer, Elizabeth	
Whoozer, Elizabeth B.	
Whyte, Hattie Douglas	
Wilder, Deshaun	
Wilder, Lila	
Wilder, Lila M. Connor	
Wilder, Mattie Barber	
Wilkes, Elliott B.	
Wilkins, Diamond Carr	235
Wilkins, Floyd	
Wilkins, James	
Wilkins, Jim	
Wilkins, Pauline	
Wilks, George	
Wilks, Louvenia Eller	
Wilks, Major	
Willett, Janet	236
Williams, Clestsus	
Williams, Edward	
Williams, Estelle Partee	
Williams, Florence L.	
Williams, James	
Williams, Janie Lee	
Williams, Johnsie.	
Williams, Mable Elaine	
Williams, Malik Almud	
Williams, Pettegrew Jr.	237
Williams, Victoria	
Williams, Winema C.	
Willoughby, Nannie M.	
Wilson, Adam Lee	
Wilson, Annie Mae	
Wilson, Billie Jean	
Wilson, David J	
Wilson, Ella Robinson	
Wilson, Franklin	238
Wilson, Harrison	
Wilson, Hezekiah E.	
Wilson, James	

Name	Page
Wilson, Malissa Foot	
Wilson, Rose Kelly	
Wilson, Saunders "Pete"	
Wilson, Terry Lee	
Wilson, William	239
Wilson, Willie	
Winford, Leonard L.	
Winfry, Bertie	
Wingate, Betty Bingham	
Wiseman, Annie E.	
Wiseman, Estella	
Wiseman, Lewis C.	
Wiseman, Mary	240
Wiseman, Ollie Gainey	
Wiseman, Robert L.	
Wiseman, Sherman	
Witherspoon, Christine J.	
Witherspoon, John	
Witherspoon, Roosevelt	
Wood, Columbus J.	
Wood, Daisy B.	
Wood, Ella Hannah	
Wood, Joann	241
Woodard, McDilla	
Woodburn, Emma M.	
Woodruff, Et. Louise	
Woodruff, Sarah Scott	
Woodruff, William	
Woodruff, William H.	
Woods, Carrie	242
Woodside, Millie	
Woodson, Ezell	
Woodson, John	
Woodson, M. Arthur	
Wooley, Elbert	
Wooley, George W	
Wooley, Georgianna	
Wooley, Grandparents	
Wooley, Mary	243
Worthy, Paul S. Jr.	
Worthy, Sadie Ruth	
Worthy, Willie Davis	
Wright, Anna Sloan	
Wright, Ethel	
Wright, Gladys W.	
Wright, S. P.	
Wright, Velva	
Wright, Will & Infant	
Yongue, Anita Blackwell	
Young, Alexander	244
Young, Irene Bevins	
Younge, James Wells	
Younge, John William	

Name	Page
Younge, M. McCrary	
Younge, Mary Elizabeth	
Younge, Pearl Shines	
Zimmerman, J. M. L.	

BURIALS

Jessie N. Acey
Died: 06/23/1972 Age: 78
Parents: Joshua Nicholson & Amanda Herd

NO MARKER

Mitchell & Fair
Funeral Home Record

Joe Collier Acey
Died: 12/07/1957 Age: 78
Certificate No. 0038,0327
Parents: Amos Acey & Mary Reeves

UH-399 -I/J [Grnt Hd Stn]
Cook: Southern Railroad
Informant: Jessie Acey

Ellis, Mangum & Fair

JOE COLLIER ACEY
OCT. 1, 1879
DEC. 7 1957

Cora Neely Adams
Died: 05/27/1996 Age: 95

Parents: UNKNOWN

NO MARKER
Homemaker
Informant: Wilhelmina Wilson
Bpl: SC

M/Fair @. N/Kelsey 240
Funeral Home Record

Gloria Adams
Died: 06/26/1925 Age: 71
Certificate No. 0013,0380
Parents: Tom Ramseure & Mary Payne

NO MARKER
Dressmaker
Informant: Tom Ramseure
Bpl: NC

Noble & Kelsey

Mary Alice Adkins
Died: 02/08/1942 Age: 24 hr.
Certificate No. 0028,0212
Parents: White Blackman & Ruth Adkins

NO MARKER
INFANT
Informant: C.A. Adkins
Bpl: Rowan Co., NC

Ellis, Mangum & Fair

Robert Adams
Died: 12./24/1918 Age. ∞36
Certificate No. 0006,0641:
Parents: Nat Adams & Unknown

NO MARKER
Section Hand @ Southern Railroad
Informant: Henry McCortell
Bpl: NC

Summersettt

Will Adams
Died: 02/01/1930 Age: 50
Certificate No. 0018,0182
Parents: UNKNOWN

NO MARKER
Laborer
Informant: Melinda Adams
Bpl: New York

Fraternal Funeral Home

Rosetta Adkins
Died at Age: 46

BT-279 -K

Ellis, Mangum & Fair

ROSETTA ADKINS
WIFE OF
PAUL SELLERS
SEPT. 28, 1920
DEC. 31, 1966

BURIALS

James E. Kwegyir Aggrey   OK-031- N Curb   Noble & Kelsey: 53
Died: 07/30/1927   Age: 52   Professor @ Livingstone College and Hood Theological Seminary, A.M.E. Zion Minister, Representative for Phelps Stokes Foundation in Africa, An Achimota College founder in Ghana, West Africa [Died in New York City] [1]
Parents: Kodwo Kwegyir Aggrey & Abna Andua
Bpl: Anamabu, Ghana West Africa

AGGREY OF AFRICA
UT OMNES UNUM SINT
JAMES E. KWEGYIR AGGREY
1875 – 1927
ANAMABU GOLD COAST
LIVINGSTONE COLLEGE
COLUMBIA UNIVERSITY
ACHIMOTA COLLEGE
PRESENTED BY THE AFRICAN
STUDENTS OF GREAT BRITAIN
AND THE UNITED STATES

Rose Douglass Aggrey   OK-032 -N Curb   Ellis, Mangum & Fair
Died: 09/25/1961   Age: 79   Teacher, Principal/Supervisor Author of Shaw University Alumni Song. "Beloved Shaw"; English teacher at Livingstone in High School Department; Principal of schools in Cleveland Co and Granite Quarry, NC
Certificate No. 0042,0001   **Informant**: Abna Lancaster, daughter
Parents: Walter E. Douglass & Martha Anne Belle   Bpl: Portsmouth, VA

AGGREY
ROSE DOUGLASS
WIFE OF
J. E. KWEGYIR AGGREY
MAY 27, 1882 SEPT. 25, 1961
BELOVED MOTHER, TEACHER AND
HUMAN EARPA I SAUS DSO

Rosebud Douglass Aggrey   OK-033 -N Curb   Noble & Kelsey 53
Died: 01/30/1990   Age: 80   Teacher
Certificate No. 0070,0106   **Informant**: Abna A. Lancaster, sister
Parents: James E. K. Aggrey & Rose Douglass

AGGREY
ROSEBUD DOUGLASS
JULY 7, 1910
JAN. 30, 1990
BELOVED BY FAMILY, STUDENTS & FRIENDS
LAOS DEO

INFANT of W. E. Agnew   NO MARKER   Fraternal Funeral Home
Died: 12/20/1929   Age: 18 hrs.   INFANT (Female)
Certificate No. 0018,0135   **Informant** W. E. Agnew
Parents: W. E. Agnew & Jennie Jones   Bpl: Salisbury, NC

BURIALS

INFANT of W. E. Agnew
Died: 12/20/1929   Age: 18 hrs.
Certificate No. 0018,0136
Parents: W. E. Agnew & Jennie Jones

NO MARKER
INFANT (Female)
Informant: W. E. Agnew
   Bpl: Salisbury, NC

Fraternal Funeral Home

James Agnew
Died: 06/03/1932   Age: 1yr.08 dys,
Certificate No. 0020,0249
Parents: W. E. Agnew & Jannie Jones

NO MARKER
Baby
Informant: Willie Agnew
   Bpl: Salisbury, NC

Mangum Funeral Home

Milford Sloan Agnew
Died: 10/31/1969   Age: 68
Certificate No. 0049,0629
Parents: William & Luella Agnew

NO MARKER
Retired
 Informant: Rosa L. Agnew, Syracuse, NY
   Bpl: SC

Noble & Kelsey

Milton L. Agnew
Died: 01/08/1943   Age: 37
Certificate No. 0028,0708
Parents: William Agnew & Luella Henderson

NO MARKER
Truck Driver @ Foster Produce Co.
Informant: Wilmer Brotherton
   Bpl: Seneca, SC

Noble & Kelsey

Betty Aldrich
Died: 08/10/1956   Age: 35

NO MARKER
Certificate Not Found, Funeral Home Record

Ellis, Mangum & Fair

Clara Bell McCullough Aldrich
Died: 07/17/1967   Age: 41
Parents: John & Francis

NO MARKER

   Bpl: North Carolina

Mitchell & Fair
Funeral Home Record

Alex Alexander
Died: 09/20/1943   Age: 61
Certificate No. 0028,0896
Parents: Adam Alexander & Frances McCorkle

NO MARKER
Laborer employed WPA
Informant: Martha Alexander, Wife
   Bpl: Mecklenburg, Co., NC

Noble & Kelsey: 86

Dawn M. Alexander
Died: 08/08/1972   Age: STILL BIRTH
Parents: Leon & Ernestine Alexander

OK-355 - I/J

Ellis, Mangum & Fair
Funeral Home Record

BABY
DAWN M. ALEXANDER
INFANT DAUGHTER OF
LEON & EARNESTINE
ALEXANDER
AUG. 8, 1972
AUG. 8, 1972

James Alexander

Died: 09/04/1924   Age: 1-Day
Certificate No. 0012,0442
Mother Unknown according to Marie Perkins, Midwife
Parents: Alex Alexander & Unknown

BN-787-M MISSING
Next to Robert L. Smith
INFANT
Informant: Martha Alexander,
   Bpl: Salisbury, NC

Noble & Kelsey

James A. Alexander
Died: 09/20/1943   Age: 66

OK-150 -O
Bricklayer

Noble & Kelsey: 86

JAMES A. ALEXANDER
SEPT. 26, 1877
SEPT. 20, 1943

BURIALS

James A. Alexander UH-581-H Ellis, Mangum & Fair
Died: 12/27/1990   Age: ∞34
Certificate Not Found

JAMES A. ALEXANDER
JAN. 5, 1966
DEC. 27, 1990

Laura Alexander OK-374 - I/J Ellis, Mangum & Fair
Died: 07/16/1942   Age: 68   Housewife
Certificate No. 0028,0331   **Informant:** Sallie Henderson
Parents: UNKNOWN   Bpl: Rowan Co., NC

LAURA
ALEXANDER
DIED
JUL. 16, 1945

Martha Johnson Alexander OK-151-O [Flush Granite] Ellis, Mangum & Fair
Died: 04/26/1979   Age: 89   Funeral Home Record

MARTHA J. ALEXANDER
SEPT. 16, 1890
APR. 26, 1979

Mary Jane Brown Alexander NO MARKER Noble & Kelsey: 343
Died: 01/23/1924   Age: 61   Laundry Work   Funeral Home Record
Certificate No. 0012,0287   **Informant:** Giles Brown
Parents: Unknown & Laura Luckey   Bpl: Davie Co., NC

Nolander A. Alexander UH-557-H MISSING (Near Alberta Chisholm)

Norman Clyde Alexander NO MARKER Noble & Kelsey: 86
Died: 03/28/1923   Age: 1 Day
Certificate No. 0011,0410   **Informant:** Alex Alexander, Father
Parents: Alexander & Martha Johnson   Bpl: Salisbury, NC

Nancy Alison NO MARKER Noble & Kelsey:
Died: 01/24/1910   Age: 54   Widow: Domestic
Certificate No. 0017,0650   **Informant:** Annie James
Parents: Henry Shaver &   Bpl: Rowan Co., NC

James A. Allen NO MARKER Noble & Kelsey: 300
Died: 01/04/1912   Age: 51   Common Laborer   Funeral Home Record
Certificate Not Found   **Informant:** Gertrude Allen
Parents: Richard Allen & Elizabeth Izzard   Bpl: SC

Jennie Allen NO MARKER Bingham & Carter
Died, 05/13/1925   Age: 59   Housewife
Certificate No.0001,0341   **Informant** Mr. S. Smith
Parents: Harrison Harris & Hosetine Thomas   Bpl: Morgan Co., GA

Francis Roseline Allison NO MARKER Ellis, Mangum & Fair
Died: 02/17/1942   Age: 44   Housework
Certificate No. 0028,0242   **Informant:** Mary Harris
Parents: Lee Walker & Mary Brice   Bpl: Blackstock, SC

BURIALS

Cicero T. Anderson — NO MARKER — Noble & Kelsey: 107

Arthur Andrews
Died: 07/18/1951   Age: 60
Certificate No. 0032,0839
NO MARKER
Laborer (city directory 1938)
Parents: Fate & Mary Andrews
Ellis, Mangum & Fair

Lucile Andrews
Died: 08/09/1946   Age: 50
Parents: Bill Nobel & Not Given
NO MARKER
Domestic
Ellis, Mangum & Fair
Funeral Home Record

James Allen Archie
Died: 04/25/1987   Age: 31
Certificate No. 0067,0322
Parents: Unknown & Ada Archie
BN-666 -P MISSING
Orderly @ Hospital
Informant: Ola M. Robins, Cousin
Bpl: Rowan Co., NC
Noble & Kelsey

Charles Ardis
Died: 11/14/1915   Age: ∞50
Certificate No. 0002,0255
Parents: UNKNOWN
OK-∞039-N
Preacher & brick mason
Informant: W. F. Kelsey
Bpl: Greenville, Alabama
Noble & Kelsey: 46

Curley Armstrong
Died: 12/17/1981   Age: 68

Parents: UNKNOWN
BT-246-K MISSING
Laborer
Informant: Annie Mae Woodson
Noble & Kelsey
Funeral Home Record

INFANT Armstrong
Died: 01/14/1912   INFANT
NO MARKER
Summersett
Funeral Home Record

John Allen Armstrong
Died: 12/24/1943   Age: ∞78
Wife Ella
OK-209 -L [Mrbl Hdston]
Helper Southern Railroad
Ellis, Mangum & Fair
Funeral Home Record

**JOHN ALLEN
ARMSTRONG
DIED DEC. 24, 1943
AGE ABOUT 78 YRS
Gone but not forgotten**

Farris G. Arnold
Died: 06/27/1990   Age: 65   Certificate Not Found
UH-567-H

**FARRIS G. ARNOLD
DEC. 23, 1925
JUNE 27, 1990**

Blanche Gable Asberry
Died: 08/21/1977   Age: 86
Certificate Not Found
Parents: Eaph Gable & Eva Rowe
BN-707-P
Noble & Kelsey
Housewife, Maid

Bpl: NC

**ASBERRY
BLANCHE GABLE ASBERRY
WIFE OF
REV. E. T. ASBERRY
MAR. 18, 1891
AUG. 21, 1977**

BURIALS

Florence Ashwood
Died: 10/06/1972   Age: 101
Certificate No. 0052,0864

NO MARKER
Midwife
Parents: John Hargraves & Unknown

Mitchell & Fair

Mrs. P. W. Ashwood

OK-141-O MISSING

Noble & Kelsey: 133

Peter A. Ashwood
Died: 04/04/1938   Age: 65
Certificate No. 0026,0108
Parents: Arthur Ashwood & Unknown
Headstone on ground 04/23/04

OK-141-O
Blacksmith
Informant: Florence Ashwood

Mangum @ Kelsey 133

PETER
ASHWOOD
DIED
APR. 4, 1938
AGE 65 YRS
Gone, but not forgotten

Emma Austin

OK-NO MARKER

Noble & Kelsey: 115

Isabella Anderson Austin
Died: 08/12/1927   Age: 39
Certificate No. 0015,0412
Parents: Lewis Anderson & Delia Hobson

NO MARKER
Housewife
Informant: Martha Hobson
   Bpl: Davie Co., NC

Noble & Kelsey: 212

Baby of Lenner/ Murry
Died: 10/17/1946   Age:
Parents: Linwood Lenner & Montana Murry

NO MARKER
STILL BIRTH

Ellis, Mangum & Fair
Funeral Home Record

Jericho Endigo Bailey

Died: 01/02/1994   Age: 18
Certificate No. 0074,0030
Parents: James Bailey, Sr. & Julia Williams

BN-647 MISSING
Next to Malik Williams
Occupation not given.
Informant: Julia Williams
   Bpl: Rowan Co., NC

Beasley's, Charlotte

Jewel Arched Bailey
Died: 09/30/1955   Age: 11m
Certificate No. 0036,0427
Parents: Unknown & Willeth Bailey

NO MARKER
Baby
Informant: Willett Bailey
   Bpl: East Spencer, NC

Ellis, Mangum & Fair

Martha Wooley Baitey
Died: 09/25/1965   Age: 57

NO MARKER
Funeral Home Record

Mitchell & Fair

Rosa S. Baker
Died: 08/20/1970   Age: ∞63
Certificate Not Found

BT-259-K

Mitchell & Fair
Funeral Home Record

ROSA BAKER
AUG. 10, 1907
AUG. 20, 1970

BURIALS

Joe Ballard

Died: 02/25/1917   Age: 92
Certificate No. 0005,0002:
Parents: Solman Cameral & Unknown

OK-N MISSING   Noble & Kelsey
Blacksmith, Teamster, Philosopher, and Chairman of the Republican Party in Rowan County, Honorary member of the Livingstone College Board of Trustees. Last name "Ballard" was taken from his owner when he was the slave of Miss Margaret Ballard
Informant: Joe Ballard Jr.
Bpl.: Fayetteville, NC

(Source Rowan Museum)

Ida Clement Banks
Died: 01/14/1910   Age: 44y11m
Certificate No. 0004,0472
Parents: Zion & Merette Clement

NO MARKER.   Noble & Kelsey
Domestic
Informant: Peter Banks

James Bernard Banks Jr.
Died: 11/05/1972   Age: 1y3m
Certificate No. 0052,0790:
Parents: James B. Banks & Mary Graham

OK-348-I/J   Mitchell & Fair
Baby
Informant: Mary G. Banks, Mother
Bpl: NC

Mary Etta Graham Banks
Died: 05/09/1991   Age: 43
Certificate No. 0071,0397
Parents: John L. Graham Sr. & Margaret Lyerly

OK-349-I/J   Noble & Kelsey
Food Preparer, Fast food restaurant
Informant: Margaret Lyerly Graham
Bpl.: Salisbury, NC

BANKS
MARY ETTA
FEB. 27, 1948
MAY 8 1991

Haskell Barber
Died: 04/09/1959   Age: 74
Funeral Home Record

BN-872-M   Ellis, Mangum & Fair
Minister

BARBER
REV. H. BARBER	MYRTILE BARBER
BORN 3-2-1885	BORN 6-9-1907
DIED 4-9-1959	DIED 8-30-1956

Linnie Infant of Barber
Died: 01/20/1918   Age: STILL BIRTH
Certificate No. 0006,0360
Parents: James Kerns & Linnie Barber

OK-NO MARKER   Noble & Kelsey: 345
INFANT
Informant: Calvin Kirkland
Bpl: Rowan Co., NC

Mr. Charlie E. Barber
Died: 03/15/1936   Age: 75
Certificate No. 0024,0132
Parents: Unknown & Sarah Barber

OK-34-39-N MISSING   Noble & Kelsey: 52
Restaurant 202 N Lee St. (1910 City Dir.)
Informant: Pearl Young, Philadelphia

Myrtile Barber
Died: 08/30/1956   Age: 49

BN-873-M   Ellis, Mangum & Fair
Funeral Home Record   (See Haskell Barber)

BURIALS

Nora Barber
Died: 11/22/1915   Age: 30
Certificate No. 0002,0262
Parents: William Barber & Mollie Barber

NO MARKER
Cook
Informant: Carrie Teasley
   Bpl: Rowan Co., NC

Noble & Kelsey: 250

Oties Barber
Died: 02/21/1945   Age: 51
Certificate No. 0029,0518
Parents: Henry Barber & Lizzie Watson

NO MARKER
Farming
Informant: Mrs. Katie Barber, Wife
   Bpl: Chester, SC

Noble & Kelsey

Harvey Barker

NO MARKER

Noble & Kelsey: 342

John Barker
Died: 04/27/1959   Age: 48

NO MARKER

Ellis, Mangum & Fair
Funeral Home Record

Sallie Barney
Died: 11/19/1963

NO MARKER

Ellis, Mangum & Fair
Funeral Home Record

Henry Howard Barret
Died: 08/01/1916   Age: 01m25d
Certificate No. 0003,0249
Parents: Unknown & Marie Dowley

NO MARKER
INFANT
Informant: William Barrett
Bpl: Salisbury, NC

Noble & Kelsey: 342

Henry Charleston Barton
Died: 05/30/1939   Age: 59y02m25
Certificate No. 0027,0145
Parents: Unknown & Ida Miller

BN-022-M
Freight Carrier Southern Railroad
Informant: Carrie T. Barton, Wife
   Bpl: Salisbury, NC

Noble & Kelsey

HENRY C. BARTON
MAR. 5, 1880
MAY 30, 1939
His memory is blessed.

Lafayette Bass

OK-NO MARKER

Noble & Kelsey: 226

John Robert Battle
Died: 10/13/1981   Age: 64
Certificate No. 0061,0858
Parents: Peter Battle & Unknown

NO MARKER Mitchell & Fair
Burlington Industries
Informant: Mrs. Mary Troutman, Sister
   Bpl: Rowan Co., NC

Daughter Baum

OK-353-I/J

Ellis, Mangum & Fair

William Baxter
Died: 09/24/1910   Age: 27
Certificate No. 0004,0260
Parents: Jake Elmore & Martha Benet

NO MARKER
Railroader
Informant: O. B. Watts,
   Bpl: Gaston Co., NC

Ellis, Mangum, & Fair

Leona M. Beattie
Died: 05/05/1929   Age: 43
Certificate No. 0017,0410

NO MARKER
Domestic
Informant: Rev. M. C. Beattie

Cheshire & Fisher

Donald Ray Beatty Jr.

Died: 03/01/1990   Age: 01m11d
Certificate No. 0070,0194
Parents: Donald Ray Beatty & Aurora D. Black

UH-579-H MISSING   Noble & Kelsey
Next to John Chambers
INFANT
Informant: Donald Ray Beatty Sr., Father
Bpl: Salisbury, NC

BURIALS

Harrison James Bell

Died: 02/11/1981   Age: 71
Certificate No. 0061,0150
Parents: Harrison Bell & Betty Holmes

BN-859-M MISSING   Noble & Kelsey
Next to Marion Brookhart
Laborer @ Brickyard
Informant: Josephine Bush, Sister
   Bpl: Rowan Co., NC

Frank Belton Sr.

Died: 08/09/1994   Age: 65
Certificate No. 0074,0792
Parents: Clarence & Sarah Belton

UH-640-G MISSING   Noble & Kelsey
Next to Richard Hargrave
Hand truck Driver @ Fertilizer Plant
Informant: Geraldine J. Belton, Wife

Eliza L. Benjamin
Certificate Not Found

UH-626-G MISSING   Ellis, Mangum & Fair
Next to Donald Sellers & Frank Belton

Mary Benjamin
Died 06/10/1910   Age 37
Certificate No. 0004,0307

NO MARKER   **Noble & Kelsey**
Housekeeping
Informant: W. F. Benjamin

Tom Bennett
Died: 01/26/1908   Age: 22yrs.

NO MARKER   Summersett
Funeral Home Records   T. W. Summersett Jr.

Creola Bernhardt
Died: 10/07/1966   Age: 72
Certificate Not Found

OK-137-N Plot [Grnt Hdstn]   Ellis, Mangum & Fair
Teacher @ Lincoln School

CREOLA BERNHARDT
WIFE OF
MERVIN S. SUMNER
JULY 12, 1894
OCT. 7, 1966

Mattie Bernhardt
Certificate Not Found

OK-137-N Plot [Grit Hdstn]   Ellis, Mangum & Fair

MATTIE BERNHARDT
WIFE OF ADAM CARUTH

Sallie Bernhardt
Died: 11/22/1930   Age: 52
Certificate No. 0018,0381
Parents: John Parker & Unknown

NO MARKER   Cheshire & Callahan
Domestic
Informant: Gertrude Bobbitt
   Bpl: Stanley Co., NC

Amions Berry
Died: 08/25/1910   Age: 80yrs.
No Certificate Found
Parents: Unknown

OK-NO MARKER   Noble & Kelsey
Farmer   Funeral Home Record
Informant: Mary Berry, Salisbury
   Bpl: Newbern, NC

Elizabeth Best
Died: 02/05/1951   Age: 70
Parents: Levi Tyson & Unknown

NO MARKER   Ellis, Mangum & Fair
Domestic   Funeral Home Record
   bd. 11/25/1880

Charles Bethea
Died: 05/26/1918   Age: 02 days
Certificate No.; 0006,0451
Parents: John Bethea & Alice Starrs (sic)

NO MARKER   Summersettt
INFANT
Informant: Alma McClain
   Bpl: Southern Pine, NC

BURIALS

James Price Biggers   BT-301-K   Ellis, Mangum & Fair
Died: 03/27/1959   Age: 36   Funeral Home Record   [1930 US Census]
Parents: James H. & Marry Biggers   Bpl: Salisbury, NC

BIGGERS
JAMES PRICE
DEC. 18, 1923
MAR. 27, 1959
OUR DEAR ONE HAS ANSWERED
THE CALL OUR HEARTS SHOULD
BE AT REST, FOR THERE BEYOND
THE STARRY SKIES A LOVING
GOD KNOWS BEST.

PLOT OK-188   THE BINGHAM FAMILY

Arthur Brown Bingham   OK-188-O Plot   Noble & Kelsey: 166
Died: 10/26/1996   Age: 93   Educator/School, Davidson Co., NC
Certificate No. 0076,1040   **Informant**: Dr. Arletta M. Verley
Parents: Lillington H. Bingham & Henrietta Browne

ARTHUR BROWNE	LUCILLE BITTING
MAY 2, 1903	JUNE 23, 1903
OCT. 26, 1996	JULY 6, 1977

TOGETHER FOREVER
BINGHAM

Charles H. Bingham   OK-188-O Plot   Noble & Kelsey: 166
Died: 1940   Certificate Not Found   Bpl: bd. ∞ 1884 NC

Henrietta Browne Bingham   OK-188 O-Plot   Noble & Kelsey: 166
Died: 10/14/1937   Age: ∞58   Housewife
Informant: Mrs. Lillian Evans
Parents: William Brown & Margaret Brown
Bpl: Rowan Co., NC

BINGHAM
L. H. BINGHAM   HIS WIFE
NOV. 16, 1858   HENRIETTA BROWN
JULY 17, 1933   BORN 1877
OCT. 14, 1937

Inez Bingham   OK-188 -O Plot   Noble & Kelsey: 166
Died: 12/16/68   Age: ∞72
Certificate Not Found   Died in New York City

INEZ BINGHAM
WIFE OF ERNEST MEDLIN

BURIALS

Juanita Elizabeth Bingham OK-188 -O Plot Noble & Kelsey: 166
Died at Age 12 in New York City
Parents: Charles & Grace Bingham

JUANITA ELIZABETH
DAU. OF
CHARLES & GRACE BINGHAM

Lillington H. Bingham OK-188- O Plot Noble & Kelsey: 166
Died: 07/17/1933 Age: 74y08m01d Fireman on Southern Railroad
(1910 City Directory)
Informant: Harvey Bingham
Parents: Henry H. Bingham & Rosa Hoshe Bpl: Rowan Co., NC

SEE HENRIETTA BROWN BINGHAM

Lucile Bitting Bingham OK-188 -O Plot Noble & Kelsey
Died: 06/06/1977 Age: ∞74 Retired school teacher, Davidson Board of Education
Certificate No. 0057,518 **Informant**: Arthur B. Bingham, Husband
Parents: Robert Bitting and Julia Gilchrist Bpl: NC

SEE ARTHUR BROWN BINGHAM

Mabel Myers Bingham OK-188- O Plot Noble & Kelsey: 166
Died: 9/16/93 Age: ∞91
Certificate Not Found

MABEL MYERS
BINGHAM

Clara Black NO MARKER
Died: 10/31/1952 Age: 68 Housewife
Certificate No. 0033,0460 **Informant**: Unknown
Parents: Jack Tutt, Unknown Bpl: Lincolnton, GA

Ernestine Black NO MARKER Ellis, Mangum & Fair
Died: 04/15/1957 Age: 1y3m Certificate Not Found, Funeral Home Record

Eula Mae Heilig Black BN- 009A-M Noble & Kelsey
Died: 07/08/2000 Age: 90 Domestic Work @ Private Home
Certificate No. 0080,0634 **Informant**: Mrs. Brenda Clark
Parents: Larin Heilig & Mamie Barnhart Bpl: Rowan Co., NC

EULA HEILIG
BLACK
MAY 5, 1910
JULY 8, 2000
A LOVING WIFE MOTHER AND SISTER

BURIALS

Florence L. Black

Died: 06/23/1922   (Male) Age: 48
Certificate No. 0010,0377
Parents: Thomas Black & Emma White

OK-161-O

Noble & Kelsey
Porter in Hotel
Informant: Lulu Black, Wife
Bpl: Cabarrus, Co., NC

Thy Will Be Done
FLORENCE L. BLACK
JAN. 16, 1874
JUNE 23, 1922
God gave-He took - He will restore - He doeth all things
(Born. 01/16/1882 died 06/21/1922 @ 40y05m06d)

Julia Rebecca Black
Died: 12/18/1977   Age: 44
Certificate No. 0057,0964
Parents: Willie Crockett & Nellie Greenlee

BN-704-P
Housewife
Informant: Mrs. Nellie C. Gable

Noble & Kelsey

JULIA R. BLACK
FEB. 27, 1935
DEC. 22, 1977

Lloyd Black

Died: 04/17/1987   Age: 78
Certificate No.   **Informant:** Eula Mae Heilig Black, Wife
Parents: John Black & Cora Miller   Bpl.: Davidson Co., NC

BN-009-M

Noble & Kelsey
Laborer: Southern Railway

LLOYD BLACK
APR. 26, 1908
APR. 17, 1987

Lula Holt Black
Died: 07/14/1962   Age: 76
Certificate No. 0042,0544
Parents: John Holt & Josephine Campbell

NO MARKER
Housewife
Informant: Josephine Mitchell
   Bpl: Rowan Co., NC

Noble & Kelsey: 123

Robert Black
Died: 04/23/1911   Age: 19y05m29
Certificate No. 0004,0215
Parents: James Black/Minnie Johnson

NO MARKER
Laborer
Informant: Minnie Johnson
Bpl: Cabarrus

Summersett

Son of Eva Black
Died: 04/24/1910
Parents: Eva Black

NO MARKER
Certificate Not Found

Summersett

Josephine Blackmer
Died: 01/08/1927   Age: 83
Certificate Not Found?

OK-369-I/J Plot

JOSEPHINE
BLACKMER
DIED
JAN. 8, 1927
AGED
83 YRS.
Gone but not forgotten (J. B.)

Ellis, Mangum & Fair

Ed Blackmon
Died: 06/10/1918   Age: ∞27
Certificate No. 0006,0453
Parents: Charles & Lula Blackmon

NO MARKER
Worked @ Transfer Shed of Southern Railroad
Informant: Isabel Blackman
   Bpl: Columbus, GA

Summersettt

BURIALS

Clarence Blackmore
Died: 03/03/1915

OK-369 -I/J Plot

Noble & Kelsey: 362
Certificate Not Found

**CLARENCE
BLACKMORE
DIED
MAR. 3, 1915
He is not dead
but sleepeth.**

Josephine Blackwell
Died: 01/25/1927   Age. ∞75
Certificate No. 0015,0289
Parents: Ben & Harriet Walker

NO MARKER
Cooking
Informant Janette Walker
    Bpl: Davidson Co., NC

Noble & Kelsey

Lillie Walker Blackwell
Died: 04/11/1956   Age: 96 65/dcert.
Certificate No. 0036,0717
Parents: Jack Walker & Unknown

UH-475-H
Housewife
Informant: Mrs. Earldena Harrison
    Bpl: NC

Noble & Kelsey

**LILLIE WALKER
WIFE OF
ABE BLACKWELL
APRIL 2, 1860
APRIL 11, 1956
AT REST**

Harry Blair
Died: 06/22/1956   Age: 66

UH-512-H

Ellis, Mangum & Fair
Funeral Home Record

**HARRY BLAIR
MARCH 15, 1890
JUNE 22, 1956**

Raymond Blair
Died: 12/20/1953   Age: 48
Certificate No. 0034,0520
Parents: Robert Blair & Maggie Williams

NO MARKER
Laborer: Isenhour Brick & Tile Co.
Informant: Mary Blair
    Bpl: East Spencer, NC

Ellis, Mangum & Fair

Henry Blair Sr.

Died: 04/30/1961   Age: 50
Certificate No. 0041,0473
Parents: Harry Blair & Dora Davis

OK-338 -I/J MISSING
Next to M. E. Bost & A. Jamison
Factory Helper
Informant: Mildred Blair, Wife
    Bpl: SC

Ellis, Mangum & Fair

Viola Harris Bluford
Parents: Cicero R. & Mariah E. Harris

OK-070-N Goler Plot

Noble & Kelsey: 13

Homer Blunt
Died: 03/12/1964   Age: 66
Certificate No. 0044,0133
Parents: Will Blunt & Unknown Blunt

NO MARKER

Informant: Delia Tugman
    Bpl: Randolph Co., NC

Mitchell & Fair

Katie Parham Blunt
Died: 12/09/1946   Age: 44
Certificate No. 0030,0411
Parents: James Parham & Georgia Brown

NO MARKER

Informant: Homer Blunt, Husband

Ellis, Mangum & Fair

BURIALS

Columbus M. Boger
Died: 03/18/1915   Age: 53
Certificate No. 0002,0118
Parents: Ben & Nancy Boger

OK-NO MARKER
Day Labor
Informant: Lydia Boger,
   Bpl: Cabarrus, Co., NC

Noble & Kelsey: 73

Dorothy E. Boger (1930 Census)

OK-NO MARKER

Noble & Kelsey: 338

May Linda May Troy Boger(sic)
Died: 02/03/1923   Age: 5 mos. 24 dys.
Certificate No. 0011,0376
Parents: William Boger & Grace Harris

NO MARKER
INFANT
Informant: William Boger
   Bpl: Salisbury, NC

Noble & Kelsey

Paul Henry Boger
Died: 03/22/1923   Age: 54
Certificate No. 0011,0422
Parents: Richard & Janie Boger

NO MARKER
Butler in Store
Informant: Mary Miller
   Bpl: Cabarrus Co., NC

Noble & Kelsey

William Byrd Boger

OK-NO MARKER

Noble & Kelsey: 243

Annie Bonepart
Died: 11/25/1939

NO MARKER

Ellis, Mangum & Fair
Funeral Home Record

Irene Clinton Booker
Died: 12/21/1975   Age: 74
Certificate No.0055,0877
Parents: Henry Clinton & Lilly Aldrich

NO MARKER
Housewife
Informant: Mr. George Booker, Husband

Mitchell & Fair

Janie Booker
Died: 1936   Age: 67

BN-862-M

Ellis, Mangum & Fair
Funeral Home Record

JANIE BOOKER
WIFE OF
JEFF RODGERS
1869 - 1936

Mr. Marion Bookhart
Died: 02/26/1981   Age: 46
Certificate No. 0061,0213
Parents: & Maggie Bookhart Patterson

BN-860-M
Laborer Textiles
Informant: Jessie Davis Bookhart, Wife
   Bpl: Richland Co., SC

Noble & Kelsey

MARION BOOKHART
SEPT. 9, 1934
FEB. 26, 1981

Bessie Harris Boozer
Died: 12/14/1964   Age: 77

BN-722-M
Housewife

Noble & Kelsey

Certificate No. 0042,0192   **Informant:** Forest Boozer, Husband
Parents: Dan Harris & Susie Boozer   Bpl: Newberry, SC

BOOZER
BESSIE HARRIS	FORREST T.
MAR. 4, 1884	MAY 1, 1880
DEC. 14, 1961	DEC. 2, 1971

Forrest Thomas Boozer
Died: 12/02/1971   Age: 94
Certificate No. 0051,0734
Parents: Henry Boger & Mattie Harris

BN-723-M
Janitor, Boyden High School, & Livingstone College
Informant: Gertrude Stoner
   Bpl: SC (See Bessie Harris)

Noble & Kelsey

BURIALS

Maggie W. Bosley
Died: 04/28/1967   Age: 58

NO MARKER

Mitchell & Fair
Funeral Home Record

Berthenia Smith Bost
Died: 09/16./1994   Age: 63
Certificate No. 0074,0888
Parents: Andy Smith & Viola Hester
Funeral Home Marker

UH-638-G
Cleaning Person @ Hospital
Informant: John A. Bost
   Bpl: Rowan Co., NC

Noble & Kelsey

BERTHA S. BOST
1931   1994
NOBLE & KELSEY FUNERAL HOME

Ella Odessa Bost
Died: 09/25/1997   Age: 60

BT-325-K
Winder/Spinner
Certificate No. 0077,0924   **Informant:** Linda Davis
Parents: Walter S. Neely & Ella J. Alexander   Bpl: Rowan Co., NC

Noble & Kelsey

BOST
WILLIS COLUMBUS	ELLA ODESSA
NOV. 13, 1937	JAN. 15, 1937
APR. 11, 1976	SEPT. 25, 1997

Ephraim Bost
Died: 01/24/1931   Age: 49
Certificate No. 0019,0139
Parents: Ephraim Bost & Lizzie Bost

OK-NO MARKER
Grocer & barber, 104 E. Council Day Labor
Informant: Minnie Campbell
   Bpl: Cabarrus Co., NC

Noble & Kelsey: 226

Francis Elizabeth Bost

OK-326-K
Died: 08/12/1938   Age: 91   Domestic
Informant: Minnie A. Campbell
Parents: Ben Boger & Elsie Boger   Bpl: Cabarrus Co., NC

Ellis, Mangum & Fair
Funeral Home Record

FRANCIS BOST

Mary Elizabeth Bost
Died: 05/24/1961   Age: 48

OK-337-I/J [Grit Fld Stn]

Ellis, Mangum & Fair
Funeral Home Record

MARY ELIZABETH BOST
JAN. 10, 1913
MAY 24, 1961

Willis Columbus Bost
Died: 04/11/1976   Age: 39

BT-324-I/J

Ellis, Mangum & Fair
Funeral Home Record
Informant: Mrs. Odessa N. Bost, Wife (See Ella Odessa.)

Alfred Burley Boyd
Died: 08/06/1930
Certificate No. 0018,0290
Parents: Henry Boyd & Unknown

NO MARKER
Cook on Dining Car
Informant: Henry Boyd
   Bpl: Mathews, NC

Fraternal Funeral Home

Artie Rose Mack Boyd
Died: 02/20/1918   Age: 11yrs, 6 mo.
Certificate No. 0006,0378
Parents: Oscar Mack & Joyce Owens

NO MARKER
School Girl
Informant: Mrs. Archibald Boyd
   Bpl.: Lexington, NC

Noble & Kelsey

BURIALS

Beulah McCorkle Boyd
Died: 02/24/1989   Age: 85
Certificate No. 0069,0159
Parents: John Fisher & Jessie McCorkle

OK-172-O   Noble & Kelsey
Teacher: Elementary, Salisbury, NC Schools
Informant: Ruth H. Price
   Bpl: Salisbury, NC

BOYD
BEULAH McCO.RKLE BOYD
MAY 10, 1904
FEB. 24, 1989
TEACHER
40 YEARS
BELMONT, LEAKSVILLE, HIGH POINT PUBLIC
SCHOOLS
EDUCATION
SCO.TIA SEMINARY-
SECO.NDARY
WINSTON SALEM STATE UNIV-A. B.
CO.LUMBIA UNIV.-M.A.
AFFILIATIONS
SOLDIERS MEMORIAL AME ZION CHURCH
ASSOCIATE TRUSTEES
NEA NCAE AARP NCESP
DRAGONETTE CLUB RITZ CLUB
TRAVELS
FIVE EUROPEAN TRIPS,
ONE AROUND THE WORLD TRIP

WELL DONE THY GOOD AND FAITHFUL SERVANT
REST AT LAST

Effie Muskelly Boyd
Died: 07/19/1952   Age: 70
Certificate No. 0033,0240
Parents: UNKNOWN

OK - NO MARKER   Noble & Kelsey: 139
Housewife
Informant: T. O. Hunt
   Bpl: Wilks Co., NC

Ida Cremonia Pearson Boyd
Died: 12/24/1924   Age: ∞40
Certificate No. 0012,0485
Parents: Daniel Pearson & Sarah Reeves

OK-MARKER   Noble & Kelsey: 144
House
Informant: J. N. Boyd
   Bpl: Salisbury, NC

INFANT of Walter Boyd
Died: 08/31/1909   Certificate Not Found

NO MARKER

Maggie Boyd
Died: 11/23/1910   Age: ∞32yrs.
Certificate No. 0004,0301
Parents: Dowell Harshane & Annie Johnson

NO MARKER   Summersett
Married Domestic
Informant: Arch Boyd
   Bpl: McDowell Co.

Maggie Boyden
Died: 10/01/1923   Age: ∞51
Certificate No. 0011,0509
Parents: UNKNOWN

OK-NO MARKER   Noble & Kelsey: 82
Domestic Housework
Informant: Ida Jones
   Bpl: Rowan Co., NC

Sarah Boyden
Died: 11/27/1926   Age: ∞34
Certificate No. 0014,0336

UH-   Cheshire & Mangum
Domestic
Informant: Laura Boyden

BURIALS

Alma Price Braithwait　　　　　OK-038-N Price Plot [Ledger]　Noble & Kelsey: 47
Died: 04/07/1945　Age: 57　Wife of Episcopal Priest
Parents: Joseph Charles & Jennie Smallwood Price

ALMA PRICE BRAITHWAIT SEPT. 28, 1888 APR. 7. 1945
WILLIAM DIEDGE PRICE MAR. 21, 1884 MAR. 1924 EMMA
LOUISE PRICE MAY 7, 1886 NOV. 12, 1915

*Emma Louise Price　　　　　OK-038-N Price Plot　　Noble & Kelsey: 47
Died: 11/12/1915　Age: 29　Certificate Not Found
Parents: Joseph Charles & Jennie Smallwood Price (See Alma Price Braithwaite)

Florence Broadway　　　　　BT-261-K　　　　Noble & Kelsey
Died: 01/15/1962　Age: 57　Housewife
Certificate No. 0042,0194　Informant: Mrs. Beulah Jones
Parents: John & Elizabeth Broadway　Bpl: NC

FLORENCE
BROADWAY
1904 -- 1962

Rosa Mae Brooker　　　　　UH-585-H MISSING　　Noble & Kelsey
Died: 02/18/1991　Age: 66　Baker @ Pie Factory
Certificate No. 0071,0124　Informant: Michael Brooker
Parents: David Dirk & Pearl Brooker　Bpl: Newberry, SC

Marion Brookhart　　　　　BN-860-M

Died: 02/26/1981　Age: ∞47　Certificate Not Found

MARION BROOKHART
SEPT. 9, 1934
FEB. 26, 1981

Tinty Brooks　　　　　UH-Fair Sub Section　Ellis, Mangum & Fair
Died: 04/02/1947　Age: 32　Domestic　Funeral Home Record
Parents: None Given

John A. Brotherton　　　　　NO MARKER　　Ellis, Mangum & Fair
Died: 02/10/1938　　　　　　　　　　　　　Funeral Home Record

Alford Brown　　　　　**NO MARKER**　　Noble & Kelsey
Died 10/16/38　Age: 29　Common Laborer
Certificate No. 0026,0523　Informant: Margaret Smith of East Spencer
Parents: Elex Brown & Luvenia Pike　Bpl.: Eastman, GA

Alice L. Brown　　　　　OK-027-N　　Noble & Kelsey: 58
Died: 12/08/1959　Age: 94　Teacher: Alice Brown School
Certificate No. 0040,0251　Informant: Rev. G. W. Rolland
Parents: Jack Rowland & Mother?　Bpl: NC

ALICE L. BROWN
BORN SEPT. 26, 1865
DIED DEC. 8, 1959
THE RIGHTEOUS SHALL BE IN
EVERLASTING REMEMBRANCE. PSALM 112 6

BURIALS

Arthur Brown
Died: 11/26/1923   Age: 28
Certificate No. 0011,0529
Parents: Unknown

NO MARKER
Tailor
Informant: Lilly Brown, Wife
   Bpl: Sumter, SC

Bingham & Carter

Calvin Brown
Died: 10/18/53   Age: 63
Parents: Gable Brown & Hester Macula

NO MARKER
Laborer, Southern Railroad
b. 1880

Ellis, Mangum & Fair
Funeral Home Record

Charles Edward Brown
Died: 04/05/1969   Age: 21
Certificate No. 0049,0217

BT-265 K
Laborer
Informant: Mrs. Debris P. Brown
Parents: John Frank Smith & Mrs. Elnora Brown   Bpl: NC

Noble & Kelsey

CHARLES E. BROWN
THIN MAN
JUNE 24, 1947
APR. 5, 1969

E. Henry Brown
Died: 06/12/1952   Age: 70
Certificate No. 0033,0244

NO MARKER

Ellis, Mangum & Fair

Ella Key Brown
Died: 09/21/1962   Age: 62

Certificate No. 0042,0663
Parents: Charles Key & Not Given

UH-
Housewife & grocery store owner of Wilson Road in
   Salisbury, NC
Informant: Mr. Amos T. Brown

Noble & Kelsey

BROWN
ELLA KEY
WIFE OF AMOS T. BROWN
SEPT. 12, 1901
SEPT. 21, 1962
SLEEP ON MOTHER SLEEP ON
LAY DOWN AND TAKE YOUR REST
WE LOVED YOU BUT GOD LOVED
YOU BEST.

Fate Brown
Died: 02/08/1942   Age: 30
Certificate No. 0028,0456
Parents: Fate Poe & Eva Brown

OK-NO MARKER
Janitor

Noble & Kelsey: 58

Goldia Brown
Died: 05/24/1986   Age: 72
Certificate No. 0066,0443

BN-881-M
Domestic - Maid @ Private Homes
Informant: Mrs. Hattie Jones, Daughter
Parents: Calvin Brown & Mattie Alexander Brown   Bpl: Rowan, NC

Mitchell & Fair

GOLDIA BROWN
JULY 4, 1914
MAY 24, 1986
WE LOVED HER BUT GOD LOVED HER BEST

Josie Brown
Died: 03/31/1924   Age: ∞34
Certificate No. 0012,0335
Parents: Glen & Bettie Suber (Sic)

NO MARKER
Housewife
Informant: W. M. Brown, Husband
   Bpl: SC.

Noble & Kelsey

BURIALS

Kalyn A. Brown UH-????
Died: 12/31/1998   Certificate Not Found

KALYN A. BROWN
DEC. 31, 1998
INFANT SON OF
DERICK BROWN
AND
DIONNE FITZGERALD

Lula Simmons Brown   UH-470-I/J   Ellis, Mangum & Fair
Died: 05/22/1953   Age: 70   Domestic
Certificate No. 0034,0217   **Informant**: Gentle Ingram
Parents: Webb Summons & Mary Hall   Bpl: Lincolnton, GA

MOTHER
LULA SIMMONS
BROWN
AUG. 9, 1882
MAY 22, 1953

Mary Brown   NO MARKER   Fraternal Funeral Home
Died: 11/29/1929   Age: 79   Housewife
Certificate No. 0017,0535   **Informant**: Jennie Johnson
Parents: Peter & Dixie Parker   Bpl: Davie Co., NC

Mary Nance Brown   BN-751-M
Died: 11/11/1978   Age: 76   Certificate Not Found

BROWN
MARY NANCE
DEC. 30, 1902
NOV. 11, 1978

Mattie Alexander Brown   NO MARKER   Mitchell & Fair
Died: 02/11/1964   Age: 73   Domestic
Certificate No. 0044,0092   **Informant**: Goldia Brown
Parents: Charlie Alexander & Martha Unknown   Bpl: Fairfield, SC

Melinda E. Brown   NO MARKER
Died: 03/4/1911   Age: 24yrs.   Cook
   Informant: Employer - Mrs. Byron Clark
Parents: Unknown   Bpl: Windsor, NC
Register of Death, Salisbury, Co. of Rowan, NC (09/1909-10/11/1911 pg 29)

Michael D. Brown   UH-400-I/J
Certificate Not Found

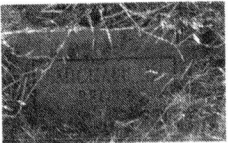   MICHAEL D. BROWN

Mildred Louise Brown   UH-NO MARKER   Ellis, Mangum & Fair
Died: 12/19/1943   Age: 4m21d   INFANT
Certificate No. 0029,0072   **Informant**: Bertha Mae Brown
Parents: Lawrence T. Brown & Bertha Mae Brown   Bpl: Salisbury, NC

BURIALS

Nathaniel Ambrose Brown   UH-
      Died: 03/15/1981   Age: 75   Certificate Not Found

NATHANIEL AMBROSE
BROWN, SR.
AUG. 7, 1906
MAR. 15, 1981

Nettie Isenhour Brown   NO MARKER
Died: 02/24/1910   Age: 38   Domestic
Certificate No. 0004,0372   **Informant:** Robert V. Brown
Parents: Charles Eisenhower & Martha Isenhour
Register of Death, Salisbury, and Co. of Rowan, NC (09/1909-10/11/1911)

Savannah Brown   NO MARKER   Ellis, Mangum & Fair
Died: 05/04/1955   Age: 54   Domestic
Certificate No. 0036,0208   **Informant:** Elizabeth Urquhart
Parents: Frank Carter & Nettie Isenhour   Bpl: Concord, NC

Will Brown   NO MARKER   Summersettt
Died: 08/01/1917   Age 24   Laborer
Certificate No. 0005,0140   **Informant:** Clyde Bameket (Sic)
Parents: UNKNOWN

William H. Brown Age 28   NO MARKER   Noble & Kelsey
Died 10/22/39   Day Laborer
North Carolina State Board of Health Certificate of Death   **Informant:** Alex Brown Jr., Brother
Parents: Alex Brown & Luvenia Pikes or Dikes, or Dukes   Bpl: Eastman, Dodge Co., GA

Sallie Browner   OK-205-L   Bingham & Carter
      Died: 02/20/1925   Age: 58   Housewife
      Certificate No. 0013,0267   **Informant:** B. Browner
      Parents: J. Webb & Unknown
            (Concrete Marker)
         SALLIE
         BROWNER
         JUL. 15, 1877
         FEB. 20, 1925
         AT REST

Charles Bruce   UH-633-G MISSING

Ruben Bruce   UH-389 -I/J   Ellis, Mangum & Fair
Died: 07/28/1948   Age: 59y08m27d   Janitor: Southern Bell Telephone Co.& Mt. Zion Baptist
   Church
Certificate No. 00310375
Parents: Jim Bruce & Julia Adams

         BRUCE
RUBEN BRUCE   ELMINA BRUCE
OCT. 1893   HOUSTON
JULY 1948   NOV. 15, 1897   (No Record of burial)

Carrie Gee Bryant   NO MARKER   Mitchell & Fair
Died: 07/08/1972   Age: 92   Funeral Home Record
Death Certificate Not Found
Parents: William Gist & Lizzie Roberson

BURIALS

Roger Bryant
Died: 04/01/1956 Age: 47
Certificate No. 0036,0720
Parents Will Bryant & Unknown

UH-437-I/J [Grnte Fldstn] Ellis, Mangum & Fair

ROGER BRYANT
JAN. 23, 1909
APR. 1, 1956

Sylvia C. Bryant

UH-601 G MISSING

William H. Bryant
Died: 10/31/1914 Age: 65y09m20d
Certificate No. 0001,0506
Parents: Not known & Emily Harrison Norris

OK-140 -N Noble & Kelsey
Pastor of Church Street Presbyterian Church (Trinity)
Informant: Emma Bryant, Daughter
Bpl: Raleigh b. 12/28/1848

William Henry Bryant
Died: 03/27/1952 Age: 73
Certificate No. 0033,0177
Parents: William Henry Bryant & Mother Unknown

UH-451-H Noble & Kelsey: 25
Minister & Teacher @ Old Lincoln School
Informant: Mrs. Nannie K. Bryant, wife
Bpl: Hertford, NC

BRYANT
REV. WILLIAM HENRY
BRYANT
DIED MAR. 27, 1952
AGED ABOUT 73 YEARS
THY GOD HAS CLAIMED THEE AS HIS OWN

Arthur Baylis Buford
Died: 10/13/1973 Age: ∞59
Certificate No. 0053,0606
Parents: Simon Buford & Mary Woodside

UH-469-H Noble & Kelsey
Teacher
Informant: Mrs. Lillian B. Perkins
Bpl: NC

ARTHUR BAYLIS
BUFORD
AUG. 2, 1914
OCT. 13, 1973

Lula Wyne Buford UH-
Died: 12/08/1938 Age: 41 Certificate Not Found

LULA WYNE BUFORD
WIFE OF EDDIE LEON
HENDERSON, SR.
JAN. 18, 1897
DEC. 8, 1938

Mary Woodside Buford
Died: 10/29/1950 Age: ∞70
Certificate No. 0032,0452
Parents: Unknown & Millie Woodside

UH-467-H Noble & Kelsey
Domestic
Informant: Mrs. Lillian Perkins
Bpl.: Iredell Co., NC

MARY W.
BUFORD
DIED
OCT. 29, 1950
AGE ABOUT
70 YRS.

BURIALS

Simon Martin Buford
Died: 02/15/1946   Age: 79
Certificate No. 0030,0243
Parents: UNKNOWN

UH-466-H
Barber
Informant: Arthur Buford.
Bpl: Danville, VA

Noble & Kelsey

SIMON M.
BUFORD
DIED
FEB. 15, 1946
AGE ABOUT
75 YRS.

John Bunyon Jr.
Died: 04/08/1932   Age: 28 days
Certificate No. 0020,0187
Parents: John Bunyon & Will Bell Butler

NO MARKER
INFANT
Informant: John Bunyon
Bpl: Rowan

Cheshire & Lynn

Willie Belle Bunyon
OK-104-N
Died: 07/18/1947   Age: 33   Certificate Not Found
Parents: Usher & Berenza Butler

WILLIE BELLE BUNYON
DAUGHTER OF
USHER & BERENZA BUTLER
AUGUST 5, 1914
JULY 18, 1947

Versey Burch
Died: 05/29/1948   Age: 26
Certificate No. 0031,0090
Parents: Carl Burch & Durlie Ross

NO MARKER

Born. 11/25/1921

Ellis, Mangum & Fair

George Burley
Died: 03/05/1918
Certificate No. 0006,0386
Parents: George Burley & Jessie Hanna

OK-NO MARKER
STILL BIRTH
Informant: George Burley
Bpl: Salisbury, NC

Noble & Kelsey: 345

Elijah Burns
Died: 03/17/1945   Age: 63
Certificate No. 0030,0282
Parents: Elijah Burns & Unknown

NO MARKER
Machinist Helper
Informant: Ola Mae Burns
Bpl: SC

Ellis, Mangum & Fair

Henrietta Burns
Died: 01/01/1959

BT-294-K
Certificate Not Found

HENRIETTA BURNS
WIFE OF
FRED DAVIS
OCT. 25, 1898
JAN. 1 1959

Neoma Burns
Died: 03/13/1939

NO MARKER
Certificate Not Found

Emma Burton
Died: 02/09/1929   Age: ∞34
Certificate No.0017,0346
Parents: William & Sallie Sutton

NO MARKER
Housewife
Informant: R. M. Burton
Bpl: Washington, GA

Noble & Kelsey

BURIALS

Baby of Jim Burton
Died: 07/03/1908   Age: 2 mo.
Parents: Jim Burton & Unknown

NO MARKER
INFANT

Summersett

R. M. Burton
Died: 06/21/1929   Age: 48
Certificate No. 0017,0432
Parents: George G. Burton & Mary Branner (Sic)

NO MARKER
Self Employed @ Café
Informant W. J. Burton
Bpl: Elburton, GA

Noble & Kelsey

Gerald Bush
Died: 06/02/2002   Age: 55
Funeral Home Marker 09/02/03

UH-xxx
Certificate Not Found
GERALD B. BUSH
Born 10-8-1946   Died 6-2-2002
MITCHELL & FAIR FUNERAL SERVICE, INC
SALISBURY, NORTH CAROLINA

Mitchell & Fair

Albert A. Butler
Died: 10/13/1988 Age: 78

ALBERT A. BUTLER
BIRTH MAR. 9, 1910
DIED OCT. 13, 1988

BN-885 -M
Certificate Not Found

Berenza Virginia Howell Butler
Died: 01/06/2001   Age: 108
Certificate No. 0081,0004:
Parents: James Howell & Marry Tyler

OK-107-N
Domestic, Private Home
Informant: Ava D. McKinney
Bpl: GA

THY KINGDOM COME   THY WILL BE DONE
BUTLER
USHER   BERENZA H.
1889 - 1966   1892 - 2001

Ida Reid Butler
Died: 1977   Age: 41 Certificate Not Found

IDA REID
BUTLER
1936 -- 1977
IN LOVING MEMORY
OF YOUR FAMILY

BN-705-M

Mary Ann Butler
Died: 02/16/1931   Age: 19 Certificate Not Found

OK-103-N [Pink Grnt Fldstn]   Noble & Kelsey

MARY ANN BUTLER
DAUGHTER OF
USHER & BERENZA BUTLER
JUNE 30, 1912
FEB. 16, 1931

Usher Butler
Died: 12/16/1966   Age: 74
Certificate No. 0046,0683
Parents: Lewis Butler & Julia Howard

OK-108-N
Retired: NC Finishing Co.
Informant: Berenza Butler, Wife
SEE BERENZA BUTLER

Noble & Kelsey: 34

BURIALS

Charles Leroy Butner
Died: 01/21/1962   Age: 69
Certificate No. 0042,0195

OK-160-O   Noble & Kelsey: 146
Retired Southern Railway Company.
Informant: Victoria Butner, Wife
Parents: Charles Butner & Fannie Morgan   Bpl: NC

BUTNER
CHARLES LEROY	VICTORIA HUFF
AUG. 15, 1892	MAY 16, 1896
JAN. 21, 1962	JUNE 29, 1971

Charles Sandy Butner
Died: 12/29/1966   Age: 94
Certificate No. 0046,0717
Parents: Sandy Butner & Unknown

OK-364-I/J [Grnt Fldstn]   Noble & Kelsey: 340
Retired: Salisbury Water Works
Informant: Dulcie Rippy, Wife
Bpl: Salisbury, NC

CHARLES S. BUTNER
MAY 10, 1872
DEC. 29, 1966
I HAVE KEPT THE FAITH.
2ND Tim. 4 7

Dulcie Rippy Butner
Died: 10/14/1986   Age: 84
Certificate No. 0066,0862

BN-865-M   Noble & Kelsey
Housemaid, Private Home
Informant: Mary A. Johnson, Washington, DC, Grand niece

Parents: Wilbur Rippy & Rachel Unknown

Bpl: Cherokee, SC

DULCIE RIPPY BUTNER
MAR. 31, 1902
OCT. 14, 1986
WELL DONE, GOOD & FAITHFUL SERVANT
MATTHEW 25: 21

Fannie Butner
Died: 09/10/1915   Age: 42
Certificate No. 0002,0222
Parents: Unknown & Margrett Hogans

OK-364-I/J   Noble & Kelsey: 340
Domestic, Housework
Informant: Margaret Hogans, Mother
Bpl: Rowan Co. b. 10/?? /1873

Lilla M. Butner
Died: 10/16/1976   Age: 93
Certificate No. 0056,0806
Parents: David Ellis & Lececilia Smith

NO MARKER   Mitchell & Fair
Retired Domestic
Informant: Mrs. Alice Henderson

Sandy Alexander Butner
Died: 02/06/1915   Age: 87
Certificate No. 0002,0503
Parents: Unknown & Melishie Butner

OK-364-I/J   Noble & Kelsey: 340
Farmer
Informant: Charles P. Butner
Bpl: Rowan

Victoria Huff Butner
Died: 06/29/1971   Age: 75 or 71
Certificate No. 0051,0416
Parents: Roy & Sallie Huff
(See Charles Leroy Butner)

OK-160-O   Noble & Kelsey
Housewife
Informant: A. R. Kelsey
Bpl: NC

BURIALS

Fannie H. Byers
Died: 03/ / 1935   Certificate Not Found
<u>Holt Family Plot</u>

ADDIE HOLT	JULIA F. HOLT
DIED MAR.7, 1965	DIED JUNE 3, 1939
HERMA K. FLEMING	FANNIE H. BYERS
DIED AUG. 30, 1979	DIED MAR. 1935
CLARENCE J. FLEMING	CARTHA H. CRAVER
DIED MAY 1, 1998	DIED OCT. 4, 1939

OK-192-L Plot   Noble & Kelsey: 163

Lorence Byers
Died: 05/13/1910   Age: 55
Certificate No. 0004,0389
Parents: George Byers & Betsy Carol

NO MARKER.
Widowed Farmer
Informant: John Opostal

Noble & Kelsey
Funeral Home Record

Nadine Yvette Byers
Died: 03/22/1980   Age: 17
Certificate No. 0060,0215
Parents: John Byers & Edna Ruthe Byers

BN-798-M
Student
Informant: Edna Ruth Byers, Mother
Bpl.: NC

NADINE YVETTE
BYERS
JULY 14, 1967
MAR. 22, 1980

Silva Byers
Died: 01/01/1910   Age: 47
Certificate No.0004,0435
Parents: Unknown

NO MARKER   Noble & Kelsey
Married: House Keeper
Informant: Torrance Byers, Salisbury
Bpl.: Macon, Ga.

Tinnie Robinson Poe Byers
Died: 08/09/1964   Age: 56
Certificate No. 0044,0455
Parents: Sam Davis & Sallie Phillips

BT-260-K MISSING   Mitchell & Fair
Cafe & Service Station Operator
Informant: John W. Byers, Husband
Bpl.: Stanley Co., NC

Albert L. Byrd
Died: 09/24/1931

OK   [Marble Military Headstone]

ALBERT L.
BYRD
NORTH CAROLINA
PVT.
422 RES. LABOR BN. OMC
SEPTEMBER 24, 1931

Janice Henderson Byrd
Died: 09/08/1992   Age: 37
Certificate No. 0072,0691
Parents: James P. Henderson & Edna Provoid

UH-616-G
Nurse's Aide @ Hospital
Informant: Ernest Byrd
Bpl: Salisbury, NC

Noble & Kelsey

JANICE HENDERSON BYRD
SEPT. 24,   SEPT. 8,
1955   1992

Clara Mashore Caldwell

Died: 12/16/1967   Certificate Not Found

UH-445-H

CALDWELL

LEWIS JAMES	CLARA MASHORE
MAY 17, 1903	DEC. 24, 1899
FEB. 25, 1951	DEC. 16, 1967

BURIALS

Dr. Edgar L. Caldwell UH-445-H
Died: 09/12/1959   Age: 52   Certificate Not Found

HUSBAND
DR. EDGAR L. CALDWELL
MAR. 26, 1907
SEPT. 12, 1959

Hazel Melchor Caldwell UH-472-H   Noble & Kelsey
Died: 04/17/1958   Age: 74y00m00d   Housewife
Certificate No. 0039,0010   **Informant:** Herman Caldwell
Parents: Amos Melchor & Adline Peck   Bpl: NC

CALDWELL
HAZEL   JAMES R.
DIED APR. 17, 1958   DIED NOV. 20, 1947

Herman Caldwell UH-460-H
Died: 07/01/1968   Age: 63   Certificate Not Found

HERMAN CALDWELL
JUNE 10, 1905
JULY 1, 1968

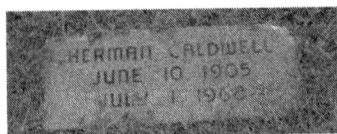

James Love Caldwell UH-445 H   Mitchell & Fair
Died: 11/16/1983   Age: 81   Employee @ NC Finishing Co.
Certificate No. 0063,0866   **Informant:** Rena Caldwell, Wife
Parents: James & Hazel Melchor Caldwell   Bpl: Rowan Co., NC

JAMES L.
CALDWELL
DEC. 6, 1902
NOV. 16, 1983

James Lewis Caldwell UH-445-H   Noble & Kelsey
Died: 02/25/1951   Age: 48   Insurance Agent
Certificate No. 0032,0663   **Informant:** Mrs. Clara Caldwell
Parents: Lewis James & Fannie Caldwell   Bpl: Chester, SC
SEE CLARA MAHORE

James Robert Caldwell UH-473-H   Noble & Kelsey
Died: 11/20/1947   Age: 63   Retired North Western Railroad Co.
Certificate No. 0030,0998   **Informant:** Mrs. Hazel Caldwell, Wife
Parents: Adolphus Caldwell & Unknown   Bpl: Rowan Co., NC

John Edward Caldwell NO MARKER   Mitchell & Fair
Died: 12/08/1970   Age: 23   Laborer
Certificate No. 0050,0774   **Informant:** Mrs. Catherine W. Caldwell
Parents: John Lee Caldwell & Catherine Waiters   Bpl: NC

Larry Eugene Caldwell NO MARKER
Died: 02/28/1957   Age: 9mos   INFANT
Certificate No. 0037,0487   **Informant:** Catherine Waiters Caldwell, Mother
Parents: John Lee Caldwell & Catherine Waiters   Bpl.: NC

BURIALS

Mary Virginia Caldwell
Died: 10/19/1952   Age: 30 days
Certificate No. 0033,0482
Parents: Richard Caldwell & Nevolia Waiters

NO MARKER
INFANT
Informant: Nevolia Waiters, Mother
Bpl: Salisbury, NC

Ellis, Mangum & Fair

Reatha Mae Caldwell
Died: 01/04/1949   Age: 01y06m
Parents: Richard Caldwell & Nevolia Waiters

NO MARKER
CHILD

Ellis, Mangum, & Fair
Funeral Home Record

Richard Caldwell Jr.
Died: 01/23/1949   Age: 01m26d
Parents: Richard Caldwell & Nevolia Waiters

NO MARKER
INFANT

Ellis, Mangum, & Fair
Funeral Home Record

Annie E. Campbell
Died: Certificate Not Found

OK-NO MARKER
Winder: Rowan Cotton Mills

Noble & Kelsey: 8
Funeral Home Record

Emma Campbell
Died: 03/20/1956   Age: 60
Certificate No. 0037,0008
Parents: Unknown & Harriet Wilson

OK-167-O [Pink Granite Fieldstone]
House Work
Informant: Isaac Campbell, Husband
Bpl: Guilford, Co. NC

Noble & Kelsey

EMMA CAMPBELL
MAR. 30. 1887
MAY 20, 1956

Gary Campbell

OK-NO MARKER

Noble & Kelsey: 8

James Campbell
Died: 11/01/1939   Certificate Not Found

BN-685-P MISSING

Lizzie Trott Campbell
Died: 02/20/1911   Age: 22y07m12
Certificate No. 0004,0154
Parents: Lon Trott/Mother Unknown

NO MARKER

Informant: Isaac Campbell
Bpl.: NC

G. W. Wright

Minnie Almeta Campbell
Died: 02/02/1948   Age: 57
Parents: Ephraim Bost & Elizabeth Boger

UH- NO MARKER
Domestic
bd. 03/11/1890

Ellis, Mangum & Fair
Funeral Home Record

Susie Campbell
Died: 01/14/1932   Certificate Not Found

??[Granite Headstone]

SUSIE CAMPBELL
WIFE OF
JOHN W. CARTER
DIED JAN. 14, 1932
HAVING FINISHED LIFE'S DUTY, SHE NOW SWEETLY RESTS.

Walter Jack Campbell
Died: 06/16/1910   Age: 18y06m12
Parents: Will Sloan & Della Campbell
Register of Death, Salisbury, and Co. of Rowan, NC (09/1909-10/11/1911)

NO MARKER
Student

Noble & Kelsey

Bpl: Salisbury

Elem Cannon
Died: 08/17/1961   Age: 76
Certificate No. 0041,0663
Parents: George Cannon & Unknown

NO MARKER
Laborer
Informant: Bertha Cannon, Wife
Bpl: NC

Ellis, Mangum & Fair

BURIALS

Dorothy Lavorn Carpenter
Died: 12/05/1988   Age: 16
Certificate No. 0068,1098
Parents: Lonzo Carpenter & Merry Leach

BN-887-M
Unloader @ Screen Printing business
Informant: Merry L. Carpenter, Mother
Bpl: Iredell Co. NC

Noble & Kelsey

MISS DOROTHY LAVORN
CARPENTER
MAR. 19, 1972
DEC. 5, 1988

Mollie Carpenter
Died: 07/17/1915   Age: 34
Certificate No. 0002,0195
Parents: Alex Cowan & Phoebe Hall

NO MARKER
Domestic: General House Work
Informant: Not Given
Bpl: Rowan Co.

Noble & Kelsey: 250

Dorothy Scott Carr
Died: 09/10/1985   Age: 81
Certificate No. 0065,0014
Parents: John Henry Scott & Cora Brooks

UH-506-H [Grnt Hdstn]
Domestic - Maid @ Stone's Studio
Informant: James E. Scott, Brother
Bpl: Rowan Co., NC

Noble & Kelsey

CARR
DOROTHY SCOTT CARR

John R. Carr
Died: 05/25/1931   Age: ∞36
Certificate No. 0019,0237:
Parents: Carr & Amanda Carr

BN-821-M [Marble]
Veteran: Mail Porter, Southern Railroad
Informant: Sirler Carr
Bpl: Rowan Co., NC

Noble & Kelsey

JOHN R.
CARR
NORTH CAROLINA
PVT. 825 CO. TRANS. CORPS
QMC
MAY 25, 1931

Katie Katherine Carr
Died: 1982

NO MARKER

Noble & Kelsey: 282

Lafayette Carr
Died: 09/13/1983   Age: 90
Certificate No. 0063,0670
Parents: Jim & Minnie Carr

BN-669-P [Grnt Hdstn]
Retired Farmer
Informant: Mrs. Josephine Leach, Daughter
Bpl: York Co., SC

Noble & Kelsey

IN LOVING MEMORY
OF
LAFAYETTE CARR
MAR. 17, 1893
SEPT. 13, 1983

Lula Rice Carr
Died: 03/18/1989   Age: 82
Certificate No. 0069,0288
Parents: James Rice & Liza Boler

BN-668-P
Homemaker

Informant: Josephine Leach
Bpl: Chesterfield, SC

Noble & Kelsey

IN LOVING MEMORY
OF
LULA RICE CARR
APR. 8, 1907
MAR. 18, 1989

BURIALS

Rita Carr
Died: 06/15/1957   Age: 83
Certificate No. 0038,0002
Parents: Neal Chunn & Unknown

NO MARKER   Ellis, Mangum & Fair
Domestic
Informant: Mrs. Julia Rankins

Scott Carr
Died: 04/26/1924
Certificate No. 0012,0349
Parents: UNKNOWN
Plot contains Scott Carr & Elizabeth Whoozer

NO MARKER   Bingham & Carter k016

Informant: Will Carson

William Scott Carr
Died: 04/29/1955   Age: 63
Certificate No. 0036,0203
Parents: Scott Carr & Charlotte Thompson

UH-507-H [Granite Headstone]   Noble & Kelsey
Helper @ Southern Railway
Informant: Mrs. Dorothy S. Carr, Wife
  Bpl: Cleveland, NC

CARR
WILLIAM SCOTT CARR
SEPT. 21, 1891
APR. 29, 1955

William Henry Carrington
Died: 06/04/1911 age: 6 mos. 8dys   Baby
Certificate No. 0004,0061
Parents: William O. Carrington & Mabel E. Simmonds (sic)

NO MARKER

Informant: William O. Carrington, Father

Beulah Crawford Carroll
Died: 06/20/1993   Age: 82
Certificate No. 0073,0599
Parents: Isaac Crawford & Mildred Provoid

UH-658-G   Noble & Kelsey
Homemaker @ Own Home
Informant: Kenneth T. Carroll
  Bpl: Gaston Co., NC

CARROLL
BEULAH CRAWFORD   THOMAS C.
AUG. 1, 1910   JAN. 13, 1914
JUNE 20, 1993   APR. 25, 1993

Thomas C. Carroll
Died: 04/25/1993   Age: 79
Certificate No. 0073,0424
Parents: James Carroll & Geneva Shanks
See Beulah Carroll

UH-659-G   Noble & Kelsey
Dye House Attendant @ Cotton Blends Mfg.
Informant: Kenneth T. Carroll
  Bpl: Cleveland Co., NC

Annie Carson
Died: 06/23/1925   Age: 39
Certificate No.0013,0374
Parents: Syie (Sic) McNair & Unknown

NO MARKER   Bingham & Carter
Housewife
Informant: Charles Carson
Bpl: Maxton, NC

Charlie Carson
Died: 02/13/1926
Certificate No. 0014,0106
Parents: Bonnie Carson & Lucy Chattman

NO MARKER   Bingham, Carter, Cheshire
Day Labor @ Southern Rail Road
Informant: Charles Carson
Bpl: NC

Dovie Staley Carson
Died: 02/02/1954   Age: 64
Certificate No. 0035,0066

NO MARKER   Ellis, Mangum & Fair
Dress Maker
Parents: James Staley

BURIALS

Ethel McIlwaine Carson   UH-458-H   Noble & Kelsey
Died: 09/16/1983   Age: 83   Homemaker
Certificate No. 0063,0671   **Informant:** Vera M. Moore, Daughter
Parents: Samuel McMullen & Bessie Hicklin   Bpl: Lancaster, SC

ETHEL M. CARSON
SEPT. 29, 1900
SEPT. 16, 1983
IN MEMORY OF MOTHER

Hattie C. Carson   UH-411-I/J   [Granite Fieldstone]
Died: 1946   Age: ∞ 62 Certificate Not Found

HATTIE C. CARSON
1884 ---- 1946

Rachel Elizabeth Carson   OK-NO MARKER   Noble & Kelsey: 10
Died: 04/24/1916   Age: ∞72   Cook/Servant   Funeral Home Record
Certificate Not Found   **Informant:** Mrs. Clyde? uers   Parents: ????

Rev. William O. Carson   UH-412-I/J   Ellis, Mangum, & Fair
Died: 08/30/1955   Age: ∞76   Minister: Hood Seminary Class of 1925 (Trinity AME Zion Church, Greensboro, NC) Presiding Elder, Died in Norfolk, VA
Certificate Not Found   Parents: Bpl: Rutherfordton, NC

REV. WILLIAM O. CARSON
1879 ---- 1955

Clare Carter   BN-675-P   [Granite Flush]   Noble & Kelsey: 345
Died: 04/24/1985   Age: 61 Certificate Not Found

CLARE CARTER
OCT. 30. 1924
APR. 24, 1985

Emiline Carter   OK-163-O MISSING Plot   Noble & Kelsey: 27
Certificate Not Found

Evaline Bernhardt Carter   OK-137-N Plot   Noble & Kelsey
Died: 06/ /1935   Age: 90   Domestic
Certificate No. 0023,0161   **Informant:** Mattie Caruth
Parents: Henry Boyden & Mary Henderson   Bpl: Rowan Co., NC

EVALINE BERNHARDT
CARTER
DEPARTED THIS LIFE
JUNE 1935

George A. Carter   OK-163-O   Noble & Kelsey
Died: 03/29/1921   Age: 41 [39 on dc]   Day Labor for Street Work
Certificate No. 0009,0346   **Informant:** John W. Carter
Parents: John A. Carter & Mickie Neely   Bpl: Davidson Co., NC

GEORGE A CARTER
DEC. 1, 1880
MAR. 29, 1921
None knew thee but to love thee.

BURIALS

John W. Carter

Died: 07/04/1926 Age: ∞53 Blacksmith Helper @ Southern Railroad
Certificate No. 0014,0603 **Informant:** M. J.Carter
Parents: Not Given & Unreadable
OK-163-O N&K109 Bingham, Carter & Cheshire

(Carter Plot) **HUSBAND
JOHN W. CARTER
DIED JUNE 4, 1926**
He died as he lived - Christian

Matthew Carter
Died: 06/04/1944   Age: 42
OK-228-K [Grnt. Hdstn]   Noble & Kelsey: 239
Certificate Not Found

**MATTHEW CARTER
DEC. 16, 1902
JUNE 4, 1940**

Samuel Carter
Died: 11/22/1909   Age: 32yrs.3mth
Certificate No. 0004,0480
Parents: Henry Carter & Laura Fowler
OK-163-O   Noble & Kelsey 14
Teamster
Informant: Laura Carter
Bpl: Davie Co., NC

Warren Carter
Died: 02/09/16   Age: ∞70
Certificate No. 0003,0370
Parents: Unknown & Elsie Parker
OK-163-O MISSING   Noble & Kelsey: 14
Cab Driver
Informant: Mrs. Josephine Carter
Bpl: Davie Co., NC

Adam Caruth
Died: 05/ /1907   Certificate Not Found
OK-137-N Plot
Carpenter

**ADAM CARUTH
DEPARTED THIS LIFE
MAY 1907**

Mattie Bernhart Caruth
Died: 12/14/1954   Age: 67   Housewife
OK-137-N Plot   Ellis, Mangum & Fair
Certificate No. 0035,0516   **Informant:** Flora Flack
Parents: James Isaac Bernhardt & Everline Henderson   Bpl: Salisbury, NC

**MATTIE BERNHART
WIFE OF
ADAM CARUTH**

Harvey Leon Chalk
Died: 06/05/1990   Age: 33
Certificate No. 0070,0450
Parents: George Johnson & Annie Ruth Chalk
UH-558 H   Noble & Kelsey
Cloth Factory Supervisor
Informant: Annie Ruth Key
Bpl: Salisbury, NC

**WE LOVE YOU
HARVEY LEON CHALK
(MICKEY)
APR. 18, 1957
JUNE 5, 1990**

BURIALS

Annie Rose Chambers NO MARKER Ellis, Mangum & Fair
Died: 01/29/1947   Age: 37
Certificate No. 0030,0742
Parents: John Summer & Florence Setzer bd. 10/23/19

Creola Cowan Chambers UH-587-H MISSING Noble & Kelsey
Died: 04/17/1991   Age: 81 Housemaid @ Private Homes
Certificate No. 0071,0346 **Informant:** Nola Angle
Parents: Neal Cowan & Katie Cuthbertson Bpl: Rowan Co., NC

Essie Chambers OK-NO MARKER Noble & Kelsey: 3

F. C. Chambers OK-126-N

Herbert Charles Chambers Jr. UH-386-I/J
Died: 07/17/1968   Age: INFANT
Certificate No. 0048,0419
Parents: Herbert C. Chambers Sr., & Gladys Dublin

HERBERT C. CHAMBERS JR.
JULY 16, 1968
JULY 17, 1968

INFANT of Amy Chambers NO MARKER Summersett
Died: 02/11/1908   Age: 4 m 15 dys INFANT Funeral Home Record

Julia Chambers OK-NO MARKER Noble & Kelsey: 325

Lester Chambers BN-769-M Ellis, Mangum, & Fair
Died: 12/14/1942   Age: 81 Certificate Not Found

LESTER CHAMBERS
NOV. 8, 1861
DEC. 14, 1942
FATHER

Lillie Chambers NO MARKER Noble & Kelsey
Died: 06/21/1927   Age ∞33 Domestic/Housework
Certificate No. 0015,0370 **Informant:** J. H. Little John
Parents: Edward & Mary Norris Bpl: Spartanburg, SC

Margie Leola Chambers OK-125-N Noble & Kelsey
Died: 01/12/1912   Age: 14 Certificate Not Found

HOWARD-CHAMBERS
MOTHER   SISTER
FANNIE CHAMBERS MARGIE LEOLA
HOWARD   CHAMBERS
JULY 25, 1877   DEC. 8, 1898
JAN 19, 1949   JAN. 12, 1912
With Christ in Heaven
(Footstone) MARGIE L. Dau. of W. C. & F. C.

Moses Chambers NO MARKER Noble & Kelsey: 325
Died: 08/16/1912   Age: 62y04m06d Trucker, Farming
Certificate No. 0001,0187 **Informant:** J. W. Hairston
Parents: Unknown & Leanna Shuman Bpl: Rowan Co., NC

BURIALS

Ethel Mae Miller Cherry
Died: 12/23/1969   Age: 48
Certificate No. 0049,0741:
Parents: Edward Miller & Beulah Sloan

NO MARKER
Housekeeper
Informant: Mrs. Clara Barger
Bpl: NC

Noble & Kelsey

James Avery Cherry
Died: 09/26/1994   Age: 50
Certificate No. 0074,0931
Parents: Leroy Ellis & Laura Cherry

UH-654 G MISSING

Informant: Margaret Leach
Bpl: Iredell Co., NC

Noble & Kelsey

Mary Lee Cherry
Died: 04/02/1918   Age: 14,07,19
Certificate No. 0006,0398
Parents: James W. Cherry & Lula Hill

NO MARKER
School Girl
Informant: James W. Cherry
Bpl: Harmony Station, SC

Noble & Kelsey

Thomas Lee Cherry

BN-778-M MISSING

Bessie Bryant Cheshire
Died: 06/03/1934   Age: 38y10m03d
Certificate No. 0022,0246
Parents: William H. Bryant & Elizabeth Maroney

OK. –025 N MISSING
School Teacher
Informant: Leroy R. Cheshire, Husband
Bpl: NC

Cheshire Funeral Home

Florence Cheshire
Died: 12/29/1958   Age: 36 Certificate Not Found   Waitress @ Kelsey's Cafe

BT-300-K

FLORENCE CHESHIRE
WIFE OF
LOUIS SMITH
AND DAUGHTER OF
CLARENCE & ANNIE
CHESHIRE
JULY 11, 1921
DEC. 29, 1958
"THE LORD IS MY SHEPARD I SHALL NOT WANT."

Leroy Cheshire
Died: 04/20/1938   Age: 46
Certificate No. 0026,0112
Parents: UNKNOWN

NO MARKER
Undertaker/Chauffeur
Informant: Alvin H. Cheshire
Bpl: Salisbury, NC

Cheshire Funeral Home

Mary Ann Childress
Died: 05/22/1929   Age: 48
Certificate No. 0017,0408
Parents: & Mary A. Allison

NO MARKER
Cook @ Private Family
Informant: Ida May Morton
Bpl: Cleveland, NC

Noble & Kelsey

Alberta Moffitt Chisholm
Died: 12/21/1991   Age: 108
Certificate No. 0071,1106
Parents: Willis Moffitt & Sarah Caldwell

UH-553-H
Housemaid @ private homes
Informant: Rosa Lee Paterson
Bpl: Chester Co., SC

Noble & Kelsey

ALBERTA MOFFITT
CHISHOLM
NOV. 16, 1883
DEC. 21, 1991
108 YRS. OF AGE

BURIALS

Cicero Christian
Died: 03/25/1915 Age: 50
Certificate No. 0002,0121
Parents: James Christian & Rachel Christian

NO MARKER -
Bellman: Empire Hotel
Informant: Wiley Christian
  Bpl: Montgomery Co., NC

Noble & Kelsey: 252

Sophronia Gaines Christian
Died: 11/27/1922 Age: 37
Certificate No. 0010,0483
Parents: George W. Gaines & Unknown

OK-NO MARKER
Domestic, Housework
Informant: Wiley Christian
  Bpl: Florida

Noble & Kelsey: 125

Wiley Christian
Died: 10/29/1934 Age: ∞46
Certificate No. 0022,0289
Parents: Cicero & Julia Christian

OK-NO MARKER
Day Laborer
Informant: Andrew Christian
  Bpl: Iredell Co., NC

Noble & Kelsey: 125

Lula Osborne Brown Chun
Died: 11/25/1938 Age: ∞68
Certificate No. 0026,0257
  Parents: Jack & Phillis Brown

OK-143-O
Housewife
Informant: Henry Osborne
  Bpl: Davie Co., NC

Noble & Kelsey

LULA
OSBORNE
CHUN
DIED
NOV. 25, 1938
AGE 68 YEARS
AT REST

Alice Clark
  Died: 08/28/1925 Age: 46
  Certificate No. 0013,0406
  Parents: Benjamin Moore &??

OK-204-L
Housewife
Informant: Will Clark, Husband
  Bpl:

Bingham & Carter

ALICE CLARK
BORN JAN 1882
DIED AUG 28
1928

Anita Archie Clark
Died: 12/22/1958 Age: 20
Certificate No. 0039,0414
Parents: Melvin Archie & Thelma Caldwell

NO MARKER
Domestic
Informant: James L. Clark
  Bpl: NC

Ellis, Mangum & Fair

Charlotte Ferron Clark   OK-098-N Ferron Plot
  Died: 07/21/1930 Age: 75 Certificate Not Found

CHARLOTTE FERRON
CLARK
AUG. 12, 1855
JULY 21, 1930
At Rest

BURIALS

Louisa Clark
Died: 01/27/1943   Age: 88
Certificate No. 0028,0721
Parents: Daniel Clark & Katie Mango

NO MARKER
Domestic
Informant: Samuel Clark
Bpl: Kershaw, SC

Ellis, Mangum & Fair

Annie Charleston Clayborn
Died: 07/19/1960   Age: 65
Certificate No. 0041,0004
Parents: Jonah Charleston & Ida Jackson

BT-NWSTN
Housewife
Informant: Mrs. Maggie Ellis
Bpl: GA

Noble & Kelsey

CLAYBORN
WILL CLAYBORN
JUNE 12, 1883
HIS WIFE
ANNIE CHARLESTON
MAR. 20, 1895
JULY 19, 1960

Della Clement
Died: 12/24/1957   Age: 63

BT-319-K
Certificate Not Found

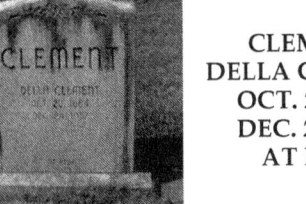

CLEMENT
DELLA CLEMENT
OCT. 20, 1884
DEC. 24, 1954
AT REST

James A. Clement
Died: 11/19/1964   Age: 85
Certificate Not Found

BT-317-K
Laborer, Southern Railroad

JAMES A. CLEMENT
DEC. 23, 1879
NOV. 19, 1964
HIS TOILS ARE PAST, HIS WORK IS DONE,
HE FOUGHT THE FIGHT -- THE VICTORY WON.

Maggie Clement
Died: 03/28/1966   Age: 86

BT-315-K
Certificate Not Found

(Top) MAGGIE CLEMENT
WIFE OF
JOSEPH GADDY
DEC. 25, 1880
MAR. 28,   1966
(Front) MOTHER OUR LOVED ONE

Marshall Clement
Died: 04/01/1913   Age: 30 yrs.
Certificate Not Found
Parents: Jess Clement & Mother Unknown

NO MARKER
Cook
Informant: Lula Bailey
Bpl: Mocksville

Summersett

Otis Lark Clement
Died: STILL BIRTH   Certificate Not Found: Parents:

NO MARKER

BURIALS

Mrs. Martha Clement
Died: 07/03/1913   Age: 63y11m
Certificate No. 0001,0321
Parents: Unknown & Ellen Smith

NO MARKER
Domestic
Informant: Sallie Rankin

Noble & Kelsey:

Effie Coil
Died: 09/19/1944   Age: no DOB
Certificate No. 0029,0229
Parents: Alexander Coil & Mollie Ellis

NO MARKER
Domestic
Informant: Willie Coil
    Bpl: Concord, NC

Blanche Elma Coleman

Died: 08/01/1951

UH-492-H
    Age: 44 Certificate Not Found

COLEMAN
BLANCHE ELMA
COLEMAN
MAY 19, 1907
AUG. 1, 1951

Caroline Coleman
Died: 05/09/1925   Age: ∞65
Certificate No. 0013,00347
Parents: Unknown & Nancy Hairston

NO MARKER
Domestic Housework
Informant: Francis Coleman
    Bpl: Davie Co., NC

Noble & Kelsey: 218

Eliza Coleman
Died: 10/09/1974   Certificate Not Found

NO MARKER

Mitchell & Fair

Ethel Warner Coleman
Died: 10/07/1987   Age: 94
Certificate No. 0067,0833

BN-07-M
Housewife, Organist @ Soldiers Memorial
Informant: Susie Moss, Daughter
    Parents: Andrew Jackson Warner/Mary Delmore
    Bpl: Mobile, AL

Noble & Kelsey

MOTHER
ETHEL WARNER
COLEMAN
NOV. 10, 1892
OCT. 7, 1987

Francis Coleman

OK-NO MARKER

Noble & Kelsey: 218

Gerhardt Sherwin Coleman
Died: 06/03/1918   Age: 01y01m04d
Certificate No. 0006,0449
Parents: Francis Coleman & Margaret Stokes

OK-NO MARKER
INFANT
Informant: Francis A. Coleman
    Bpl: Salisbury, NC

Noble & Kelsey: 218

John Coleman
Died: 09/11/1925   Age: 54
Certificate No. 0013,0354
Parents: UNKNOWN

NO MARKER
Day Labor
Informant Frank Colman
    Bpl: Baker Co., GA

Noble & Kelsey

John Wesley Coleman
Died: 05/07/1957   Age: 62

UH-NO MARKER
Certificate Not Found

Ellis, Mangum, & Fair

BURIALS

Vernan Heifetz Coleman
Died: 12/12/1919   Age: 08m12d
Certificate No. 0007,0105
Parents: F. H. Coleman & Margaret Stokes

NO MARKER
INFANT
Informant: F. H. Coleman
 Bpl: Salisbury, NC

Noble & Kelsey: 218

John Hillard Collins
Died: 12/14/1966   Age: 76
Certificate No. 0046,0685
Parents: Hilliard Collins & Patty Linder

BT-314-K
Minister & Retired from Southern Railway
Informant: Annie Laney

Noble & Kelsey

REV. JOHN H. COLLINS
DEC. 25   DEC. 14
1890   1966

Rosie Blair Collins
Died: 07/04/1958   Age: 56
Certificate No. 0039,0151
Parents: Allen Blair & Sallie Faulkner

UH-416-H
Domestic
Informant: Elveree Witherspoon
 Bpl: Lancaster, SC

Ellis, Mangum & Fair

MOTHER
ROSIE BLAIR
COLLINS
JUNE 6, 1902
JULY 4, 1958
GONE, BUT NOT FORGOTTEN.

John Colston
Died: 10/15/1915   Age: 56
Certificate No. 0002,0236
Parents: Gooding Colston & Unknown

OK-NO MARKER
General Labor
Informant: Sara Colston
 Bpl: Montgomery Co., NC

Noble & Kelsey: 191

John V. Colston
Died: 12/04/1960   Age: 72
Certificate No. 0041,0219
Parents: Fred Colston & Mary Kendall

NO MARKER
Machinist Helper
Informant: Mrs. Ollie Bingham
 Bpl: NC

Ellis, Mangum & Fair

Clyde M. Coltson
Died: 01/11/1969   Age: 55

NO MARKER

Mitchell & Fair
Funeral Home Record

Azellee M. Connor
Died: 05/15/1971

NO MARKER

Mitchell & Fair
Funeral Home Record

Emanuel Connor

NO MARKER

Noble & Kelsey: 252

James L. Connor
Died: 10/21/1980   Certificate Not Found

BN-762-P

JAMES L. CONNER
JAN. 2, 1909
OCT. 21, 1980

BURIALS

Arthur Clinton Cook OK-141-O Noble & Kelsey: 132
Died: 09/22/1918   Age: 29y06m22   Photographer (Self employed)
Certificate No. 0006,499   **Informant**: May Troy Cooke
Parents: Mitt Cook, born Africa & Roda, born Spain   Bpl: Born @ Sea

A. C. COOK
FEB. 29, 1890
SEPT. 22, 1918
Tho last to sight to memory dear

Clyde Innis Cook OK-NO MARKER Noble & Kelsey: 10

Tyrice Deshawn Cook UH-543-H MISSING

May Troy Cook OK- 141-O MISSING Noble & Kelsey: 132
Certificate Not Found   Teacher @ Livingstone College Public School 1921-1922

Felicia Michelle Corpening OK-356 -I/J Noble & Kelsey
Died: 02/14/1977   Age: 4ms.   INFANT
Certificate No. 0057,0135   **Informant**: Murphy Corpening
Parents: Murphy Corpening & Marie Granford   Bpl: NC

FELICIA MICHELLE
CORPENING
OCT. 10, 1976
FEB. 14, 1977

Andrew Lee Cowan OK-164-O MISSING Plot Noble & Kelsey: 98
Died: 05/10/1923   Age: 90   Carpenter   Funeral Home Record
Certificate Not Found   **Informant**: Roxie Cowan
Parents: Not Known & Arnienta Brown   Bpl: Rowan Co., NC

Annie Milton Cook NO MARKER Mitchell & Fair
Died: 10/06/1974   Age: 51   Domestic - Housewife
Certificate No. 0054,0633:   **Informant**: Mrs. Maggie Gadson, Mother
Parents: Unknown & Maggie Alexander   Bpl: NC

Annie Ruth Cowan NO MARKER Ellis, Mangum & Fair
Died: 01/07/1958   Age: 21d   Certificate Not Found   Funeral Home Record

Arthur Cowan UH-609-G MISSING Noble & Kelsey
Died: 06/29/1992   Age: 57   Hand truck Laborer @ Roofing Company
Certificate No. 0072,0476   **Informant**: Esther Edwards
Parents: Son Woods & Esther Rosetta Cowan   Bpl: Cleveland, NC

Carrie Neely Cowan BN-021-N MISSING Noble & Kelsey:
Died: 07/??/1946   Certificate Not Found

Carry Cowan NO MARKER Bingham & Carter
Died: 03/10/1924   Age: None Given   Housewife
Certificate No. 0012,0356   **Informant**: Adam Cowan, Husband
Parents: Ed. Thomas &??   Bpl: NC

BURIALS

Launa Cowan　　　　　　　　　　NO MARKER　　　　　　　　Noble & Kelsey: 225

Roxie Cowan　　　　　　　　　　OK-164-O　　　　　　　　　Noble & Kelsey: 98
Died: 08/12/1934　　Age: 75　　　Domestic
Certificate No. 0022,0239
Parents: Jack & Laura Walker　　　　　　Bpl: Weldon, NC
Date Read: 08/15/2003　(Damaged Stone Marker – broken – in front of Duncan Sr. Plot)

Annie Mae Cowen　　　　　　　UH- NO MARKER　　　　　　Mitchell & Fair
Died: 10/06/1974　　Age: 51　　　Domestic/Housewife
Certificate No. 0066,0596
Parents: Unknown & Maggie??

Frank Charles Craige　　　　　　UH-463-H　　　　　　　　　Noble & Kelsey
Died: 12/17/1977　　Age: 64　　　Presser @ Star Laundry & Worker @ Cone Mills
　　　　　　　　　　　　　　　　Certificate No. 0057,0968　　**Informant**: Mrs. Willie Mae Hornes
　　　　　　　　　　　　　　　　Craige
　　　　　　　　　　　　　　　　Parents: Unknown & Laura Craig　　Bpl: NC

　　　　　　　　　　　　　　　　　　CRAIGE
　　　　　　　　　　　　　FRANK CHARLES　　WILLIE HORNES
　　　　　　　　　　　　　JUNE 21, 1913　　APR. 7, 1916
　　　　　　　　　　　　　　　　DEC. 17, 1977

Mr. John C. Craige　　　　　　　OK-NO MARKER　　　　　　Noble & Kelsey: 51
Died: 03/18/1918　　Age: 45,08m　　Cook @ boarding house
Certificate No. 0006,0394　　　　**Informant**: Stephen Noble
Parents: Frank & Adeline Craige　　　Bpl: Rowan Co., NC

Kerr Craige　　　　　　　　　　OK-NO MARKER　　　　　　Noble & Kelsey: 51
Died: 11/15/1913　　Age: 31　　　Machinist Helper: Southern Railway Shops
Certificate No. 0001,0732　　　　**Informant**: Anna Craig
Parents: Matt Craig & Lucy Kerr　　　Bpl: Rowan Co., NC

Laura Smith Craige　　　　　　UH-465-H　　　　　　　　　Noble & Kelsey
Died: 05/19/1947　　Age: 65　　　Housewife
Certificate No. 0030,0860　　　　**Informant**: Frank Craige
　　　　　　　　　　Parents: Obadiah Smith & Amanda Long　　Bpl: Rowan, NC

　　　　　　　　　　CRAIGE
　　　　　　　　　LAURA SMITH
　　　　　　　　　　WIFE OF
　　　　　　　　JEFFERSON CRAIGE
　　　　　　　　DIED MAY 19, 1947
　　　　　　　　　AGE 65 YRS.
　　　　　　GONE, BUT NOT FORGOTTEN

Lula Craige　　　　　　　　　　OK-NO MARKER　　　　　　Noble & Kelsey: 51

Willie Hornes Craige　　　　　　UH-464-H
Died: 04/07/1916　　Age: 61　Certificate Not Found　(See Frank Charles Craige)

Wille Mae Craige　　　　　　　UH-463-H　　　　　　　　　Noble & Kelsey
Died: 2003　　Age: 88　　Certificate Not Found　　　　　　Funeral Home Marker

　　　WILLE MAE
　　　　CRAIGE
　　　1915　2003

BURIALS

Annie Walker Crane
Died: 04/19/1911 Age: 38yrs.
Certificate No. 0004,0214
Parents: John Walker & Cresie McDonald

NO MARKER.
Domestic
Informant: Cresie Walker
 Bpl.: SC

Carthia Holt Craver
Died: 10/02/1939 Age: 47
Certificate No. 0027,0226
Parents: John Holt & Julia F. Miller
(See Fannie Byers)

OK-192-L
Housewife
Informant: Roy B. Craver, Husband
 Bpl: Davidson, Co., NC

Noble & Kelsey: 163

Caroline Johnson Crawford
Died: 02/23/1956 Age: 71
Parents: James Johnson & Unknown

NO MARKER
Domestic

Ellis, Mangum & Fair
Funeral Home Record

John E. Crawford
Died: 01/09/1969 Certificate Not Found

NO MARKER

Mitchell & Fair
Funeral Home Record

Mable Macie Crawford
Died: 01/09/1969 Age: 73
Certificate No. 0049,0022
Parents: John Holland & Elizabeth Stowe

NO MARKER
Domestic
Informant: Claude Crawford
 Bpl: SC

Mitchell & Fair

Susie Crawford

BT-264-K
Died: 07/30/1962 Age: 42
Certificate No. 0042,0550

Parents: John Beatty & Eliza McCullough

Noble & Kelsey
Domestic
Informant: George Crawford, Husband
 Bpl: Chester, SC

SUSIE CRAWFORD
SEPT. 11, 1917
JULY 30, 1962

Miss Lizzie Crittenden
Died: 12/06/1948 Age: 53
Certificate No. 0031,0488
Parents: William B. Crittenden & Julia Moore

OK-NO MARKER
Domestic
Informant: Miss Minnie Howe (928 W. Monroe Street)
 Bpl: Savannah, Ga.

Noble & Kelsey: 7

William Bentley Crittenden

OK-NO MARKER

Noble & Kelsey: plot 7

He is probably buried in the same plot with his daughter Lizzie since he purchased it from W. F. Kelsey
Died: Between 1924 & 1929 Age Unknown
He was a teacher @ Livingstone College & Pastor of St. Phillips Episcopal Church in Salisbury, NC according to the Census and the 1905 Livingstone College Cat. & City Directory
No Certificate for Rowan County or Savannah, GA. Could be located.

Will Crittinden
Died: 10/08/1923 Age. 38
Certificate No. 0011,0508
Parents: UNKNOWN

OK-NO MARKER
Day Labor
Informant: Vera Crittinden

Noble & Kelsey

BURIALS

Julie Crosby
Died: 01/03/1925   Age: 49
Certificate No. 0013,0257
Parents: Cyrous Alexander & ????? Smith

OK-NO MARKER   Noble & Kelsey: 227
Domestic Housework
Informant: Thomas Crosby, Husband
   Bpl: Rowan Co., NC

Thomas Crosby
Died: 06/28/1946   Age: ∞68
Certificate No. 0030,0316
Parents: Berry Crosby & Sarah Thorpe

OK-NO MARKER   Noble & Kelsey: 227
Day Laborer
Informant: John Crosby
   Bpl: Fairfield Co., SC

Willie Crosby

Died: 12/25/1917   Age: 14
Parents: Thomas & Julia Crosby

OK-217-L [Marble]
Certificate Not Found

WILLIE
Son of
THOMAS & JULIA CROSBY
FEB. 1, 1903
DEC. 25, 1917

Miss Willie G. Crowell
Died: 02/25/1920   Age: 21y03m20
Certificate No.0008,0127
Parents: William Crowell Gold Hill, NC

OK-NO MARKER   Noble & Kelsey: 35
Student
Informant: Mrs. Janie Reid
& Janie Walker   Bpl: Chester, SC

Charles Edward Culbertson
Died: 02/29/1960   Age: 24

OK-341-I/J
Certificate Not Found

CHARLES EDWARD
CULBERSTON
SEPT. 30, 1936
FEB. 29, 1960
THO LOST TO SIGHT
TO MEMORY DEAR.

Clyde C. Culp

UH-602-G   MISSING

Lula Ferguson Culp
Died: 02/08/1971   Age: 52
Certificate No. 0051,0080
Parents: Plumie Ferguson & Gertrude Ferguson

OK-248-L   Noble & Kelsey
Housewife
Informant: Gertrude Ferguson
   Bpl: SC

LULA FERGUSON CULP
JULY 13, 1919
FEB. 8, 1971

Mary Burns Cureton
Died: 11/06/1964   Age: 80
Certificate No. 0044,0629
Parents: Dudley Burns & Francis Montgomery

NO MARKER   Ellis, Mangum & Fair
Housewife
Informant: Janie B. Neely
   Bpl: Lancaster, SC

John Curley
Died: 09/18/1922   Age:
Certificate No. 0010,0516
Parents: Not Given

NO MARKER   George W. Wright
Laborer
Informant: R. P. Russill (Sic)
   Bpl: Wadesboro, NC

BURIALS

Ella Harriet Glenn Currence
Died: 07/16/1964   Age: 77
Certificate No. 0044,0410
Parents: Frank Glenn & Louis Meeks

OK-155-O
Housewife
Informant: Helen C. Bennett

Noble & Kelsey

Bpl: NC

CURRENCE
ELLA GLENN
WIFE OF
FRANK M. CURRENCE
NOV. 20, 1886
JULY 16, 1964

Frank Leonard Daniel
Died: 4/29/1926   Age: 58
Certificate No. 0014,0228
Parents: Unknown & Ellie Daniel

OK-NO MARKER
Prescription druggist & Physician until 1924
Informant: Selene Daniel, Wife
Bpl: Goldsboro, NC

Noble & Kelsey: 23

John Daniel, III
Died: 10/21/1969   Age: 3 m
Parents: J. D. & Ermine Jefferies

UH-
Certificate Not Found

JOHN DANIEL, III
SON OF
J. D. & ERMINE
JEFFERIES
JULY 17, 1969
OCT. 21, 1969

Fannie Payne Daniels
Died: 01/22/1977   Age: 86
Certificate No. 0057,0065:
Parents: Jim & Delia Rankin

OK-168-O Duncan Sr. Plot
Housewife
Informant: Georgia Hipps
Bpl: NC

Noble & Kelsey

MOTHER
FANNIE PAYNE
DANIELS
JULY 28, 1890
JAN. 22, 1977

Ollie Daniels

OK-NO MARKER

Noble & Kelsey: 23

Rev. C. R. Davidson
Died: 12/21/1923   Age: 57
Certificate No. 0011,0552:
Parents: Alfred & Ellen Davidson

OK-NO MARKER
Minister, Plasterer
Informant: Essie Davidson
Bpl: Union Co.

Noble & Kelsey: 149

Alice Johnson Davis
Died: 10/12/1953   Age: 38
Parents: Clarence & Lula F. Johnson

OK-NO MARKER
Maid in store

Ellis, Mangum & Fair
Funeral Home Record

Bessie Davis
Died: 10/07/1940   Age: 37
Certificate No. 0027,0775
Parents: Sam Hall & Sara Hairston

OK-NO MARKER
Domestic
Informant: Sara Hairston
Bpl: Rowan Co., NC

Noble & Kelsey: 147

BURIALS

Charlotte Davis
Died: 05/10/1923   Age: 90
Certificate Not Found
Parents: Unknown & Arnienta Brown

OK-NO MARKER
Housework
Informant: Lee Davis

Noble & Kelsey: 249
Funeral Home Record

Daisy Fletcher Wilkerson Davis
Died: 10/28/1968   Age: 40
Certificate No. 0048,0631
Parents: John Wilkerson & Mary Unknown

NO MARKER
Domestic
Informant: Mr. Ray Davis, Husband
   Bpl: GA

Mitchell & Fair

Delia Davis
Died: 03/11/1947   Age: 64
Certificate No. 0030,0793
Parents: Andy Biggers

NO MARKER
Domestic

Ellis, Mangum, & Fair

Edward Davis

Died: 10/27/1918   Age: 30
Condition on 08/12/2003

EDWARD DAVIS
JAN 6, 1888
OCT. 27, 1918

OK-130-N

Certificate Not Found

Edward Davis
Died: 09/09/1987   Age: 74
Certificate Not Found
Parents: Robert Davis & Sudie Hobson

OK-N NO MARKER
Janitor @ Newspaper
Informant: Maggie Davis, Wife
   Bpl: NC

Noble & Kelsey: 9

Edward Luther Davis
Died: 01/18/1971   Age: 68
Certificate No. 0051,0045
Parents: Luther Davis & Laura Greed

NO MARKER
Retired Laborer
Informant: Mary Neely, Winston Salem, NC
   Bpl: NC

Mitchell & Fair

Harrison P. Davis
Died: 03/30/1944   Age: 45
Certificate No. 0029,0133
Parents: Unknown & Wench Davis

NO MARKER
Truck Driver
Informant: Maude Davis, Wife
   Bpl: New London, NC

Ellis, Mangum & Fair

Harry James Davis
Died: 08/02/1969   Age: 26
Certificate No. 0049,0472
Parents: Rally & Jessie Mae Davis

BT-268-K [Grnt Fldstn]
Laborer @ Johnson Concrete
Informant: Jessie Mae Davis, Mother
   Bpl: NC

Noble & Kelsey

HARRY JAMES DAVIS
AUG. 19, 1943
AUG. 2, 1969

Harvey Lee Davis
Died: 05/06/1972   Age: 65
Certificate No. 0052,0318
Parents: John Davis & Betty (Unknown) (From Funeral Home Record)

NO MARKER
Retired Foundry

Mitchell & Fair

BURIALS

Hattie Dunlap Davis
Died: 02/09/1947   Age: 37
Certificate No. 0030,0941
Parents: Bob Dunlop & Annie Guest

UH-387-I/J   Ellis, Mangum & Fair
Domestic
Informant: Bubber Davis, Husband
Bpl: Rock Hill, SC

HATTIE DUNLAP
DAVIS
MAY 5, 1910
FEB. 9, 1947
MOTHER OF MARY ELIZABETH FERGUSON

Hattie Rainey Davis

UH ∞ 387-I/J   Ellis, Mangum & Fair
Died: 09/09/1947   Age: 37   Domestic   Funeral Home Record
Certificate Not Found
Parents: Bob Dunlap & Annie Guest

HATTIE DAVIS
BORN MAY 5, 1910
DIED SEPT. 9, 1947
AT REST

Jesse Davis
Died: 07/14/1988   Age: 75
Certificate No. 0068,0618
Parents: Not Given

BN-838-M [Grnt Fldstn]   Noble & Kelsey
Track man @ Railroad
Informant: Mattie L. Wood Davis, Wife

JESSE DAVIS
ON EARTH   IN HEAVEN
DEC. 25   JULY 14
1912   1988

Joe Davis
Died: 11/01/1961   Age: 71
Certificate No. 0042,0113
Parents: Jim & Wennie Davis

BT-272-K [Grnt Fldstn]   Noble & Kelsey
Operator of Wood Yard, Wood & Fuel Business
Informant: Nannie M. Davis, Wife
Bpl: Gillesville, GA

JOE DAVIS
JAN. 15, 1883
NOV. 1, 1961

John M. Davis
Died: 02/02/1954   Age: 61
Certificate No. 0035,0075
Parents: George Davis & Not Known

OK-NO MARKER   Noble & Kelsey: 147
Railway
Informant: Mary Davis
Bpl: Mecklenburg Co., NC

Leon Davis
Died: 05/20/1913   Age: 10 days
Certificate No. 0001,0296
Parents: Sam Moore & Georgia Davis

OK-NO MARKER   Noble & Kelsey: 9
INFANT
Informant: Roxy Davis
Bpl: Rowan Co., NC

BURIALS

Lillie M. Mason Davis OK-362 -I/J [Mason Plot & Curb]

MASON
REV. FISHER R. MASON
HIS WIFE
FANNIE B. MASON
SON
EVERETTE H. MASON
1905 - 1909
DAUGHTER
LILLIE M. MASON DAVIS

Margaret Davis UH-383-I/J Mitchell & Fair
Died: 07/09/1993 Age: 82 General Maintenance @ Private College
Certificate No. 0073,0669 **Informant:** Ruth Davis Camp
Parents: Robert E. Davis & Sudie Hobson Bpl: Salisbury, NC

Marie A. Kelley Davis OK-128-N Ellis, Mangum & Fair
Died: 10/16/1949 Age: 54 Teacher: Livingstone College Public School
Certificate No. 0039,0284

DAVIS
MARIE A. DAVIS   VIVIAN RAY
KELLY   DAVIS, D. D. S.
OCT. 15 1895   APR. 30, 1892
OCT 16, 1949   APR. 22, 1928

Mattie Wood Davis UH-NEW Noble & Kelsey
Died: 03/15/1999 Age: 84 Homemaker @ Own Home
Certificate No. 0079,0317 **Informant:** Juanita D. Tucker
Parents: Henry & Mattie Wood Bpl: GA

MATTIE W. DAVIS
ON EARTH   IN HEAVEN
AUG. 17   MAR. 15
1914   1999

Odessa Francis Davis NO MARKER Ellis, Mangum & Fair
Died: 03/15/1955 Age: 52 Nurse
Certificate No. 0036,0122
Parents: Noah Reid & Frances Mors

Rashayla Taleea Davis UH-537-H MISSING Noble & Kelsey
Died: 04/11/1995 Age: 01m INFANT
Certificate No. 0075,0440 **Informant:** Lashonda L. Bush, Mother
Parents: Dennis Lamont Davis & Lashonda Lee Bush Bpl: Rowan Co., NC

Richard Davis NO MARKER Noble & Kelsey: 249
Died: 03/27/1915 Age: 86 Shoe Maker
Certificate No. 0002,0123 **Informant:** Lee Davis
Parents: UNKNOWN Bpl: Fayetteville, NC

Rose Douglas Davis BN-748-P MISSING Noble & Kelsey
Died: 01/04/1980 Age: 83 Housewife
Certificate No. 0060,0017 **Informant:** Mary Davis, Daughter
Parents: William Douglas & Katie Crawford Bpl: Mecklenburg Co., NC

BURIALS

Ruth Bonner Davis UH-471-H
Died: 05/11/1952   Age: 30   Certificate Not Found
Parents: Lewis Bonner & Viola Oglesby   bd. 10/23/1922

MOTHER
RUTH BONNER
DAVIS DIED MA.........

Sarah Davis Certificate Not Found   BT-313-K MISSING

Shawn Demont Davis   BT-249-K   Noble & Kelsey
Died: 09/23/1972   Age: 2   CHILD
Certificate No. 0052,0646   **Informant**: Mrs. Sandra Lyes Davis
Parents: Not Given & Sandra Lyes   Bpl: NC

SHAWN DEMONT
DAVIS
MAY 2, 1970
SEPT. 23, 1972

Sudie C. Davis   UH-382-I/J   Ellis, Mangum & Fair
Died: 06/22/1952   Age: 57   Domestic
Certificate No. 0033,0251   **Informant**: Robert E. Davis
Parents: Adam Hobson & Lucinda Barber   Bpl.: Davie Co., NC

MOTHER
SUDIE DAVIS
AUG. 10, 1894
JUNE 22, 1952
AT REST

Dr. Vivian Ray Davis D. D. S.   OK-129-N   Cheshire & Mangum
Died: 04/27/1928   Age: 36y04m30   Dentist
Certificate No. 0016,0334   **Informant**: Marie Davis, Wife
Parents: Lee Davis & Virginia Gooding   Bpl: Rowan Co., NC   (See Marie Davis)

William Davis   NO MARKER   Bingham & Carter
Died: 10/27/1923   Age: ∞48   Day Laborer for Contractor
Certificate No. 0011,0512   **Informant**: Lorten Gh?? t
Parents: Wilson & Zilphia Davis

William Thomas Davis Sr.   BN-835-M
Died: 03/12/1940   Age: 62   Certificate Not Found
Headstone on ground 08/24/2003

WILLIAM
THOMAS
DAVIS, Sr.
DEC. 7, 1878
MAR. 12, 1940
Gone, but not forgotten.

Wilson Davis   OK-NO MARKER: Noble & Kelsey: 339
Stonecutter /Mason – (55 years old, born in 1845 according to the 1900 US Census) He was a member of the Soldiers Memorial AME Church Zion Board of Trustees. He died before death Records were kept. Death occurred after 1903.

BURIALS

Zilpha Davis   OK-NO MARKER   Noble & Kelsey: 339
Housewife & Mother – (53 years old/ born in 1847 and wife of Wilson Davis according to 1900 Census) She died before death Records were kept. Death occurred after 1903.

Rudolph Dawkins   NO MARKER   Noble & Kelsey
Died: 08/21/1918   Age: ∞71   Stone Cutter @ Granite Quarry
Certificate No. 0006,0489   **Informant:** Susan Dawkins
Parents: UNKNOWN   Bpl: SC

Georgia Foust Dean   NO MARKER.   Noble & Kelsey
Died: 11/30/1010   Age: 37   Domestic
Certificate No. 0004,0316   **Informant:** Lula Watkins
Parents: Tom Foust & Mary Gibson   Bpl: Davidson Co., NC

Louise Holt Diggs   BT-280-K
Died: 12/31/1966   Age: 48   Certificate Not Found

> **LOUISE HOLT DIGGS**
> MAR. 17, 1918
> DEC. 31, 1966
> AT REST

Cecelia Giles Dodge   OK-N Plot NO MARKER   G. W. Wright
Died: 02/20/1912   Age: ∞77   not given
Certificate No. 0001,0126   **Informant:** Wiley E. Dodge, Husband
Parents: Allen Giles/Mother Unknown

Grace M. Dodge   OK-061-N Plot   Noble & Kelsey: 45
Died: 03/08/1916   Age: 23y10m29   Teacher
Certificate No. 0003,0382   **Informant:** Wiley Dodge
Parents: Wiley Dodge & Mary Gray   Bpl: Salisbury, NC

Mary A. Gray Dodge   OK-061-N Plot   Noble & Kelsey: 45
Died: 12/14/1923   Age: 66   Public School Teacher
Certificate No. 0011,0307   **Informant:** W. E. Dodge Husband
Parents: Charles Gray/Jane Gray   Bpl: Randolph Co., NC

Wiley E. Dodge Jr.   OK-061-N Plot   Noble & Kelsey: 45
Died: 08/09/1928   Age: 71   Teacher: Conducted The Union Hill Unincorporated Graded School 1904 – 1905: Trustee Board Member of Soldiers Memorial A.M.E. Zion Church (118th Anniversary Soldiers Memorial AM.E. Zion Church: 1983 pg. 3)
Certificate No. 0016,0426   **Informant:** Annie B. Dodge Ellis, Daughter
Parents: Wiley Dodge Sr. & Cecelia Giles   Bpl: Rowan Co., NC

Wiley E. Dodge Sr.   OK-061-N Plot NO MARKER Noble & Kelsey: 45
Died: 12/19/1920   Age: ∞93   Shoe maker & member of the Board of Trustees @ Soldiers Memorial A. M. E. Zion Church (118th Anniversary Soldiers Memorial AME. Zion Church: 1983 pg. 3) He was one of the towns people who contributed money to move Zion Wesley Institute from Concord to Salisbury in 1881. Zion Wesley became Livingstone College
Certificate No. 0009,0307   **Informant:** Wiley E. Dodge Jr. Son
Parents: A. Dodge & Unknown   Bpl: Rowan Co., NC

BURIALS

James Samuel Donald Sr.
Died: 10/18/1988 Age: 75
Certificate No. 0068,0907
Parents: None Given

BN-840-M Noble & Kelsey
Stock clerk @ Retail drug Store
Informant: Virginia Spencer
Bpl: Rowan Co., NC

Ollie Lee Carr Donald (Female)
Died: 12/13/1969 Age: 63
Certificate No. 0049,0711
Parents: Unknown & Alice Miller

OK-111-N Ellis, Mangum & Fair
School Teacher, Rowan Co. Schools
Informant: Lyonell C. Donald Salisbury, NC
Bpl: NC

DONALD
OLLIE LEE CARR
DONALD
1907 – 1969

James Donaldson
Died: 05/25/1937 Age: 43
Certificate No. 0025,0149
Parents: Enoch Donaldson & Fannie Williamson

NO MARKER Noble & Kelsey
Day Laborer
Informant: Nannie Donaldson
Bpl: Davidson Co., NC

James Donaldson
Died: 04/24/1985 Age: 83
Certificate No. 0065,0349
Parents: Henderson & Della Donaldson

NO MARKER Noble & Kelsey: 31
Retired Shipping Clerk @ Cannon Mills Co.
Informant: Meryl Donaldson, Daughter
Bpl: Orangeburg, SC

Mrs. Nannie Smith Donaldson
Died: 05/09/1988 Age: 96
Certificate No. 0068,0441
Parents: Souie (Sic) & Clara Smith

OK-NO MARKER Noble & Kelsey: 31
Housemaid
Informant: Geneva James

Ella Dixon Dorsey
Died: 02/29/1952 Age: 72
Certificate No. 0033,0027
Parents: William Dixon & Adeline Scott

NO MARKER Ellis, Mangum & Fair
Domestic

Funeral Home Records

Dorothy Ann Douglas
Died: 01/12/1950 Age: 4m
Certificate No. 0032,0228
Parents: Eddie Rivers & Josephine Douglas

NO MARKER Ellis, Mangum & Fair
INFANT
Informant: Josephine Douglas, Mother

Mary Kitchen Douglas
Died: 01/25/1973 Age: 66
Certificate No. 0053,0038
Parents: Frank & Classie Kitchen

BT-242-K Noble & Kelsey
Housewife
Informant: Grace L. Johnson
Bpl: SC

MARY KITCHEN
DOUGLAS
MAY 9, 1902
JAN 25, 1973

William Douglas
Died: 05/07/1925 Age: ∞54
Certificate No.: 0013,0361
Parents: UNKNOWN

NO MARKER Summersettt
Day Labor
Informant: M. Eagle
Bpl: Waynesboro, NC

BURIALS

Lucille Davie Drafton BN-837-M
Died: 1988   Age: 71 Certificate Not Found:

LUCILLE DAVIE
DRAFTON
1917 - 1988

Jim Draper   NO MARKER   Noble & Kelsey
Died: 02/03/1908   Summersett
Marker could not be found. The information was obtained from the Records of Summersett Funeral Home. T. W. Summersett Jr. Proprietor. The body was turned over to Noble & Kelsey after it was embalmed.

Laura Draper   NO MARKER   Noble & Kelsey:
Died: 06/01/1933   Age: ∞53   House Wife
Certificate No. 0021,0080   **Informant**: name unreadable
Parents: James Linden & Harriet Stacey   Bpl: Cowpens, SC

Alice Dudley   NO MARKER.   Noble & Kelsey
Died: 02/21/1910   Age: 37
Certificate No. 0004,0403   **Informant**: Charles Dudley
Parents: Alex Dudley/Marie Dudley   Bpl: Rowan

Connie INFANT of Dudley   NO MARKER   Noble & Kelsey: 346
Died: 02/08/1920   Age: STILL BIRTH   INFANT
Certificate No. 0008,0110   **Informant**: Connie Dudley
Parents: Charlie Bates & Connie Dudley   Bpl: Salisbury, NC

Mary Dumas   NO MARKER
Died: 01/27/1959   Age: 65   Certificate Not Found

Aileene Wade Duncan   OK-176-O Duncan Sr., Plot   Noble & Kelsey
Died: 02/06/1988   Age: 70   Teacher
Certificate No. 0068,0088   **Informant**: Joseph C. Duncan
Parents: Horace Wade & Mary Frances Marrow   Bpl: Edgecombe Co.

AILEENE WADE   JOSEPH C.
MAY 5, 1918   MAY 31, 1917
FEB. 6, 1988   AUG. 30, 1989
ZΦB::   ΦBΣ
DUNCAN

Annie Ruth Elizabeth Duncan   OK-168-O Duncan Plot   Ellis, Mangum & Fair
Died: 09/17/1944   Age: one day   INFANT
Certificate No. 0029,0026   **Informant**: Fred Duncan
Parents: Fred Duncan Jr. & Ruth Anna Rustin   Bpl: Rowan Co., NC

BURIALS

Baby Michael Payne Duncan OK-168-O Duncan Plot Noble & Kelsey
Died: 02/12/1952 Age: 4mos INFANT
Certificate No. 0033,0028 **Informant**: Catherine Duncan, Mother
Parents: William Duncan & Catherine Payne Bpl: Salisbury, NC

BABY
MICHAEL PAYNE
DUNCAN
NOV. 21. 1951
FEB. 12, 1952

Frederick Deberry Duncan OK-176-O Duncan Sr., Plot w Curb
Died: 11/26/1978 Age: 63 Certificate Not Found
Parents: Samuel E. Duncan Sr. & Lena Jordan

FREDERICK DEBERRY
DUNCAN
JAN. 29, 1915
NOV. 26, 1978

President Duncan– Hauser Plots

Ida Hauser Duncan OK198-L Duncan Jr. Plot w Curb Noble & Kelsey
Died: 11/23/1980 Age: 76 Teacher, Public schools & wife of President S. E. Duncan of Livingston College
Certificate No. 0060,0905 **Informant**: Mrs. Johnie E. Brown, Sister
Parents: Sanford Hauser & Anna Spease Bpl: Yadkin Co., NC

IDA HAUSER
OCT 1, 1904 - NOV. 23, 1980
FISK UNIVERSITY 1927
EDUCATOR - HUMANITARIAN

DEDICATED TO HIGH PURPOSES
OF
RELIGIOUS, CIVIC AND SOCIAL
ORGANIZATIONS

ARDENT TEACHER
SUPPORTER OF CHURCH SCHOOL
AND COMMUNITY
A FOUNDER OF
L.C. POETS AND DREAMERS GARDEN
MEMBER CITY BD OF EDUC.

BURIALS

John Bonner Duncan OK-178-O Noble & Kelsey
Died: 06/21/1994 Age: 84 Certificate Not Found District Commissioner of Washington, DC before the district began electing mayors Died in DC.
Parents: Samuel E. Duncan Sr. & Lena B. Jordan Bpl: Salisbury, NC

J. B.
JOHN BONNER
DEVOTED HUSBAND,
CHERISHED FATHER & GRANDFATHER
FEBRUARY 6, 1910
JUNE 21, 1994
HUMANITARIAN TIRELESS CIVIC
WORKER
AND CO.MMUNITY LEADER
RECO.RDER OF DEEDS
CO.MMISSIONER DISTRICT OF CO.LUMBIA
ASSISTANT TO THE SECRETARY OF THE
U. S. DEPARTMENT OF THE INTERIOR
FOR URBAN AFFAIRS
BRIDGE MASTER & AUTHOR
DOCTOR OF LAWS LIVINGSTONE CO.LLEGE
DOCTOR OF PUBLIC SERVICE GEORGE WASHINGTON UNIVERSITY

Joseph Duncan NO MARKER Noble & Kelsey
Died: 06/08/70 Age: 48 Laborer, Earnhardt Construction Company
Certificate No. 0050,0320 **Informant:** Mrs. Louise Harden, Brooklyn, NY
Parents: Joseph Duncan Sr. & Unknown Bpl: Rowan Co., NC

Joseph Cottene Duncan OK-176-L Duncan Sr. Plot
Died: 08/30/1989 Age: 72
Certificate No. 0068,0737
Parents Samuel Edward Duncan Sr. & Lena B. Jordan (See Aileen Wade Duncan)

Julia Belle Duncan UH-404-H Belle Duncan Plot Noble & Kelsey
Died: 04/04/1976 Age: 70 Retired Registrar @ Livingstone College, Founder & advisor of the Julia B. Duncan Players @ Livingstone College
Certificate No. 0056,0224 **Informant:** Elizabeth Duncan Koontz, Sister
Parents: Samuel Duncan Sr. & Lena B. Jordan Bpl: KY

JULIA BELL DUNCAN
JAN. 28, 1906 ---- APR. 4, 1976
SECRETARY, REGISTRAR ---- TREASURER
LIVINGSTONE COLLEGE. 1923 ---- 1973
REMEMBERED FOR
LOYALTY
DEVOTION
SERVICE
FAMILY, FRIEND, CHURCH, COMMUNITY
A.K.A. SORORITY

BURIALS

Lena Belle Jordan Duncan
Died: 01/30/1967   Age: 86
Certificate No. 0047,0091

UH 404-H   Belle Duncan Plot   Mitchell & Fair
Teacher (Retired)
Parents: Samuel Jordan & Ellen B. Satchelle

LENA B. JORDAN DUNCAN
DEDICATED TEACHER, WISE COUNSELOR
ARDENT CHURCH WORKER
SOLDIERS' MEMORIAL A. M. E. ZION CHURCH
SUNDAY SCHOOL
STEWARDESS BOARD 2 B
SHE LIVED WITH A LOVE FOR GOD, FAMILY, CHURCH
AND ALL MANKIND SHE RESTS IN PEACE

Samuel Edward Duncan
192
Died: 07/10/1968   Age: 64
Certificate No. 0048,0400
Parents: Samuel Edward Duncan Sr. & Lena B. Jordan

OK-198-L Plot w Curb   Nobel/Kelsey:
President of Livingstone College
Informant: Ida Hauser Duncan, Wife
Bpl: KY

SAMUEL EDWARD
APRIL 27, 1904 - JULY 10, 1968
PRESIDENT LIVINGSTONE COLLEGE
1958   1968
CIVIC AND RELIGIOUS LEADER
SCHOLAR - EDUCATOR
HUMANITARIAN AND FRIEND
DEDICATED TO BROTHERHOOD
SERVED MANKIND UNSELFISHLY

Samuel Edward Duncan Sr.
Died: 05/21/1931   Age: 57-51y9, 24d

Certificate No. 0019,0216
Parents: Sam Duncan & Julia Stone

OK-176-O Duncan Sr. Plot   Noble & Kelsey
School Teacher, Professor of graded school, Professor
   @ Livingstone College
Informant: Lena Belle Jordan, Wife
   Bpl: Blumfield, KY.

SAMUEL EDWARD
DUNCAN SR.
JULY 29, 1874
MAY 21, 1931

BURIALS

William Francis Duncan OK-168-O Duncan Plot w Curb   Noble & Kelsey
Died: 03/31/1990   Age: 59   never worked
Certificate No. 0070,0267   **Informant:** Catherine P. Duncan, Wife
Parents: William J. Duncan & Catherine Payne   Bpl: Salisbury, NC

SON
WILLIAM FRANCIS
DUNCAN
OCT. 20, 1931
MAR. 31, 1990

Hope Dunlap   UH-482-H
Died: 07/31/1974   Age: 75   Certificate Not Found

DUNLAP -- TATE
HOPE DUNLOP	ELLA LOUISE TATE
DEC. 26, 1899	AUG. 28, 1923
JULY 31, 1974	MAY 5, 1949

Walter Cornell Dunlap   UH-484-H
Died: 05/26/1984   Age: 58   Certificate Not Found

WALTER CORNELL
DUNLAP
JULY 21, 1926
MAY 26, 1984

Marie H. Dunlop   NO MARKER   Mitchell & Fair
Died: 12/09/1968   Age: 65   Funeral Home Record

Amos Willie Ealy   UH-511-H   Noble & Kelsey
Died: 06/27/1956   Age: 17   Laborer @ Construction Company
Certificate No. 0037,0089   **Informant:** Mrs. Florence Ealy
Parents: Emmanuel Ealy & Florence Brown   Bpl: Burke Co., GA

EALY
AMOS WILLIE EALY
AUG. 21, 1938
JUNE 27, 1956

Anthony Brown Ealy   UH-511-H
Died: 08/04/1966   CHILD   Certificate Not Found

ANTHONY BROWN
EALY
JAN. 29, 1953
AUG. 4, 1966
DARLING, WE MISS THEE.

BURIALS

Florence Brown Ealy   UH-511-H
           Died: 06/02/1993   Age: 74   Certificate Not Found

EALY
FLORENCE BROWN
JUNE 8, 1919
JUNE 2, 1993

Camilla Rogers Eddy   NO MARKER   Mitchell & Fair
Died: 06/12/1985   Age: 82   Certificate Not Found:

Pearl Edge   NO MARKER   Cheshire & Callahan
Died: 01/12/1930   Age: 19   Domestic
Certificate No. 0018,0185   **Informant:** Willie M. Johnson
Parents: Walter Hilton & Pearl Hairston   Bpl: Salisbury

Will Edwards   NO MARKER
Died: 03/24/1947   Age: 52   Laborer
Certificate No. 0030,0795
Parents: UNKNOWN

Nancy Beadie Eigner   BT-283-K   Noble & Kelsey
Died: 06/17/1960   Age: 42
         Certificate No. 0040,0581   **Informant:** Mrs. Robert Fox
         Parents: David Eigner & Lizzie Hodges   Bpl: SC

EIGNER
MOTHER
NANCY BEADIE
EIGNER
JAN. 14, 1918
JUNE 17, 1960

James Melton Elder   NO MARKER   Ellis, Mangum & Fair
Died: 09/09/1943   Age: 34   Laborer @ Buick Motor Company
Certificate No. 0028,0859   **Informant:** Ruby Lee Elder, Wife
Parents: Edgar Eller & Fannie Hester   Bpl: Madison, GA

Ruby Lee Elder   NO MARKER   Ellis, Mangum & Fair
Died: 04/18/1956   Age: 46   Domestic
Certificate No. 0036,0733   **Informant:** Jean Carol Elder
Parents: Thomas Mason & Sophia Andrews   Bpl: GA

Irma Alexander Eller   UH-578-H   Noble & Kelsey
Died: 11/12/1990   Age: 78   Domestic @ Private Homes
Certificate No. 0070,0939   **Informant:** Betty E. Black   *Cause unreadable*
         Parents: Mark Alexander & Mary Unknown   Bpl: Rowan Co., NC

IRMA ALEXANDER
ELLER
APR. 8, 1912
NOV. 12, 1990

BURIALS

Ulysess Snappy Eller
Died: 03/13/1980   Age: 44
Certificate No. 0060,0198
Parents: Richard Eller & Irma Alexander

BN-754-P
Salisbury Country club
Informant: Dennis R. Eller, Brother
Bpl: Rowan Co., NC

Noble & Kelsey

**ULYSESS SNAPPY
ELLER
APR. 28, 1935
MAR. 13, 1980**

Sara C. Holly Elliot
Died: 11/11/1926   Age: not given
Certificate No. 0014,0330
Parents: Isom Holly & Unknown

OK-NO MARKER
Domestic Housework
Informant: Hattie C. Jeffries
Bpl: Edenton, NC

Noble & Kelsey: 174

Annie B. Dodge Ellis
Died: 11/28/1961   Age: 78

Certificate No. 0042,0120
Parents: Wiley E. Dodge Jr. & Mary Grey

OK- 061-N Dodge Plot
Teacher employed @ Ellis, Mangum & Fair Funeral
  Home & Grand Daughter of Wiley E. Dodge Sr.
Informant: Liddell Fitzgerald, Mt. Vernon, NY
Bpl: NC

Ellis, Mangum & Fair

**ANNIE B ELLIS
WIFE OF
CHARLES A. ELLIS
OCT. 7, 1883
NOV. 28. 1961
THE BEAUTY OF HER LIFE LAY IN SERVICE TO GOD AND HUMANITY.**

Wiley Dodge, Grace Dodge, and Mary Dodge are also in this plot according to the Kelsey map
Charles A. Ellis was part owner of Ellis Mangum & Fair and is buried in the U.S. National Cemetery @ Salisbury, NC

Edward Ellis
Died: 1945   Age:

NO MARKER

Ellis, Mangum, & Fair
Funeral Home Record

Emma Lee Ellis

UH-619-G MISSING

Willie L. Ellis
Died: 01/15/1991   Age: 85
Certificate No. 0071,0054
Parents: Unknown & Melinda Ellis

UH-583-H MISSING
Shoe Repairman @ Shoe Repair Shop
Informant: Emma Lee Ellis
Bpl: Rowan Co., NC

Noble & Kelsey

Catherine Emmason
Died: 03/02/1915   Age: 59
Certificate No. 0002,0108
Parents: Lewis & Fannie Hall

NO MARKER
Farmer and Domestic
Informant: Mary Banger
Bpl: SC

Noble & Kelsey

Geneva Ervin
Died: 05/02/1943   Age: 24

NO MARKER
Certificate Not Found

Audy Eury
Died: 06/23/1929   Age: 28
Certificate No. 0017,0438
Parents: Noah Eury & Eliza Cartha

NO MARKER
Common Laborer
Informant: John Eury
Bpl: Salisbury, NC

Noble & Kelsey

BURIALS

Lillian Eury
Died: 05/23/1929   Age: 32
Certificate No. 0017,0424
Parents: Thomas Peeler & Rosa Perkins

NO MARKER
Domestic
Informant: Thomas Peeler
Bpl: Salisbury, NC

Cheshire & Callahan

A. L. Evans
Died: 11/13/1940   Certificate Not Found

NO MARKER

Carter & Joseph Evans

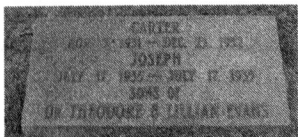

OK-188-O Plot
Carter Died: 12/02/1931 Age: 1 yr
Joseph Died: 07/17/1935 Age: 1 yr
Parents: Dr. Theodore & Lillian Evans
Bingham Plot

Noble & Kelsey

Francis Lucille Evans
Died: 03/28/1928   Age 17
Certificate No. 0016,0383
Parents: Robert Evans and Lillie Mae Hargrave

NO MARKER
School Girl
Informant: Robert Evans, Father
Bpl: Salisbury, NC

Noble & Kelsey

Jimmy David Evans

UH-590-G
Died: 1992   Age: Certificate Not Found

JIMMY DAVID
EVANS

Lillie Mae Ellison Evans
Died: 02/05/1993   Age: 72
Certificate No. 0073,0121
Parents: Joseph Ellison & Ada Austin

UH-592-G
Twist machine operator @ Glass Mfg.
Informant: Willie Evans, Husband
Bpl: Rowan Co., NC

Noble & Kelsey

Mother
LILLIE MAE ELLISON EVANS
MAY 8,   FEB. 5,
1920   1993

Lillie Mae Hargrave Evans
Died: 03/27/1979   Age: 84
Certificate No. 0059,0247
Parents: Hodge Hargrave & Lie Ella Knox

OK-NO MARKER
Widowed Housewife
Informant: Freddie M. Evans, Son
Bpl: Rowan Co., NC

Noble & Kelsey

Margaret Evans
Died: 03/15/1957   Age: 77
Certificate No. 0037,0503
Parents: Henry Shamrock (Shimpock, Shimpoch, or Shimpop) & Unknown   Bpl: NC

OK-NO MARKER
Housewife
Informant: Robert L. Evans

Noble & Kelsey

Margaret Lucille Evans
Died: 02/20/1969   Age: 50
Certificate No. 0049,0128:
Parents: Henry Hairston & Fannie Unknown

OK- NO MARKER   Mitchell & Fair @N. & Ksy: 71
Cafeteria Worker, Salisbury City Schools
Informant: Wayne S. Evans, Detroit, Michigan
Bpl: NC

BURIALS

Mattie Evans
Died: 10/26/1925   Age: 57
Certificate No. 0013,0445
Parents: Arron Morris &??

NO MARKER
Domestic
Informant: Sarah Boyden
   Bpl: Cabarrus Co., NC

Bingham & Carter

Otho Evans

NO MARKER

Noble & Kelsey: 360

Robert L. Evans
Died: 06/21/1961   Age: 65
Certificate No. 0041,0579
Parents: Harry & Margaret Shinpool Evans

OK-NO MARKER
Grocer: Grocery business in Dixonville
Informant: Lillie Evans, Wife
   Bpl: NC

Ellis, Mangum & Fair

Warren Evans
Died: Age: Ill/Infant

OK-NO MARKER
Certificate Not Found

Noble & Kelsey: 71

Bradley Everhardt
Died: 06/13/1965   Age: 60
Certificate No. 0045,0350
Parents Bradley & Martha Everhardt

NO MARKER

Mitchell & Fair

Pearl Everhart
Died: 06/04/1958   Age: 59
Certificate No. 0039,0076

NO MARKER

Parents UNKNOWN

Cornelia Mills Fagatt
Died: 12/09/1923   Age: 4 mos.
Certificate No. 0011,0542
Parents: John Fagatt & Millie Bell

NO MARKER
INFANT
Informant: John X Fagatt
   Bpl: NC

Summersettt

Millie Bell Fagatt
Died: 01/18/1924   Age: ∞ 32
Certificate No. 0012,0402
Parents: UNKNOWN

NO MARKER
Domestic
Informant: John X Fagatt
   Bpl: NC

Summersettt

Joseph Faggart
Died: 08/29/1980   Age: 48
Certificate No. 0060,0679
Parents: Phifer B. Faggart & Rosa Lockhart

BN-758-P
Unemployed - disabled
Informant: Mrs. Rosa Faggart, Mother
   Bpl: Cabarrus Co., NC

Noble & Kelsey

JOSEPH FAGGART
   1932 -- 1980

Lucille Faggart
Died: 05/26/1916   Age: 01m07d
Certificate No. 0003,0442
Parents: L. H. Hall & Sadie Faggart

NO MARKER
INFANT
Informant: Sadie Faggart
   Bpl: Cabarrus Co., NC

Noble & Kelsey: 342

Rose Lockhart Faggart
Died: 07/07/1985   Age: 77
Certificate No. 0065,0592
         Parents: Thomas Lockhart & Isabelle Brooks

BN-763-P
Homemaker
Informant: Archie Faggart, Son
   Bpl: Cabarrus Co., NC

Noble & Kelsey

ROSA LOCKHART
FAGGART
NOV. 7, 1907
JULY 7, 1985

98 BURIALS

Bertha Faggatt
Died: 06/15/1909 Age: 28 yrs.

NO MARKER

Summersett
Funeral Home Record

Charlie Fair

NO MARKER

Noble & Kelsey: 342

Delbert Sepheria Fair (Male)
Died: 06/04/1923 Age: 01y09m02d
Certificate No. 0011,0455
Parents: J. C. Fair & Sadie Davis

OK-NO MARKER
CHILD
Informant: J. C. Fair
    Bpl: Salisbury, NC

Noble & Kelsey: 134

James C. Fair
Died: 04/25/1952 Age: 70
Certificate No. 0033,0187
Parents: William Blair & Annie Provough

UH-410-H
Minister, Undertaker, Teacher, and entrepreneur
Informant: Sadie Fair, Wife
    Bpl: Swansboro, NC
Foot Stone resting on base

Ellis, Mangum & Fair

REV. JAMES C. FAIR
MAY 3, 1881
APR. 25, 1952
HE WAS THE SUNSHINE OF OUR HOME.

James C. Fair Jr.
Died: 01/31/1980 Age: 65

UH-∞413-H

Mitchell & Fair
Funeral Home Record

(BABY BOY)
J. C. FAIR, JR.
JUNE 7, 1915
JAN. 31, 1980

Mrs. Charles Fair

OK-NO MARKER

Noble & Kelsey: 344

Robert William Fair
Died: 01/12/1921 Age: 01y06m05d
Certificate No. 0009,0311
Parents: J. C. Fair & Sallie Davis

OK-NO MARKER
CHILD
Informant: J. C. Fair, Father
    Bpl: Salisbury, NC

Noble & Kelsey: 339

Sadie Davis Fair
Died: 05/24/1981 Age: 92

Certificate No. 0061,0478
Parents: Wilson & Zilpha Davis

UH-409-H
Retired Teacher: Dunbar High School, E. Spencer, NC
    Founded Carver High School, Kannapolis, NC
    Founded Pric High School Band, Salisbury, NC
Informant: Avis F. Wilkins Monroe, Daughter
    Bpl: Rowan Co., NC

Mitchell & Fair

SADIE DAVIS
FAIR
MAY 24, 1981
AT REST
REST IN PEACE DARLING MOTHER
MAY GOD RICHLY BLESS YOU.

BURIALS

Bertha Roberts Falls
Died: 10/26/1982   Age: 67

BN-854-M
Certificate Not Found

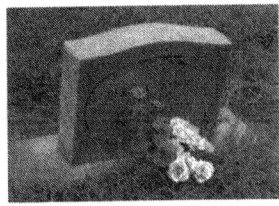

BERTHA ROBERTS
FALLS
JUN. 25, 1915
OCT. 26, 1982

James Edwards Falls

NO MARKER
INFANT

Bishop Feanster
Died: 12/22/1927   Age: 38
Certificate No. 0015,0486
Parents: Right Feamster & A Feamster

UH-NO MARKER   Cheshire & Mangum
Laborer @ Southern Railroad Shop
Informant: Lessie McNinch[Sic]
   Bpl: Yorkville, SC

Albert Joel Feaster
Died: 06/02/1945   Age: 82y08m29d
Certificate No. 0029,0698
Parents: Primas & Jane Feaster

NO MARKER   Noble & Kelsey
Granite Work/ Blacksmith
Informant: Helen Feaster, Wife
   Bpl: Feasterville, SC

Henry Feaster
Died: 03/05/1914   Age ∞ 21
Certificate No. 0001,0406
Parents: Hough Feaster & Hattie Feaster

NO MARKER   Summersett
Laborer @ Southern Railroad
Informant: Hattie Feaster
   Bpl: SC

Walton Febby
Died: 10/01/1922   Age: 63

OK-
Certificate Not Found

FEBBY
WALTON
APR. 17 1859
OCT. 1 1922
AT REST

William Coley Ferbee
Died: 08/09/1929   Age: ∞35
Certificate No. 0017,0473
Parents: John & Rebecker [Sic] Ferbee

UH-NO MARKER   Fraternal Funeral Home
Laborer @ Southern Railroad Transfer shed
Informant: Ida Ferbee
   Bpl: Davidson Co., NC

Plumie Ferguson
Died: 04/08/1970   Age: 69
Certificate No. 0050,0206
Parents: Mr. Ed Ferguson & Unknown

BT-247-K
Retired Southern Railway
Informant: Miss Lula Ferguson

PLUMIE FERGUSON
FEB. 15, 1892
APR. 8, 1970

Clarence Ferriber
Died: 02/24/1910   Age: 20
Certificate No. 0004,0371
Parents: Mac (?) Mother's name Unknown

NO MARKER.
Certificate Not Found
Informant: Callie Ferriber

BURIALS

John M. Ferron   OK-101-N Plot   Noble & Kelsey: 28
Died: 07/30/1933   Age: 73   Employee @ Southern Railway Company
Certificate Not Found

JOHN M. FERRON
MAY 9, 1860
JULY 30, 1933
Weep not he is at rest

Maria Ferron   OK∞101&102-N
Died: 01/12/19   Age: 83   Certificate Not Found

MARIA FERRON
SEPT. 18, 1837
JAN. 12, 1919

Marial or Mollie Ferron   NO MARKER   Noble & Kelsey: 28
Died: 10/13/1937   Age: 72,05m12   House Wife
Certificate No. 0025,0396   **Informant:** Lottie Mae Carr
Parents: Rankin F. Haynes

Walter L. Ferron   OK-98-N
Died: 03/25/1927   Age: 54
Certificate Not Found

WALTER L.
FERRON
MAR. 10, 1873
MAR. 25, 1927

William A. Ferron   NO MARKER   Noble & Kelsey: 28
    Porter   Funeral Home Record

William Onslow Ferron   OK-102-N Plot   Noble & Kelsey: 56
Died: 10/13/1943   Age: 72y00m11   Supt. of Grounds @ Livingstone College & City School Grounds: He was a grocer on 331 N. Lee St. in1901 & a cabman on Council Street near the Southern Railroad Depot in 1910 according to the city directory.
Certificate No. 0028,0917   **Informant:** Mrs. Willie Paris
Parents: William Ferron & Maria Baldin   Bpl: Salisbury, NC

W. O. FERRON
APR. 2, 1871
OCT. 13, 1943
MAY HE REST IN PEACE

Henrietta Parker Field   NO MARKER   Noble & Kelsey
Died: 07/13/1912   Age: 70
Certificate Not Found
Parents: Charles Porterfield   Bpl: Davidson Co., NC

BURIALS

Charles Fields Jr. III   OK-342 -I/J   Noble & Kelsey
Died: 01/27/1961   Age: 1yr   CHILD
Certificate No. 0041,0301   **Informant**: Elizabeth Fields
Parents: Charles Fields II & Elizabeth Pearson   Bpl: NC

CHARLES FIELDS, JR. III
SON OF
CHARLES & ELIZABETH
FIELDS
SEPT. 19, 1960
JAN. 27, 1961

Annie Irene Garwood Fisher   OK-232-K
Died: 02/24/1996   Age: 106   Certificate Not Found

FISHER
ANNIE IRENE GARWOOD   H. CARL
MAR. 24, 1890   AUG. 13, 1892
FEB. 24, 1996   JUNE 23, 1963
MARRIED OCT. 15, 1914

Baby of Maggie Fisher   NO MARKER   Summersett
Died: 12/20/1908   Age: 3 m.   INFANT
Certificate Not Found.   **Informant**: Maggie Fisher

Carr Harold Fisher   UH- NO MARKER   Noble & Kelsey: 213
Died: 06/26/1963   Age: 68   Retired from Southern Railroad
Certificate No. 0043,0346   **Informant**: Rena Fisher, Wife
Parents: Stokes Fisher & Unknown

Catherine Mariah Fisher   BN-420 –M Plot
Died: 01/19/1932   Age: 22   Certificate Not Found

CATHERINE MARIAH
FISHER
JAN. 8, 1910
JAN. 19, 1932

Charles Fisher   NO MARKER   Bingham, Carter, & Cheshire
Died: 01/14/1926   Age: 43,04,20   Waiter
Certificate No. 0014,0084   **Informant**: Gladys Fisher, Wife
Parents: William Fisher & Julia Lloyd   Bpl: Rowan Co., NC

Clyde Verner Fisher   NO MARKER
Died: 02/05/1949   Certificate Not Found
Parents: James Fisher & Maggie Rose

Deborah Fisher   NO MARKER   Noble & Kelsey: 350
Died: 01/28/1910   Age: 17y 01m 12dys   Single Domestic
Certificate No.   **Informant**: Norah Fisher
Parents: Henry Williams/Norah Fisher   B.pl. Rowan Co. NC

Dorothy M. Fisher   UH-pst.96
Died: 11/18/1997   Age: 71   Certificate Not Found

DOROTHY M. FISHER
APR. 2, 1919
NOV. 18, 1997

BURIALS

H. Carl Fisher
Died: 06/23/1963   Age: 71
Certificate No. 0043,0346
Parents: Will Murphy & Minnie Tutterow
(See Annie Irena Garwood)

OK-233-K
Domestic
Informant: Ray Pinkston
  Bpl: NC

Ellis, Mangum & Fair

James Fisher
Died: 10/14/1959   Age: 73

NO MARKER
Funeral Home Record

Ellis, Mangum & Fair

Jessie McCorkle Fisher
Died: 11/23/1966   Age: 81

OK-171-O
Certificate Not Found

Noble & Kelsey: 137

FISHER
JESSIE McCORKLE FISHER
NOV. 15, 1885
NOV. 23, 1966
A PIONEER SPIRIT
A LOVER OF MANKIND
SHE LIVED HER CREED MAKING OTHERS HAPPY BY HER
GENEROSITY
A LIFETIME SPENT IN SERVICE TO HER CHURCH AND
COMMUNITY
EMERGENCY CLUB HAPPY HEARTS
"NOW I LAY ME DOWN TO SLEEP."

John Fisher
Died: 03/18/1914   Age: 64
Certificate No. 0001,0411
Parents: Kerr Fisher & Unknown

NO MARKER
Day Laborer
Informant: H.L. Fisher
  Bpl: Rowan Co., NC

Noble & Kelsey: 268

Josie Partee Fisher
Died: 11/01/1959   Age: 80
Certificate No. 0040,0316
Parents: Livi Partee/Name Unknown

BN-014-N
Housewife
Informant: Nonnie F. Johnson, Salisbury
  Bpl: NC

Noble & Kelsey

JOSIE PARTEE
FISHER
MAR. 15, 1872
NOV. 1, 1959

Laura Fisher
Died: 01/09/1920   Age: 05m26d
Certificate No. 0008,0098
Parents: Kerr Fisher & Rena Garwood

OK-NO MARKER
INFANT
Informant: Kerr Fisher, Father
  Bpl: Salisbury, NC

Noble & Kelsey:213

Maggie Rose Fisher
Died: 03/15/1955   Age: 65
Certificate Not Found
Parents: Charlie Rose & Alice Gaither

OK-NO MARKER
Domestic

Noble & Kelsey 149

Miss Lovagoos Fisher
Died: 12/03/1922   Age: 01m02d
Certificate No. 0010,0472
Parents: Kerr Fisher & Rena Garwood

OK-NO MARKER
INFANT
Informant: Rena Fisher
  Bpl.: Salisbury, NC

Noble & Kelsey: 213

BURIALS

Mrs. Rose Sloan Fisher
Died: 07/29/1956   Age: 75
Certificate No. 0037,0153

OK--
Domestic
Informant: Mrs. Anna Wright, Salisbury, NC
Parents: Martin Sloan & Lina McCorkle   Bpl: Rowan Co., NC

Ellis, Mangum & Fair

<u>Wright Plot</u>
MRS. ROSE SLOAN
FISHER
DIED JULY 29, 1956
WE WILL MEET AGAIN.

Nonie Springs Johnson Fisher
Died: 02/08/1996   Age: 93

BN-420 -M Plot
Certificate Not Found

Noble & Kelsey: 350

NONNIE SPRINGS
JOHNSON
JUNE 12, 1903
FEB. 8, 1996

Samuel Fisher
Died: 12/26/1922   Age: 38
Certificate No. 0011,0308
Parents: UNKNOWN

NO MARKER
Tailor
Informant: Maggie Fisher, Wife
Bpl: Reidsville, NC

Noble & Kelsey

Arthur Fisher. Sr.
Died: 07/03/1926   Age: 43

OK-170-O
Certificate Not Found

ARTHUR FISHER, SR
DEC. 3, 1883
JULY 3, 1926

Carl Fitzgerald

UH-517-H MISSING

Fannie Mae Fitzgerald
Died: 08/30/1966   Age: 47
Certificate No. 0046,0429
Parents: Robert Wilson & Lydia Wennmon

UH-515-H MISSING
Housewife
Informant: John Fitzgerald, Husband
Bpl: Davidson Co., NC

Noble & Kelsey

Jeanett Fitzgerald
Died: 04/05/1957   Age: 72

UH-516-H
Certificate Not Found

Ellis, Mangum & Fair

MOTHER
JEANETT FITZGERALD
WIFE OF WESLEY FOX
MAY 9, 1884
APR. 5, 1957

Flora Bernhardt Flack
Died: 03/19/1989   Age: 96

OK-137-N Bernhardt Plot   Noble & Kelsey
Elementary Teacher, City of Salisbury Elementary
Schools & principal of Dixonville Graded School
in the 1920's

Certificate No. 0069,0296   **Informant**: Melvin J. Rush
Parents: Adam Caruth & Mattie Bernhardt   Bpl: Rowan Co., NC

FLORA BERNHARDT
WIFE OF
REV. E. REX FLACK
APR. 21, 1892

BURIALS

Neal Roy Flack
Died: 06/03/1915   Age: 04 days
Certificate No. 0002,0162
Parents: P. R. Flack & Hattie Neal

OK-NO MARKER
INFANT
Informant: P. R. Flack
  Bpl: Salisbury, NC

Noble & Kelsey: 342

Rev. E. Rex Flack
Died: 1937   Certificate Not Found

OK-137-N   Bernhardt Plot
Minister

HUSBAND
REV. E.
REX FLACK
1893 - 1937
GONE
BUT NOT
FORGOTTEN

Clarence J. Fleming
Certificate Not Found

OK-192-L   Holt Plot
(See Fannie H. Byers)

Noble & Kelsey 163

Herman Koontz Fleming
Died: 08/30/1979   Age: 63
Certificate No. 0059,0595
Parents: Robert Lee Holt & Mamie Holt

OK-192-L Holt Plot
Retired, Board of Education
Informant: Clarence J. Fleming
  Bpl: Davidson Co., NC (See Fannie H. Byers)

Noble & Kelsey: 163

Ada Graham Flowe
Died: 08/03/1961   Age: Certificate Not Found

OK-138-N   Flowe Plot

Noble & Kelsey: 25

ADA GRAHAM
WIFE OF
REV. C. L. FLOWE
DIED
AUG. 3, 1961

Christopher L. Flowe & (1 yr. Old Child)
Died: 12/03/1939   Certificate Not Found

OK-138-N Flowe Plot
Minister

Noble & Kelsey 25

REV. CHRISTOPHER L. FLOWE
DIED
DEC. 3, 1939

Theodore Dewey Flowe
Died: 1933   Age: 19 Certificate Not Found

OK-138 -N Flowe Plot

Noble & Kelsey 25

THEODORE DEWEY FLOWE
1914 – 1933

Adelaide Malone Flowers
Died: 06/14/1914   Age: 26
Certificate No. 0001,0447
Parents: Julius Malone & Lula Clement

OK-NO MARKER
Domestic
Informant: Lula Malone
  Bpl: Salisbury, NC

Noble & Kelsey: 65

Jim Floyd
Died: 08/24/1926   Age: 27
Certificate No. 0014,0284
Parents: John Holt & Sarah Floyd

NO MARKER
Laborer @ Swift & Co.
Informant: Eliza Floyd

Peoples Undertaking Co.

BURIALS

Sarah Floyd
Died: 08/21/1911   Age: 45
Certificate No. 0004,0086
Parents: UNKNOWN

NO MARKER
Domestic, Cook
Informant: W. F. Kelsey
   Bpl: Unknown

Noble & Kelsey: 178

Sarah V. Hayden Foard
Died: 04/16/1010   Age: 71y11m15
Certificate No. 0004,0343:
Parents: Ben Hayden & Maria Smith

NO MARKER
Domestic
Informant: Alice Hall
   Bpl.: Davidson Co., NC

Noble & Kelsey

Joe Foil
Died: 03/26/1927   Age: ∞50
Certificate No. 0006,0416
Parents: Lawson Foil &??

NO MARKER
Day Laborer @ Southern Railroad Transfer Shed
Informant: Alice White
   Bpl: Cabarrus Co., NC

Noble & Kelsey: 346

Alean Goins Ford
Died: 02/01/1990   Age: ∞80
Certificate No. 0070,0109
Parents: Peter Goins & Lula Kennedy

UH-550-H
Foster Grandmother @ State Hospital for Retarded
Informant: Gladys Jones
Bpl: Ridgeway, SC

Noble & Kelsey

MOTHER
ALEAN G. FORD
1910 ---- 1990

Catherine Ford

NO MARKER

Noble & Kelsey: 316

Mollie Ford *(White Female)*
Died: 05/24/1911   Age: 22
Certificate No.0004, 0101
Parents: Unknown & Catherine Ford

NO MARKER
Domestic
Informant: Stephen Noble

Stokes Ford
Died: 08/18/1924   Age: 77
Certificate No. 0012,0428
Parents: UNKNOWN

NO MARKER
Labor, Southern Railroad
Informant: Henry Sire, Son In Law
   Bpl: NC

Noble & Kelsey: 250

Charlie Fore
Died: 03/26/1927   Age: ∞57
Certificate No. 0015, 0325
Parents: UNKNOWN

NO MARKER
Cook @ Restaurant
Informant: Charlie Cowan

Noble & Kelsey

Brynda Fortune
UH-604-G
Died: 08/04/1991   Age: ∞41 Certificate Not Found

BRYNDA FORTUNE
NOV. 19, 1950
AUG. 4, 1991

Edgar Eugene Fowler
Certificate Not Found

BN-662-P MISSING

Sadie Fowler
Died: 08/08/1947   Age: 37   Domestic
Parents: Alexander Smith & Eveline Hudson

NO MARKER

Ellis, Mangum & Fair
Funeral Home Record

BURIALS

Israel Jeremiah Fox UH-540-H Noble & Kelsey
Died: 09/09/1995   Age: 20 days   INFANT
Certificate No. 0075,0884   **Informant:** Clara Boger
Parents: Billy Fox Sr., & Karen Miller   Bpl: Raleigh, NC

Baby of Francis Lyerly   NO MARKER   Summersett
Died: 06/24/1909   Age: 2 yrs.   INFANT   Funeral Home Record

Robert Freeman   BN-855 M [Marble]
Died: 09/19/1949   Age: 54   Certificate Not Found   WW I Veteran

ROBERT
FREEMAN
NORTH CAROLINA
PVT. 813 PIONEER INF.
WORLD WAR 1
AUGUST 29, 1894
SEPTEMBER 19, 1949

Thomas Frohock   OK-nmrk.   Unknown
Died: ∞ 1794   Age: Mill Plantation Owner @ Grants Creek, Rowan Co., NC
Parents: John Frohock Sr. &????   Bpl: Unknown

Michael Derick Frost   UH-   Noble & Kelsey
Died: 12/14/1971   Age: INFANT
Certificate No. 0051,0766   <u>Certificate of Fetal Death</u>
Parents: Valerie Lavern Frost age 19   Place of delivery: Rowan Hospital

MICHAEL DERICK FROST
DEC. 14, 1971

George Washington Gaddy   BT-318-K
Died: 08/23/1961   Age: 54   Certificate Not Found

GADDY
GEORGE WASHINGTON GADDY
OCT. 18, 1907
AUG. 23, 1961
WE'LL JOIN THEE IN THAT HEAVENLY LAND
NO MORE TO TAKE THE PARTING HAND.

Annie Gains   UH-NO MARKER   Ellis, Mangum & Fair
Died: 11/20/1944   Age: 64   Sewing
Certificate No. 0029,0268   **Informant:** Willie Connors
Parents: Joe Bailey & Unknown   Bpl: Cummings, GA

Edward Gaines   BT-236-K   Noble & Kelsey
Died: 10/01/1979   Age: 42   Laborer
Certificate No. 0059,0646   **Informant:** Mrs. Victoria Gaines, Mother
Parents: Unknown & Victoria Gaines
EDWARD GAINES
1937 -- 1973

Jerry Gaines Certificate Not Found   UH-630 MISSING

BURIALS

Paul A. Gains BT-237-K

Died: 1975
Age: 34

PAUL A. GAINES
1941 -- 1975

Willie Lee Gaines (Female) UH-NO MARKER Ellis, Mangum & Fair
Died: 06/05/1952 Age: 49 House Keeper
Certificate No. 0033,0256 **Informant**: Odessa Gaines
Parents: Ben Harris & Annie Bailey bd. 10/07/1902

Geneva Gaither OK-NO MARKER Noble & Kelsey: 240
Died: 03/13/1944 Age: 42 Domestic
Certificate No. 0029,0129 **Informant**: Leon Gaither
Parents: Frank Pryor & Carrie Adams Bpl: Gastonia, NC

Laura Sloan Gaither OK-146-O Noble & Kelsey: 94
Died: 04/23/1915 Age: 27 Dressmaker
Certificate No. 0002,0143 **Informant**: Anna S. Wright
Parents: Martin Sloan & Lina McCorkle Bpl: Rowan Co., NC

LAURA SLOAN
GAITHER
DIED
APRIL 23, 1945
WE WILL MEET AGAIN

INFANT Gaither NO MARKER
Died: 05/05/1947 Age: Premature INFANT Certificate Not Found
Parents: Leon Gaither & Arrilee Patterson

Van Galloway BT-2?? Noble & Kelsey
Died: 09/05/1960 Age: 60 Brick Mason
Certificate No. 0041,0054 **Informant**: Annie Galloway
Parents: Charlie Galloway & Nancy Broadenax Bpl: NC

VAN GALLOWAY
JUNE 17 SEPT. 5
1900 - 1960

Edna Mae Gantt NO MARKER Mitchell & Fair
Died: 02/14/1965 Age: 74 Teacher
Certificate No. 0045,0128 **Informant**: Mary Lash
Parents: Henry Smith & Maria Ellis Bpl: Salisbury, NC

John Henry Gantt OK-177-O Noble & Kelsey: 140
Died: 04/09/1960 Age: 59 Certificate Not Found

GANTT
JOHN HENRY
NOV. 11, 1901
APRIL 9, 1960

BURIALS

Mary Holmes Gantt
Died: 12/03/1951   Age: 64
Certificate No. 0032,1002
Parents: Louis & Bettie Holmes

NO MARKER

bd. 10/03/1887

Ellis, Mangum & Fair

Mr. A. Garner

OK-NO MARKER

Noble & Kelsey: 78

Linda Fay Garner
Died: 01/18/1954   Age: 17 days
Certificate No. 0035,0020
Parents: Elijah & Beulah Mae Garner

NO MARKER
INFANT
Informant: Beulah Mae Garner
    Bpl: Salisbury, NC

Ellis, Mangum & Fair

Logan Garner
Died: 06/06/1941   Age: ∞4

NO MARKER
Certificate Not Found

Ellis, Mangum & Fair

Willie Garrison Sr.
Died: 10/20/1972   Age: 67
Certificate No. 0052,0730
Parents: Garrison & Julia Watkins

BT-245-K
Retired: Southern Railway Co.
Informant: Mrs. Annie Walker Garrison
    Bpl: SC

Noble & Kelsey

    WILLIE GARRISON, SR.
       MAY 19, 1904
       OCT. 20, 1972

Berry Garwood
Died: 04/20/1951   Age: 82
Certificate Not Found
Parents: Green Berry Garwood

NO MARKER
Machinist Helper

Green Berry Garwood
Died: 04/07/1958   Age: 56
Certificate No. 0039,0015
Parents: Berry Garwood & Martha Peck

NO MARKER
Laborer
Informant: Mrs. Rena Fisher
    Bpl: NC

Ellis, Mangum & Fair

Lena Lyerly Garwood
Died: 01/19/1951   Age: 49
Certificate No. 0032,0539
Parents: Ralph Lyerly & Sallie Sloan

NO MARKER
Domestic
Informant: Leola Garwood
bd. 05/30/1901

Ellis, Mangum & Fair

Leola Garwood
Died: 04/14/1952   Age: 32
Certificate Not Found
Parents: Green Berry Garwood & Lena Lyerly

NO MARKER
Domestic

Ellis, Mangum & Fair
Funeral Home Record

William Garwood
Died: 08/19/1925   Age: 07,04,28
Certificate No. 0013,0407
Parents: Robert Patterson & Fannie Reudle

NO MARKER
CHILD
Informant: Ola Brown
    Bpl: Rowan Co., NC

Summersettt

BURIALS

Harvey Henry Gee BN-871-M
  Died: 05/20/1950   Age: ∞38 Certificate Not Found

HARVEY
HENRY
GEE
NORTH CAROLINA
PVT
784 TANK BN
WORLD WAR II
AUGUST 20, 1912
MAY 20, 1950

Lizzie Poe Gibson UH-419 H
Died: 08/10/1952   Age: ∞78   Certificate Not Found

LIZZIE POE
WIFE OF FRONTIS GIBSON
DEC. 11, 1874
AUG. 10, 1952
CHILDREN
LAURA, DAVID & JOSHUA

Amos Gill BT-276 -K   Noble & Kelsey
Died: 01/08/1961   Age: 60   Retired from Southern Railroad Shops
Certificate No. 0041,0303   **Informant**: Mary Gill
Parents: James Gill & Martha Leach   Bpl: NC

AMOS GILL
FEB. 8, 1900
JAN. 8, 1961
MEET ME IN HEAVEN

Ella Gill   NO MARKER   Summersett
Died: 09/23/1909   Age: 61 yrs.
Certificate Not Found

Nannie Bromfield Gill   NO MARKER   Mitchell & Fair
Died: 06/28/1965   Age: 67   Housewife
Certificate No. 0045,0395   **Informant**: Sarah Woodard
Parents: Henry Blake & Sally McCullough   Bpl: Chester Co., SC

Romis Morris Gill   BN-742-P   Noble & Kelsey
Died: 10/25/1980   Age: 28   Laborer @ General Construction
Certificate No. 0060,0829   **Informant**: Essie Mae Huff, Grandmother
Parents: Unknown & Loraine Gill   Bpl: Rowan Co., NC

ROMIS GILL
(DUCK)
1952 - 1980

BURIALS

Augusta L. Gillespie
Died: 08/12/1987   Age: 85

UH-446-H
Certificate Not Found

```
         GILLESPIE
AUGUSTA L.      JOHN ROBERT
JAN. 6, 1902    SEPT. 2, 1897
AUG. 12, 1987   DEC. 4, 1949
     TO A DEVOTED HUSBAND
```

John Robert Gillespie
Died: 12/04/1949   Age: 52
(See Augusta L. Gillespie)

UH-446-H

Della Gist / Douglas Gist
Died: 03/21/1940   Age: 58
Certificate No. 0027,0726
Parents: Unknown & Fannie Worthy

BN-777 & 776-P   Noble & Kelsey

Informant: Annie B. Gilmore
   Bpl: Santuck, SC

```
            GIST
   SON           MOTHER
 DOUGLAS          DELLA
JAN. 24, 1905   JULY 6, 1882
 JUNE 5, 1940   MAR. 21, 1940
```

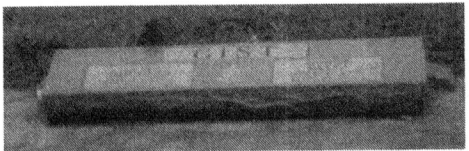

Douglas Gist
Died: 06/05/1940   Age: 38
Certificate No. 0027,0721
Parents: William Gist & Della Worther

BN-776-P   Noble & Kelsey
Section Hand, Southern Railroad
Informant: Annie Gilmore
   Bpl: Union, SC

Elsa Winslow Gist

Died: 05/02/1984   Age: 22

BN-845-M

Certificate Not Found

```
ELSA WINSLOW GIST
  JUNE 28, 1962
   MAY 2, 1984
```

James Gist
Died: 03/06/1927   Age: 41,07,27
Certificate No. 0015,0314
Parents: William & Lizzie Gist

NO MARKER   Noble & Kelsey
Shoe Maker
Informant: Rev. W. W. Gist
   Bpl: Union, SC

Lizzie Gist
Died: 02/17/1960   Age: 101
Certificate No. 0040,0364
Parents: Lewis Gee & Unknown

NO MARKER   Ellis, Mangum & Fair

Informant: Carrie G. Bryant
   Bpl: SC

Nora F. Gist
Died: 02/05/1954   Age: 64
Certificate No. 0045,0132
Parents: Jasper Fowler & Unknown

BN-868-M   Noble & Kelsey
Housewife
Informant: Zeola
   Bpl: Union Co., SC

Lula Glasco
Died: 10/06/1923   Age: ∞38
Certificate No. 0011,0506
Parents: Albert Smith & Delia Gillespie

NO MARKER   Summersettt
Domestic
Informant: R. G. Glasco, Husband
   Bpl: Charlotte, NC

BURIALS

Rufus G. Glasco
Died: 09/12/1930   Age: 50
Certificate No. 0018,0298
Parents: UNKNOWN

NO MARKER
none given
Informant: None Given

Noble & Kelsey; 216

Willie Glasco
Died: 08/05/1911   Age: 19
Certificate No. 0004,0052
Parents: Rufus Glasco/Lizzie Wilson

NO MARKER
Cook
Informant: R. G. Glasco (or Glasca)
B.pl. GA

James Gleen
Died: 08/07/1923   Age: 1 day
Certificate No.0011,0461

OK-NO MARKER
INFANT
Informant: Della Green

Noble & Kelsey: 89

Willie M. Gleen (Male)
Died: 05/20/1969   Age: 65
Certificate No.0049,0327
Parents: John Gleen & Frances Adams

OK-NO MARKER
Carolina Rubber Company employee
Informant: Lubertha Gleen, Wife
Bpl: SC

Noble & Kelsey: 106

Annie A. Glenn
Died: 08/14/1952   Age: 57
Certificate No. 0033,0397
Parents: Ephron Anderson & Loretta Hall

OK-157-O
Beautician
Informant: Clayton Glenn
Bpl: Salisbury, NC

Ellis, Mangum & Fair

ANNIE A. GLENN	L. CLAYTON GLENN
OCT. 10, 1894	FEB. 2, 1883
AUG. 14, 1952	OCT. 16, 1964
GLENN	

Isabel Glenn
Died: 10/23/1957   Age: 56
Certificate No. 0038,0219
Parents: Lewis & Fannie Caldwell

UH-527-H
Domestic

Informant: Miss Willie Glenn
Bpl: SC

Noble & Kelsey

MOTHER
ISABELL GLENN

James Glenn
Died: 0048,0005   Age: one day
Certificate No. 0011,0461
Parents: Emanuel Glenn & Della McKelley

NO MARKER
CHILD

Bpl: Salisbury, NC

Noble & Kelsey: 89

Lambeth Clayton Glenn
Died: 10/16/1964   Age: 76
Certificate No. 0044,0572
Parents: Frank Glenn & Louise Meeks

OK-157-O
Salesman for Wallace Manufacturing Company
Informant: Margaret Belton
Bpl: Gaston Co., NC

Ellis, Mangum & Fair

Louise Meeks Glenn
Died: 12/29/1944   Age: 73
Certificate No. 0029,0561
Parents: Samuel & Mamie Meeks

NO MARKER
Housewife
Informant: Clayton Glenn
Bpl: SC

Noble & Kelsey

BURIALS

Will Glenn
Died: 05/20/1969 Age: 66
Certificate Not Found

BT-266-K

WILL GLENN
DEC. 27, 1903
MAY 20, 1969

Willie Glenn
Died: 02/07/1920
Certificate No. 0008,0109
Parents: Clayton L. Glenn & Annie Anderson

NO MARKER
INFANT
Informant: Clayton Glenn, Father

Noble & Kelsey

Maggie Kendrick Glover
Died: 07/24/1952 Age: 73
Certificate No. 0033,0258
Parents: Joshua Kendrick & Unknown

NO MARKER
Domestic
Informant: Mason Scott

Ellis, Mangum & Fair

William Harvey Goler

OK-070-N Plot   Noble & Kelsey: 18
Died: 01/11/1939 Age: 96   A.M.E. Zion Minister @ Soldiers
Memorial &, Second Livingstone College President 1893-1917

GOLER
REV. W. H. GOLER
JAN. 1, 1843
JAN. 11, 1939

Emma U. Unthank Goler

John Goode
Died: 02/05/1939   Age: 63 Certificate Not Found

UH-NO MARKER

Ellis, Mangum & Fair

John Edward Goodlett
Died: 10/21/1994 Age: 61

BN-683-P   Mitchell & Fair
Motor pool @ Duke Power Co.
Certificate No. 0074,1033   **Informant:** Roy L. Goodlet
Parents: John H. Goodlett & N. Witherspoon   Bpl: Rowan, NC

FATHER
JOHN E. GOODLETT
(BUCK)
JUNE 13, 1933
OCT. 21, 1994

Modest Elizabeth Goodlett
Died: 02/13/1949 Age: 03m
Certificate No. 0031,0792
Parents: David Goodlett & Mary Chapel

UH-NO MARKER
INFANT
Informant: David Goodlett, Father

Ellis, Mangum & Fair

BURIALS

Nancy Goodwin OK-121-N
Died: 07/26/1913   Age: 42 Certificate Not Found

MOTHER
NANCY
GOODWIN
JULY 5, 1871
JULY 26, 1913

Yvonne Goodwin   UH-NO MARKER   Ellis, Mangum & Fair
Died: 01/10/1952   Age: 5m5d   INFANT   Funeral Home Record
Certificate Not Found
Parents: Odell Camp Jr. & Peggy Goodwin

Frank Graham   NO MARKER   Bingham & Carter
Died: 05/17/1924   Age: 41   Laborer @ Southern Railroad
Certificate No. 0012,0371   **Informant**: Rose Graham
Parents: Julius Graham & Cilices Hyde   Bpl: Rowan Co., NC

Hezekiah Graham   NO MARKER   Noble & Kelsey: 231

James Banks Graham   OK-348-I/J
Died: 11/05/1972   Age: 1 year   CHILD   Certificate Not Found
(See John Lee Graham)

John Lee Graham Sr.   OK-347-I/J   Mitchell & Fair
Died: 05/08/1964   Age: 44   Janitor for Dr. J.D. Corpening: Porter @ Rowan
      Hospital
Certificate No. 0044,0259   **Informant**: Margaret L. Graham, Wife
Parents: Brodie & Etta Graham   Bpl: Rowan Co., NC

GRAHAM
JAMES B. BANKS, JR.	JOHN LEE, SR.	RAYFORD A.
JULY 25, 1971	SEPT. 7, 1918	FEB. 11, 1949
NOV. 5, 1972	MAY 8, 1964	JULY 14, 1979

Rayford Alexander Graham   OK-346-I/J   Noble & Kelsey
Died: 07/14/1979   Age: 30   Industries, Lyon-Shaw
Certificate No. 0059,0502   **Informant**: Mrs. Margaret L. Graham, Mother
Parents: John Lee Graham & Margaret Lyerly   Bpl: Rowan Co., NC
(See John Lee Graham)

Ever Grasty   NO MARKER
Died: 02/18/1911   Age: 25yrs.
Certificate Not Found   **Informant**: Sam Grasty
Parents: Frank C. Miller/Mattie Craven   Bpl: Randolph Co. NC

BURIALS

Mabel Harris Graves　　　　　　OK-095-N　　　　　　Nobel & Kelsey: 13
　　Died: 04/19/1963　　Age: 70　Livingstone College & Hood Seminary Librarian
　　Certificate No. 0043,0200
　　Parents: Cicero R. & Mariah E. Harris

MABEL HARRIS GRAVES
SEPT. 17, 1893
APRIL 19, 1963

John W. Gray　　　　　　UH-385 -I/J
　　Died: 01/10/1952　　Age: 81　　Laborer
　　Certificate No. 0033,0078　　**Informant**: Mary Lou Brunson
　　Parents: Daniel Gray & Sylvia Gray　　Bpl: Rowan Co., NC

GRAY
JOHN W. GRAY
OCT. 15, 1870
JAN. 15, 1952

Luther Junior Gray　　　　　　NO MARKER　　　　　　Mitchell & Fair
Died: 01/11/1982　　Age: 55　　Truck Driver @ Jack B. Wooten Co.
Certificate No. 0062,0029　　**Informant**: Bertha W. Gray, Wife
Parents: Adam Click & Mildred Goosebee

Sallie Gray　　　　　　NO MARKER
Died: 11/10/1910　　Age: 56y06m19　　Widowed Domestic
Certificate No. 0004,0297　　**Informant**: Sinnis Dunn, Salisbury
Parents: Alex Gibson & Eliza Pethral　　Bpl: Cabarrus Co., NC

INFANT of John & Ellen Green　　NO MARKER　　　　Noble & Kelsey: 345
Certificate Not Found　Parents: John & Ellen Green　　Funeral Home Record

Jennie Green　　　　　　NO MARKER　　　　　　Cheshire & Callahan
Died: 06/05/1929　　Age: 53　　Domestic
Certificate No. 0017,0449　　**Informant**: James King
Parents: Jessie Green &??　　Bpl: SC

Jessie Greenlee　　　　UH-661-H MISSING
Certificate Not Found

Jessie James Greenlee Sr.　　BN-646 -H MISSING　　Mitchell & Fair
Died: 11/30/1993　　Age: 73　　General Laborer
Certificate No.0073,1117　　**Informant**: Patricia Jackson
Parents: Julius Greenlee & Julia Tate　　Bpl: Marion, NC

Julia Tate Greenlee　　　　NO MARKER　　　　Mitchell & Fair
Died: 03/27/1966　　Age: 74　　Domestic
Certificate No. 0046,0150　　**Informant**: Nelle Gable
　　　　Bpl: McDowell Co., NC

BURIALS

Mildred E. Ingram Griffin
Died: 11/27/90   Age: 38
Certificate No. 0070,0110
Parents: Milden Ingram & Jessie Heggins

UH-556-H MISSING   Noble & Kelsey
Stitcher @ cloth plant
Informant: Timothy Ingram
   Bpl: Salisbury, NC

Stanley Jerome Griffin
Died: 02/18/1989   Age: 33
Certificate No. 0069,0178
Parents: Curtis E. Griffin Sr. & Mary Miller

BN-785-P   Noble & Kelsey
Worker @ Clay Products Co.
Informant: Mary Miller Griffin, Mother
   Bpl: Salisbury, NC

STANLEY JEROME
GRIFFIN
NOV. 17, 1955
FEB. 18, 1989
WITH OUR LOVE

Beulah Turner Guider
Died: 01/04/1954   Age: 44
            Certificate No. 0035,0022

UH-395-I/J   Ellis, Mangum & Fair
Maid @ Rustine Johnson Furniture
Parents: James Turnipseed & Charlotte Green

BEULAH TURNER GUIDER
WIFE OF
EUGENE GUIDER
DEC. 20, 1909
JAN. 14, 1954

Ola Harper Guy
Died: 04/27/1959   Age: 54 Certificate Not Found

UH-2??
OLA HARPER GUY
MAR. 30, 1905
APR. 27, 1959

Adam Forest Hairston
Died: 11/01/1939   Age: 39
Certificate No.0027,0238
Parents: Henry Hairston & Fannie Hairston

NO MARKER   Ellis, Mangum & Fair
Mechanic
Informant: Nellie Hairston, Wife
   Bpl.: Davidson Co., NC

Shalene Evon Hairston
Died:09/03/1967   STILL BIRTH
Certificate No.0047,0555
Parents: Pennix Hairston & Juanita Bush

NO MARKER   Mitchell & Fair

Informant: Mrs. Pennix Hairston, Jr., Mother
   Bpl.: Salisbury, NC

Alice Maria Hargrave Hall
Died:06/20/1914   Age: 51
Certificate Not Found
Parents: John Lewis Hargrave & Amanda Hayden

NO MARKER   Noble & Kelsey: 49
Domestic, Housework   Funeral Home Record
Informant: Janet Hargrave
   Bpl.: Unknown

Bessie Corpening Hall
Died:09/29/1940   Age: 50y08m13d
Stewardess & dietitian of Livingstone College Boarding Department.
Certificate No.0027, 0778   **Informant:** L. H. Hall, Husband
Parents: Unknown & Minerva Corpening   Bpl.: Lenior, NC

BN-812-P   Noble & Kelsey
Housewife & Former

BESSIE CORPENING
WIFE OF L. H. HALL
FEB. 16, 1890
SEPT. 29, 1940

BURIALS

Betty L. Hall
Died: 12/12/1959   Age: 64
Certificate Not Found

NO MARKER

Edmonia Kent Hall
Died: 04/02/1961   Age: 63
Certificate Not Found
Parents: Father - Tom Kent: Mother - Margie Banks

OK-086-N
Teacher, wife of O. C. Hall

Ellis, Mangum & Fair

Condition on 08/15/03

EDMONIA KENT HALL
MAR. 7, 1897
APR. 2, 1961
FAITHFUL TO HER TRUST
EVEN UNTO DEATH

Florence Hall
Died: 1945   Certificate Not Found

NO MARKER

Henry Buford Hall
Died: 06/10/1955   Age: 85
Parents: Abraham & Harriet Hall

NO MARKER
Pharmacist

Ellis, Mangum & Fair
Funeral Home Record

Henry D. Hall
Died: 02/15/1934   Age: ∞52
Certificate No. 0022,0442
Parents: Gun & Amanda Hall

UH- NO MARKER
Farmer
Informant: Samuel Hall
  Bpl.: NC

Noble & Kelsey: 338

John Gus Hall
Died: 12/30/1914   Age: 72
Certificate No. 0001,0847
Parents: John Hall & Unknown

OK- NO MARKER
Contractor, Carpenter
Informant: Willis M. Hall
  Bpl.: Gainesville, Ala

Noble & Kelsey: 49

Louicio (sic) Hamilton Hall

BN-813-P   Noble & Kelsey
Died: 04/11/64   Age: 84   Retired Teacher: Principal Salisbury Graded School 1911 – 1922 Principal of Price High School, Member of Moores Chapel AME Zion Church, Graduate of Livingstone College
Certificate No. 0044,0228   **Informant:** Miss A. B. Pharr
Parents: Unknown   Bpl.: Cabarrus Co., NC

L. H. HALL
MAY 3, 1879
APR. 11, 1964

Oliver Cleveland Hall
Died: 05/06/1953   Age: 48
Parents: Father - Mack Hall: Mother - Dinah Shields

OK-085-N
Teacher: Principal, Price High School.

Ellis, Mangum & Fair

OLIVER CLEVELAND HALL
NOV. 26, 1904
MAY 6, 1953
NOT LOST TO SIGHT, TO MEMORY DEAR

BURIALS

Alice Hambrick
Died: 09/09/1946   Age: 52
Certificate No.0030,0343
Parents: John Jamison & Not Given

NO MARKER   Ellis, Mangum & Fair
Domestic
Informant: Emma Ellis

Lottie Perry Hamilton
Died: 09/25/1959   Age: 48
Certificate No.0040,0114
Parents: Henry Mooney & Fannie Jones

BT-292-K MISSING   Noble & Kelsey
Housewife @ Own Home
Informant: Willie Hamilton, Husband
Bpl.: NC

Marie Hampton
Died: 05/13/1966   Age: 71
Certificate No.0046,0285
Parents: George Johnson & Unknown

UH-431-H MISSING   Noble & Kelsey
Housewife
Informant: Gad Johnson
Bpl.: Anderson, SC

Richard E. Hancock
Died: 06/30/1952   Age: 85
Certificate No.0033,0263
Parents: Adam Hancock & Nora Eveligh

UH-453-H Plot   Noble & Kelsey
Farmer: Livingstone College Farm
Informant: Emma Laney
Bpl.: Liberty Hill, SC

```
           HANCOCK
   HUSBAND            WIFE
RICHARD E. HANCOCK   SARAH B. COOK
   JAN. 6, 1877       JAN. 3, 1881
   JUNE 30, 1952      OCT. 3, 1970
THY PRESENCE SHALL GO WITH THEE AND I WILL GIVE THEE REST
```

Sarah B. Cook Hancock
Died: 10/03/1970   Age: 89
(See Richard E. Hancock)

UH-453-H
Farmers wife

Alexander Hannum
Died: 09/10/1922

OK-152-O   Noble & Kelsey: 96
Minister & Member of the Livingstone College Board
  of Trustees

```
REV. ALEXANDER
   HANNUM
    DIED
 SEPT. 10, 1922
 HE DID HIS BEST
```

William Henry Hannum
Died: 08/03/1942   Age: 73
Certificate No. 0034,0027
Parents: Samuel Hannum & Eliza Gay
(Photo: 1930 Blue Bear Year Book of Livingstone College)

OK-N NO MARKER   Noble & Kelsey: 19
Professor & treasurer of Livingstone College & part
  owner of Eureka Drug Store
Informant: Mrs. J. E. Westlong
Bpl.: Maryville, TN

Bester Harbison
Died: 07/22/1910   Age: ∞29yrs
Certificate No. 0004,0228
Parents: Neete Harbison & Meg Harbison

UH-unmark.
Railroad Hand
Informant: Florence Harbison
Bpl.: NC

BURIALS

James Hardback
Died: 03/07/1926   Age: ∞40
Certificate No. 0014,0139
Parents: Jackson Hardback & Flora Greene

NO MARKER   Noble & Kelsey
Day Laborer @ Plaster Construction
Informant: Jackson Hardback
Bpl.: NC

Clarence Hargrave
Died: 12/11/1910   Age: 33y04m15
Certificate No.0004,0202
Parents: Henry Hargrave/Annie Ferrar

NO MARKER   Noble & Kelsey
Tobacco Worker
Informant: R. L. Wiseman
Bpl.: Salisbury

Frank Hargrave
Died:03/16/1916   Age: ∞23   Certificate Not Found

BN-026-M

FRANK HARGRAVE
OCT. 8, 1892
FEB. 20, 1915

Jack Hargrave
Died: 03/25/1926   Age: 07 mos.
Certificate No. 0014,0164
Parents: Abe Hargrave & Willie Mae Johnson

NO MARKER   Noble & Kelsey
INFANT
Informant: Abe Hargrave
Bpl.: Salisbury, NC

Jesse Lee Hargrave
Died:03/17/1959   Age: 74
Certificate No.0040,0021
Parents: UNKNOWN

BT-293-K   Noble & Kelsey
Retired from Southern Railroad
Informant: Lillie Hargrave, Wife

HARGRAVE
JESSE LEE HARGRAVE
JULY 25, 1885
MAR. 17, 1959
THO LOST TO SIGHT TO MEMORY DEAR.

John Hargrave
Died: 01/26/1930   Age: ∞60
Certificate No. 0018,0156
Parents: Lindsey Hargrave & Amanda Eller

NO MARKER   Noble & Kelsey
Mail Messenger @ Southern Railroad
Informant: Mary Hargrave, wife
Bpl.: Davidson Co., NC

Lena Brown Hargrave
Died:04/03/1948   Age: 71

UH-415-H
Laundress

LENA BROWN HARGRAVE
MAR. 30, 1877
APR. 3, 1948
ASLEEP IN JESUS

Lizzie Hargrave
Died:04/02/1955   Age: 76
Certificate Not Found:

UH- NO MARKER
Seamstress
Parents: George Chandler &??

BURIALS

Mary L. Hargrave
Died: 10/26/1944   Age: 82
Certificate No.0027,0062
Parents: Frank & Amanda Clodfelter

UH- NO MARKER
Housework
Informant: Mrs. Grace Kelly
Bpl.: Davidson Co., NC

Richard Hargrave
Died:08/16/1993   Age: 59
Certificate No.0073,0790
Parents: Theodore Hargrave & Willie Johnson

UH-641-G MISSING   Noble & Kelsey
Grounds Keeper @ Country club
Informant: Betty W. Hargrave
Bpl.: Salisbury, NC

William Hargrave
Died:05/03/1910   Age: 30y20d
Certificate No. 0004,0366
Parents: Henry Hargrave & Annie Ferron

NO MARKER

Informant: Mrs. R. L. Wiseman

Jonathan Hargrove
Died:08/27/1963   Age: 47
Certificate Not Found

BT-296-K

HARGROVE
JONATHAN HARGROVE
BORN MAY 12, 1916
JACKSON CO, GA.
DIED AUG. 27, 1963
ALAMANCE CO., NC
GONE BUT NOT FORGOTTEN.

Geneva Marie Miller Harley
Died: 10/20/1970   Age: 43
Certificate No.0059, 0733
Parents: Alonzo & Marie Miller

OK-182-O Plot   Noble & Kelsey: 160
Retired
Informant: Miss Ruby Lee Miller, Sister
Bpl.: Rowan Co. NC

<u>Miller Family Plot</u>
GENEVA M. HARLEY
NOV. 25, 1913
OCT. 20, 1970

Lillie May Harley
Died: 03/28/1929   Age: 19
Certificate No. 0017,0383
Parents: Paul & Mattie Harley

NO MARKER   Noble & Kelsey
School Girl
Informant: Eva Mays
Bpl.: Allendale, SC

Paul Harley
Died: 12/20/1946   Age: 70
Certificate No.0030,0739
Parents: Unknown & Martha Harley

NO MARKER   Noble & Kelsey: 128
Farmer
Informant: Walter Harley

Benjamine Church Harris
Died:07/31/1981   Age: 74
Certificate No.0061,0690
Parents: Charles Harris & Florence Johnson

NO MARKER   Mitchell & Fair
Handyman - Maintenance
Informant: Oscar E. Johnson, Brother
Bpl.: Rowan Co., NC

Charles Frank Harris
Died: 12/17/1992   Age: 73
Certificate No.0072,1001
Parents: John Harris & Estella Johnson

OK-323-K MISSING   Noble & Kelsey
Picker operator @ Cotton Cloth Mill
Informant: Fannie S. Harris
Bpl.: Rowan Co., NC

BURIALS

Charles Henry Harris
Died: 01/06/1966

UH-440-H
Age: 71 Certificates Not Found

CHARLES HENRY
HARRIS
MAY 22, 1895
JAN. 6, 1966

Cicero Richardson Harris
Died: 06/24/1917

OK-080-N   Noble & Kelsey -13
Age: 73 Certificate Not Found
Principal, teacher, A.M.E. Zion Bishop. Held the first classes of Zion Wesley Institute at his home in Concord, NC in December 1879. When Zion Wesley Institute, the progenitor of Livingstone College, moved to Salisbury, NC in October of 1882, he was an instructor at the Institute along with his wife Mariah during the presidency of J. C. Price.
Parents: Jacob & Charlotte Harris   Bpl.: Fayetteville, N.C

BISHOP C. R. HARRIS
AUG. 25, 1844 - JUNE 24, 1917
HIS WIFE
MARIAH E. HARRIS
MAR. 10, 1856 - JAN. 9, 1921

Mariah E. G. Harris

Cleo Harris
Died: 02/16/1911   Age: 37
Certificate No. 0004,0043
Parents: Malinda Wiseman & Wilson

NO MARKER   Noble & Kelsey
Domestic
Informant: Edward Harris
    Bpl.: Rowan Co., NC

Eva Harris
Died: 07/14/1956

UH-
Age: 77 Certificate Not Found

Florence Johnson Harris
Died: 03/22/1980   Age: 98
Certificate No. 0060,0221
Parents: Caleb Johnson & Ester Gray

NO MARKER -   Mitchell/Fair @Kelsey: 315
Retired teacher
Informant: Benjamine Church Harris
    Bpl.: Rowan Co., NC

Florence Willard Harris
Died: 06/13/1920   Age: 12
Certificate No.0008,0211
Parents: William C. Harris & Florence S. Johnson

NO MARKER   Noble & Kelsey
Schoolgirl
William C. Harris
    Bpl.: Salisbury, NC

George Harris
Died: 10/12/1937   Age:

OK-373-I/J
Certificate Not Found

GEORGE HARRIS
DIED OCT. 12, 1937

BURIALS

Henry Harris
Died: 02/07/1934   Age: 61 or 59
Certificate No.0022,0108
Parents: William Harris & Malinda Harris

OK-180-O [Harris – Morant Plot] Noble & Kelsey: 151
Office Helper @ Southern Railroad
Informant: Mrs. Rena Morant
Bpl.: Rowan Co., NC

HARRIS
HENRY HARRIS
MAR. 8, 1873 – FEB. 7, 1934
HIS WIFE
LONNIE HARRIS
MAR. 15, 1875 - APR. 2, 1934

INFANT Of John Harris
Died: 03/16/1910   Age: 6 mths, 12 dys
Certificate No. 0004,0322
Parents: Robert & Bertha Harris

NO MARKER   Summersett
INFANT
Informant: Robert Harris, Father
Bpl.: Rowan Co., NC

Isabella Harris

NO MARKER   Noble & Kelsey: 283

James C. Harris
Died: 02/17/1910   Age: 39y07m13
Certificate No. 0004,0407
Parents: Wilson Harris & Malinda Hugans

OK- NO MARKER   Noble & Kelsey
Shoe Maker
Informant: Henry Harris

Lee Harris
Died: 12/25/1919   Age: ∞30
Certificate No.0007,0117
Parents: William Holmes & Pauline Harris

OK-NO MARKER   Noble & Kelsey: 80
Day Laborer
Informant: Mrs. Nellie Harris
Bpl.: Rowan Co., NC

Lillie Harris
Died: 01/05/1923   Age: ∞32
Certificate No. 0011,0357
Parents: Hill Greene & Bettie Floyd

NO MARKER   Summersettt
Domestic
Informant: Robert Harris, Husband
Bpl.: Greenville, SC

Lonnie Harris
Died: 04/02/1934   Age: 59
Parents: Westley Harris & Daisy McKenzie
(See Henry Harris)

OK-180-O   Noble & Kelsey: 151
Certificate Not Found
Bpl.: Lock Township, Rowan Co., NC

Lula Harris

NO MARKER   Noble & Kelsey: 345

Malinda Harris

NO MARKER   Noble & Kelsey: 283

Margaret Peck Harris
Died: 06/30/1916   Age: 54
Certificate No.0003,0234
Parents: Anderson & Emeline Peck

OK-361-I/J   Noble & Kelsey: 315
Domestic Housework
Informant: William Charles Harris

MARGARET PECK
HARRIS
1862 - 1916

MARGARET PECK
HARRIS
1862 — 1916

BURIALS

Mariah Elizabeth Gion Harris OK-079-N Noble & Kelsey: 13
Died: 01/09/1921 Age: 65 Certificate Not Found She was the first matron of Livingstone College and Zion Wesley Institute, the first General Recording Secretary of The Women's Home and Foreign Missionary Society of the A. M. E. Zion Church, and Bishop C. R. Harris's wife. [The word 'Foreign' was replaced with over seas WHOMS]
Bpl.: Lincolnton, North Carolina

(See Cicero R. Harris for marker and photo.)

Marjorie Harris OK-376-I/J
Died: 04/01/1934 Age: 27 Certificate Not Found

MARJORIE A. HARRIS
WIFE OF
REV. JULIUS P. JOHNSON
FEB. 28, 1907
APR. 1, 1934

Martha Harris OK-NO MARKER Noble & Kelsey: 353

Mattie Harris OK-NO MARKER Noble & Kelsey: 248
Died: 08/19/1916 Age: 19y4m19d Domestic, Housework
Certificate No.0003,0258 **Informant:** Nellie Harris
Parents: Willie & Lizzie Wise

Robert Harris Family Plot OK Concrete Family Plot Marker in poor Condition

ROBT
HARRIS
FAMILY

Robert Harris OK-200-L (Cement Marker) Noble & Kelsey
Died: 08/27/1951 Age: 60 Laborer
Certificate No.0032,0878 **Informant:** Mrs. Martha A. Harris
Parents: Unknown Bpl.: Mecklenburg Co., NC bd. **12/25/1891**

So (female) Harris OK NO MARKER
Died: 02/16/1911 Age: 37y11m16 Single Domestic
Certificate Not Found: **Informant:** Edward Harris
Parents: Wilson & Melinda Wiseman Bpl.: Rowan Co. NC
Register of Death, Salisbury, Co. of Rowan, NC (09/1909-10/11/1911 pg.28)

Steven Harris NO MARKER Noble & Kelsey
Died: 03/03/1922 Age: ∞74 Farmer
Certificate No. 0011,0316 **Informant:** Angeline Neely

Susie Warner Harris UH-NO MARKER Ellis, Mangum & Fair
Died: 01/29/1947 Age: 65 Practical Nurse Funeral Home Record
Certificate No. 0030,0753
Parents: Bishop A. J. Warner & Unknown bd. 01/28/1882

BURIALS

William Harris
Died: 06/04/1961   Age: 61
Certificate No. 0041,0581
Parents: UNKNOWN

BT-278-K   Noble & Kelsey: 264
Cook @ Rowan Memorial Hospital
Informant: Lucille Harris, Wife

WILLIAM J. HARRIS
JAN. 30, 1900
JUNE 4, 1961

Emily N. Harrison
Died: 04/29/1911   Age: 96
Certificate No. 0004,0091
Parents: William Norris & Unknown

OK-NO MARKER   Noble & Kelsey: 25
Mother
Informant: W. H. Bryant
Bpl.: Raleigh, NC

James Bell Harrison
Died: 02/11/1981   Age: 71
Certificate No. 0061,0150
Parents: Harrison Bell Sr. & Betty Holmes Bell

BN-859-M   MISSING   Noble & Kelsey
Laborer @ Brick Yard
Informant: Mrs. Josephine Bush, Sister
Bpl.: Rowan Co., NC

Lizzie Mae Harrison
Died: 08/23/1917

BN-792-P
Certificate Not Found

LIZZIE MAE HARRISON
AUG. 1917

Samuel James Harrison
Died: 08/15/1981   Age: 66
Certificate No. 0061,0691
Parents: Emory Harrison & Minnie Strickland

BN-791-P   Mitchell & Fair
Retired from Southern Railway
Informant: Mrs. Lizzie Mae Harrison
Bpl.: GA

SAMUEL J. HARRISON
AUG. 12, 1915
AUG. 15, 1981

Mary Anna Speas Hauser
Died: 11/09/1974   Age: 90

OK-197-L Plot   Noble & Kelsey: 192
Housewife and General Missionary   President who
  made the motion to establish the Chair of
  Missionary Education at Hood Theological
  Seminary

Certificate No. 0054,0681
Parents: John & Ida Matthews

Informant: Mrs. Samuel E. Duncan, Daughter
Bpl.: Yadkin Co., NC

HAUSER
SANFORD HENRY HAUSER
APRIL 8, 1880 - DECEMBER 21, 1953
AND WIFE MARY ANNA SPEAS HAUSER
APRIL 10, 1884 - NOVEMBER 9, 1974
W.H. & F.M. SOCIETY A.M.E. ZION CHURCH
VICE PRESIDENT 1932 -1943 PRESIDENT 1943 –1951
Back. DEVOTED WIFE AND MOTHER
CHRISTIAN AND FRIEND[2]

Nancy N. Hauser
Died: 1953   Age: ∞81

UH-???
Certificate Not Found:

NANCY N. HAUSER
1872   1953

BURIALS

Sanford Henry Hauser
Died: 12/21/1953   Age: 72
Certificate No.0034,0524
Parents: Columbus Hauser & Mary Shores
(See Mary Anna Speas Hauser)
  Back.
    REST COMES TO A LABORING MAN
    DEATH IS THE CROWN OF LIFE

OK-197-L Plot   Nobel & Kelsey: 192
Retired from Southern Railway
Informant: Mrs. Mary Anna Hauser, Wife
    Bpl.: Yadkin Co., NC

Derrick Hawkins Jr.
Died: 2003

UH-xxx
Certificate Not Found   Funeral Home Marker

Eliza Hawkins

OK-NO MARKER   Noble & Kelsey: 345

Pollie Hayes
Died: 04/09/1930   Age: 55
Certificate No. 0018,0201
Parents: Elex Hartman &??

NO MARKER   Fraternal Funeral Home
Domestic
Informant: W. W. Watson
    Bpl.: Rowan Co., NC

Price Hayes
Died: 03/14/1917   Age: ∞30
Certificate No. 0005,0302
Parents: Isaral (Sic) Hayes & Harriett (Sic) Hoskins

NO MARKER   Summersettt

Informant: H. S. Kerrnerly
    Bpl.: Rowan Co., NC

Lizzie Mae Moore Headen
Died:02/21/1998   Age: 96   Certificate Not Found

BN-### (Marker placed after 1996 survey)

    LIZZIE MAE MOORE HEADEN
    BORN   DIED
    MAY 2,1902   FEB. 21, 1998

Adam Dewitt Hearne
Died: 10/05/1982   Age: 74   Laborer @ Cannon Mills
            Certificate No.0062,0734   **Informant**: Birdie Guthledge Hearne, Wife
            Parents: Jake Hearne & Maggie Oates   Bpl.: Rowan Co., NC

BN-852-M   Noble & Kelsey

        ADAM DEWITT
        HEARNE
        JAN. 3, OCT. 5
        1908   1982

Kathleen G. Johnson Hearns
Died 10/22/1992   Age 82
Certificate No. 0072,0859
Parents Charlie & Mary Jane Johnson

UH-628-G MISSING

William Henry Hebrew
        Died:07/29/1922   Age: 71
        Certificate Not Found

OK-039-N   Noble & Kelsey: 46
            Teacher @ Hood Seminary

            W. H. HEBREW
            MAY 5, 1851
            JULY 29, 1922

(Buried also with no marker: Charles Artis and Mary Smyre)

BURIALS

Gladys Irene Heilig UH-577-H
Died: 10/25/1990   Age: 76   Certificate Not Found

GLADYS IRENE
HEILIG
AUG. 9, 1914
OCT. 25, 1990

Raymond Lloyd (Black) Heilig   BN-863-M   Noble & Kelsey
Died: 06/02/1985   Age: 50   Janitor for City of Salisbury
Certificate No. 0065,0475   **Informant**: Eula M. Black, Mother
Parents: Lloyd Black & Eula Heilig   Bpl.: Rowan Co., NC

RAYMOND L. HEILIG
DEC. 8, 1935
JUNE 2, 1985

Elijah J. Hemphill   NO MARKER
Died: 04/16/19   Age: 68   Farmer
Certificate No. 0028,0102   **Informant**: Odessa Mourrey
Parents: Unknown & Sylvia Burgin   Bpl.: NC

Ella Hemphill   NO MARKER   Ellis, Mangum & Fair
Died: 02/16/1941   Age: 36   Domestic
Certificate No. 0027,1346   **Informant**: Odessa Murry
Parents: Elijah Hemphill & Lula Steps   Bpl.: McDowell Co.

Abraham Henderson   OK-NO MARKER.   Noble & Kelsey: 11
Died: 06/17/1936   Age: 75   Brick Layer/Mason
Certificate No. 0024,0215   **Informant**: Mamie Henderson
Parents: Alex Henderson & Ellen Henderson   Bpl.: Salisbury, NC
Plot also Contains Abraham Henderson, Douglas Henderson, and Susan Henderson bd. 01/1852

Alice Ellis Henderson   UH-402-I/J   Mitchell & Fair
Died: 04/10/1980   Age: 87   Homemaker
Certificate No. 0060,0295   **Informant**: Mrs. Grace Littlejohn, Daughter
Parents: David and Letitia Ellis   Bpl.: Davison Co., NC
(See Clanton Henderson for marker)

ALICE ELLIS HENDERSON
JUNE 20, 1892
APRIL 10, 1980

Annie Faye Henderson   BN-794-P   Noble & Kelsey
Died: 11/05/1980   Age: 30   Cafeteria worker @ hospital
Certificate No. 0060,0865   **Informant**: Bobby Smith, Father
Parents UNKNOWN

HENDERSON
ANNIE FAYE
MOTHER OF
SHONTELL MONIQUE
WIFE OF
ARCHIE L. HENDERSON
DEC. 6, 1949 -- NOV. 5, 1980

BURIALS

Arthur Henderson
Died: 06/26/1951   Age: 60
Certificate No.0032,0821
Parents: Phifer Henderson & Eliza Graham

NO MARKER
Janitor, Spencer Shops Southern Railroad
Informant: Joe Henderson
bd. 08/20/1890

Ellis, Mangum & Fair

Caroline (P.) Henderson
Died: 11/23/1910   Age: 74
Certificate Not Found

OK-081-N
Laundress

Noble & Kelsey: 55

CAROLINE HENDERSON
Feb. 15, 1836
Nov. 23, 1910:
She died as she lived
a Christian

Buried also in Kelsey plot 55: Annie B. Lawrence and Mr. L. B. Henderson (unmark.)

Cecelia Hall Henderson
Died: 01/24/1955   Age: 90
Certificate No.0036,0020
Parents: Jule Hall & Unknown

UH-525-H
Housewife
Informant: Miss Elizabeth Henderson
Bpl.: Rowan Co., NC

Noble & Kelsey

MOTHER
CECELIA
HENDERSON
DEC. 12, 1865
JAN. 24, 1955

Clanton Eugene Henderson
Died: 10/12/1957   Age: 66
Certificate No.0038,0225

UH-402-I/J
Southern Railroad Shops
Informant: Mrs. Alice Henderson, Wife
Parents: John Henderson & Nellie Jenkins   Bpl.: NC

Ellis, Mangum & Fair

CLANTON E. HENDERSON   ALICE ELLIS HENDERSON
SEPT. 13, 1881
OCT. 12, 1957

Curlee Greer Henderson
Died: 09/05/1993   Age: 84
Certificate No.0073,0835
Parents: Stewart Greer & Maggie Clark

UH-656-G MISSING
Homemaker @ Own Home
Informant: Rosa Mae Cuthrell
Bpl.: Salisbury, NC

Noble & Kelsey

Dottie Henderson
Died: 12/18/1924   Age: 35
Certificate No. 0012,0484
Parents: Thomas Henderson & Lucy Davis

NO MARKER
Teacher in Rowan County Schools
Informant: Lucy Henderson
Bpl.: Rowan Co., NC

Bingham & Carter

Douglas Henderson
Died: 03/18/1916   Age: 25

OK-N
Certificate Not Found

Noble & Kelsey: 011

DOUGLAS HENDERSON
BORN
SEPT. 1, 1891
DIED
MARCH 18, 1916

BURIALS

Elizabeth Lizzie Henderson OK-250-K Noble & Kelsey
Died:09/16/1976   Age: 79   Retired
Certificate No.0056,0681   **Informant**: Leo Henderson   M
Parents: William Henderson & Cecelia Hall   Bpl.: NC
Marker off base – 09/07/03

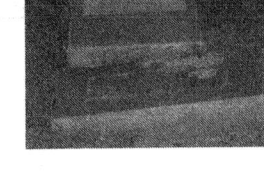

ELIZABETH (LIZZIE)
HENDERSON
APRIL 2, 1897
SEPT. 16, 1976

Elizabeth Perry Henderson BT-289-K Noble & Kelsey
Died:06/29/1971   Age: 60   Cook @ Carolina Diner
Certificate No. 0051,0423   **Informant**: Mrs. Dorothy Colbert
Parents: Henry Henderson & Maria Perry   Bpl.: SC

HENDERSON
ELIZABETH PERRY
HENDERSON
JUNE 15, 1900
JUNE 29, 1971

Henry Henderson NO MARKER Mitchell & Fair
Died:09/26/1967   Age: 93   Retired   Funeral Home Record
Certificate Not Found
Parents: Caslem Henderson & Mary Ann Perry

Isaac Henderson NO MARKER Ellis, Mangum & Fair
Died:01/23/1953   Age: 03m09d   INFANT
Certificate No.0035,0083   **Informant**: James Henderson
Parents: James Henderson & Marie Powell   Bpl.: Salisbury, NC

John Alexander Henderson BN-677-P Noble & Kelsey
Died: 12/13/1982   Age: 80   Retired Laborer @ Cannon Mills
Certificate No.0062,0976   **Informant**: Dorothy A. Henderson, Wife
Parents: Unknown & Charlotte Johnson   Bpl.: Rowan Co., NC

HENDERSON
LULA C.   JOHN A.
1913 - 1985   1911 - 1982

John Lacie Henderson NO MARKER Noble & Kelsey
Died: 05/29/1918   Age: 26,08,16   Shoemaker in Shoe Shop
Certificate No. 0006,0444   **Informant**: Abraham Henderson
Parents: Abraham Henderson & Susan Baker

Judy Blackwell Henderson BN-733 Noble & Kelsey
Died: 10/21/1938   Age: 46   Housework
Certificate No.0026,0230   **Informant**: Alice Horton
Parents: Bill Blackwell & Not Given   Bpl.:Rowan Co., NC

JUDY BLACKWELL
HENDERSON
AT REST

BURIALS

Laura Henderson
Died: 05/21/1939 Age: 54
Certificate No. 0027,0135
Parents: Bob Gibson & Laura Neely

NO MARKER
Laundress, Domestic
Informant: George Henderson (widow)
Bpl.: Rowan Co., NC

Ellis, Mangum & Fair

Leon Eddie Henderson, Sr.
Died: 05/28/1954 Age: ∞62
Certificate No. 0035,0231
Parents: Eddie Leon Henderson & Nellie Jenkins

UH-468-H
Janitor
Informant: Mrs. Louise Pharr
Bpl.: Salisbury, NC

Noble & Kelsey

EDDIE LEON
HENDERSON, Sr.
SEPT. 7, 1894
MAY 28, 1954

Lula Cook Henderson
Died: 02/12/1985 Age: 71
Certificate No. 0065,0120
Parents: Unknown & Alberta Cook
(See John Alexander Henderson)

BN-676-P
Retired Maid
Informant: Linda Hosch, Daughter
Bpl.: Newberry, SC

Noble & Kelsey

Lula D. Henderson
Died: 12/10/1976 Age: 79
Certificate No. 0056,0892
Parents: Nelson Davis & Mary Hall

UH-501-H
Domestic
Informant: Major Hampton, Washington, DC
Bpl.: SC

Noble & Kelsey

LULA D. HENDERSON
NOV. 29, 1892

Martin Kennedy Henderson
Died: 11/13/1981 Age: 16
Certificate No. 0061,0945
Parents: James P. Henderson & Edna Provoid

BN-799
Informant:
(TICES)
MARTIN KENNEDY
HENDERSON
APR. 12, 1965
NOV. 13, 1981

Marvin Paul Henderson
Died: 04/20/1960 Age: 13
Certificate No. 0040,0498
Parents: Unknown & Elizabeth Henderson

BT-290-K
Student
Informant: Elizabeth Henderson, Mother
Bpl.: NC

Noble & Kelsey

HENDERSON
MARVIN PAUL
SON OF
ELIZABETH HENDERSON
JULY 14, 1946
APR. 20, 1960
GONE SO SOON

Mary Henderson
Died: 07/02/1910 Age: 33
Certificate No. 0004,0287
Parents: S. L. Kelly & Linda Wiseman

NO MARKER
Domestic
Informant: S. L. Kelly, father
Bpl.: Rowan Co., NC

BURIALS

William Henderson
Died: 09/20/1946   Age: 67
Parents: Elijah Henderson & Laura S. Kelley

NO MARKER
Laborer, Farm Laborer

Ellis, Mangum & Fair
Funeral Home Record

Henry Henderson Jr.
Died: 02/05/1933   Age: 18
Certificate No. 0021,0112
Parents: Henry Henderson & Mariah Perry

OK-379-I/J
Laborer
Informant: Mrs. Laurence Hartley
Bpl.: Chester Co., SC

Cheshire & Harris

HENRY JR. SON OF
HENRY & MARIA
HENDERSON
JULY 10, 1915
FEB. 5, 1933
Our beloved son

George Washington Henry
Died: 05/23/1947   Age: 74
Certificate No. 0030,0861
Parents: George Henry & Marie Huggan

NO MARKER
Carpenter
Informant: Will Henry
Bpl.: Clover, SC

Noble & Kelsey

David Wayne Herndon
Died: 05/11/1990   Age: 34
Certificate No. 0070,0526
Parents: James Herndon & Mary Jean Ross
(See Mary Jean Ross Herndon.)

BN-782-P
Doffer @ Cotton Cloth Mill
Informant: Mary Jean Herndon
Bpl.: Salisbury, NC

Noble & Kelsey

DAVID WAYNE
HERNDON
APR. 9, 1959
MAY 11, 1990

James Edward Herndon
Died: 04/10/1982   Age: 61
Certificate No. 0062,0321
Parents: Jim Herndon & Polly Smith

BN-823-M
Retired Laborer @ Southern Railroad
Informant: Jean Herndon, Wife
Bpl.: Rowan Co., NC

Noble & Kelsey

JAMES EDWARD
HERNDON
NOV. 21, 1921
APR. 10, 1982

Mary Jean Ross Herndon
Died: 03/22/1991   Age: 55
Certificate No. 0071,0256
Parents: William & Irene Ross

BN-781-P
Homemaker @ Own Home
Informant: Terry Diane Torrence
Bpl.: Rowan Co., NC

Noble & Kelsey

We Love You
MARY JEAN ROSS
HERNDON
APR. 28, 1936
MAR. 22, 1991
AT REST

BURIALS

Polly Herndon
Died: 01/03/1954 Age: 57
Certificate No.0035,0024
Parents: Henry Smith & Not Known

NO MARKER
Housework
Informant: William Herndon
Bpl.: Columbia, SC

Ellis, Mangum & Fair

Priscilla Herndon

BN-667-P MISSING

Dossie Stowers Hickman
Died: 01/11/1940 Age: 61
Certificate No.0027,0607
Parents: George Stowers & Nancy Stith

OK-
Housewife
Informant: George Hickman
Bpl.: Lexington, NC

Noble & Kelsey: 158

HICKMAN		
LOUICO	DOSSIE STOWERS	WILLIAM LEE
FEB. 3, 1858	JUNE 5, 1879	AUG. 28, 1905
NOV. 9, 1928	JAN. 11, 1940	JAN. 2, 1961

Loucio Hickman
Died: 11/09/1928 Age: 70
Certificate No. 0016,0481
Parents: Joseph & Sallie Hickman
(See Dossie Stowers Hickman)

OK--
Day Laborer
Informant: Susie Hickman
Bpl.: Salisbury, NC

Noble & Kelsey: 158

Margie Hickman
Died: 05/10/1924 Age: None Given
Certificate No.0012,0372
Parents: Loucio Hickman & Dossie Stowers

OK-NO MARKER
Housewife
Informant: Louico Hickman, Father
Bpl.: NC

Bingham & Carter

Rosetta Hickman
Died: 03/08/1926 Age: 18
Certificate No. 0014,0188
Parents: Loucio Hickman & Dossie Stowers

OK-NO MARKER
Domestic
Informant: Dossie Hickman, Mother

Bingham, Carter, & Cheshire

William Lee Hickman
Died: 01/02/1961 Age: 55
Certificate No.0041,0308
Parents: Louicio Hickman
(See Dossie Stowers Hickman)

OK--
Laborer, Foil's Grocery Store
Informant: William Hickman
Bpl.: NC

Noble & Kelsey: 158

William Ray Hickson
Died: 1983 Age: ∞29

BN-????

Noble & Kelsey

Nina Higgins
Died: 08/28/1911 Age:

NO MARKER
Certificate Not Found

Summersett

BURIALS

Amanda Lee Hill
Died: 02/19/1978   Age: 54
Certificate No.0058,0045
Parents: Willie Lee & Mary Weeks

BN-703-P   Noble & Kelsey
Housewife
Informant: Walter Hill, Husband
   Bpl.: Rowan Co., NC

AMANDA L. HILL
FEB. 15, 1924
FEB. 19, 1978

Annie Mae Simpson Hill
Died: 03/23/1983   Age: 83
Certificate No.0063,0256
Parents: Benjamin Hamilton & Janie Gilyard

BN-757-M   Noble & Kelsey
Retired Laborer @ Wiley School Cafeteria
Informant: Mrs. Alene Arnold, Daughter
   Bpl.: Rowan, NC

ANNIE M.
SIMPSON HILL
OCT. 30, 1900
MAR. 23, 1983

Aron Hill
Died: 11/07/1947   Age: 58
Certificate No.0030,0639
Parents: Unknown & Laura Hill

NO MARKER   Noble & Kelsey: 345
Laborer
Informant: Ruth Baldwin
   Bpl.: Winnsboro, SC

Harvest L. Hill
Died: 06/21/1994   Age: 86
Certificate No.0074,0673
Parents: UNKNOWN

UH-635-G   Noble & Kelsey
Farmer @ Own Farm in China Grove
Informant: Mayola Darden
   Bpl.: GA

Walter June Hill
Died: 10/26/1989   Age: ∞66

UH-545-H
Certificate Not Found

WALTER JUNE
HILL
SEPT. 21, 1923
OCT. 26, 1989

Nolia Smith Hines
Died: 09/14/1992   Age: 91
   Certificate No.0072,0732
   Parents: James Smith & Lisha Andrews

UH-625-G   Mitchell & Fair
Minister: Baptist
Informant: Lorene H. Heath
   Bpl.: Worthen, GA

NOLIA SMITH
HINES
1901 ---- 1992

Eddie Hipps, Jr.
Died: 07/05/77   Age: 33
Certificate No.: 0057,0518
Parents: Eddie Hipps & Nettie Earl

UH-NO MARKER   Noble & Kelsey
Prisoner
Informant Nettie Hipps, Mother
   Bpl.: North Carolina

BURIALS

Georgia Payne Hipps
Died: 04/05/1997   Age: 89
Certificate No.0077,0369
Parents: George Payne & Fannye Rankins
Duncan Sr. Family Plot

OK-168-O Plot
Seamstress, Self-employed
Informant: Alonzo Payne
   Bpl.: Salisbury, NC

Noble & Kelsey: 124

DAUGHTER
GEORGIA PAYNE HIPPS
FEB. 11, 1908
APR. 5, 1997

Beatred Hobson
Died: 01/08/1923   Certificate Not Found

OK-NO MARKER

Noble & Kelsey: 212

Eugene Hobson
Died: 12/05/1944   Age: 61
Certificate No.0029,0288
Parents: Adam Hobson & Lucinda Barber

OK-NO MARKER
Butcher
Informant: Sadie Davis
   Bpl.: Davie Co., NC

Noble & Kelsey: 231

Isabell Barringer Hobson
Died: 08/28/1925   Age: 19y1m22d
Certificate No.0013,0416
Parents: Henry Barringer & Martha Hobson

OK-NO MARKER
Cook
Informant: Martha Hobson, Mother
   Bpl.: Salisbury, NC

Noble & Kelsey: 212

Josephine E. Henderson Hobson
Died: 02/12/2002   Age: 74 Certificate Not Found

UH-xxx

Mitchell & Fair

JOSEPHINE ELAINE
HENDERSON HOBSON:
Born 4-25-1927   Died 2-12-2002

Lillie Davis Hobson
Died: 09/21/1920   Age: ∞40
Certificate No.0008,0236
Parents: Charlie Davis & Zoo Hobson

OK-NO MARKER
Cook for private family, employer Col. Scales
Informant: Mrs. H. D. S??ter
   Bpl.: Davie Co., NC

Noble & Kelsey: 39

Maggie Hobson
Died: 08/25/1923   Age: 49
Certificate No. 0011,0485
Parents: P. & Julia Ramsey

NO MARKER
Domestic/Housework
Informant: A. R. Shay
   Bpl.: Rowan Co., NC

Noble & Kelsey

Martha Hobson
Died: 03/06/1943   Age: 50
Certificate No.0028,0734
Parents: Warrick Hobson & Martha Morris

OK-NO MARKER
Housework
Informant: Lizzie Sharpe

Noble & Kelsey: 302

Mary Hobson
Died: 03/22/1926   Age: 22
Certificate No.0014,0224
Parents: Ed. Hobson & Annie Hobson

OK-NO MARKER
Domestic
Informant: Arthur Hobson
   Bpl.: Salisbury

Noble & Kelsey: 212

Phoebe Carr Hobson
Died: 12/04/1957   Age: 94

NO MARKER
Certificate Not Found

Ellis, Mangum, & Fair
Funeral Home Record

BURIALS

Rachel Hobson　　　　　　　　　BT-234-K　　　　　　　Ellis, Mangum, & Fair
　　　Died: 1956　　Age: 73　　　　　　　　　　　　　　Funeral Home Record

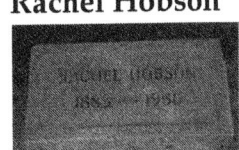
　　　　　　RACHEL HOBSON
　　　　　　　1883 -- 1956

Bernice Foster Hoffman　　　　　OK-NO MARKER　　　　Noble & Kelsey: 345
Died:04/18/1912　　Age: 8y3m18d　　CHILD
Certificate No.0001,0136　　　　　　**Informant:** Will Hoffman
Parents: George Foster & Cora Crisp　　　Bpl.: Salisbury

Carrie Hogan　　　　　　　　　　BT-NO MARKER　　　　Noble & Kelsey: 282
Died:08/ /1957　　　　　　　　　　　Certificate Not Found

Robert J. Hoke　　　　　　　　　BN-727-M　　　　　　　Ellis, Mangum, & Fair
Died: 12/22/1943　　Age: 72　　　　　　　　　　　　　　Funeral Home Record

　　　　　　　　HOKE
　　　　　ROBERT J. HOKE
　　　　　　　OCT. 1871
　　　　　　DEC. 22, 1943

S. D. Holce　　　　　　　　　　　NO MARKER
Died:02/13/1958　　Age: 58　　　　　Unknown
Certificate No.0038,0470　　　　　　**Informant:** <u>Lapsed Policy</u>: Winston Mutual Life
　　　　　　　　　　　　　　　　　　　　Insurance, Winston Salem, NC
Parents: UNKNOWN

Mamie McNair Holie　　　　　　NO MARKER
Died:09/11/1956　　Age: 53
Certificate Not Found

Madline Carter Holland　　　　　OK-229-K　　　　　　　Noble & Kelsey: 239
Died: 12/31/1981　　Age: 72　　　　Homemaker
Certificate No.0061,1071　　　　　　**Informant:** Johnnie Holland
　　　　Parents: Samuel Carter & Rebecca Pedrick　　Bpl.: Rowan, NC

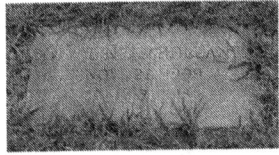
　　　　　　MADLINE C. HOLLAND
　　　　　　　NOV. 22, 1909
　　　　　　　DEC. 31, 1981

Johnnie Holland Sr.　　　　　　　OK-230-K　　　　　　　Noble & Kelsey: 239
Died:09/05/1985　Age: 77　　　　　Certificate Not Found

　　　　　　JOHNNIE HOLLAND, Sr.
　　　　　　　OCT. 22, 1908
　　　　　　　SEPT. 5, 1985

Barbara Holmes　　　　　　　　BT-309-K　　　　　　　Noble & Kelsey
Died: 12/21/1964　　Age: 24　　　　Housewife
Certificate No.0044,0699　　　　　　**Informant:** Lester Holmes
Parents: Bishop Barber & Wilma Finger　　Bpl.: Rowan Co., NC

BURIALS

Ella Rankins Holmes
Died: 05/26/1953 Age: 63
Certificate No.0034,0232
Parents: John Rankins & Delia Rankins

UH-522-H
Housewife
Informant: Tommie Holmes
Bpl.: Rowan Co., NC

Noble & Kelsey

IN LOVING REMEMBRANCE
OF MOTHER
ELLA HOLMES
JULY 28, 1890
MAY 26, 1953

Addie Gertrude Holt
Died: 03/07/1965 Age: 78
Certificate No.0045,0161
Parents: John Holt & Julia Miller
(See Fannie H. Byers)

OK-192-L
Domestic
Informant: Mr. C. J. Fleming
Bpl.: Linwood, NC

Mitchell & Fair @ Kelsey 163

Anna Noble Holt
Died: 12/12/1961
Age: 62
Certificate No.0042,0165
Parents: Caleb Johnson & Ester Grey

OK-191-L Holt Plot
Housewife
Informant: John Holt
Bpl.: NC

Noble & Kelsey: 175

ANNA NOBLE
HOLT
DEC. 12, 1961

Baby Edwin Allen Holt
Died: 02/20/1925
Certificate No.0013,0340
Parents: John Holt & Odessa Colman

OK-191-L Holt Plot
CHILD
Informant: John Holt
Bpl.: Salisbury, NC

Noble & Kelsey: 175

BABY
EDWIN A. HOLT
1925

Helen Sauté Waugh Holt
Died: 08/13/1965 Age: 71

Certificate No.0045,0409
Parents: James Henry Waugh &?

OK-097-N
Retired teacher @ Livingstone College Public School
1921 - 1922
Informant: Mr. Francis Holt, Husband
Bpl.: Rowan Co., NC

Noble & Kelsey

HELEN WAUGH HOLT
WIFE OF FRANCIS H. HOLT
MAR. 23, 18--
AUG 13, 1965

John Anderson Holt
Died: 01/11/1973 Age: 62
Certificate No.0053,0030
Parents: Edward & Susan Holt

BT-255-K
Barber/Self Employed
Informant: Sarah Holt, Daughter
Bpl.: NC

Noble & Kelsey

John Calvin Holt
Died: 07/14/1977 Certificate Not Found

OK-191-L Holt Plot

JOHN C. HOLT
JULY 14, 1977

BURIALS

Josephine Campbell Holt
Died: 06/25/1930   Age: ∞70
Certificate No.0018,0246
Parents: Calvin & Rachel Campbell

OK-NO MARKER
Domestic
Informant: Mr. Francis Holt
   Bpl.: Davidson Co., NC

Noble & Kelsey: 8

Julia F. Holt
Died: 06/01/1939   Age: ∞82
Certificate No.0027,0146
Parents: Sam & Emma Miller
(See Fannie H. Byers)

OK-192-L Holt Plot
Housework
Informant: Mrs. Katie Craven
   Bpl.: Davidson Co., NC

Noble & Kelsey: 163

Kenneth Baby of Wilson Holt
Died: 07/16/1918
Certificate No.0006,0466
Parents: Mrs. Wilson Holt

NO MARKER
INFANT

Noble & Kelsey: 346

Melba Darrel Holt
Died: 06/08/1947   Age: 9hrs
Parents: A. Holt & Doris Smith

NO MARKER
INFANT

Ellis, Mangum, & Fair
Funeral Home Record

Nellie Holt
Died: 05/14/1944   Age: 52

BN-877-M
Certificate Not Found

(Marker is broken & on the ground)

NELLIE HOLT
DIED
MAY 14, 1944
AGED 52 YEARS
GONE BUT NOT FORGOTTEN

Odessa Manuel Holt
Died: 12/03/1932   Age: 40

OK-191-L Holt Plot
Certificate Not Found

Noble & Kelsey: 175

ODESSA M. HOLT
AUG. 24 1892
DEC. 3, 1932

Azree Headen Hoover
Died: 03/22/1991   Age: 81
Certificate No.0071,0284
Parents: Taylor & Lula Headen

UH-586-H
Presser @ Commercial Laundry
Informant: Doris Douglas
   Bpl.: Rowan Co., NC

Noble & Kelsey

Frank Hoover
Died: 08/16/1926   Age: 18y6m8d
Certificate No.0014,0285
Parents: Pink Hoover & Maudy Scott

OK-NO MARKER
Day Laborer, Southern Railway Shops
Informant: Pink Hoover
   Bpl.: Rowan Co., NC

Noble & Kelsey: 177

Pink INFANT of Hoover
Died: 11/18/1917

OK-NO MARKER
INFANT

Noble & Kelsey: 177
Funeral Home Record

BURIALS

Clara Mitchell Hopkins
Died: 11/02/1960   Age: 48
Certificate No.0041,0186
Parents: Horace & Unknown

OK-218-K [Grnt Fldstn]
Housewife
Informant: James Hopkins, Husband
Bpl.: NC

Noble & Kelsey: 238

CLARA MITCHELL
HOPKINS
1912 - 1960

Luke Horne
Died: 07/26/1939   Age: 51

NO MARKER
Certificate Not Found

Ellis, Mangum, & Fair
Funeral Home Record

Alice Harris Horton
Died: 01/19/1952   Age: 49
Certificate No.0033,0063
Parents: George Harris & Eva Barnhardt

BN-734-M
Housewife
Informant: Jesse Horton
Bpl.: Rowan Co., NC

Noble & Kelsey

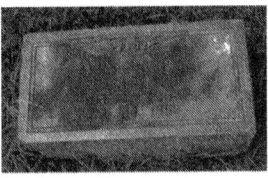

ALICE HARRIS
HORTON
JAN. 16, 1902
JAN. 19, 1952

Evelyn Inez Horton
Died: 10/24/1943   Age: 20y4m24d
Certificate No.0028,0887
Parents: Jesse & Alice Horton

BN-732-M
Student
Informant: Alice Horton
Bpl.: Salisbury, NC

Noble & Kelsey

EVELYN INEZ
HORTON
MAY 29, 1923
OCT. 24, 1943

Henry Robert House
Died: 07/10/1947   Age: 63
Certificate No. 0030,0894
Parents: Judge House & Sidney Heath   bd. 08/04/1883

UH- NO MARKER
Laborer

Ellis, Mangum, & Fair

Mary Heilig House
Died: 05/07/1912   Age: 60y06m28
Certificate No. 0001,0140
Parents: David & Eliza Heilig

OK-NO MARKER
Domestic
Informant: Henry Johnson
Bpl.: Stanley Co., NC

Noble & Kelsey: 24

Elmina Bruce Houston
Died: 05/17/1975   Age: 76
Certificate No.0055,0355
Parents: Julius Sumner & Nancy Bridges

UH-390- I/J
Housewife
Informant: Louis Houston
Bpl.: NC

Noble & Kelsey

Ida Houston
Died: 02/15/1908   Age: 20 yrs.

NO MARKER

Summersett
Funeral Home Record

James Houston
Died: 10/25/1945   STILL BIRTH

UH- NO MARKER

Ellis, Mangum, & Fair
Funeral Home Record

BURIALS

Andrew R. Houze
Died: 2002

ANDREW
HOUZE
2002
NOBLE & KELSEY
FUNERAL HOME

uh-xxx (Post 1996 Survey)
Certificate Not Found

Nobel & Kelsey
Funeral Home Marker

Fannie Chambers Howard
Died: 01/19/1949

OK-125-N   Age: 72

HOWARD-
MOTHER
FANNIE CHAMBERS
HOWARD
JULY 25, 1877
JAN . 19, 1949

CHAMBERS
SISTER
MARGIE LEOLA
CHAMBERS
DEC. 8, 1898
JAN. 12, 1912

Noble & Kelsey: 4
Certificate Not Found

Gerard Howard
Died: 03/27/1961   Age: 58

NO MARKER
Certificate Not Found

Ellis, Mangum, & Fair
Funeral Home Record

Henry Howard

NO MARKER

Noble & Kelsey: 342

Malinda Howard
Died: 05/01/1955

Age: 55
Certificate No.0036,0178
Parents: James Smith & Lishia Andrews

UH-396 -I/J
Domestic

HOWARD
MALINDA HOWARD
DECEASED
MAY 1, 1955
IN MEMORY OF OUR MOTHER

Ellis, Mangum, & Fair

Informant: Mrs. Lorene Heath
Bpl.: Warthen, GA

Rev. William Henry Howard
Died: 02/17/1954   Age: 85
Wadesboro District, Western North Carolina Conference

Certificate No.0035,0192
Parents: ??

REV. WILLIAM H.
HOWARD
JUNE 6, 1869
FEB. 17, 1954

OK-127-N   Noble & Kelsey
Minister: AME ZION Church, Presiding Elder,

Informant: Aurther Howard
Bpl.: Wilmington, NC

Eliza Poe Howie
Died: 08/05/1919   Age: 36y4m29d
Certificate No.0007,0248
Parents: Richard Poe & Rosa Ramseur

OK-NO MARKER
Laundry Work
Informant: Alice Roberts
Bpl.: Salisbury, NC

Noble & Kelsey: 325

Gordon A. Hull
Died: 09/23/1968   Age: 48

AT REST
GORDON A. HULL
AUG. 11, 1920
SEPT. 23, 1968

BT-332 -I/J
Certificate Not Found

BURIALS

Francis Hunt
Died: 06/06/1913 Age: 09m.
Certificate No. 0001,0305

NO MARKER Summersett
INFANT
Parents: Robert Hunt & Mollie Dowel

Fred Robert Hunt
Died: 02/08/1986 Age: 82
Certificate No. 0066,0110
Parents: Robert & Lottie Hunt

UH-481-H MISSING Noble & Kelsey
Butler for Medical Doctor
Informant: Dr. Frank B. Marsh, Friend
    Bpl.: Rowan Co., NC

Julia Hunt
Died: 02/09/1929 Age: ∞ 49
Certificate No. 0017,0345
Parents: Sam Wallace & Tisha Ganies (Sic)

NO MARKER Noble & Kelsey
Housework @ Home
Informant: Thomas Hart
    Bpl.: Albemarle

Lizzie Benton Hunt
Died: 04/20/1924 Age: 46
Certificate No. 0012,0362
Parents: Prince Berton & Martha Ford

OK-NO MARKER Noble & Kelsey: 215
Cook
Informant: May Clement
    Bpl.: Rowan Co., NC

Charles Wilson Hunter
Died: 06/03/1988 Age: 69
Certificate No. 0068,0527
Parents: Hosea Diggs & Alice Hunter

BN-839-M MISSING Noble & Kelsey
Equipment Operator @ Lumber Company
Informant: Rev. Jimmy Hunter
    Bpl.: Wadesboro, NC

Josephine Kelsey Hunter
Died: 08/02/1941

OK-426-N Mitchell & Fair:
Certificate Not Found Funeral Home Record

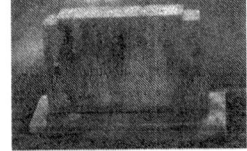

JOSEPHINE KELSEY
HUNTER
DIED AUG. 2, 1941
GOD IS AND ALL IS WELL.

Bishop Francis R. Ivey
Died: 07/01/1989 Age: 68

BN – P (Post 1996 survey) Mitchell & Fair
Minister Certificate Not Found

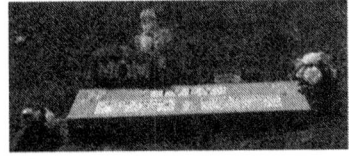

IVEY
MATTIE ABRAMS BISHOP FRANCIS R.
NOV. 9, 1934 OCT. 16, 1921
MAY 23, 2003 JULY 1, 1989

Mattie Abrams Ivey
Died: 05/23/03 Age: 69
(See Bishop Francis R. Ivey)

BN-P Noble & Kelsey
    Certificate Not Found

Arthur James Jackson
Died: 11/16/1957
Certificate No. 038,0295
Parents: Ned Jackson & Unknown

NO MARKER Noble & Kelsey
Bingham Lumber Company
Informant: Desie Mae Jackson, Wife
    Bpl.: NC

Israel Joseph Jackson
Died: 02/15/53 Age: 52
Certificate No.: 0034,0042
Parents: Henry Jackson &?????

NO MARKER Noble & Kelsey
Teacher: Livingstone High School - (1925-26 Cat.) & Bible
    History and Sunday school Teacher Training

Mattie Jackson
Died: 09/03/1981 Age: 75
Certificate No. 0061,0747
Parents: Henry Jackson & Unknown

NO MARKER Mitchell & Fair
Domestic
Informant: Mrs. Ionia Morrison
    Bpl.: Atlanta, GA

BURIALS

Pearl C. Jackson
Died: 11/17/1983   Age: 85

NO MARKER
Certificate Not Found

Mitchell & Fair
Funeral Home Record

Ellen James
Died: 07/28/1910
Certificate No.0004,0267
Parents: Henry Shaver &????

NO MARKER
Laundry
Informant: Annie James
   Bpl.: Salisbury

Noble & Kelsey

Alice B. Jamison
Died:03/16/1959   Age: 65

OK-339-I/J
Certificate Not Found

ALICE JAMISON
MAR. 9, 1884
MAR. 16, 1959

Effie Phifer Jamison
Died: 10/17/1982   Age: 77:

BT-235-K
Cook Lakewood Cafe

JAMISON
FRANCIS SYLVESTER
FEB. 23, 1900 - SEPT. 7, 1957
EFFIE PHIFER
SEPT. 11, 1905 -- OCT. 17, 1982

Francis Sylvester Jamison
Died:09/07/1957   Age: 57
Certificate No.0038,0178
Parents: Wade Jamison & Emma Pinkson

BT-235-K
Laborer, Southern Railroad
Informant: Mrs. Effie Jamison
   Bpl.: NC   (See Effie Phifer Jamison)

Noble & Kelsey

John Jamison
Died:04/10/1950   Age: 40
Certificate No.0032,0276
Parents: Judge Jamison & Hattie Segal

NO MARKER
Section hand for Southern Railroad
Informant: Ray Williams
   Bpl.: Clover, SC

Ambrose Leroy Jefferies
Died: 09/29/1967   Age: 80
Certificate No. 0047,0596

OK-193-L Jefferies Plot
Retired.Heartline Cleaners
Informant: Mrs. Doris Jones
Parents: Henry Jefferies & Unknown   Bpl.: Gaffney Co., SC

Noble & Kelsey

JEFFERIES
HIS WIFE
HATTIE C. ELLIOT   AMBROSE LEROY
FEB. 29, 1884   DEC. 3, 1881
OCT. 14, 1950   SEPT. 29, 1967
RESTING IN HOPE OF A GLORIOUS RESURRECTION

Hattie C. Elliot Jeffries
Died: 10/14/1950   Age: 66
Certificate No. 0032,0436
Parents: Luke Elliot & Sarah Horley

OK-193-L Plot
Housewife
Informant: Ambrose Jefferies
   Bpl.: Edenton, NC (See Ambrose Leroy)

BURIALS

Windsor H. Jefferies   OK-193-L Plot   Noble & Kelsey
Died: 03/08/1952   Age: 41
Certificate No. 0033,0067   **Informant:** Ambrosis(sic) Jefferies
Parents: Ambrose & Hattie Jefferies

<u>Family Plot</u>   JEFFERIES
JULY 28, 1910
MAR. 8, 1952
HE HAS GONE TO THE MANSIONS OF REST

Hallie Jefferson   NO MARKER   Noble & Kelsey: 201
Died: 10/14/58   Certificate Not Found

Ethel Beatrice Tucker Jeffrey   UH-406-I/J   Ellis, Mangum & Fair
Died: 08/15/1951   Age: 71
Certificate No. 0032,0869
Parents: George Tucker & Unkown

ETHEL TUCKER
JEFFREY
DIED AUG. 15, 1951
BELOVED "NANA" OF ADRIENNE & ELAINE LASH.

Alberta Moore Jenkins   OK-NO MARKER   Noble & Kelsey: 61
Died: 05/24/1911   Age: 24   Domestic
Certificate No. 0004,0102   **Informant:** E. K. Jenkins
Parents: Edward Moore MD & Serena L. Suggs

Granddaughter of Wesley Jenkins   NO MARKER   Summersett
Died: 11/25/1908   Age: INFANT

Henry Jenkins   OK-NO MARKER.   Noble & Kelsey: 44
Died: 07/08/1911   Age: 77   Hack man (Driver) Member of Soldiers Memorial
Certificate No. 0004, 0027   **Informant:** Laura Jenkins, Wife
Parents: Samson Hide & Mother Unknown   Bpl.: Iredell Co., NC

Laura Jenkins   NO MARKER
Died: 03/19/1911   Age: 27y08m07
Certificate No. 0004,0190   **Informant:** Bessie Walters
Parents: Ben Barger/Mary Sumner   Bpl.: Rowan Co. NC

Laura Jenkins   NO MARKER   Bingham, Carter, & Chesire
Died: 03/31/1926   Age: ∞78   Domestic
Certificate No. 00014,162   **Informant:** E. H. Jenkins
Parents: Unknown   Bpl.: Rowan Co., NC

Lillie Jenkins   OK-
Died: 08/07/1910   Age: 58   Certificate Not Found
     Off of pedestal – 08/15/03

LILLIE JENKINS
DIED AUG 7, 1910
AGE 58 YRS.
FAITHFUL UNTO DEATH

BURIALS

Willie Jenkins
Died: 12/01/1919   Age: 1y6m19d
Certificate No.0007,0104
Parents: Cale Jenkins & Jane Hunt

NO MARKER
CHILD
Informant: Jane Hunt
Bpl.: Rowan Co., NC

Noble & Kelsey: 346

Willie Mae Crockett Jenkins
Died:08/27/1990   Age: 59
Certificate No.0070,0736
Parents: Willie Crocket & Nellie Greenlee

UH-573-H
Housemaid @ Private homes
Informant: Pattie Ann Jenkins
Bpl.: Salisbury, NC

Noble & Kelsey

WILLIE MAE
JENKINS
JUNE 16, 1931
AUG. 27, 1990

Amanda Tucker Jennings
Died: 11/08/1988   Age: 56
Certificate No.0068,0960
Parents: Fred Tucker & Carrie Bell Ricks

BN-886-M

Informant: Johnie Tucker
Bpl.: Camden, SC

Mitchell & Fair

AMANDA T.
JENNINGS   JAN. 25, 1932
NOV. 8, 1988

Norris Thomas Jennings
Died:08/17/1985
Certificate No.0065,0685
Parents: Harry Jennings & Hattie Palmer

NO MARKER
Oiler @ Cannon Mills - Cotton Textiles
Informant: Amanda Tucker Jennings, Wife
Bpl.: Fairfield Co., SC

Noble & Kelsey

Arthur L. Jeter

OK-NO MARKER
Student

Noble & Kelsey: 99
Certificate Not Found

Florence Jeter
Died:05/15/1930   Age: 53
Certificate No.0018,0237
Parents: Unknown & Martha George

OK-NO MARKER
Domestic, Housework
Informant: Mary Ellen Croom
Bpl.: Patterson Springs, NC

Noble & Kelsey: 99

Andrew Johnson
Died:08/10/1965   Age: 74
Certificate No.0045,0411
Parents: Robert Johnson & Ellen Unknown

NO MARKER
Mill Worker
Informant: Edna Johnson, Wife
Bpl.: Mecklenburg Co., NC

Ellis, Mangum & Fair

Annie Johnson
Died:04/01/1908   Age: 14 yrs.

NO MARKER

Summersett
Funeral Home Record

Cicero Johnson
Died: 06/20/1924   Age: ∞39
Certificate No. 0012,0505
Parents: Father?, Charlotte Crowell

NO MARKER
Chain Gang for Rowan County
Informant: Mary Johnson, Wife
Bpl.:Salisbury, NC

Summersett

BURIALS

David Allen Johnson UH-526-H Noble & Kelsey
Died:03/26/1972   Age: 85   Retired
Certificate No.0052,0253   **Informant:** Mrs. Didelia B. Johnson
Parents: Postelle Johnson & Elvie Murphy   Bpl.: SC

DAVID ALLEN
JOHNSON, JR.
JAN. 16, 1917
SEPT. 18, 1952
NOT OUR WILL, BUT
THINE BE DONE

Dock Johnson BN-775-P Ellis, Mangum & Fair
Died: 1944   Age: ∞83   Certificate Not Found Funeral Home Record

JOHNSON
ESTHER JOHNSON   DOCK JOHNSON
1866 -- 1952   1861 -- 1944

Dupree Johnson BT-274-K Noble & Kelsey
Died:05/11/1961   Age: 48   Laborer @ Southern Railroad Co.
Certificate No.0041,0534   **Informant:** Naomi P. Johnson, Wife
Parents: Jesse Johnson & Mary Tabor   Bpl.: Georgia

JOHNSON
DUPREE JOHNSON
DEC. 1, 1912
MAY 11, 1961
I FROM PAIN AND SORROW FREE,
LIVE FOREVERMORE WITH THEE.

Esther Sarah Johnson BN-774-P Ellis, Mangum & Fair
Died:04/16/1952   Age: 87   Domestic
Certificate No. 0033,0200
Parents: Unknown & June Gray
(See Dock Johnson)

J. T. Johnson BN-883-M
Died:04/17/1983   Age: 69   Certificate Not Found

J. T. JOHNSON
JULY 5,   APRIL 17,
1914   1983

James H. Johnson OK-158-O Noble & Kelsey: 121
Died: 10/04/1931   Age: 57 Certificate Not Found   Treasurer of Livingstone College &
principal of Livingstone High School before it was phased out

JAMES H.
JOHNSON
DIED OCT. 4, 1931
AGE 57 YRS.
HE IS NOT DEAD BUT SLEEPETH

BURIALS

Jarrie Martin Johnson
Died: 12/07/1947   Age: 56
Certificate No.0030,1013
Parents: Fred Martin & Henrietta Summers

NO MARKER
Housework
Informant: Susie Johnson

Jesse James Johnson
Died: 10/23/1955   Age: 65

UH-417-H

Certificate No.0036,0438   **Informant:** Dupree Johnson
Parents: Richard Johnson & Caroline Clark   Bpl.: Madison Co., GA

JESSE JAMES
JOHNSON
MAY 2, 1889
OCT. 23, 1955
" HE THAT BELIEVETH ON ME HATH EVERLASTING LIFE."

John Johnson
Died:01/04/1909   Age: 35 yrs.
Parents: Unknown

NO MARKER

Summersett
Funeral Home Record

Julius Percival Johnson
Died: 11/19/1986   Age: 84
Certificate No.0066,1014

UH-376 -I/J   Noble & Kelsey
6th Minister: Trinity Presbyterian Church, Salisbury, NC
Informant: Nonie F. Johnson, 2NDWife
Parents: Peter P. Johnson & Lula Amie   Bpl.: Robeson Co., NC

JOHNSON
REV. JULIUS P.
DEC. 20, 1901
NOV. 19, 1986

Lillie Johnson
Died: 12/21/1961   Age: 69
Certificate No.0042,0231
Parents: Bird Coplen & Susan Davis

NO MARKER
Domestic
Informant: Susie C. Smith
Bpl.: SC

Ellis, Mangum & Fair

Lillie Johnson
Died:05/12/1952   Age: 70
Parents: Silas McDonald & Pollie Pearson

NO MARKER

bd. 07/27/1881

Ellis, Mangum & Fair
Funeral Home Record

Lizzie Lewis Johnson

UH-487-H   Ellis, Mangum & Fair
Died:05/04/1947   Age: 50   Domestic   Funeral Home Record
Parents: Ned Lewis & Harriet Lipscombe   bd.10/28/1896

LIZZIE LEWIS
WIFE OF
ANDY JOHNSON
OCT. 27, 1897
MAY 4, 1947

Lottie Johnson
Died:01/28/1912   Age: 25 yrs
Certificate No. 0001,0093
Parents: John McCall Johnson

NO MARKER   Summersett

BURIALS

Lucious Johnson
Died: 12/28/1942   Age: 57
Certificate No.0028,0450
Parents: Wyatt Johnson & Susan Hinton

NO MARKER
Blacksmith Helper
Informant: Jannie Johnson
   Bpl.: Chester, SC

Noble & Kelsey: 137

Melvin Johnson

UH-636-G   MISSING

Mildred Jordan Parham Johnson
Died:06/28/1947   Age: 31
Certificate No.0030,0883
Parents: Joseph Jordan & Lula Jones

OK-176 -O   Duncan Sr, Plot
Domestic
Informant: Lena Duncan
   Bpl.: Philadelphia, PA

Ellis, Mangum & Fair

MILDRED JORDAN
PARHAM JOHNSON
APRIL 28, 1916
JUNE 27, 1947
BELOVED MOTHER

Nonie Fisher Springs Johnson
Died:02/08/1996   Age: 92

BN-017-M   Noble & Kelsey
Elementary School Teacher: Salisbury Schools, 2ND Wife
   of J. P. Johnson & a founder of The Lend a Hand
   Club @ Trinity Presbyterian Church

Certificate No. 0076,0194
Parents: John Fisher & Josie Partee

Informant: Luella J. Graves, Greensboro, NC
   Bpl.: Rowan Co., NC

NONIE SPRINGS
JOHNSON
JUNE 12, 1903
FEB. 8, 1996

Thomas W. Johnson
Died:05/25/1956   Age: 71

NO MARKER

Ellis, Mangum & Fair
Funeral Home Record

Velma Branch Johnson

BN-741-M (Broken Curb 08/24/03)   Noble & Kelsey

Died: 11/11/1937   Age: 24
Certificate No.0025,0273
Parents: Will Branch & Frances Davidson

Housework
Informant: Frank Johnson
Bpl.: York Co., SC

VELMA BRANCH
JOHNSON
DEC. 6. 1913
NOV. 10, 1937

Walter Louis Johnson
Died:09/22/1949   Age: 59
Certificate No.0031,0993
Parents: Unknown

BN-831-M   Noble & Kelsey
Porter, Southern Railway
Informant: Annie J. Johnson

JOHNSON
WALTER L. JOHNSON
MAY 13, 1890
SEPT. 22, 1949
GONE BUT NOT FORGOTTEN

Washington Johnson
Died:01/16/1915   Age: ∞72
Certificate No.0002,0085
Parents: UNKNOWN

NO MARKER   Noble & Kelsey: 24
Day Laborer
Informant: Henry Johnson
   Bpl.: Cabarrus Co., NC

BURIALS

John R. Johnston
Died: 02/18/1911   Age: 25
Certificate No. 0004,0152
Parents: John & Mary Sterling

NO MARKER
Tailor
Informant: Wife
  Bpl.: Chester, SC

Noble & Kelsey

Adline Curry Jones
Died: 10/23/1964   Age: 89

Certificate No.0044,0585

OK-028-N
Retired, Board of Education
between 1914 - 1919
Informant: A. R. Kelsey

Noble & Kelsey: 54
Once ran private school

Parents: John Robinson & Laura Curry

ADLINE C. JONES
JULY 8, 1875
OCT. 23, 1964

Alice Nicholson Jones
Died: 11/22/1979   Age: 78   Certificate Not Found

UH 439-H

JONES
LEE CLARENCE   ALICE NICHOLSON
SEPTEMBER 2, 1895   MARCH 25, 1901
OCTOBER 27, 1961   NOVEMBER 22, 1979
RESTING IN THE HOPE OF A GLORIOUS RESURRECTION

Arthur Jones
Died: 11/27/1909   Age: 22 yrs.
Certificate No. 0004,0452
Parents: Unknown

NO MARKER

Informant: Arthur Carter
  Bpl.: Atlanta, Ga.

Summersett

Carrie Lena Jones
Died: 11/21/1955   Age: 55
Certificate No.0036,0499
Parents: Hercules Smith & Sujette Harris

UH-498-H
1ST Wife of Bishop R. L. Jones
Informant: Bishop R. L. Jones, Husband
  Bpl.: SC

Noble & Kelsey

CARRIE LENA
WIFE OF
BISHOP R. L. JONES
APR. 28, 1900 -- NOV. 21, 1955

Courtney M. Harris Jones
Died:08/06/1993   Age: 64
Certificate No.0073,0732

UH-610-G
Winder @ Cotton Mill
Informant: Alice H. Jones

Noble & Kelsey

Parents: George Harris & Alice Lindsay   Bpl.: Rockwell Co., NC

APR. 10,   FROM   AUG. 6,
1929   LOVED   1993
          ONES
COURTY M. HARRIS JONES

Daisey Jones
Died: 10/29/1918   Age: ∞ 32
Certificate No.: 0006,0542
Parents: Daniel Pierce & Sara Reeves

NO MARKER
Housewife
Informant: Umphrey Jones
  Bpl.: Salisbury, NC

Noble & Kelsey

BURIALS

Edna Marie Jones
Died:04/30/1967   Age: 16
Parents: Willie C. Jones & Alberta Robinson

NO MARKER

Mitchell & Fair
Funeral Home Record

Ellen Jones
Died:07/28/1910   Age: 60
Parents: Henry Shaver & Not Given
Register of Death, Salisbury, Co. of Rowan, NC (09/1909-10/11/1911)

NO MARKER
Informant: Annie James
   Bpl.: Salisbury, NC

Ernest Maurice Jones
Died:04/16/1994   Age: 28
Certificate No.0074,0400
Parents: Ernest J. Lockett & Marion Jones

BN-688-G   MISSING
Cook @ College
Informant: Marion V. Jones
   Bpl.: Manhattan, NY

Noble & Kelsey

Gabe Jones
Died: 11/18/1939   Age: 65

BN-766-P
Certificate Not Found

GABE JONES
BORN
JULY 25, 1874
DIED
NOV. 18, 1939
AGE 65 YRS.
3 MOS, 23 DYS

Henry (Red) Jones
Died:05/02/1951   Age: 36

BN-874-M
Certificate Not Found

JONES
HENRY (RED) JONES
APR. 7, 1915
MAY 2, 1951

I. Jones
Died:05/18/1915   Age: 10 days
Certificate Not Found
Parents: Edward Jones & Hortense Tinnen

NO MARKER
INFANT
Informant: Hortense Jones
   Bpl.: Salisbury, NC

Noble & Kelsey

John Elvester Jones
Died: 10/30/1938   Age: ∞30
Certificate No. 0026,0253
Parents: George & Caroline Jones

BN-P
Hospital Orderly
Informant Alice Jones, Wife
   Bpl.: Laurence, SC

Noble & Kelsey

JOHN E.
JONES
DIED
OCT. 30, 1938
AGE
ABOUT 30 YEARS
DYING BUT
GOING HOME

BURIALS

Julius Jackson Jones
Died: 01/11/1958   Age: 67
Certificate No.0038,0412
Parents: Felix Jones & Unknown

OK-029-N
Retired: Jones Cafe: 828 W. Horah Street
Informant: Adline Jones, Wife
   Bpl.: NC

Noble & Kelsey: 54

JONES
JULIUS J.
1891 – 1958

L. V. Jones
Died: 06/03/1956   Age: 56

NO MARKER

Ellis, Magnum, & Fair
Funeral Home Record

Latisha Elizabeth Jones
Died: 01/27/1984   Age: 4mos.
Certificate No.0064,0078
Parents: Larry Jones & Tammy Davis

NO MARKER
INFANT
Informant: Larry Jones, Father
   Bpl.: Rowan Co., NC

Mitchell & Fair

Lee Clarence Jones
Died: 01/27/1961   Age: 66
(See Alice Nicholson Jones)

UH-439-H
Dentist

Certificate Not Found

Mary Heilig Jones
Died: 11/02/1992   Age: 67
Certificate No.0072,0923
Parents: Arch Heilig & Unknown

UH-629-G   MISSING
Sweeper @ Cotton Mill
Informant: Tammy Kirkley
   Bpl.: Rowan Co., NC

Noble & Kelsey

Minnie C. Jones
Died: 08/16/1983   Age: 90
Certificate No.0063,0640
Parents: Archie & Mattie Carough

NO MARKER
Homemaker
Informant: Mrs. Willie Mae McDaniel, Guardian-
   Bpl.: Jackson Co., GA

Mitchell & Fair

Mrs. Ida Jones
Died: 06/03/1928   Age: Unknown
Certificate No.0016,0363
Parents: UNKNOWN

NO MARKER
Cook
Informant: W. F. Kelsey
   Bpl.: UNKNOWN

Noble & Kelsey: 83

Robert M. Jones
Died: 12/26/1986   Age: 58
Certificate No.0063,1019
Parents: Unknown & Lula Trillon

NO MARKER
Retired Mill Worker
Informant: Julia B. Jones, Wife
   Bpl.: Newberry, SC

Mitchell & Fair

George W. Judge
Died: 02/13/1963   Age: 50
Certificate No.0043,0136
Parents: Quary Judge & Fannie Cherry

NO MARKER
Laborer
Informant: Annie Pitts
   Bpl.: Chester Co., SC

Ellis, Mangum & Fair

Arthur C. Kelly
Died: 12/25/1967   Age: 78
Certificate No.0047,0742
Parents: Nathaniel Kelly & Unknown

BT-312-K
Retired
Informant: A.G. Kelly
   Bpl.: Union Co., SC

Noble & Kelsey

BURIALS

Daisy Lyles Kelly
Died: 10/06/1986 Age: 47

BT-254-K
Certificate Not Found

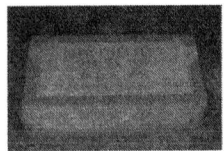

DAISY LYLES KELLY
FEB. 23, 1939
OCT. 6, 1986
IN LOVING MEMORY YOUR SONS & FAMILY

Eula Kelly
Died: 03/24/1975 Age: 61

OK-359-I/J
Certificate Not Found

EULA KELLY
MAR. 1. 1914
MAR. 24, 1975

Grace H. Kelly
Died: 08/08/1950 Age: 53

UH-477-H
Housewife
Certificate No. 0032,0385
Parents: Lewis Hargrave & Mary Clodfelter

Noble & Kelsey

Informant: James Kelly Sr.
Bpl.: Davidson Co., NC

GRACE H. KELLY
OCT. 4, 1897
AUG. 8, 1950

James S. Kelly
Died: 06/18/1979 Age: 86

UH-476-H
Certificate Not Found

JAMES KELLY
APR. 27, 1893
JUNE 18, 1979

Margarine Margie Kelly
Died: 02/19/1988 Age: 75
Certificate No. 0068,0178

BN-008-M
Never Worked

Noble & Kelsey

Informant: Geronia Drain
Parents: Arthur Kelly & Pettie Littlejohn Bpl.: Rowan Co., NC

MARGARINE MARGIE
KELLY
MAY 1, 1912
FEBRUARY 19, 1988

Marie A. Davis Kelly
Died: 10/16/1949 Age: 54
Certificate No. 0031,0722
Parents: Leon Davis & Addie Todd
(See Vivian Ray Davis)

OK-129-N
Teacher
Informant: Louis Kelly
Bpl.: Philidelphia, PA

Noble & Kelsey: 9

Mary Kelly
Died: 1966 Age: 72

UH-509-H

Noble & Kelsey
Funeral Home Marker

MRS. MARY KELLY
1894   1966
NOBLE AND KELSEY

BURIALS

Mr. Savannah Kelly
Died: 06/19/1982   Age: 85
Certificate No.0062,0487
Parents: James & Bertha Kelly

UH-434-H
Laborer @ Southern Railroad
Informant: Doris M. Roberts, Granddaughter
Bpl.: Union Co., SC

Noble & Kelsey

SAVANNAH K.
KELLY
OCT. 22, 1896
JUNE 19, 1982
AT REST

S. L. Kelly
Died: 09/03/1926   Age: 1yr., 6 mos., 23 days
Certificate No. 0014,0287
Parents: Early Kelly & Ida Bell Hall

OK
Baby Boy
Informant: Early Kelly, Father
Bpl.: Salisbury, NC

Noble & Kelsey

Alex Kelsey
Died: 05/23/1905   Age: 80   Died before Records were kept

OK-428-N

Noble & Kelsey

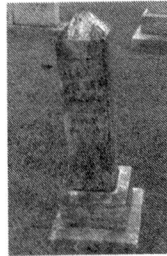

ALEX KELSEY
BORN
MAY. 15, 1825
DIED
MAY 23, 1905
Asleep in Jesus,
blessed sleep, From which never ever wake to weep

Alexander Spaulding Kelsey
Died: 10/19/1908   Age: 61

OK-428-N

Noble & Kelsey

KELSEY
ALEXANDER SPAULDING
KELSEY
OCT. 19, 1908
MAY 29, 1969

Amanda Banks Kelsey
Died: 07/17/1911   Age: 76
Certificate No.0004,0034
Parents: Moses Banks & Lucinda Rosebough

OK-427-N
Domestic
Informant: W. F. Kelsey
Bpl.: SC   bd. **07/09/1835**

Noble & Kelsey

MRS.
AMANDA
KELSEY
DIED
JULY 17,
1911
AGE 76 YRS.

BURIALS

Amanda Lucille Kelsey OK-421-N Noble & Kelsey
Died: 12/03/1915   Age: 1 yr. 9 mos.   Baby
Certificate No.0002,0271:   **Informant:** W. F. Kelsey
Parents: W. F. Kelsey & Lula Spaulding   Bpl.: Salisbury, NC

A. LUCILE KELSEY
DIED DEC. 3, 1915
AGE 1 YR. 9 MOS.
Our darling baby.

Harvey Alexander Kelsey OK-429-N Noble & Kelsey
Died:01/10/1944   Age: 82y07m23d   Postal Clerk, Government Office
Certificate No.0029,0070   **Informant:** W. F. Kelsey
Parents: Alexander Kelsey & Amanda Clark   Bpl.: Chester Co., SC

HARVEY A. KELSEY
MAY 18, 1861
JAN. 10, 1944

Lula Spaulding Kelsey OK-425-N Noble & Kelsey
Died:04/09/1947   Age: 66   Mortician, Undertaker, and First Lady embalmer in the State of North Carolina. President of the State Federation of Negro Women's Clubs
Certificate No.0030,0823   **Informant:** A.R. Kelsey, Son
Parents: John & Lucy Ann Spaulding
Bpl.: Bladen Co., NC

WIFE
LULA SPAULDING KELSEY
AUG. 26, 1881
APR. 9, 1947

William Francis Kelsey OK-424-N Noble & Kelsey: 80
Died:02/15/1944   Age: 76   Mortician, Barber, & Umbrella Repairman. Leader of the Negro Civic League, President of the Kelsey Burial Association
Certificate No.0029,0092   **Informant:** Lula S. Kelsey
Parents: Alexander Kelsey & Amanda Kelsey   Bpl.: Chester Co., SC

HUSBAND
WILLIAM F. KELSEY
JUNE 28, 1867
FEB. 15, 1944

Alexander Spaulding Kelsey Jr. OK-N NO MARKER Noble & Kelsey
Died:08/09/1930   Age: 13 days   INFANT
Certificate No.0018,0293   **Informant:** Alexander Kelsey
Parents: Alexander Kelsey & Gertrude Halloway   Bpl.: Salisbury, NC

Hattie Anderson Kendall UH-637-G
Died:08/25/1992   Age: 69   Certificate Not Found

HATTIE ANDERSON
KENDALL
AUG. 15, 1923
AUG. 25, 1992

BURIALS

Annie Letitia Kennedy
Died:07/29/1911   Age: 01y09m15d
Certificate No.0004,0046
Parents: John Kennedy & Annie L. Moore

OK-069-N MISSING
Baby
Informant: E. Moore
 Bpl.: NC

Noble & Kelsey

Annie Moore Kennedy
Died:08/30/1942   Age: 59

OK-069-N
Certificate Not Found

Noble & Kelsey: 60

ANNIE L. MOORE
WIFE OF
REV. J. E. KENNEDY
FEB. 23, 1883
08/30/1942
KENNEDY
Back
A star has faded away in the night but the light of that star lives on.

Rev. J. E. Kennedy Sr.
Died:05/05/1944   Pastor

OK-068-N
Certificate Not Found

Noble & Kelsey: 60

REV. J. E. KENNEDY
DIED MAY 5, 1944
Blue Ribbon Aux Board
Hood Temple A. M. E. Zion

Charles Kenny
Died: 03/07/1930   Age.: ??
Certificate No. 00018,0186
Parents Unknown

NO MARKER
Truck man
Informant: T. V. Mangum
 Bpl Unknown

Fraternal Funeral Home

Caroline Kent
Died:03/08/1929 Age: ∞76 Certificate Not Found
 Condition on 08/18/03

OK-N   broken marble headstone

Noble & Kelsey: 300

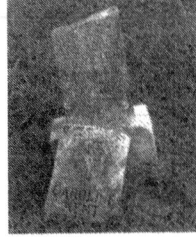

CAROLINE
KENT
DIED
MAR. 8 1929
AGE ABOUT
76 YEARS
A sleep in Jesus

Pleasant Kent (Male)
Died: 06/12/1918   Age: 67 ,9 ,18
Certificate No. 0006,0450
Parents: William Kent & Elijah Valentine

NO MARKER
Farmer
Informant: Caroline Kent, Wife
 Bpl.: Davie Co., NC

Noble & Kelsey

Brutus Kerns
Died:02/21/1955   Age: 72
Parents: Adam Kerns

NO MARKER
Laborer @ NC Finishing Co.

Ellis, Mangum & Fair
Funeral Home Record

Ella Hobson Kerns
Died:02/16/1942   Age: 45
Certificate No.0028,0243
Parents: Adam Hobson & Lucinda Barber

NO MARKER
Housewife
Informant: Brutus Kerns, Husband
 Bpl.: Davie Co., NC

Ellis, Mangum & Fair

James Bernard Kerr
Died: 11/13/1996   Age: 44

UH-
Certificate Not Found

BURIALS

Sussie Key
Died: 06/23/1960   Age: 28

NO MARKER
Funeral Home Record

Noble & Kelsey Map

Inez Rivers King
Died: 07/06/1991   Age: 76
Certificate No. 0071,0610
Parents: Reuben Benjamin Rivers & Daughter Mack

UH-599-G
Cook @ Restaurant
Informant: Mary R. Thompson
Bpl.: Cornesville, GA

Mitchell & Fair

INEZ R. KING
JULY 13, 1915
JULY 6, 1991

Janie Efrium King
Died: 12/19/1957   Age: 71
Certificate No. 0038,0352
Parents: Peter Ephram & Unknown

OK-331-K
Housewife
Informant: Daisey Gregg
Bpl.: Blacksville, SC

Noble & Kelsey

Toleda Elease Kiser
Died: 05/18/1981   Age: 1-Hour
Certificate No. 0061,0458   **Informant:** James N. Kiser, Father
Parents: James N. Kiser & Addie Bryant   Bpl.: Rowan Co., NC

BN-728-M
INFANT

Noble & Kelsey

TOLEDA ELEASE
KISER
MAY 18, 1981
MAY 18, 1981

Amanda Lucinda Knox
Died: 03/11/1943   Age: 98
Certificate No. 0028,0743
Parents: UNKNOWN

NO MARKER
Domestic
Informant: Mrs. Mary O. Lincoln
Bpl.: Mocksville, NC

Ellis, Mangum & Fair

Columbus C. Knox
Died: 12/24/1915   Age: 31 Certificate Not Found
Condition on 08/15/03

OK- N

COLUMBUS
C. KNOX
MAY 11, 1884
DEC. 24, 1915

Ella Knox
Died: 11/06/1912   Age: 2y3m3d
Certificate No. 0001,0255
Parents: Robert Earnhardt & Pollie Standard

OK-NO MARKER
CHILD
Informant: Martin
Bpl.: Salisbury

Noble & Kelsey: 134

Emma Knox
Died: 08/04/1930   Age: 52
Certificate No. 0018,0339
Parents: Not Given & Annie Steel

OK-NO MARKER
Domestic
Informant: Creola Knox
Bpl.: NC

Noble & Kelsey: 129

BURIALS

Henry Knox
Died:07/09/1971   Age: 56
Certificate No.0051,0427
Parents: James Knox & Hattie Wright

OK-NO MARKER
Southern Converting Company
Informant: Mrs. Hattie Sims
   Bpl.: NC

Noble & Kelsey: 129

Infant of Lewis Walker Knox
Died: 11/07/1910   Age: 1 mth. 2 days
Parents: Lewis & Della Knox

OK-NO MARKER
Certificate Not Found.

INFANT Son

Julia Butler Knox
Died:01/20/1969   Age: 58

OK-106-N
Certificate Not Found.

KNOX
JULIA BUTLER KNOX
MAY 25, 1911
JAN. 20, 1969

Otis Knox
Died: 11/17/1993   Age: 73
Certificate No.0073,1062
Parents: George S. Knox & Janie Thomas

UH-645-G
Worked @ Cotton Mill
Informant: Margaret K. Archie
   Bpl.: Rock Hill, SC

Noble & Kelsey

Elizabeth Duncan Koontz
Died:01/06/1989   Age: 70   Educator, President of NEA, Under Secretary of Labor
Certificate No.0069,0017   Informant: Carl T. Duncan
Parents: Samuel E. Duncan Sr. & Lena B. Jordan

OK-176-O Duncan Sr. Plot   Noble & Kelsey

KOONTZ
ELIZABETH DUNCAN   HARRY LEE
JUNE 3, 1919   NOV. 1, 1914
JAN. 6, 1989   APR. 21, 1986

Harry Lee Koontz
Died:04/21/1986   Age: 72

OK-176-O Duncan Sr. Plot   Noble & Kelsey
Certificate Not Found
Educator: First African American teacher elected as a
   faculty member of Lutheran College, Greensboro,
NC , Coach at Dunbar High School in E. Spencer, NC

(See Elizabeth Duncan Koontz)

James Eddie Koontz
Died: 11/10/1993   Age: 77
Certificate No.0073,1039
Parents: George Koontz & Lena Boyd

UH-660-G
Truck Driver @ Retail fuel oil & Coal
Informant: Doretha W. Scarborough
   Bpl.: Rowan Co., NC

Noble & Kelsey

Lonnie Wilson Koontz
Died: 11/16/1981   Age: 83

BN-800-M
Certificate Not Found

LONNIE WILSON
KOONTZ
SEPT. 21, 1898
NOV. 16, 1981

Florence Pemberton Krider
Died:07/24/1947   Age: 18y10m16d
Parents: Willie Pemberton & Florence Wise

UH- I/J Fair SubSec
Domestic

Ellis, Mangum & Fair
Funeral Home Record

BURIALS

Abna Aggrey Lancaster
Died: 01/09/97   Age: 89

OK-N *NO MARKER (Yet)*   Noble & Kelsey: 53
Retired High School & College Teacher
[Price High School-Livingstone College]
Certificate No.0077,0060 **Informant:** Raemi Lancaster Evans, Daughter
Parents: James Emman Kwegyir Aggrey & Rose Rudolph Douglas Aggrey
Bpl.: Salisbury, NC

Aggrey Family Plot w curb
In Family curb Containing sister Rosebud, Mother Rose, aunt Hattie Whyte, Father James Aggrey, and Husband Spencer Wellington Lancaster

Spencer Wellington Lancaster
Died: 01/10/1996   Age: 91

OK-N *NO MARKER (Yet)*.   Noble & Kelsey: 53
Retired Price High School Teacher &
former principal of Bear Poplar Elementary School
Certificate No.0076,0061 **Informant:** Abna A. Lancaster, Wife
Parents: Spencer Wellington Lancaster & Hattie Johnson
Bpl.: New London Co., CT

Aggrey Family Plot w curb
In Family curb Containing sister-in-law; Rosebud, Mother-in-law Rose Aggrey, aunt Hattie Whyte, Father-in-law James Aggrey, and next to wife Abna

Emma Land
Died: 02/10/1925 Age: none given
Certificate No. 0013,0278
Parents: Jerry Coleman &??

NO MARKER   Bingham & Carter
Housewife
Informant: Charles Land
Bpl.: SC

Dora Hoover Lanear
Died: 05/29/1990   Age: ∞72
Certificate No.0070,0437

UH-565-H   Noble & Kelsey
Homemaker
Informant: Evelyn Johnson
Parents: William Pinkney Hoover & Maude Scott   Bpl.: Rowan Co., NC

IN LOVING MEMORY OF MOTHER
DORA HOOVER
LANEAR
OCT. 21, 1918
MAY 29, 1990

Emma J. Hancock Laney
Died: 12/03/1998   Age: 95
Certificate No.0078,1180
Parents: Richard E. HanCock & Sarah Barns

UH-453-H   Noble & Kelsey
Teacher, School System
Informant: Darrell Hancock
Bpl.: Lancaster Co., SC

LANEY
EMMA J. HANCO.CK
OCT. 27, 1903
DEC. 3, 1998
THERE'S A GARDEN WHERE JESUS IS WAITING AND HE BIDS YOU TO
CO.ME MEET HIM THE RE JUST TO BOW AND RECEIVE E A NEW
BLESSING IN THE BEAUTIFUL GARDEN OF PRAYER.

BURIALS

Mayzonetta Grundy Lash
Died: 12/24/1967   Age: ∞81:

UH-405-H
Industrial Dept. @ Livingstone College in 1905,
Housewife, and geocery store owner

(See Wiley Hezikiah Lash for picture of monument)

LASH

OUR
BELOVED
FATHER AND PASTOR
THE REVEREND WILEY H. LASH
NOV. 13, 1880
JUNE 12, 1950

OUR BELOVED MOTHER
COUNSELOR AND CONTINUING
INSPIRATION
MAYZONETTA GRUNDY
WIFE OF REV. WILEY H. LASH
MAY 30, 1886
DEC. 24, 1967

Wiley Hezikiah Lash
Died:06/12/1950   Age: 69

UH-405-H   Ellis, Mangum & Fair
Lutheran Minister & Teacher @ St. John's Lutheran
School 1905
Certificate No.0032,0342
Parents: Jacob Lash & Eliza Oglesby   Bpl.: Kernersville, NC

(See Mayzonetta Grundy Lash for inscription)

Kenderick R. Dawan Lassiter
Died:08/11/1994   Certificate Not Found

UH-533-H
INFANT

KENDERICK RASHEEN DAWAN
INFANT SON
OF
CELESTINE LASSITER
APR. 20, 1994
AUG. 11, 1994

Annie B. Shaver Lawrence
Died:03/10/1914   Age: 58y6m11d
Certificate No.0001,0758
Parents: Levi Saver & Carolina Carr

OK-NO MARKER -   Noble & Kelsey: 55
Housewife, Domestic
Informant: Jennie E. Hargrave
Bpl.: Salisbury, NC

Annie Henderson Lawrence
Died:03/10/1913   Age: 58

OK-082-N
Certificate Not Found
Condition on 04/23/03

ANNIE HENDERSON
LAWRENCE
Sept. 29, 1855
Mar. 10, 1913
A tender mother and a faithful friend

Ervin Vinson Leach
Died:01/08/1994   Age: 89
Certificate No.0074,0012
Parents: UNKNOWN

BN-650-G   Noble & Kelsey
Farmer @ Own Farm
Informant: Vivian A. Norman
Bpl.: Iredell Co., NC

LEACH

LOIS I. HINSON BROWN
MAY 25, 1914
MAR. 25, 1994

ALLISON ERVIN VINSON "JACK"
OCT. 30, 1905
JAN. 8, 1994

BURIALS

Lois I. Hinson B. Allison Leach
Died: 05/25/1994 Age: 79
Certificate No.0074,0323
Parents: Ned Hinson & Annie Leake

BN-649-G
Homemaker @ Own Home
Informant: Vivian Norman
  Bpl.: Anson, NC

Noble & Kelsey

(see Ervin Vinson Leach)

Samuel Leach
Died: 02/07/1909 Age: 13 yrs.

NO MARKER

Summersett

Silas Leach Jr.
Died: 08/05/1931 Age: 12
Certificate No. 0019,0120
Parents: Silas Leach/Sallie Reid

BN-019-M
School Boy
Informant: Sallie Leach, Mother

Noble & Kelsey

SILAS
LEACH JR.
JUNE 30, 1919
AUG. 5, 1931
Budded on earth
to bloom in Heaven

Virginia Leach
Died: 01/06/1926 Age: 23
Certificate No. 0024,0532
Parents: Silas Leach & Sallie Dans

BN-020-M
Domestic
Informant: Sallie Leach
Bpl.: York Co., SC

Noble & Kelsey

VIRGINIA
LEACH
DEC. 12, 1912
JAN. 16, 1936
Tis sunbeam from the world has vanished

Pattie Leak
Died: 06/08/1942 Age: 75
Certificate No.0028,0316
Parents: UNKNOWN

OK- N
Laundress
Informant: Alice Kelly

Noble & Kelsey

MRS. PATTIE
LEAK
DIED
JUNE 8, 1942
AGE 75 YRS.
Asleep in Jesus

Will Leazer
Died: 01/20/1910 Age: 17
Certificate No.0004,0469
Parents: Dave Leazer & Unknown

NO MARKER
Rail roader
Informant: Green White
  Bpl.: Mecklenburg Co., NC

Noble & Kelsey: 300

Betty Lee
Died: 05/15/1915 Age: 34
Certificate No. 0002,0152
Parents: Moses Chambers & Julia

NO MARKER
Dressmaker
Informant: John W. Lee
  Bpl.: Rowan Co., NC

Noble & Kelsey

Emma Lee
Died: 04/11/1954 Age: 70
Certificate No.0035,0195
Parents: John Wells & Unknown

NO MARKER
Domestic
Informant: Mrs. Otelia Summer

Ellis, Magnum, & Fair

BURIALS

John Wesley Lee
Died: 02/27/1922   Age: ∞49
Certificate No.0010,0321
Parents: John Wesley Lee & Betsy Ann McFadden

NO MARKER
Blacksmith Helper @ Southern Railway Shops
Informant: E. Spurgeon Lee
Bpl.: Caswell, Co., NC

Noble & Kelsey: 325

Livonia Clark Lee
Died: 12/30/1954   Age: 54
Certificate Not Found
Parents: James Muskelley & Louise Love

NO MARKER
Domestic

Ellis, Mangum, & Fair
Funeral Home Record

Lucille Hoke Legree

Died: 05/23/1964   Age: ∞52

BN-725-M

Certificate Not Found

LUCILLE HOKE
LEGREE
APR. 23, 1912
MAY 23, 1964

Ethel Lewis

OK-175-O MISSING

Noble & Kelsey: 90

Rena Lewis
Died: 03/02/1928   Age: ∞36
Condition on 08/19/03

OK-186-O
Certificate Not Found marble grvstn on ground

RENA LEWIS
BORN -1892
DIED MAR. 2, 1928
Buellah Chamber – G 147
Salisbury, NC

LillieFord   Certificate Not Found

BT-301-K

LILLIEFORD

Julius Lindsay
Died: 04/02/1911   Age: 27yrs.
Certificate No. 0004,0194
Parents: Julius Lindsay & Lizzie Holman

NO MARKER
Laborer
Informant: Alice Lindsay

Robt. (Robert) Lindsey
Died: 10/12/1909   Age: 40 yrs.

NO MARKER
Certificate Not Found

Summersett
Funeral Home Record

Calvin Henry Lineburger
Died: 08/11/1993   Age: ∞41
Certificate No.0073,0762
Parents: John Henry Lineberger & Hester Hall

UH-663-G
Cook @ Restaurant
Informant: James Lineberger
Bpl.: Rowan Co., NC

Noble & Kelsey

CALVIN HENRY LINEBUGER
BORN OCT. 11 1951
DIED AUG. 11 1993

BURIALS

Cynthia Denette Lineberger OK-179-O Plot Noble & Kelsey 115
Died: 11/21/1962 Age: 7 CHILD
Certificate No.0042,0782 **Informant:** Mrs. Hester Lineberger
Parents: J. H. Lineberger & Hester Bpl.: Salisbury, NC
Lineberger Family Plot

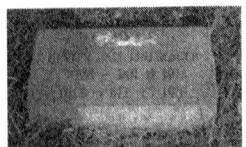

CYNTHIA DENETTE LINEBERGER
BORN - JUNE 5, 1955
DIED - NOV. 21, 1962

Hester Hall Lineberger BN-797-M
Died: 12/25/1981 Age: 70
Certificate No. 0061,01076
Parents: Robert Hall & Mae B. Jackson

HESTER HALL LINBERGER
BORN - JAN. 11, 1911
DIED - DEC. 25, 1981

J. D. Lineberger OK-179-O MISSING Noble & Kelsey: 115

John Henry Lineberger OK-179-O Plot
Died:08/28/1962 Age: 57 Southern Railroad Company
Certificate No.0042,0626 **Informant:** Hester Lineberger, Wife
Parents: J. D. Lineberger & Maggie Neely Bpl.: Rowan Co., NC
Lineberger Family Plot

JOHN HENRY LINEBERGER
BORN - MAY 8, 1905
DIED - AUG. 28, 1962

William David Lineberger BN-761-P
Died: 10/31/1917 Age: 63 Certificate Not Found

WILLIAM DAVID LINEBERGER
BORN -- MAY 25, 1917
DIED -- OCT. 31, 1980

Alta Mills Litaker UH-448-H
Died:04/19/1982 Age: 76 Certificate Not Found

	LITAKER	
DANIEL	JULIA	ALTA MILLS
APRIL 16, 1875	APRIL 29, 1879	JULY 3, 1906
MAY 13, 1949	JAN. 19, 1978	APRIL 19, 1982

Angeline Knoble Litaker OK-123-N MISSING Noble & Kelsey: 10
Plot Contains: E. D. Saunders; Minnie G. Knoble: Stephen Knoble; James Knoble; Rachel E. Carson; Clyde Innis Cook Sr.

Angeline Wilson Litaker OK-NO MARKER- Noble & Kelsey: 10
Died:02/17/1919 Age: 69 Domestic
Certificate No.0007,0161 **Informant:** Julius Litaker
Parents: Jake Wilson & Angelie Wilson Bpl.: NC

BURIALS

Charles Garfield Litaker
Died: 01/27/1925 Age: 43
Certificate No. 0013,0388
Parents: John Litaker & Angeline Wilson
[Concrete Marker – Inscription poor]

OK-189-O Noble & Kelsey
Laborer @ Salisbury Hardware Company
Informant: Blanch Litaker, Wife
Bpl.: Salisbury, NC

CHARLES
LITAKER
MAR. 17, 1881
JAN. 27, 1924
PRESENTED BY HIS
WIFE …. [Unreadable]

Daniel Litaker
Died: 05/16/1949 Age: 74
(See Alta Mills Litaker)

UH-448-H
Certificate Not Found

Elliott Litaker
Died: 02/19/1911 Age: 01y11m12d
Certificate No. 0004,0153
Parents: William Litaker & Lizzie Smith

OK-NO MARKER Noble & Kelsey
Baby
Informant: William Litaker
Bpl.: Rowan Co., NC

Julia Litaker
Died: 01/19/1978 Age: 98
Certificate No. 0038,0414
Parents: William Tott & Unknown

UH-448-H Noble & Kelsey: 258
Housewife
Informant: Mrs. Alta Mills
Bpl.: NC   (See Alta Mills Litaker)

Lizzie Litaker
Died: 08/20/1910 Age: 28

NO MARKER
Married Domestic
Informant: William Litaker

Parents: Ambrose Smith & Not Known   Bpl.: Davidson Co., NC
Register of Death, Salisbury, Co. of Rowan, NC (09/1909-10/11/1911)

Margaret Litaker

UH-448-H MISSING Noble & Kelsey: 258

Mary Jane Litaker
Died: 03/23/1926 Age: ∞57
Certificate No. 0014,0163
Parents Unknown

OK-NO MARKER Bingham, Carter, & Chesire
Domestic
Informant: William Litaker
Bpl.: Monroe

David Eugene Little
Died: 08/19/1985 Age: 51
Certificate No. 0065,0729
Parents: James Neely & Zettie R. Little

NO MARKER Mitchell & Fair
Brick Layer & repair Kiln - Brick Mfg.
Informant: Isabel Belton Little, Wife
Bpl.: Rowan Co., NC

Donald Ray Little
Died: 02/07/1989 Age: 32
Certificate No. 0069,0128
Parents: James Robert Little & Janie Daughters Little

BN-785-P MISSING Noble & Kelsey
Rip Saw Operator @ Lumber Company
Informant: James R. Little
Bpl.: Rowan Co., NC

George Locke
Died: 12/20/1927 Age: ∞31
Certificate No. 0017,0300
Parents: Lewis & Sallie Luke

NO MARKER Noble & Kelsey: 135
Day Laborer
Informant: Lydia McConnaughey
Bpl.: High Point, NC

Annie C. Long
Died: 01/10/1929 Age: 26,7,10
Certificate No. 0018,0309
Parents: Humphrey Jones & Daisy Pierce

OK-NO MARKER Noble & Kelsey
Housewife
Informant: King Long, Husband
Bpl.: Salisbury, NC

BURIALS

Ben David Long UH-634-G Noble & Kelsey
Died: 06/19/1994   Age: 61   Janitor @ Electric light & power Utility
Certificate No.0074,0628   **Informant**: Marcie Long
Parents: George Long & Avara Chavis   Bpl.: Rowan Co., NC

BEN DAVID
LONG
DEC. 12, 1932
JUNE 19, 1994

George W. Long NO MARKER Noble & Kelsey: 172
Died: 01/07/1952   Age: 65   Retired from Southern Railway
Certificate No.0033,0121   **Informant**: Avery Long
Parents: Bud Long & Harriet (Unknown)   Bpl.: Burlington, NC

Lallage Bost Long UH-489-H
Died: 09/17/1945   Age: 48   Domestic
Certificate No.0029,0738   **Informant**: Jesse Long
Parents: Ray Ramseur & Lizzie Thunderburk   Bpl.: Shelby, NC

LALLAGE BOST
LONG
AUG. 26, 1897
SEPT. 17, 1945
GONE BUT NOT FORGOTTEN

Leroy Jones Long NO MARKER Noble & Kelsey: 144
Died: 09/29/1923   Age: 1y9m23d   CHILD
Certificate No.0011,0507   **Informant**: Leroy Long
Parents: Leroy Long & Anna Jones   Bpl.: Salisbury, NC

Robert Long NO MARKER Noble & Kelsey
Died: 06/18/1927   Age: 10yrs, 11mos.   School Boy
Certificate No. 0015,0158   **Informant**: George Long
Parents: George Long &. ...Chavis   Bpl.: NC

Malvina Lord NO MARKER Noble & Kelsey
Died: 08/04/1910   Age: 60   Laundress
Certificate No.0004,0240   **Informant**: James Roundtree
Parents: Unknown

Clinton Luckey NO MARKER Noble & Kelsey
Died: 07/06/1910   Age: 2   Baby Boy
Certificate Not Found   **Informant**: Daisey Luckey
Parents: Jessie Lock & Nelia Luckey   Bpl.: Salisbury, NC

Raymond Albert Luckey UH-554-H Noble & Kelsey
Died: 09/26/1991   Age: 83   Janitor @ Cotton Cloth Mill
Certificate No.0071,0890   **Informant**: Viola Wilkerson Lucky, Wife
Parents: Enoch Luckey & Mary Knox   Bpl.: Rowan Co., NC

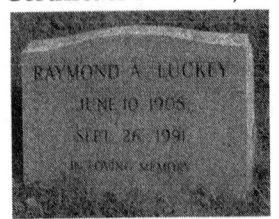

RAYMOND A. LUCKEY
JUNE 10, 1908
SEPT. 26, 1991
IN LOVING MEMORY

BURIALS

Etta Lee Lyerly
Died: 01/21/1920 Age: 34
Certificate No.0008,0100
Parents: Henry & Cora Lee

OK-NO MARKER Noble & Kelsey: 36
Housekeeper
Informant Thaddeus Lyerly
Bpl.: Rowan Co., NC

John Henry Lyerly
Died: 12/14/1985 Age: 82
Certificate No.0065,1088
Parents: George Lyerly & Francis Barber

BT-352-I/J Lyerly Subsection Mitchell & Fair
Fireman Laborer, U.S. Post Office
Informant: Betty L. Holt, Daughter
Bpl.: Rowan Co., NC

LOVING FATHER
JOHN HENRY LYERLY
AUG. 3, 1903
DEC. 14, 1985

Mary Rosie Lyerly
Died: 03/17/1918 Age: 14
Certificate No. 0006,0393
Parents: Alfred Lyerly &??

NO MARKER Noble & Kelsey
No Occupation Given
Informant: Harrison Lyerly

Mary White Lyerly
Died: 09/08/1958 Age: 53
Certificate No.0039,0260
Parents: Locke White & Rosa Boger

BT-350-I/J Lyerly Subsection
Housewife
Informant: John Henry Lyerly
Bpl.: NC

LYERLY
MARY WHITE LYERLY
SEPT. 26, 1905
SEPT. 8, 1958
SHE WAS THE SUNSHINE OF OUR HOME.

Earnest Edward Lyles
Died: 11/12/1993 Age: 81
Certificate No.0073,1030
Parents: John & Laura Lyles

UH-615-G Noble & Kelsey
Dough Mixer @ Retail Bakery
Informant: Jean R. Miller
Bpl.: Blair, SC

EARNEST EDWARD
LYLES, SR.
DEC. 3, 1911
NOV. 12, 1993
IN LOVING MEMORY

Adolphus Lyttle
Died: 08/13/1970 Age: 72
Certificate No. 0070,0473
Parents: Nelson Lyttle &???? Born 08/14/1897 [Birth date given by informant is different from that of the stonecutter] Bpl.: NC

BT- K Noble & Kelsey
Retired from Martin Construction Company
Informant: Mrs. Napoleon Krider

ADOLPHUS LYTLLE
AUG. 14, 1885
AUG. 1970

Louise Maaks
Died: 12//1944: Certificate Not Found

OK-156-O MISSING

BURIALS

Elizabeth Pauline Mack
Died: 11/13/1956   Age: 1 day
Certificate No.0037,0288
Parents: Paul Mack & Gladys Hays

NO MARKER
INFANT
Informant: Paul Mack, Father

Willie Mack
Died: 10/18/1957   Age: 49
Certificate No.0038,0296
Parents: Isaac Mack & Rena Watson

UH-401-I/J
Janitor @ Duke Power
Informant: Gussie Mack, Wife
Bpl.: SC

MACK
WILLIE MACK
MAR. 14, 1908
OCT. 28, 1957
GONE BUT NOT FORGOTTEN

Lula Malone
Died:05/26/1944   Age: 74
Certificate No.0029,0161
Parents: John & Jane Clement
    Julius Malone, Love Malone, Adelaide Flowers, Mary Malone, Dorothy Samuel, Babies

OK-NO MARKER   Noble & Kelsey: 65
Housewife
Informant: Juanita Broadway
Bpl.: Davie Co., NC

Thenia Manuel
Died:07/07/1920   Age: ∞70
Certificate No.0008,0204
Parents: UNKNOWN

OK-NO MARKER   Noble & Kelsey: 359
Home Laundress
Informant: Theodore Manuel
Bpl.: Greensboro, NC

John Wesley March
Died:08/27/1907   Age: 4 mth. 1 day

NO MARKER   Summersett
INFANT   Funeral Home Record

Mary Marlin
Died: 12/24/1943   Age: 66
Certificate No.0029,0051
Parents: Cedric Brice & Charlotte Sterling

NO MARKER
Domestic
Informant: Annie Mae Little
Bpl.: Blackstork, SC

George W. Marsh
Died:07/17/1946   Age: 82
Certificate Not Found
Parents: Harry Marsh & Not Known   bd. 03/30/1864

NO MARKER
Laborer
Informant: Estella Marsh, Wife

Stella Marsh
Died:01/03/1947   Age: 62
Certificate No.0030,0722
Parents: Willie Williams & Amanda Wiseman

NO MARKER   Ellis, Mangum, & Fair
Domestic
Informant: Annie Henderson
Bpl.: Salisbury, NC

Daisy Martin
Died: 1920   Certificate Not Found

OK-059-N

Condition on 08/18/03

DAISY
MARTIN
BORN 189?
DIED 1920

BURIALS

Earl Martin
Died: 10/12/1918   Age: 4
Certificate No. 0006,0510
Parents: Zema Martin & Pinky S. Daniels

NO MARKER   G. W. Wright
CHILD
Informant: Zema Martin (sic)
   Bpl.: GA

Eva Barksdale Martin
Died: 03/26/1982   Age: 72
Certificate No.0062,0259
Parents: Tranham Barksdale & Emma Brown

BN-829-M   Noble & Kelsey
Domestic @ Defense Plant
Informant: Harvey L. Rice, Nephew
   Bpl.: Spartanburg, SC

Francis Martin, dau of
Died: 07/22/1911   Age: 4 yrs.
Certificate Not Found
Parents: Jake & Mary Dulin Martin

NO MARKER   Summersett
CHILD   Funeral Home Record

Jake Martin
Died: 06/26/1929   Age: 57
Certificate No.0017,0434
Parents: UNKNOWN

OK-NO MARKER   Noble & Kelsey: 72
Day Laborer, Employer: G.W.Martin
Informant: Tom Brown
   Bpl.: Wilks Co., NC

Lizzie Martin
Died: 10/23/1941   Age: ∞90
Certificate No.0027,1565
Parents: William Burnett

NO MARKER
Farming
Informant: Ethel Miller

Thomas Martin
Died: 05/01/1923   Age: 45
Certificate No. 0011,0437
Parents Unknown

OK-NO MARKER   Noble & Kelsey
Bank work
Informant: Steven Noble
   Bpl.: Salisbury, NC

Everette H. Mason
Died: 1909   Age: 4
Parents: Fisher R. & Fannie B. Mason
(See Lillie M. Mason Davis or Everette H. Mason for marker.)

OK-362 -I/J Mason Plot
CHILD   Certificate Not Found

```
         MASON
   REV. FISHER R. MASON
        HIS WIFE
     FANNIE B. MASON
          SON
    EVERETTE H. MASON
       1905 - 1909
        DAUGHTER
   LILLIE M. MASON DAVIS
```

Fannie Bryant Mason
Certificate Not Found

OK-362-I/J Plot
Teacher @ Fannie Mason School @ Mt. Zion Baptist
Church in 1922

Fisher Robert Mason
Died: 11/26/1965   Age: 86
Died in High Point, NC
Parents: Caldwell Mason & Lucinda Burrel
(See Everett H. Mason)

OK-362-I/J Mason Plot
Minister of Mt. Zion Baptist Church &Principal
of Salisbury Graded School 1909 –11
   Bpl.: Mocksville, NC

Maggie Mason

OK-362- I/J MISSING Mason Plot   Noble & Kelsey: 35
Certificate Not Found   Nurse

BURIALS

Abe Massey
Died: 02/02/1960   Age: 73
Certificate No.0040,0382
Parents: Henry Massy & Maria McCullough

NO MARKER

Informant: Mrs. Carrie Scott
Bpl.: SC

Freddy Massey
Died: 04/19/1948   Age: 30

NO MARKER

Ellis, Mangum, & Fair
Funeral Home Record

Julia F. Massey
Died: 10/29/1958   Age: 76
Certificate No.0039,0299
Parents: George H. Massey & Marie McCullough

NO MARKER
Laundress
Informant: Elmon Massey
Bpl.: SC

Naomi Henderson Massey
Died: 01/12/1914   Age: 1y4m13d
Certificate No.0001,0744
Parents: Crafford Henderson & Julia Massy

NO MARKER
Baby
Informant: Sam Massy
Bpl.: Salisbury, NC

Noble & Kelsey: 353

Samuel Massey
Died: 11/04/1961   Age: 77
Certificate No.0042,0123
Parents: Henry Massey & Marie McCullough

OK-NO MARKER
Textile, N. C. Finishing Co.
Informant: Willie M. Massey, Wife
Bpl.: Rock Hill, SC

Noble & Kelsey: 49

Urnette Mathews

UH-622-G MISSING

David H. Maxwell
Died: 12/13/1957   Age: 88
Certificate Not Found

UH-510-H

MAXWELL
DAVID H.
MAR. 4, 1869
DEC. 13, 1957
WE LOVED YOU BUT GOD LOVED YOU BEST
BY FAMILY

Elizabeth Maxwell

UH-494-H
Died: 09/10/1970   Age: 75   Certificate Not Found

ELIZABETH MAXWELL
MAY 30, 1895
SEPT. 10, 1970

Minnie Maxwell
Died: 04/11/1961   Age: 56
Certificate No.0041,0483
Parents: Ellison Howie & Lottie Frazier

NO MARKER
Domestic
Informant: George Maxwell, Husband
Bpl.: NC

Cora Pratt McCain
Died: 11/24/1923   Age: ∞44
Certificate No.0011,0530
Parents: Ned Pratt & Mollie Heileg

OK-NO MARKER
Domestic Housework for Smith
Informant: John McCain
Bpl.: Rowan Co., NC

Noble & Kelsey: 30

BURIALS

Mack McCluney

UH-397- I/J
Died: 12/27/1955   Age: 70   Certificate Not Found

MACK McCLUNEY
AUG. 15, 1885
DEC. 22, 1955

Nettie McConnaughey (sic)
Died: 03/11/1918   Age: 15,4,9
Certificate No. 0006,0439
Parents: Mitchell McConnaughey & Diana McCoskey

OK-NO MARKER   Noble & Kelsey
Laundress @ Steam Laundry
Informant: Bertha McConnaughey
Bpl.: Rowan Co., NC

Gertrude Amanda McCorkle
Died: 06/23/1957   Age: 51
Certificate No. 0038,0028
Parents: John Rowe & Lillie Mae Stockton

NO MARKER
Domestic
Informant: Beatrice Holt
Bpl.: NC

Harold J. McCorkle
Died: 07/06/1948   Age: 46

HAROLD MCCORKLE
MAY 22, 1902
JUNE 6, 1948

OK-169-O   Noble & Kelsey: 137
Certificate Not Found

Jennette Alexander McCorkle
Died: 04/15/1923   Age: 38
Certificate No. 0011,0424
Parents: Adam Alexander & Fannie Griffin

OK-NO MARKER   Noble & Kelsey: 48
Day Labor, Housework
Informant: Alex Alexander
Bpl.: Charlotte, NC

John McCorkle
Died: 03/26/1910   Age: 28y02m22
Certificate No. 0004,0325
Parents: Winslo Henderson & Magritte McCorkle

NO MARKER   Noble & Kelsey
Laborer
Informant: Margritte McCorkle

Johnsie Lyerly McCorkle

Died: 12/10/1980   Age: 40   Certificate Not Found

OK-351-I/J Lyerly Subsection

JOHNSIE LYERLY
McCORKLE
AUG. 19, 1940
DEC. 10, 1980

Laura McCorkle
Died: 03/02/1925
Certificate No. 0013,0300
Parents: Walter McCorkle & Lorene Douglas

OK-NO MARKER   Noble & Kelsey: 148
CHILD
Informant: Rev. P. A. McCorkle

BURIALS

Miss Alma McCorkle
Died: 09/26/1916   Age: 22
Certificate No. 0003,0283
Parents: James McCorkle & Dewilla Pope

OK-NO MARKER
Student & School Teacher
Informant: J. A. McCorkle
   Bpl.: Rowan Co., NC

Noble & Kelsey: 48

Pinkney Armstrong McCorkle
Died: 09/07/1928   Age: ∞57

Certificate No. 0016,0428
Parents: Aaron & Candace McCorkle

OK-N NO MARKER
Minister of Trinity A.M.E. Zion Church & Soldiers
   Memorial A. M. E. Zion Church 1893-1897
   Graduated from theological department @
   Livingstone 1907
Informant: Laura McCorkle, Wife
   Bpl.: Iredell Co., NC

Noble & Kelsey: 148

Thomas L McCorkle
Died: 07/16/1924   Age:
Certificate No. 0012,0400
Parents: P. A. McCorkle & Laura E. Todd

OK-N NO MARKER
Day Laborer in Lumber Yard
Informant: P. A. McCorkle
   Bpl.: Mooresville birthday not given

Noble & Kelsey: 148

Richard McCowan
Died: 08/ /1950   Certificate Not Found

OK-N NO MARKER
   4 people in plot

Noble & Kelsey: 130

Miles McCoy
Died: 03/30/1927   Age: 39
Certificate No. 0015,0324
Parents Unknown

NO MARKER
Farmer
Informant: Sarah Witherspoon

Cheshire & Mangum

William McCoy
Died: 07/23/1969   Age: 43
Parents: Unknown & Effie McCoy

NO MARKER

Mitchell & Fair
Funeral Home Record

Willie Lyerly McCoy
Died: 01/17/1983   Age: 79
         Certificate No. 0063,0049
         Parents: John Lyerly & Lena Harris

BN-846-M
Homemaker
Informant: Mrs. Willie E. Stout, Daughter
   Bpl.: Rowan Co, NC

Noble & Kelsey

WILLIE LYERLY
McCOY
JULY 3, 1903
JAN. 17, 1983

Bettie McCrarie
Died: 02/25/1919   Age: ∞85
Certificate Not Found
Parents: UNKNOWN

NO MARKER
Washing & Ironing – Laundry
Informant: W. F. Kelsey
   Bpl.: UNKNOWN

Noble & Kelsey
Funeral Home Record

Younge Madison McCrary
Died: 05/27/1969   Age: 86
Parents: Younge M. McCrary & Unknown

NO MARKER
Coal Miner

Mitchell & Fair
Funeral Home Record

Noah McCubbins
Died: 01/30/1910   Age: 60
Certificate No. 0004,0494
Parents: Silvous McCubbins Mother Unknown

NO MARKER
Fish Dealer
Informant: Helen Fisher
   Bpl.: Iredell Co., NC

Noble & Kelsey: 350

BURIALS

James Edward McCullough
Died: 12/06/1985   Age: 37
Certificate No.0064,0345
Parents: John Junior McCullough & Lavonia Boyd

BN-848-M
Laborer- Block Mach. @ Johnson Concrete Company
Informant: Mrs. Lovenia McCullough, Mother
Bpl.: Rowan Co., NC

Noble & Kelsey

JAMES E. MCCULLOUGH

Komika Denise McDowell
Died:05/18/1988   Age: 8

BN-843-M
Certificate Not Found

McDOWELL
KOMIKA DENISE
MARCH 6, 1980
MAY 18, 1988
THE LORD REPLIED,
MY PRECIOUS CHILD I LOVE AND I WOULD NEVER LEAVE
YOU DURING YOUR TIMES OF TRIALS AND SUFFERING
WHEN YOU SEE ONLY ONE SET OF FOOTPRINTS
IT WAS THEN THAT I CARRIED YOU

Joe McGarity
Died:02/28/1952   Age: 66
Certificate No.0033,0102
Parents: Wilson A & Ambress McGarity

UH-478-H
Laborer @ Southern Railway
Informant: Mamie
Bpl.: Chester, SC

Noble & Kelsey

JOE
McGARITY
FEB. 28, 1952

Minnie McGill
Died:: 08/03/1924   Age: 45
Certificate No. 0012,0419
Parents: Len Garner & Ida Miller

OK-NO MARKER
Cook for Carry Roberts
Informant: Thelma McGill
Bpl.: York, SC

Noble & Kelsey

Marion Setzer McGraw
Died:06/18/1941   Age: 20

UH-NO MARKER

Ellis, Mangum, & Fair
Funeral Home Record

Booker T. McGriff
Died:12/04/1970

NO MARKER

Mitchell & Fair
Funeral Home Record

John Howard McIlwaine
Died:12/27/1949   Age: 56

UH-457-H
Certificate Not Found

Noble & Kelsey

IHS
JOHN HOWARD McILWAINE
DECEMBER 18, 1893
DECEMBER 27, 1949
OUR LOVE FOR HIM WHO SLEEPS
BENEATH SHALL NEVER FADE

[Front]

IHS

McILWAINE

JESUS KEEP ME
NEAR THE CROSS

Dorothy Davis McIntyre
Died:08/03/1992   Age: 56
Certificate No.0072,0634
Parents: Unknown & Janie Davis

UH-618 G MISSING
Never Worked
Informant: Carol D. Thomas
Bpl.: Rowan Co., NC

Noble & Kelsey

BURIALS

Grace McKennzie
Died: 01/18/1923   Age: ∞20
Certificate No. 0011,0382
Parents: Ceaser McKennzie & Susie Cornelia

NO MARKER
Cook
Informant: Susie McKennzie

Summersett

Bpl.: Mooresville, NC

Bud McKinney
Died: 01/19/1964   Age: 80 (73@dcrt.)
Certificate No.0044,0027
Parents: Father not given & Mary McIllwain

UH-447-H
Yard Man
Informant: Mrs. Laura McKinney, Wife

Noble & Kelsey

Bpl.: Salisbury, NC

McKINNEY
BUD   LAURA
NOV. 28, 1884   MAY 10, 1895
JAN. 19, 1964   NOV. 16, 1975

Charlie McKinney
Died: 12/20/1950   Age: 63
Certificate No. 0032,0497
Parents: Isaac McKinney & Mary McIlwain

UH-NO MARKER
House Cleaning

Ellis, Mangum, & Fair
Funeral Home Record

db.05/19/1887

James McKinney
Died: 11/09/1955   Age: 66
Certificate No.0036,0503
Parents: Isaac McKinney & Mary McCain

UH-398-I/J
Laborer
Informant: Serlena McKinney

Ellis, Mangum & Fair

Bpl.: SC

JAMES McKINNEY
AUG. 18, 1889
NOV. 9, 1955

John McKinney
Died: 01/23/1942   Age: 55
Certificate No.0028,0233
Parents: Isaac McKinney & Mary McIlwain

UH-NO MARKER
Cement Finisher
Informant: Katie McKinney, Wife
Bpl.: Lancaster, SC

Ellis, Mangum, & Fair

Laura McKinney
Died: 11/16/1975   Age: 80
(See Bud McKinney)

UH-447-H
Certificate Not Found.

Ms. Erssell Butler McKinney
Died: 12/25/1978   Age: 46
Certificate No.0058,0981
Parents: Usher Butler & Brenza Howell

OK-105-N
Laborer in Hospital
Informant: Ava McKinney, daughter
Bpl.: Rowan Co., NC

Noble & Kelsey

ERSSELL BUTLER
MCKINNEY
JAN. 28, 1932
DEC. 25, 1978

Hurbert Grant McLaughlin
Died: 10/28/1952   Age: 42
Parents: Clark McLaughlin

UH-NO MARKER

Ellis, Mangum, & Fair
Funeral Home Record

BURIALS

Hattie McLillie
Died: 10/31/1946   Age: 55
Certificate No.0030,0395
Parents: Adam Blake & Eliza Thompson

OK-NO MARKER
Housewife
Informant: Pearl Blake
   Bpl.: Chester, SC

Noble & Kelsey: 127

Ben McMahan
Died:02/04/1941

NO MARKER

Ellis, Mangum, & Fair
Funeral Home Record

John J. McMoris
Died: 12/12/1923   Age: 51
Certificate No. 0011,0551
Parents Unknown

NO MARKER
Brick Mason
Informant: Maude McMoris, Wife
   Bpl.: S.C.

Bingham & Carter

Carrie Logan McNeely
Died: 08/18/1957   Age: 55
Certificate No.0038,0191
Parents: Wilson Harris &??

OK-223-L
Housewife
Informant: Charlie McNeely, Husband

Noble & Kelsey

CARRIE LOGAN
WIFE OF
CHARLIE MCNEELY
DEC. 20, 1890
AUG. 18, 1967
GREAT LOVES LIVE ON

Charlie McNeely

BT-298-K
Died:02/21/1964   Age: 72 (65@dcrt.)
Certificate No.0044,0106
Parents: Will & Nancy McNeely

Noble & Kelsey
Laborer @ Lumber Yard
Informant: William Logan
Bpl.: Mecklenburg Co., NC

CHARLIE McNEELY
AUG. 18, 1892
FEB. 21, 1964
GREAT LOVES LIVE ON

Maria Dodge McNeely
Died:09/23/1947   Age: 72
Parents: Wiley E. Dodge Sr. & Cecelia Giles

OK-153-O

Bpl.: Salisbury, NC

Ellis, Mangum & Fair
Funeral Home Record

MARIA DODGE
MCNEELY
DIED SEPT, 1947
Death is another life.

BURIALS

Robert Burton McNeely   OK-154-O   Noble & Kelsey: 96
Died: 04/02/1920   Age: 79yrs, 02 mos. 20 dys   Certificate Not Found
Barber: Made a Contribution to move Zion Wesley Institute from Concord to Salisbury, North Carolina in 1881   bd. 03//1840

ROBERT BURTON
MCNEELY
MAR. 12, 1841
APR. 2, 1920
AGED 79 YRS.
2 MOS. 20 DYS.

Hester Medlock   OK-NO MARKER   Cheshire & Mangum
Died: 11/11/1927   No age or birth date given   Nurse
Certificate No. 0015,0458   **Informant:** Jeminia Penn
Parents: Ike Connelly & Amanda Jones   Bpl.: GA

Louisa J. Meeks   OK-156-O
Died: 12/29/1944   Age: 77y19m07d   Certificate Not Found

LOUISA J. MEEKS
WIFE OF
R. F. GLENN
FEB. 22, 1867
DEC. 29, 1944
AGE 77 YRS. 10 MOS, 7DYS
YOUR MEMORIES WILL REMAIN WITH US ALWAYS

Minie Meniers   NO MARKER   G. W. Wright
Died: 08/28/1910   Age: 32   Domestic
Certificate No.0004,0225   **Informant:** J. A. Meniers
Parents: J. A. Meniers & Marita Fuetez   Bpl.: Rowan Co., NC

Mack Meisenheimer   UH-NO MARKER   Ellis, Mangum, & Fair
Died: 03/13/1960   Age: 78   Funeral Home Record

Vernon Melton   BT-282-K   Noble & Kelsey
Died: 08/11/1963   Age: 33   Carpenter
Certificate No.0043,0445   **Informant:** Mrs. Bernice M. Melton
Parents: Carl Melton & Mae Helen Goinnes   Bpl.: Chesterfield Co., SC

Janie Merritt   NO MARKER   Cheshire & Mangum
Died: 03/09/1928   Age: 50   Cook
Certificate No.0016,0317   **Informant:** Mrs. Ida Exum
Parents: Elizah Merritt & Unknown

Melrose Metz   UH-NO MARKER   Ellis, Mangum, & Fair
Died: 02/16/1954   Age: 46   Cook
Certificate No.0035,0090   **Informant:** Mrs. Maggie Clemmons
Parents: John Metz & Ella McDowel   Bpl.: East Spencer, NC

Henry Miles   UH-NO MARKER   Ellis, Mangum, & Fair
Died: 09/08/1951   Age: 59   Plaster
Certificate No. 0032,0886
Parents: Henry Miles & Unknown

BURIALS

Allen Miller
Died: 01/31/1911   Age: 80
Certificate No.0004,0135
Parents: Parents Not Given

NO MARKER
Laborer
Informant: Wife
   Bpl.: Stanly Co., NC

Noble & Kelsey

Alonzo M. Miller
Died: 12/03/1953   Age: 70
   Certificate No.0034,0537
   Wife
Parents: James Wilson & Julia Holt   Bpl.: Davidson Co., NC

OK-182-O
Taxi Driver

Ellis, Mangum, & Fair @ Kel 160
Informant: Mrs. Marie Miller,

MILLER
ALONZO M. MILLER
OCT. 24, 1882
DEC. 3, 1954
Gone But Not Forgotten

Arthur Mack Miller
Died: 12/15/1982   Age: 75
Certificate No.0062,0988
   Parents: John Miller & Annie Holt   Bpl.: Rowan Co., NC

BN-789-P
Retired Laborer from Southern Railroad
Informant: Mrs. Doris Roberts, Daughter

Noble & Kelsey

ARTHUR MACK
MILLER
MAY 19, 1907
DEC. 15, 1982

Demond Dray Miller

UH-541-H MISSING   Certificate Not Found

Fannie Miller
Died:07/14/1942   Age: ∞73
Certificate No.0028,0335
Parents: Don Fisher & Laura Pinkston

OK-NO MARKER
Housewife
Informant: Mrs. M. A. Houser
   Bpl.: Rowan Co., NC

Noble & Kelsey: 343

Francis Pinkston Miller
Died:01/16/1914   Age: 23y5m11d
Certificate No.0001,0746
Parents: Martin Pinkston & Eliza Miller

NO MARKER
Domestic
Informant: Jamie Miller
   Bpl.: Rowan Co., NC

Noble & Kelsey: 343

George Miller
Died:03/18/1945   Age: 80
Certificate No.0002,0129
Parents: Edward Miller & Margrett Miller

NO MARKER
Farmer
Informant: Margrett Miller
   Bpl.: Rowan Co., NC

Noble & Kelsey: 219

George Miller
Died: 12/08/1919   Age: 4days
Certificate No.0007,0111
Parents: Will Miller & Jannie Patterson

OK-NO MARKER
INFANT
Informant: Maria Miller
   Bpl.: Salisbury, NC

Noble & Kelsey: 151

BURIALS

Hattie Lattimore Miller
Died: 12/08/1965   Age: 87

OK- 173-O

Noble & Kelsey 90
Certificate Not Found

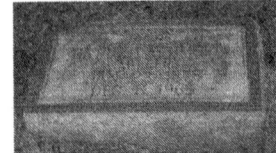

HATTIE LATTIMORE
MILLER
JAN. 22, 1878
DEC. 8, 1965

Helen Abernathy Miller
Died:04/27/1957   Age: 34

UH-NO MARKER

Ellis, Mangum, & Fair
Funeral Home Record

Ida Miller
Died: 01/12/1923   Age: None Given
Certificate No. 0012,0284
Parents: Father Unknown & Salina Summer

NO MARKER
General Housework
Informant: Charleston Barton

James Henry Miller
Died:09/14/1990   Age: 70

UH-574-H

Certificate Not Found

JAMES HENRY MILLER
"DREEK"
AUG. 13, 1920
SEPT. 14, 1990

John Miller
Died:05/02/1912   Age: 41yy07m3
Certificate No. 0001,0139
Parents: Sebastian Mills & Sarah Crafford

NO MARKER
Railroader Southern Shop Work
Informant: Eliza Mills
    Bpl.: Chester, SC

Noble & Kelsey

Julia D. Miller
Died:06/29/1923   Age: 44
Certificate No.0011,0453:
Parents: Calmeus Cowan & Charlotte Partee

NO MARKER
Teacher, Rural Schools
Informant. P. Miller
    Bpl.: Cabarrus Co., NC

Noble & Kelsey

Lavenia Miller
Died: 11/28/1982   Age: 71
Certificate No.0062,0953
Parents: William Miller & Lillia Ellis Butner

NO MARKER
not given
Informant: Salisbury Police Dept.
    Bpl.: Rowan Co., NC

Mitchell & Fair

Lee Miller
Died:01/26/1976   Age: 74
Certificate No.0056,0165
Parents: Alex Miller & Lottie Torrence

NO MARKER
Retired Hotel Worker
Informant: Mrs. Ruth Miller Cherry, Sister
    Bpl.: NC

Mitchell & Fair

Lonnie B. Miller
Died:06/22/1949   Age: 37
Certificate No.0031,0897
Parents: Alonzo Miller & Marie Jones

OK-182-O   Ellis, Mangum, & Fair @ Kelsey 160
Cook
Informant: Alonzo Miller, Father
    Bpl.: Salisbury, NC

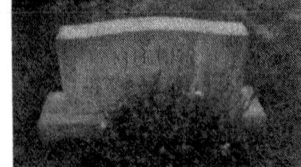

MILLER
LONNIE B.
MAR. 19, 1912
JUNE 22, 1949
Son

MARIE JONES
FEB. 2, 1894
JUNE 28, 1960
Mother

BURIALS

Maria Miller
Died: 07/28/1925   Age: 45
Certificate No. 0013,0421
Parents: George Miller & Eliza Scott

OK-NO MARKER   Noble & Kelsey
Domestic Housework
Informant: Miller

Marie Jones Miller
Died: 06/28/1960   Age: 76
Certificate No.0049,0413
Parents: George J. Jones & Carolina Jones
(See Lonnie B. Miller)

OK-182-O   Noble & Kelsey: 160

Informant: Miss Ruby L. Miller
Bpl.: SC

Martha Miller
Died: 04/13/1911   Age: 24yrs.
Certificate No. 0004,0209
Parents: Jack Gregory & Missouri Garris

NO MARKER   Summersett
Domestic
Informant: Broadus Gregory
Bpl.: Lancaster, SC

Mildred Miller
Died: 04/19/1925   Age: 9
Certificate No. 00013,0329
Parents: Alonzo Miller & Marie Jones

OK-NO MARKER   Bingham & Carter

Informant: Alonzo Miller, Father
Bpl.: Rowan Co., NC

Morris Miller

OK-166-O
Died: Age: 43   Certificate Not Found

MORRIS MILLER
MAY 13, 1907
APR. 1, 1950

Norris Jennie Miller
Died: 03/29/1977   Age: 34

BT-239-K   MISSING
Certificate Not Found

William Lawrence Miller
Died: 09/28/1937   Age: 28

OK-375-I/J
Certificate Not Found

WILLIAM LAWRENCE
MILLER
APR. 13, 1909
SEPT. 28, 1937
WE WILL MEET AGAIN

Beatrice Milton
Died: 08/11/1986   Age: 90

OK-251-K
Certificate Not Found

MOTHER
BEATRICE MILTON
APR. 4, 1896
AUG. 11, 1986

BURIALS

Andrew Thomas Mitchell BN-767-P Noble & Kelsey
Died: 01/23/1948 Age: 17 Student/Laborer
Certificate No. 0031,0244 **Informant:** Mrs. Martha Mitchell
Parents: Otis Mitchell & Martha Boler Bpl.: Winnsboro, NC

ANDREW THOMAS
SON OF
OTIS & MARTHA MITCHELL
FEB. 20, 1931
JAN. 23, 1948
HE HAS GONE TO THE MANSIONS OF REST

Annie Lee Mitchell BT-271-K Noble & Kelsey
Died: 12/05/1968 Age: 43 Laborer @ Ideal Laundry
Certificate No. 0048,0702 **Informant:** Mrs. Mae Bell Smith
Parents: Willie Mitchell & Nina White Bpl.: GA

AT REST
ANNIE LEE MITCHELL
OCT. 15, 1925
DEC. 5, 1968

Anthony Bryant Mitchell BN-684-P Mitchell & Fair
Died: 05/08/1994 Age: 35 Owner of Pest Control Company
Certificate No. 0074,0492 **Informant:** Harry Mitchell
Parents: Unknown & Annie June Mitchell Bpl.: Mecklenburg Co., NC

Horace Greely Mitchell OK-220-K Noble & Kelsey: 238
Died: 1945 Age: 50 Certificate Not Found

HORACE GREELY
MITCHELL
1885 - 1945

Ira Bell Mitchell UH-NO MARKER Ellis, Mangum, & Fair
Died: 11/09/1941 Certificate Not Found

John Hamilton Mitchell UH-419-K Noble & Kelsey
Died: 11/19/1976 Age: 93 Retired U. S. Customs
Certificate No. 0056,0827 **Informant:** Mrs. Laura G. Mitchell
Parents: Frank & Silver Mitchell Bpl.: SC
(See Laura Gibson Mitchell)

Laura Gibson Mitchell UH-419-K
Died: 12/18/1985 Age: 92 Certificate Not Found

MITCHELL
LAURA GIBSON MITCHELL   JOHN HAMILTON MITCHELL
JAN. 2, 1893   DEC. 1, 1883
DEC. 18, 1985   NOV. 19, 1976
DAUGHTER OF   SON OF
F & LIZZIE GIBSON   FRANK & SILVER MITCHELL
I HAVE FOUGHT A GOOD FIGHT, I HAVE COMPLETED MY WORK
I HAVE FINISHED MY COURSE IN HELPING OTHERS TO SUCCESS
I HAVE KEPT THE FAITH. 2 TIMOTHY 4

BURIALS

Maggie Shuford Mitchell   OK-219-L   Noble & Kelsey: 238
Died: 1917   Age: 29   Certificate Not Found

MAGGIE SHUFORD
MITCHELL
1888 - 1917

Mary Elizabeth Johnson Mitchell   UH-591-G   Noble & Kelsey
Died: 12/10/1992   Age: 78   Beautician @ Beauty Salon - Self Employed
Certificate No.0072,1002   **Informant:** Sarah Oglesby
Parents: Emmanuel Johnson & Leliah Boyd   Bpl.: Charlotte, NC

William (Bud) Mitchell   OK-NO MARKER   Noble & Kelsey
Died: 08/05/1929   Age: 56   Teamster
Certificate No. 00017,0472   **Informant:** Cora Graham
Parents: Trot Mitchell & Jossie Graham   Bpl.: Rowan Co., NC

William Wadewright Mitchell   OK-221-L
Died: 11/16/1981   Age: 77   Certificate Not Found

WILLIAM WADEWRIGHT
MITCHELL
MAY 16, 1904   NOV. 16, 1981

Willie Louice Mitchell Sr.   OK-   Noble & Kelsey
Died:07/26/1940   Age: 60   Brakeman, Southern Railroad
Certificate No.0027,0750   **Informant:** Lula Mitchell
Parents: Neal Mitchell & Janet Fisher   Bpl.: Rowan Co., NC

W. L.
MITCHELL
FEB. 28 1880
JULY 26 1940
His Record is on high.

Norma Jene Mobley   NO MARKER
Died:03/03/1941   Age: 7mos   INFANT
Certificate No.0027,1343   **Informant:** William Mobly
Parents: William Anderson Mobly & Etta Moore   Bpl.: Salisbury, NC

Mamie Patterson Monroe   UH-388-I/J
Died: 10/26/1947   Age: 43y07m24d   Domestic
Certificate No.0030,0976   **Informant:** Nancy Payne
Parents: William Patterson & Lula Harris

MAMIE PATTERSON
MONROE
DIED OCT. 26, 1947

Charles White Montgomery   BN-012-M
Died: 10/03/1960   Age: 50   Certificate Not Found

CHARLES WHITE
MONTGOMERY
JAN. 18, 1910
OCT. 3, 1960

BURIALS

George Montgomery　　　　　　　　OK-NO MARKER　　　　Noble & Kelsey: 6
　Buried with Sara Montgomery, Lewis Pitts, INFANT of Lewis Pitts & Erhane Montgomery

Marry Callie Montgomery　　　　　UH-420-H
　　　　Died: 02/17/1964　　Age: 63　　　　Certificate Not Found

　　　　　　MARY CALLIE
　　　　　　MONTGOMERY
　　　　　　SEPT. 13, 1901
　　　　　　FEB. 17, 1964

Mary White Montgomery　　　　　BN-011-M
Died: 10/26/1965　　Age: 91　　　　Certificate Not Found

　　　　　　MARY WHITE
　　　　　　MONTGOMERY
　　　　　　OCT. 26, 1865
　　　　　　OCT. 21, 1956

Sandy Daring Montgomery　　　　BN-010-M　　　　Noble & Kelsey
Died: 02/24/1937　　Age: 62　　　　Cook
Certificate No. 0023,0070　　　　**Informant:** Marie Callie Montgomery
　　　Parents: George Montgomery & Unknown　Bpl.: NC

　　　　　　SANDY DEARING
　　　　　　MONTGOMERY
　　　　　　DEC. 24, 1864
　　　　　　FEB. 24, 1937

Sarah Davis Montgomery　　　　OK-134-H　　　　Noble & Kelsey: 8
Died: 03/28/1911　　Age: 59　　　　Married
Certificate No. 0004,0191　　　　**Informant:** Margerett Hampton
　　　Parents: Elious David & Margerett Leonard　Bpl.: Rowan Co., NC
　　　Buried with Lewis Pitts, George Montgomery, INFANT of Lewis Pitts & Erhane
　　　Montgomery

　　　　　　SARAH
　　　　　　MONTGOMERY
　　　　　　DIED
　　　　　　MAR. 28, 1911

Willie Montgomery　　　　　　　NO MARKER　　　　Summersett
Died: 05/05/1908　　Age: 21 yrs.　　　　　　　　　Funeral Home Record

Alberta Guest Moore　　　　　　NO MARKER　　　　Ellis, Mangum, & Fair
Died: 01/28/1955　　Age: 53
Certificate No. 0036,0093　　　　**Informant:** Kirk Moore
Parents: Dave Jeter & Eliza Robbins　　Bpl.: Chester, SC

Ed Moore　　　　　　　　　　UH-NO MARKER　　　Ellis, Mangum, & Fair
Died: 04/20/49　　Age: 57　　　　Laborer
Certificate No. 0031,0725　　　　**Informant**
Parents: Ed Moore Sr. & Unknown　　Bpl.: Mississippi

BURIALS

Edward Moore Jr.   OK-076-N   Noble & Kelsey: 60
Died: 03/1905   Age: 20   Certificate Not Found
Parents: Edward & Serena Moore

EDWARD MOORE JR.
MARCH 1885
MARCH 1905

Edward Moore Sr.   OK-074-N   Noble & Kelsey 60
Died: 10/20/1927   Age: 74y04m06
Medical Doctor & Teacher @ Livingstone College Received PhD from Princeton through Lincoln University, PA
Certificate No. 0015,0453   **Informant**: Serena Moore, Wife
Parents: James Moore & Peggie Keyes   Bpl.: Washington, NC
(See Serena L. Moore for inscription & marker)

Emma Moore   Loc.: UH-xxx
Died: 08/15/2002   Certificate Not Found

George Moore   NO MARKER   Mitchell & Fair
Died: 06/16/1970   Age: 54   Laborer
Certificate No.0050,0342   **Informant**: Mrs. Eva Moore, Wife
Parents: Edward Moore & Lena Anderson   Bpl.: GA

Harvey Moore   NO MARKER   Ellis, Mangum, & Fair
Died: 011/22/1951   Age: 39   Truck Driver   Funeral Home Record
Parents: Edward Moore & Lenna Anderson   db. 05/30/1911

Maggie Campbell Moore   OK-162-O

Died: 04/05/1930   Certificate Not Found
Marker Inscription Poor

MAGGIE CAMPBELL
MOORE
DIED APR. 5, 1930
FAITHFUL TO HER TRUST EVEN UNTO DEATH

Mary Moore   OK-N NO MARKER   Noble & Kelsey: 108
Died: 05/15/1940   Age: 71   Domestic
Certificate No.0027,0697   **Informant**: Anna Dowans
Parents: Albert & Nellie Neely   Bpl.: Rowan Co., NC

Mary C. Moore   UH-NO MARKER   Ellis, Mangum, & Fair
Died: 01/26/1961   Age: 60   Domestic
Certificate No.0041,0332   **Informant**: Kirk Moore, Husband
Parents: Samuel Burris & Roxie McDonald   Bpl.: SC

BURIALS

Oscar James Moore
Died: 07/18/1922   Age: 26y7m1d
Certificate No.0010,0397
Parents: Walter Moore & Mary Strong

OK- N NO MARKER   Noble & Kelsey: 108
Trucker @ Southern Railroad Shed
Informant: Mary Moore
   Bpl.: Chester, SC

Serena L. Moore
Died: 08/1930 Age: 75

OK-075-N   Noble & Kelsey: 60
Certificate Not Found

MOORE
DR. EDWARD MOORE   SERENA L. MOORE
JUNE 1855   NOVEMBER 1865
OCTOBER 1927   AUGUST 1930

Arminta C. Morant
Died: 03/15/1964   Age: 85
Certificate Not Found

OK-366 -I/J

ARMINTA C. MORANT
WIFE OF
WILLIAM P. PEMBERTON
OCT. 7, 1879
MAR. 15, 1964

Harvey Alexander Morant
Died: 12/01/1970   Age: 78
Certificate No.0050,0700
Parents: Charlie Morant & Mary Kelsey

OK-180-O   Morant - Harris Plot   Noble & Kelsey 151
Retired Barber Self-Employed
Informant: Mrs. Rena Harris Morant
   Bpl.: SC

MORANT
HARVEY A.   RENA HARRIS
JUNE 28, 1892   DEC. 11, 1901
DEC. 1, 1970   MAR. 23, 1977

Rena Harris Morant
Died: 03/23/1977   Age: 73dc-76
Certificate No.0057,0265
Parents: Henry & Lona Harris
(See Harvey Alexander Morant)

OK-180-O   Morant –Harris Plot   Noble & Kelsey: 151
Housewife
Informant: Mrs. Annette Morant Mathes
   Bpl.: NC

Rosa Lee Morant
Died: 10/10/1980   Age: 90

BN-760-P   Noble & Kelsey
Homemaker

Certificate No.0060,0789   **Informant:** Mrs. Alma Clark, Daughter
Parents: Henry Hickumbotton & Mary Welch   Bpl.: Richland Co., SC

ROSA LEE MORANT
1889 -- 1980
WIFE OF WILLIAM FRED MORANT, SR.

William Fred Morant
Died: 10/01/1947   Age: 63
Certificate No. 0030,0952
Parents: Charlie & Mary Morant

NO MARKER   Noble & Kelsey
Laborer @ Spencer Shops
Informant: Rosa Morant, wife
   Bpl.: Chester, SC

BURIALS

Adam Morgan
Died: 09/15/1918   Age: ∞50
Certificate No. 0006,0497
Parents: Jessie Morgan & Annie Faggott

NO MARKER
Worker @ Transfer Shed @ Southern Railroad
Informant: Amery Chinbard (sic)
   Bpl.: NC

Summersettt

Bessie Morris
Died: 04/03/1948   Age: 59
Certificate No. 0031,0291
Parents: George Aubry & Annie Hostery

UH-NO MARKER
Laundress

Ellis, Mangum, & Fair
Funeral Home Record

bd. 02/03/1889

Edward Morris
Died: 02/15/1955   Age: 60
Certificate No. 0036,0095
Parents: Sedie Morris & Sarah Clehorne

UH-NO MARKER
Laborer
Informant: Hattie Blackwell
   Bpl.: Monroe, NC

Ellis, Mangum, & Fair

Mamie Morris
Died: 07/15/1918   Age: STILL BIRTH
Certificate No. 0006,0467
Parents: Ed Morris & Bessie Andrew

NO MARKER

Informant: Ed Morise
   Bpl.: Salisbury, NC

Noble & Kelsey: 342

Mike Morrison
Died: 01/29/1909   Age: 50 yrs.

NO MARKER

Summersett
Funeral Home Record

Emma C. Morton
Died: 03/20/1977   Age: 92
Certificate No. 0057,0264
Parents: Alexander Cundiff & Mary Jane Warden

OK-114-N
Practical Nurse
Informant: Eugene Morton
   Bpl.: NC

Noble & Kelsey: 40

EMMA C.
MORTON
MAY 26 1885
MAR 20 1977

Miles Linwood Morton
Died: 10/25/1924   Age: 16
Certificate No. 0012,0458
Parents: James M. Morton & Emma Condiff

OK-112-N
School Boy
Informant: J. M. Morton, Father

Noble & Kelsey: 40

MILES LINWOOD
MORTON
AUG. 8, 1908
OCT. 25, 1924

Rev. James M. Morton
Died: 06/17/1934   Age: 62

Certificate No. 0022,0233
Parents: William Morton & Rhoda Taylor

OK-113-N
Minister & Teacher Pastor of Trinity Presbyterian
   Church, Salisbury, NC 1910 - 1930
Informant: Emma C. Morton
Bpl.: Granville Co., NC

Noble & Kelsey: 40

REV. JAMES M.
MORTON
MAY 12, 1872
JUNE 17, 1934

BURIALS

Mattie Lucille Moton
Died: 06/17/1943   Age: 18

BN-880-M
Certificate Not Found

MATTIE LUCILLE
DAU. OF
LUCILLE MOTON
FEB. 16, 1925
JUNE 17, 1943
THO LOST TO SIGHT
TO MEMORY DEAR.
ERECTED BY
JOE B. MOTON
BROTHER OF
MATTIE MOTON
MOTON

Eke (sic) Mowery
Died: 02/26/1925   Age: 63
Certificate No. 0013,0303
Parents and birth place not given

NO MARKER   Bingham & Carter
Day Laborer @ Walker Lumber Company
Informant Cleo McKinzie (sic)

Rilla Mullen
Died: 07/01/1939   Age: 48   Housekeeper
    Certificate No.0027,0170   **Informant:** Leola Miller
    Parents: Jack Mullen & Lizzie Roland   Bpl.: Spartanburg, SC

OK-372-I/J   Ellis, Mangum, & Fair

RILLA MULLEN
MAY 30, 1892
JULY 1, 1939
SHE IS NOT DEAD
BUT SLEEPETH

Sallie Henderson Murdock
Died: 11/18/1970   Age: 60
Certificate No.0050,0701
Parents: John & Charlotte Henderson

NO MARKER   Mitchell & Fair
Cook in the City Schools
Informant: C. Z. Murdock
    Bpl.: NC

Mary Jane Howard Musgrave
Died: 08/01/1918   Age: 59
Certificate No.0008,0413
Parents: Prince Howard & Unknown

OK-NO MARKER   Noble & Kelsey: 29
Seamstress
Informant: Rev. T. G. Musgrave
    Bpl.: Washington, DC

Ellen Myers
Died: 01/21/1924   Age: ∞29
Certificate No. 0012,0293
Parents: Cahill & Sallie Gray

OK-NO MARKER   Summersettt
Cook
Informant: Sim Dunn
    Bpl.: Rowan Co., NC

Maybell Myers
Died: 08/07/1952   Age: 46
Certificate No.0033,0427
Parents: Peter Small & Margaret Walker

UH-

Informant: Carrie Bradford

BURIALS

Elizabeth Worthey Neely BT-262-K Plot
Died: 09/12/1973 Age: 77
Certificate Not Found

NEELY
LEONARD ALBERT   ELIZABETH WORTHEY
JAN. 7, 1901   MAY 19, 1896
OCT. 9, 1961   SEPT. 12, 1973

Frank Solomon Neely BT-262-K Plot   Noble & Kelsey
Died: 04/27/1957 Age: 80   Retired Laborer
Certificate No. 0039, 0030   **Informant:** Ivory Neely
Parents: Frank Neely Sr. & Unknown   Bpl.: Rowan Co., NC

Father
**FRANK SOLOMON
NEELY**
MAY 4, 1877
APR. 27, 1957

John K. Neely   BN-784-P
Died: 02/19/1989 Age: 80   Certificate Not Found

JOHN K. NEELY
APR. 6, 1909
FEB. 19, 1989
IN LOVING MEMORY

Leonard Albert Neely   BT-262-K Plot   Noble & Kelsey
Died: 10/09/1961 Age: 60   Laborer China Grove Cotton
Certificate No. 0042, 0082   **Informant:** Elizabeth Neely, Wife
Parents: Robert Neely & Margaret Clark   Bpl.: NC
(See Elizabeth Worthey Neely)

Margie Neely   UH-NO MARKER   Ellis, Mangum, & Fair
Died: 02/02/1958 Age: 29

Milton Neely   OK-216-L
Died: 06/22/1925   Certificate Not Found

**MILTON NEELY
DIED JUNE 22, 1925**

BURIALS

Robert Neely BN-721-M   Bingham & Carter
Died:04/17/1924   Age: 36 Soldier, Infantry WWI   Laborer after war
Certificate No.0012,0347   **Informant**: Arthur Hopkins
Parents: Richard & Margaret Neely (1900 census)   bd. 09/1887

ROBERT
NEELY
NORTH CAROLINA
PVT. 366 INF. 92 DIV.
APRIL 17, 1924

James J. Nicholson   BN-817-P
Died:07/24/1937   Age: 66   Certificate Not Found

JAMES NICHOLSON
AUG. 22, 1871
JULY 24, 1937
HIS RECORD IS ON HIGH

Angeline Noble   OK-124-N   Noble & Kelsey 10
Died: 02/03/1944   Age: 70   Housewife
Certificate No. 0029,0089   **Informant**: Eura (sic) Wilborne
Parents:?? & Caroline Wilson   Bpl.: Rowan Co., NC
(See Stephen Noble)

Annie Noble   OK-NO MARKER   Noble & Kelsey: 50

Eloise (sic) Noble   OK-NO MARKER   Noble & Kelsey
Died: 01/31/1927   Age: 22, 5, 9   Cook
Certificate No. 0015, 0294   **Informant**; Rachel Evans
Owens Evans & Rachel Summers   Bpl.: Salisbury, NC

James Noble   OK-NO MARKER   Noble & Kelsey: 50
Died: 09/12/1918   Age: Died @ birth
Certificate No. 0006,0494   **Informant**: Frank Noble of 1218 W. Monroe St.

Margaret J. Whitaker Noble   OK-NO MARKER   Noble & Kelsey: 50
Died:08/15/1916   Age: 85   Domestic
Certificate No.0003,0257   **Informant**: Annie Noble
Parents: Lewis Whitaker & Unknown   Bpl.: CT

Minnie Garfield Noble   OK-122-N   Noble & Kelsey: 10
Died:07/1908   Age: 28   Certificate Not Found
Lot Contains: E. D. Saunders; Angeline Litaker; James Knoble; Rachel E. Carson; Clyde Innis Cook Sr.; Stephen Knoble according to Kelsey map

MINNIE
GARFIELD
NOBLE
Born
Oct. 24, 1880
Died
July 18, 1908

BURIALS

Stephen Noble
Died: 05/02/1940   Age: 92

Certificate No. 0027,0691

OK-124-N   Noble & Kelsey: 10
Undertaker / teamster @ Kelsey Funeral Home &
G. W. Wright Funeral Homes
Informant: Angeline Noble
Parents: UNKNOWN   Bpl.: Washington, DC

**STEPHEN
NOBLE
MAY 2, 1940
AGED 92 YRS.** (RIGHT SD BLANK
ERECTED BY SERGEANT WILLIAM F. KELSEY Jr.

Columbus Norman   OK-380-I/J MISSING   Noble & Kelsey: 245

Emma Norman   OK-380-I/J   Noble & Kelsey: 245

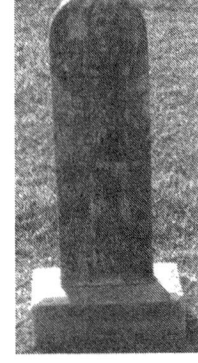

Died: 19/14/1938   Age: 54
Certificate No. 0026,0227
Parents: UNKNOWN

Informant: Mrs. Francis McElvin
Bpl.: Spartanburg, SC

**EMMA
NORMAN
DIED
OCT. 14, 1938
AGE
54 YEARS
AT REST**

John Norman
Died: 11/01/1929   Age: 43
Certificate No. 0017,0525
Parents: John W. Norman & Ella Benson

OK-145 -I/J MISSING   Noble & Kelsey
Freight Packer @ Transfer Shed
Informant: Mrs. Jessie Norman, Wife
Bpl.: Willington, SC

Rosa Lee Norman
Died: 02/07/1915   Age: 18y3m7d   Cook
Certificate No. 0002,0094
Parents: Columbus Norman & Rosa Lee Morman

OK-380 -I/J -MISSING   Noble & Kelsey: 245

Informant: Columbus Norman
Bpl.: Enoree, SC

Ruby Louise Wilks Norris
Died: 06/14/1978   Age: 72
Certificate No. 0058,0467
Parents: John Wilks & Unknown

BN-820-M   Noble & Kelsey
Retired E. L. Foil
Informant: Mr. T. R. Norris, Husband
Bpl.: Oconne Co., SC

NORRIS
THEODORE R.   **RUBY W.**
NOV. 29, 1901   **MAY 10, 1904**
JAN. 10, 1998   **JUNE 14, 1978**

Ruby Mae Norris   BN-819/820-M
Died: 1935   Certificate Not Found
(See Ruby Louise Wilks Norris)   **RUBY MAE
1935**

BURIALS

Theodore Roosevelt Norris Sr.
Died:01/30/1998   Age: 97
Certificate No.0078,0103
Parents: John Norris & Samantha Kirk
(See Ruby Louise Wilks Norris)

BN-819-M   Noble & Kelsey
Laborer @ Railroad
Informant: Theodore R. Norris Jr., Son
   Bpl.: Taccoa, GA

Sarah J. Oakley
Died:07/10/1947   Age: 53
Certificate No.0030,0890
Parents: Robert Crawford &??

NO MARKER   Ellis, Mangum, & Fair
Domestic
Informant: Sarah Smarr [sic]
   Bpl.: York Co., SC

Adam Otha Oglesby
Died: 10/31/1949   Age: 48

NO MARKER   Ellis, Mangum, & Fair
Section hand @ Southern Railroad   Funeral Home Record

Nelle Ormand
Died: 08/02/1926   Age: 11 mos.
Certificate No. 0014,0260
Parents: Jessie Ormand & Ollie Bridge

NO MARKER   Peoples Undertaker
INFANT
Informant: Jessie Ormond
   Bpl.: Not Given

Isabella Moss Osborne
Died: 06/01/1918   Age: 26, 10, 18
Certificate No. 0006,0445
Parents: Freeman Osborne & Lula Brown

NO MARKER   Noble & Kelsey
Cook for Private family
Informant: Lula Chun
   Bpl.: Davie Co., NC

John J. Osborne
Died: 10/11/1929   Age: ∞63
Certificate No.0018,0233
Parents: Osborne & Adline Brown

OK-NO MARKER   Noble & Kelsey: 105
Caller @ Southern Railroad Shops
Informant: Alice Osborne
   Bpl.: Farmville, VA

Walter Osborne
Died: 11/17/1909   Age: 22y10m17
Certificate No. 0004,0482
Parents: Alex Osborne & Magritte Hobson

NO MARKER.   Noble & Kelsey
Railroad Hand
Informant: Matilda Brown
   Bpl.: Davie Co., NC

Ellen Owens
Died: 11/25/1909   Age: 70 yrs.

NO MARKER   Summersett
Wash Woman

Register of Death, Salisbury, and County of Rowan, NC (09/1909-10/11/1911)

Johnson Toto Pajibu   UH-612-G

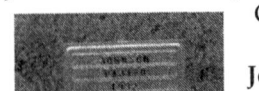

Certificate Not Found

Johnson Pajibu
1992

Palmer Plot   OK-043-N Family Plot   Noble & Kelsey 67

PALMER
(Marker off pedestal & face down on ground 2006)

Katherine Palmer Certificate Not Found   NO MARKER

Mr. Zelpale Palmer Certificate Not Found   NO MARKER

BURIALS

Georgia Parham
Died: 12/14/1939   Age: 52
Certificate No. 0027,0278
Parents: UNKNOWN

NO MARKER
Domestic
Informant: James Parham, Husband

Ellis, Mangum, & Fair

Thomas Lee Parham
Died: 06/23/1938   Age: 2y9m

NO MARKER
Baby

Ellis, Mangum, & Fair
Funeral Home Record

Hugh Ernest Parker
Died: 09/04/1960   Age: 72

NO MARKER

Ellis, Mangum, & Fair
Funeral Home Record

Ruby Lee Parker
Died: 10/09/1990   Age: ∞79 Certificate Not Found

UH-576-H

RUBY LEE
JULY 28, 1921
OCT 9, 1990

Sadie Fisher Parker
Died: 03/04/91   Age: 86
Certificate No. 0071,0233
Parents: John Fisher & Josie Partee Fisher

BN-015-M
Presser
Informant: Nonie Johnson
   Bpl.: Rowan Co., NC

Noble & Kelsey

SADIE FISHER
PARKER
DEC. 12, 1904
MAR. 4, 1991

Walter Parker
Died: 09/19/1925   Age: 45
Certificate No. 0012,0415
Parents; William Parker & Ava Montgomery

NO MARKER
Laborer
Informant: not given
   Bpl.: Cabarrus Co., NC

Bingham & Carter

Janie Parks
Died: 11/30/1931   Age: 49 Certificate Not Found grvstn
Condition on 08/19/2003

OK-046-N

JANIE PARKS
OCT. 17, 1882
NOV. 30, 1931
AT REST

Jasper P. Parks
Died: 01/03/1982   Age: 66
Certificate No. 0062,0042
Parents: John Henry Parks & Mary Lizzie People

NO MARKER
Maintenance Dept. @ Catawba College
Informant: Elsie L. Parks, Wife
   Bpl.: Clarke Co., GA

Mitchell & Fair

Moses Parks
Died: 12/31/1938   Age: 25

NO MARKER

Noble & Kelsey
Funeral Home Record

Elisie Partee
Died: 11/03/1939   Age: 31
Certificate No. 0027,0246
Parents: William Partee & Carrie Cruze

NO MARKER
Domestic
Informant: Virginia James
   Bpl.: Rowan Co., NC

BURIALS

Frank Partee
Died: 11/10/1923 Age: 29,5,5
Certificate No. 0011,0526
Parents: Robert Partee & Margrett Summ??

NO MARKER
Laborer @ Lumber Company
Informant: M. H. Partee
Bpl.: NC

Bingham & Carter

Harry Leroy Partee
Died: 05/16/1982 Age: 56
Certificate No. 0062,0401
Parents: William Partee & Carrie Stirewalt

BN-828-M MISSING
Laborer
Informant: Mrs. Virginia James, Sister
Bpl.: Rowan Co., NC

Noble & Kelsey

Mariah Bost Partee
Died: 08/27/1937 Age: Certificate Not Found

BN-014-M

MARIAH BOST
PARTEE
DIED
AUG. 27, 1937

Odessa Coleman Pate
Died: 06/05/1991 Age: 78
Certificate No. 0071,0531
Parents: Arthur Coleman & Ethel Warner

UH-595-G
Housemaid @ Private Homes
Informant: William A Frost
Bpl.: Charlotte, NC

Noble & Kelsey

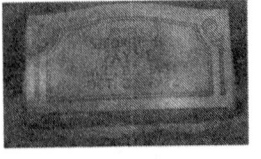

DEC. 10,   JUNE 5,
1913   1991
ODESSA COLEMAN PATE

Rosia Chisolm Patterson
Died: 06/08/1994

UH-552 H
Certificate Not Found

PATTERSON
ROSIA CHISOLM
BORN DEC. 16, 1916   DIED JUNE 8 1994

Willie Patterson
Died: 01/22/1957 Age: 86

NO MARKER

Ellis, Mangum, & Fair
Funeral Home Record

George H. Payne
Died: 10/22/1922 Age: 38
Certificate No. 0010,0443
Parents: Alonzo Payne & Alexena Beau

OK-168-O Plot
Freight Caller, Southern Rail Road
Informant: Alexena Anderson
Bpl.: Philadelphia, PA

Noble & Kelsey 124

FATHER
GEORGE H. PAYNE
AUG. 27, 1884
OCT. 22, 1922

Willie C. Payne
Died: 1943 Age: 41

OK-044-N
Certificate Not Found

PAYNE
WILLIE C.
1902 - 1943
A DEVOTED WIFE

BURIALS

Nancy Payseur   OK-O (Knox Plot)   Certificate Not Found
Died: 11/20/1944   Age. 80
Unearthed 07/15/2004

NANCY PAYSEUR
JANUARY 28, 1864
DECEMBER 20, 1944
On that bright immortal shore
We shall meet to part no more

Danil Peake   OK-144-O   Noble & Kelsey
Died: 10/08/1929   Age: ∞50   Day Laborer, City of Salisbury
Certificate No. 0017,0507   **Informant:** Lelia Peaks
Parents: Franklyn Peake & Mary Woodard   Bpl.: Fairfield Co., SC
(See Lela Josephine Peake for additional marker)

DANIL PEAKE
DIED OCT. 8, 1929

Lela Josephine Peake   OK-144-O   Noble & Kelsey
Died: 08/29/1941   Age: 50   Housework
Certificate No. 0027,1495   **Informant:** Miss Myrth Peake
Parents: Amos Tate & Emma Tate   Bpl.: York, SC

PEAKE
HIS WIFE

LELA J. PEAKE   DANIEL PEAKE
DIED AUG. 29, 1941   DIED OCT. 8, 1929
AGE 48 YRS.   AGE 50 YRS.
Life's race well run life's work well done, life's victory won, now Cometh rest.

Mrs. Lilia Peakes   OK-NO MARKER   Noble & Kelsey: 93

Ida Bell Gee Pearson   BN-06-M   Noble & Kelsey
Died: 11/08/1987   Age: 79   Maid: Private Homes
Certificate No. 0067,0901   **Informant:** Jesse Pearson
Parents: Kemper Gee & Carrie Guest   Bpl.: Union Co., SC

Jesse Edward Pearson   NO MARKER   Ellis, Mangum, & Fair
Died: 07/16/1960   Age: 57   Truck Driver
Certificate No. 0041,0019   **Informant:** Ida Bell Pearson, Wife
Parents: Joseph Pearson & Ollie Hawkins

Judge Pearson   NO MARKER   Noble & Kelsey
Died: 11/27/1925   Age: 89   Day Laborer
Certificate No. 0013,0464   **Informant:** Jack Pearson
Parents: Henry Adkins & Nancy Pearson   Bpl.: Davie Co., NC   bd∞1836

Mary D. Pearson   NO MARKER   Ellis, Mangum, & Fair
Died: 08/22/1966   Age: 64   Domestic
Certificate No. 0046,0449   **Informant:** Josephine Davis
Parents: Sandy Bickson & Jennie Farmer   Bpl.: Mt. Avery, NC

BURIALS

Elizabeth J. Peddrew
Died: 12/01/1937   BN-830-M
Age: 22 `Certificate Not Found

ELIZABETH J. PEDDREW
DAU. OF
WALTER L. JOHNSON
AUG. 4, 1915
DEC. 1, 1937

Rosa Peeler
Died: 07/29/1915   Age: 37y6m1d
Certificate No. 0002,0204
Parents: Frank Reeves & Laura Perkins
NO MARKER
Laundress & Housewife
Informant: Laura Vinson
Bpl.: Salisbury, NC
Noble & Kelsey: 385

Arnous Pemberton
Died: 01/26/1919   Age: 25
Certificate No. 0007,0169
Parents: Sandy Pemberton & Millie Christian
OK-NO MARKER
Laborer
Informant: Martha McCoanlley
Bpl.: Salisbury, NC
Noble & Kelsey: 37

Matthew Pearson Pemberton
Died: 07/18/1959   Age: 47
Certificate No. 0040,0034
Parents: William Pemberton & Arminta Morant   Bpl.: NC
OK-367-I/J
Presser @ Fair Cleaners
Informant: Angeline Hall
Noble & Kelsey: 37

MATTHEW P. PEMBERTON
MAY 2, 1912
JULY 18, 1959

Sandy Pemberton
Died: 10/17/1937   Age: 60
Certificate No. 0025,0257
Parents: Hubert Pemberton & Alice Pemberton
OK-NO MARKER
Peddler
Informant: Mrs. Mattie McCauley
Bpl.: Montgomery Co., NC
Noble & Kelsey: 37

Stanly S. Pemberton
Died: 03/04/1963   Age: 1 yr.
Certificate No. 0043,0159
Parents: Rinthie Pemberton & Maria Barker
OK-343-I/J
CHILD
Informant: Rinthie Pemberton
Bpl.: Washington, DC
Noble & Kelsey

STANLY S. PEMBERTON
OCT. 4, 1962
MAR. 4, 1963

William P. Pemberton
Died: 05/02/1953   Age: 90   Retired Laborer @Southern Railroad
Certificate No. 0034,0253
Parents: Herbert & Alice Pemberton
OK-368-I/J
Informant: Arminta Pemberton
Bpl: Montgomery Co., NC
Noble & Kelsey

WILLIAM P. PEMBERTON
MAY 2, 1863
MAY 29, 1953

Lottie Pennington
OK-NO MARKER
Noble & Kelsy: 100

Tom Pennington
Died: 03/16/1930   Age: 50+
Certificate No. 0018,0188
Parents: Jacob Pennington & Jane Pennington
OK-NO MARKER
Truck Driver
Informant: Lottie Pennington
Bpl.: Stanly Co., NC
Noble & Kelsy: 100

BURIALS

Lititia Mae Peoples
Died: 03/29/1963   Age: 1 Dy

UH-NO MARKER
INFANT

Ellis, Mangum, & Fair
Funeral Home Record

Howard Perkins
Certificate No. 0082,0550
Parents: William Perkins & Katie Faggart

BN-888-M

HOWARD   ILLA H.
1913 -   1917 - 1993
PERKINS

Illa A. Heggins Perkins
Died: 03/22/1993   Age: 75
Certificate No. 0073,0325
Parents: John Heggins & Annie Brown

BN-889-M
Domestic Worker in Private Homes
Informant: Howard Perkins
    Bpl.: Rowan Co., NC

Mitchell & Fair

Lillian Buford Perkins
Died: 03/30/1978   Age: 77
Certificate No. 0058,0258
Parents: Simon Buford & Mary Woodside

OK-132-N
Retired Lunch Room Manager
Informant: Mrs. Lula M. Cowan, Dau.
    Bpl.: Rowan Co., NC

Noble & Kelsey

PERKINS
ROY   LILLIAN BUFORD
JULY 9, 1900   APR. 16, 1900
NOV. 9, 1965   MAR. 1978
DEATH IS THE INN ON THE ROAD TO GOD

Roy Perkins
Died: 11/19/1965   Age: 65
Certificate No. 0045,0621
Parents: John Perkins & Unknown

OK-133-N
Unemployed
Informant: Mrs. Lillian Perkins, Wife
    Bpl.: Salisbury, NC (See Lillian B. Perkins.)

Noble & Kelsey

Edith Elizabeth Davis Perry
                Died: 08/08/1963   Age: 36

BN-Brand New
Certificate Not Found

EDITH ELIZABETH
DAVIS PERRY
SEPTEMBER 25, 1927
AUGUST 8, 1963

John W. Perry
Died: 02/13/1949   Age: 67
Certificate No. 0031,0798

NO MARKER
Minister - Janitor
Informant: Ella Tomlin

Ellis, Mangum, & Fair

Parents: UNKNOWN

Louise Henderson Pharr
Died: 08/30/1994   Age: 80

OK-131-N
Certificate Not Found

PHARR
LOUISE HENDERSON
SEPT. 17, 1914
AUG. 30, 1994
ALTHOUGH SHE SLEEPS HER MEMORY LIVES ON

BURIALS

Perreal Conner Pharr
Died: 01/08/1991   Age: 79
Certificate No. 0071,0026
Parents: Olden Connor & Gertrude Shipp

UH-582-H
Packer @ Frozen Food Company
Informant: Lubertha C. Glenn
Bpl.: Iredell Co., NC

Mitchell & Fair

PHARR
PERREAL C.
JULY 15, 1911
JAN. 8, 1991

Raymond James Pharr
Died: 07/09/1990   Age: 62
Certificate No. 0070,0590
Parents: Walter Pharr & Lizzie Miller

UH-570-H MISSING
Car Cleaner @ Railroad
Informant: Elfrances Ellis
Bpl.: Spencer, NC

Noble & Kelsey

Robert Beverly Phifer
Died: 01/29/1922   Age: 40y5m1da
Certificate No. 0010,0296
Parents: William Phifer & Mary J. Caldwell

NO MARKER
Dumper Transfer Shed @ Southern Railroad Co.
Informant: William Phifer, Father
Bpl.: Mecklenburg Co., NC

Noble & Kelsy: 281

Alberta Phillips
Died: 08/30/1935   Age: 34   Certificate Not Found

BN-764-P

ALBERTA PHILLIPS
AUG. 13, 1901
AUG. 30, 1935
AT REST

Ed Phillips
Died: 11/11/1953   Age: 86

NO MARKER
Laborer: City Street Dept.

Ellis, Mangum, & Fair
Funeral Home Record

Edward Luther Phillips
Died: 01/19/1974   Age: 32

NO MARKER

Mitchell & Fair
Funeral Home Record

Marcus Jermaine Phillips
Died: 05/20/1972

OK-354-I/J
Certificate Not Found

MARCUS JERMAINE
PHILLIPS
MAY 20, 1972
MAY 20, 1972

Sallie Ann Tomlinson Phillips

Died: 03/02/1961   Age: 69
Certificate No. 0041,0431
Parents: Walter Tomlinson & Unknown

BT-275-K
Housewife
Informant: Mrs. Tiney Byers
Bpl.: NC

Noble & Kelsey

MRS. SALLIE
ANN PHILLIPS
DEC. 23, 1892
MAR. 2, 1961

BURIALS

Willie Mills Phillips
Died: 02/22/1992   Age: 69
Certificate No. 0072,0150
Parents: Melvin Phillips & Katie Douglas

NO MARKER   Noble & Kelsey
Spin Draw Operator @ Cotton Cloth Mill
Informant: Willie Phillips Jr., Son
   Bpl.: Rock Hill, SC

Clarence Pierce
Died: 06/09/1926   Age: 18y9m25d
Certificate No. 0014,0606
Parents: John Pierce & Harriett Reynolds

NO MARKER   Noble & Kelsy: 176
Southern Railroad
Informant: Julius Pierce
   Bpl.: Wanthen, Ga.

Cordia P. Pierce
Died: 03/19/1928   Age: 27y1m18d
Certificate No. 0016,0315
Parents: Dan Pierce & Sarah Pierce

NO MARKER   Noble & Kelsy: 144
Barber
Informant: Daisy Pierce
   Bpl.: NC

Julian Pierce
Died: 02/28/1950   Age: 61
Certificate No. 0032,0258
Parents: Robert Pierce & Anna Archer

OK-NO MARKER   Noble & Kelsy: 176
Laborer: City Street Dept. Wagoner Const.ruction Co.
Informant: Janie Boyd, Newark, NJ
   Bpl.: Warthe, GA

June Brown Pierce
Died: 04/23/1910   Age: 61,4,19
Informant: Mrs. E. C. Bost
Parents: Dave Brown & Persila Haughton
(Joe Frick: Register of Deeds in 1965)   (Book 1- September 1909 to February 1910)

OK-NO MARKER
Widow/Domestic

   Bpl: Rowan Co., NC

Marie Sanford Pierce
Died: 04/27/1940   Age: ∞47
            Certificate No. 0027,0675
            Parents: Burl Sanford & Julia Ann Monroe

OK-139-N   Noble & Kelsey
Housewife
Informant: James Sanford
      Bpl.: Griffin, GA

MARIE
PIERCE
DIED
APRIL 27
1940

Margaret Pilgram
Died: 03/15/1939   Age: no dob
Certificate No. 0027,0114
Parents: UNKNOWN

NO MARKER   Ellis, Mangum, & Fair
Domestic
Informant: Wade Pilgram, Husband
   Bpl.: GA

BURIALS

David H. Pinkston   OK-053-N   Noble & Kelsey
          Died: 04/20/1976   Age: 87   Laborer   Certificate Not Found

DAVID PINKSTON
8-26-1889
4-20-1976

John Pinkston   NO MARKER   Noble & Kelsy: 221
Died: 01/29/1921   Age: 1 day   INFANT
Certificate No. 0009,0314   **Informant:** Walter Pinkston
Parents: Walter Pinkston & Eunice Torrance   Bpl.: Salisbury, NC

Nancy Chambers Pinkston   OK-054-N   Noble & Kelsey
          Died: 03/18/1986   Age: 87   Maid: Private Homes
          Certificate No. 0066,0268   **Informant:** Mary A. Johnson, Daughter

Parents: Lester Chambers & Mary Butner   Bpl.: Rowan Co., NC

NANCY C. PINKSTON
5-27-1899
3-18-1986

Thomas Alexander Pinkston   OK-NO MARKER   Noble & Kelsey
Died: 06/12/1927   Age: 76   Day Laborer
Certificate No. 0015,0386   **Informant:** Dave Pinkston
Parents: & Malinda Graham   Bpl.: Nashville, TN

INFANT of Pitts & Montgomery   OK-NO MARKER   Noble & Kelsy: 6
Died: 03/24/1920   STILL BIRTH
Certificate No. 0008,0195   **Informant:** Lewis Pitts
Parents: Lewis Pitts & Dora Montgomery   Bpl.: Salisbury, NC

Amie H. Judge Pitts   BN-747-M   Noble & Kelsey
Died: 12/18/1985   Age: 72   Domestic – Maid: Private Homes
Certificate No. 0065,1086   **Informant:** Donald Judge, Son
Parents: Quay Judge & Fannie Cherry   Bpl.: Chester Co., SC
    Condition on 09/01/2003

	PITTS	
JERRY LEE	and his wife	**AMIE JUDGE**
DEC. 6, 1894		OCT. 13, 1913
JUNE 24, 1980		DEC. 18, 1985

Frank R. Pitts   NO MARKER   Noble & Kelsey
Died: 05/10/1926   Age: ∞55   Blacksmith helper @ Southern Railway Shop
Certificate No. 0014,0229   **Informant:** Lewis F. Pitts
Parents: Richard Pitts & Sarah Anderson

BURIALS

Jerry Lee Pitts
Died: 06/24/1980   Age: 82
Certificate No. 0060,0532
Parents: Unknown
Date Read: 09/01/2003 (See Amie H. Judge Pitts)

BN-746-M   Noble & Kelsey
Retired, Proctor Chemical Company
Informant: Gerolene Pitts, Daughter
   Bpl.: Chester Co., SC

Lewis Frank Pitts Jr.
Died: 03/19/1988   Age: 78
Certificate No. 0068,0279
Parents: Lewis Frank Pitts Sr. & Dora Montgomery

OK-NO MARKER   Noble & Kelsey: 6
Mechanic Helper on Railroad
Informant: Lewis Frank Pitts III. Chicago, Illinois
   Bpl.: Rowan Co., NC

Lewis Frank Pitts Sr.
Died: 05/13/1956   Age: 69
Certificate No. 0037,0024
Parents: Frank Pitts & Mary Jane Anderson

NO MARKER   Noble & Kelsey
Painter @ Wallace Realty Co.

   Bpl.: Columbia, SC

Mae Troy Pitts
Died: 01/13/1921   Age: 2y19m11d
Certificate No. 0009,0029
Parents: Rosco Williams & Sophia Pitts

OK-NO MARKER   Noble & Kelsey: 97
CHILD
Informant: Frank Pitts
   Bpl.: Salisbury, NC

Florence Irene Woods Poag
Died: 02/08/1988   Age: 65

BN-001-M   Noble & Kelsey
Cook

Certificate No. 0068,0134   **Informant**: James G. Poag Jr.
Parents: Sandy Woods & Laura Catholic   Bpl.: Cleveland, NC

**IN LOVING MEMORY
POAG
FLORENCE IRENE
APR. 13, 1907
FEB. 8, 1988**

James Poag
Died: 03/09/1956   Age: 50
Certificate No. 0036,0703
Parents: John Poag & Sallie Reid

NO MARKER   Ellis, Mangum, & Fair
Janitor

Rose Poe
Died: 01/13/1920   Age: ∞62
Certificate No. 0008,0097
Parents: Lewis Ramseur & Jane Ramseur

OK-NO MARKER   Noble & Kelsy: 317
Laundry Work
Informant: Alice Williams
   Bpl.: Lincolnton, NC

Baby Polk

OK-NO MARKER   Noble & Kelsey: 68
                                     Funeral Home Record

Hannah Polk
Died: 09/19/1922   Age: 73
Certificate No. 0010,0305
Parents: Steve Stevenson & Charity Caldwell

OK-NO MARKER   Noble & Kelsey; 68
Domestic & Laundry work
Informant: Miller McCorkle
   Bpl.: SC

Amelia Pope
Died: 02/15/1926   Age: ∞31
Certificate No. 00014,0116
Parents: Frank Williams & Laura??

NO MARKER   Bingham, Carter, & Cheshire
Domestic
Informant: Charles Pope
   Bpl.: NC

BURIALS

Mary Francis Powell OK-187-O Summersettt
Died: 12/16/1923   Age: 47   Domestic
Certificate No. 0011,0549   **Informant:** Oliver Powell, Husband
Parents: Sam Webster &????   Bpl.: Forsyth Co., NC
Condition on 08/19/2003 Concrete grvstn

MARY
FRANCIS POWELL
MAY 25, 1876
DEC. 6, 1923
AT REST

Oliver P. Powell OK-NO MARKER Noble & Kelsey: 167
Died: 05/07/1957   Age: 79   Cook
Certificate No. 0037,0623   **Informant** Joseph Powell, Braddock, Pa
Parents: Prince Powell & Unknown   Bpl.: Iredell Co., NC

Gwendolyn Fair Preasha UH-414-I/J Mitchell & Fair
Died: 07/18/1979   Age: 64   Dietician @ New York University
Certificate No. 0059,0565   **Informant:** Mrs. Avis Fair Wilkins Monroe
Parents: Rev. James Fair & Mrs. Sadie Davis Fair   Bpl.: Rowan Co., NC

(DOLL)
GWENDOLYN F. PREASHA
JULY 28, 1912
JULY 18, 1979

Emma Louise Price OK-036-N Noble & Kelsey: 47
Died: 11/12/1915   Age: 29   Librarian: Livingstone College: Teacher
Certificate No. 0002,0250   **Informant:** William Dodge Price, brother
Parents: Joseph C. Price & Jennie Smallwood Price   Bpl.: Salisbury, NC
(See Alma Price Braithwaite for photo of marker)

EMMA LOUISE PRICE	WILLIAM DODGE PRICE	ALMA PRICE BRAITHWAITE
MAY 7, 1886	MAR. 21, 1884	SEPT. 28, 1888
NOV. 12, 1915	MAR. 6, 1924	APR. 7, 1945

Jennie Smallwood Price OK-040-N Noble & Kelsey: 47
Died: 06/23/1945   Age: 83   House Wife & Widow of Joseph Charles Price

JENNIE SMALLWOOD   JOSEPHINE PRICE SHERRILL   RICHARD W.
WIFE OF JOSEPH C. PRICE   DEC. 28, 1893   SHERRILL
FEB. 14, 1862 - JUNE 23, 1945   DEC. 6, 1887

Josephine Price NO MARKER George A. Wright
Died: 03/21/1925   Age: 48   Domestic
Certificate No. 0013,0169   **Informant:** Robert Price
Parents: None Given   Bpl.: NC

BURIALS

Louise Moore Price — OK-NO MARKER — Noble & Kelsey: 47

Robert M. Price — UH-NO MARKER — Ellis, Mangum, & Fair
Died: 01/01/1942   Age: 75   Minister
Certificate No. 0028,0307   **Informant:** Luther Price
Parents: Rufus Price & Unknown   Bpl: Mecklenburg Co., NC

William Dodge Price — OK-037-N — Noble & Kelsey: 47
Died: 03/06/1924   Age: 40   Certificate Not Found   Physician
Parents: Joseph C. Price & Jennie Smallwood Price   Bpl.: Salisbury, NC
See Alma Price Braithwaite for marker

Mary Propst — OK-096-N — Noble & Kelsey: 2
Died: 03/28/1910   Age: 17
Certificate No. 0004,0330   **Informant:** Isaiah Johnson
Parents: Robert Propst & Mother Unknown
Date Read: 08/30/2000 (No Monument: Plot also Contains Annie Wiseman & Robert Wiseman)

Carrie Mae Barber Pruitt — BN-853-M — Noble & Kelsey
Died: 01/05/1994   Age: 61   Spinner of Cotton Cloth
Certificate No. 0074,0019   **Informant:** Ronald Barber
Parents: John Roberts & Bertha Unknown   Bpl.: Rowan Co., NC

CARRIE MAE PRUITT
MAR. 5, 1932
JAN. 5, 1994
IT IS WELL WITH MY SOUL

JJ Quattlebaum (female) — OK- — Noble & Kelsey
Died: 05/29/1971 STILL BIRTH   Place of fetal death, Salisbury, NC
Certificate No. 0051,0358
Parents: Edward Quattlebaum, 31 & Jennie Mae Davis, 31

INFANT DAU. OF
EDWARD & JENNIE
QUATTLEBAUM
MAY 29, 1921

Alec Ramsuer — NO MARKER — Mitchell & Fair
Died: 06/10/1968   Age: 71   Funeral Home Record

Alvah Randall — OK-NO MARKER — Noble & Kelsey: 62
Died: 04/23/1915   Age: 17   School Boy
Certificate No. 0002,0144   **Informant:** Mrs. Sujette Smith
Parents: Thomas Randall & Fannie Harris   Bpl.: Madison, Ga.

BURIALS

Kathleen Jones Randall

UH-575-H
Died: 04/06/1993 Age ∞ 84 Beautician

RANDALL		
THOMAS JEFFERSON	MARRIED	KATHLEEN JONES
MAR. 5, 1907	JULY 14,	SEPT. 30, 1909
DEC. 1, 1992	1930	APR. 6, 1993

Thomas Jefferson Randall UH-575-H Mitchell & Fair.
Died: 12/01/1992 Age: 85 Self Employed Barber @ Randall Barber & Beauty Shop with wife Kathleen
Certificate No. 0072,1056 **Informant**: Kathleen Jones Randall, Wife
Parents: Thomas Randall & Haseltine Harris Bpl.: Madison, GA
(See Kathleen Jones Randall)

Otto Rankin NO MARKER- G. W. Wright @ Noble & Kelsey: 329
Died: 02/07/1910 Age: ∞38 Railroad Man
Certificate No. 0004,0387 **Informant** William Pemberton
Parents: No family information

Nathalee B. Reese UH-548-H
Died: 06/02/1988 Age: 94 Certificate Not Found

NATHALEE B. REESE
JULY 18, 1894
JUNE 2, 1988

Dorothy Reeves BT- K Noble & Kelsey

Died: 02/10/1943 Age: 36 Worker @ Star Laundry
Certificate No. 0028,0727 **Informant**: Annie Galloway
Parents: Herman Reeves & Lethis Reeves Bpl.: Salisbury, NC

DOROTHY REEVES
SEPT. 3, 1907
FEB. 10, 1943
GONE BUT NOT FORGOTTEN
REEVES

Bertha Pearl Reid NO MARKER Ellis, Mangum, & Fair
Died: 12/06/1951 Age: 68 Domestic Funeral Home Record
Parents: James Reid & Martha Trusdel bd. 05/08/1883

Janie Walker Reid NO MARKER Noble & Kelsey: 35
Died: 03/21/1923 Age: 42 Seamstress: Self Employed
Certificate No. 0011,0407 **Informant**: Alberta Brown
Parents: Sam Walker & Pauline McLilly Bpl.: Chester, SC

John C. Reid BN-670 P MISSING Ellis, Mangum, & Fair
Died: 03/19/1963 Age: 79 Laborer
Certificate No. 0043,0177 **Informant**: Willie Reid
Parents: Joseph Reid & Rosette Jordan Bpl.: Rowan Co., NC

BURIALS

Maggie Johnson Reid
Died:03/09/1956   Age: 77
Parents: George & Alice Washington

BN-670 P MISSING

Ellis, Mangum, & Fair
Funeral Home Record

Nancy Bennett Reid
Died:06/17/1910   Age: ∞35
Certificate No. 0004,0281
Parents: Jack & Rachel Bennett

UH-NO MARKER

Informant: Ed. Reid of Salisbury, NC
Bpl.: Unknown

Summersettt

Bertha Mae Clodfelter Reid-Craig   BN-670-P
Died: 1983   Age: ∞81 Certificate Not Found

BERTHA MAE
CLODFELTER
REID -- CRAIG
1902 -- 1983
IN LOVING MEMORY FROM YOUR FAMILY

LaKendra Monchel Reliford   BN-780-P
Died:08/07/1992   Age: 6   CHILD   Certificate Not Found

LaKENDRA MONCHEL
RELIFORD
JAN. 30, 1986
AUG. 7, 1992

William Leon Reliford   BN-793-P   Noble & Kelsey
Died:07/08/1980   Age: 37   Laborer for City of Salisbury
Certificate No. 0060,0533   **Informant**: Mrs. Mae H. Reliford, Wife
Parents: Henry Reliford & Hattie Thompson
Condition on 09/06/2003   WILLIAM RELIFORD
                                   SEPT. 5, 1942
                                   JULY 8, 1980

Frank N. Richardson   OK-328-K   Noble & Kelsey
Died:05/12/1958   Age: 60   Retired from Southern Railway Company
Certificate No. 0039,0083   **Informant**: Rossalie M. Richardson, Wife
Parents: James E. Richardson & Josephine Hyler   Bpl.: SC

RICHARDSON
FRANK N. RICHARDSON   ROSSALIE M. RICHARDSON
   MAY 6, 1898   JUNE 1, 1896
   MAY 12, 1958   DEC. 7, 1961
        GONE BUT NOT FORGOTTEN

Martha Richardson   NO MARKER   Summersettt
Died: 01/13/1923   Age: ∞65   Domestic
Certificate No. 0011,0365   **Informant**: Willie Boler
Parents: Peter Allison &???   Bpl.: Cleveland, SC

Rosalie Massey Richardson   OK-328-K   Noble & Kelsey
Died: 12/07/1961   Age: 65   Instructor, State Board of Education
Certificate No. 0042,0175   **Informant**: Frank Richardson, Son
Parents: William Massey & Marcy A. Miller   Bpl.: SC   (See Frank N. Richardson)

BURIALS

Victoria Richardson
Died: 08/01/1928   Age: 72
Certificate No. 0016,0395
Parents: Cicero Richardson & Sarah Harris

OK-196-L
College teacher @ Livingstone College
Informant: Mrs. May Graves
    Bpl.: Cleveland, Ohio

Noble & Kelsy: 192

**IN MEMORY OF
VICTORIA RICHARDSON
JANUARY 12, 1856
AUGUST 1, 1928
FOUNDER AND FIRST GENERAL
SECRETARY OF THE Y.H.&F.M.
SOCIETY - FROM MAY 1912 UNTIL HER DEATH.
ERECTED BY THE W.H.&F.M.
SOCIETY OF THE A.M.E. ZION
CHURCH - AUGUST 1942**

Elizia Riggs
Died: 07/14/1928   Age: ∞80
Certificate No. 0016,0392
Parents: UNKNOWN

OK-NO MARKER
Domestic
Informant: C. L. Danley
    Bpl.: Staunton, VA

Noble & Kelsy: 135

Clarence Rippy
Died: 01/01/1955   Age: 73
Certificate No. 0036,0039
Parents: UNKNOWN

UH-NO MARKER
Laborer, Gas Plant
Informant: Welfare Dept.

Ellis, Mangum, & Fair

Lela C. Ritchie
Died: 04/05/1969   Age: 67
Certificate No. 0049,0239
Parents: Dock Carlton & Sallie Unknown

NO MARKER
Typist
Informant: Mr. Thomas Lassiter
    Bpl.: TN

Mitchell & Fair

Sarah A. Walker Ritchie
Died: 1945   Certificate Not Found

NO MARKER

Elder V. Leak Rivers
Died: 01/12/1923   Age: 31,11,12
Certificate No. 0011,0416
Parents: A. D. Leak & Pattie Kelly

NO MARKER
Dressmaker
Informant: Pattie Leak
    Bpl.: Ashville, NC

Noble & Kelsey

Jane Roberson
Died: 10/28/1918   Age: None Given
Certificate No. 0006,0555
Parents: William Lewis &????

No Marker
Cook for Private family
Informant: Henrietta Roberson
    Bpl.: Chester, SC

Noble & Kelsey

Minnie Roberson
Died: 06/16/1910   Age: 15 yrs.
Parents: Jim Black & Minnie Hurley

NO MARKER

Summersett

William Alex Roberson
Died: 09/17/1918
Certificate No. 0006,0500
Parents: Tom Roberson & Louise Hairston

NO MARKER

Informant: Tom Roberson
    Bpl.: Salisbury, NC

Noble & Kelsey

Coatny Massey Roberts
Died: 03/18/1967   Age: 69

NO MARKER
Certificate Not Found

Mitchell & Fair
Funeral Home Record

BURIALS

Orr Ulysses Milton Roberts
Died:08/01/1981   Age: 56

NO MARKER

Mitchell & Fair
Funeral Home Record

Samuel Roberts
Died:07/02/1911   Age: 64
Certificate No. 0004,0023
Parents UNKNOWN

NO MARKER
General Laborer
Informant: Please Roberts, Rowan Co., NC

Laura Curry Robertson
Died:04/12/1928   Age: 57y07m28
Certificate No. 0016,0329
Parents: Nicholas Pea & Adline Izzards

OK-030-N
Housewife
Informant: Adline Jones
Bpl.: Lancaster Co., SC

Noble & Kelsey: 54

LAURA CURRY
ROBERTSON
Aug. 1865
Apr. 12, 1928
Erected by her
daughter

Mary Rose Robertson
Died: 11/02/1978   Age: 98
Certificate No. 0058,0867
Parents: Charles & Alice Rose

NO MARKER
Housewife
Informant: Henry Fisher, Nephew
Bpl.: Davie Co., NC

Mitchell & Fair

Charlie Robinson
Died: 01/18/1929   Age: 29,7,10
Certificate No. 0017,0312
Parents: Tom & Charity Robinson

NO MARKER
Day Labor
Informant: David Roberson
Bpl.: Salisbury, NC

Noble & Kelsey

Clarence Robinson
Died:07/23/1974   Age: 75
Certificate No. 0054,0513
Parents: Mott & Fannie Robinson

NO MARKER
Retired Southern Railway
Informant: Mrs. Beatrice M. Robinson, Wife
Bpl.: SC

Noble & Kelsey

Eva Mae Twitty Robinson
Died:07/28/1958   Age: 49
Certificate No. 0039,0216
Parents: Samuel Twitty & Unknown

BT-303-K
Housewife @ Home
Informant: Clarence Robinson, Husband
Bpl.: SC

Noble & Kelsey

ROBINSON
EVA MAE TWITTY
WIFE OF CLARENCE ROBINSON
AUG. 15, 1908
JULY 28, 1958
THOUGH I WALK THROUGH THE VALLEY OF
THE SHADOW OF DEATH, I WILL FEAR NO EVIL,
FOR THOU ART WITH ME.   PSALM 23, 4

James Leroy Robinson
Died:09/13/1986   Age: 76
Certificate No. 0066,0824
Parents UNKNOWN

NO MARKER
Janitor @ City Junior High School
Informant: Loretta Robinson, Wife

Noble & Kelsy: 384

BURIALS

James W. Robinson
Died: 10/28/1929   Age: 48
Certificate No. 0017,0561
Parents: Pierce Robinson & Mary Hunter

NO MARKER   Cheshire & Callahan
Blacksmith Helper @ Spencer Shops
Informant: Mary Robinson, Wife
   Bpl.: SC

Minnie Robinson
Died:06/15/1910   Age: ∞15yrs.

Parents: Jim Black & Mammie Heilig
Register of Death, Salisbury, County of Rowan, NC (09/1909-10/11/1911)

UH-NO MARKER
Teenager
Informant: Lee Robinson
   Bpl.: Cabarrus Co., NC

Rubye Kennedy Robinson
   Died: 12/31/1993

OK-067-N
Age: 76   Certificate Not Found

ROBINSON
RUBYE KENNEDY
JULY 23, 1917
DEC. 31, 1993

Tom Robinson
Died: 11/26/1927
Certificate No. 0015,0479
Parents: Jacob & Fannie Robinson

NO MARKER   Noble & Kelsey
Day Laborer
Informant: E. D. Robinson
   Bpl.: Fairfield, SC

Paul Agustus Rhodes
Died:07/24/1990   Age: 51
Certificate No. 0070,0601
Parents: Henry Rhodes & Bertha Ratsford

UH-571 H MISSING
Truck Driver
Informant: Josephine Cowan Rhodes, wife
   Bpl: Davie Co., NC

Sarah Simpson Roseboro
Died:06/18/1964   Age: 69
Certificate No. 0044,0384
Parents: Ned Simpson & Phoebe McCullough

NO MARKER   Mitchell & Fair
Domestic
Informant: Robert Roseboro, Husband
   Bpl.: Chester, SC

Kiana Lashae Ross
Died:03/09/1995   Age: 2 days
Certificate No. 0075,0256
Parents: Lonnie Ray Carpenter & Maudine Mardella Ross

UH-535-H MISSING   Noble & Kelsey
INFANT
Informant: Maudine M. Ross, Mother
   Bpl.: Rowan Co., NC

Laura Rousseau
Died:02/24/1920   Age: 54
Certificate No. 0008,0128
Parents: Giles & Charlotte Nichols

OK-148-O MISSING   Noble & Kelsey
Nurse: Red Cross Epidemic
Informant: W. G. Rousseau, Husband
   Bpl.: Rowan Co., NC

Nora Rowe
Died: 11/07/1942   Age: 48
Certificate No. 0028,0414
Parents: John Connor & Mira McCorkle

NO MARKER
Domestic
Informant: Gilder Rowe
   Bpl.: Catawba Co., NC

Amelia Rucker Rozzell
Died: 11/28/1975   Age: 81
Certificate No. 0055,0800
Parents: UNKNOWN

AMELIA RUCKER ROZZELL
   AUG. 18, 1894
   NOV. 28, 1975

BT-288-K   Noble & Kelsey
Housewife
   Informant: Mrs. Margaret Brown

BURIALS

Dan Russell
Died: 01/09/1927   Age: ∞67
Certificate No. 0014,0284
Parents: Unknown

UH-NO MARKER
Laborer
Informant: Eva Russell, Wife
Bpl.: MISS.

Bingham & Carter

Eva Harris Russell
Died:07/14/1956   Age: 76
Certificate No. 0037,0117
Parents: James I Berngardt & Eveline Henderson

BN-735-M
Teacher
Informant: Mrs. Flora Flack
Bpl.: NC

Ellis, Mangum, & Fair

EVA HARRIS
RUSSELL
AUG. 6, 1879
JULY 14, 1956

Lucy Sampson
Died:05/22/1944   Age: 89

OK-422-H

Noble & Kelsy
Certificate Not Found

LUCY SAMPSON
WIFE OF
ANDREW SPAULDING
OCT. 4, 1855
MAY 22, 1944

Annie Belle Sanders
Died: 09/10/1924   Age: 24
Certificate No. 0015,0457
Parents: John Sanders & Sarah Simpson

UH-NO MARKER
Laundress
Informant: Sarah Sanders
Bpl.:SC

Cheshire & Mangum

E. D. Sanders
Died:04/08/1916   Age: ∞56
Certificate No. 0003,0279
Parents: Henry & Mary Sanders

OK-NO MARKER
Blacksmith
Informant: Mrs. I.J. Sanders
Bpl.:Vance Co., NC

Noble & Kelsey: 10

Julia Sanders
Died: 09/06/1923   Age: 41
Certificate No. 0011,0489
Parents: West Saunders & Hardin ????

NO MARKER
Domestic Housework
Informant: Jannie Kendrick
Bpl.: SC

Noble & Kelsey

Kenneth Napoleon Sanders
Died:01/04/1989   Age: 33
Certificate No. 0069,0024
Parents: Jessie Bridges & Ruth Sanders

BN-678-P
Cleaning Person @ Cement Company
Informant: Charles E. Sanders
Bpl.: Wake Co., NC

Noble & Kelsey

SANDERS
KENNETH NAPOLEON
JULY 21, 1956
JAN. 4, 1989

Julia Sanford
Died: 07/05/1918   Age: Not Given
Certificate No. 0006,0461
Parents: Jim Row & Mattie Bailey

NO MARKER
Domestic
Informant: Mowery Pierce
Bpl.: GA

George W. Wright

BURIALS

Josephine Saunders
Died: 1942   Age: 61

BN-808-P
Certificate Not Found

SAUNDERS
ROBERT SAUNDERS
1881 - 1942
HIS WIFE
JOSEPHINE SAUNDERS 1890 -

H. H. Savage
Died, 10/24/1924   Age: 58
Certificate No. 0017,0514
Parents: Willis & Harriett Savage

NO MARKER   Fraternal Funeral Home
Spencer Shops
Informant: Allace (sic) Savage
Bpl.: Rowan Co., NC

Mamie L. Saunders
Died: 08/15/1963   Age: ∞50

BN-
Certificate Not Found

MAMIE L. SAUNDERS
WIFE OF
MATTHEW J. HILL
FEB. 4, 1913
AUG. 15, 1963

Robert Saunders
Died: 09/17/1942   Age: 63
Certificate No. 0028,0371
Parents: Jordan & Janie Saunders
(See Josephine Saunders)

BN-807-P   Noble & Kelsey
Freight Packer for Southern Railroad
Informant: Mrs. Josyline Sanders
Bpl.: SC

Ardelia Scott
Died: 03/19/1961   Age: 39
Certificate No. 0041,0434
Parents: George Jeffers & Georgiana Goosby

UH-NO MARKER   Ellis, Mangum & Fair
Informant: Odell Scott, Husband
Bpl.: Danville, VA

Arthur Harry Scott
Died: 06/04/1949   Age: 62
Certificate No. 0031,0893
Parents: John Scott & Unknown

UH-NO MARKER   Ellis, Mangum, & Fair
Janitor
Informant: Bessie Scott
Bpl.: Mecklenburg Co., NC

Bessie Scott
Died: 03/29/1954   Age: 56
Certificate No. 0035,0206
Parents: Richard Smith & Emma Summer

NO MARKER
Domestic
Informant: Arthur Scott
Bpl.: Rowan Co., NC

Henryetter Scott
Died: 12/22/1918   Age: 13
Certificate No. 0006,0594
Parents: Vance Scott & Fannie Pearson
Poor condition on 08/19/03

OK-060-N   George W. Wright
Domestic
Informant: Vance Scott, father
Bpl.: Salisbury, NC

HENRYETTER
SCOTT
AUG. 5, 1905
DEC. 22, 1918
AT REST

BURIALS

John Scott

Died: 12/08/1916   Age: 62
Certificate No. 0003,0313
Parents: UNKNOWN
Condition on 08/15/2003

OK-215-L
Laborer
Informant: Mrs. John Scott
Bpl.: NC

G. W. Wright @ N. & Kelsey 236

JOHN SCOTT
DIED
DEC. 8, 1916
AGE 62
AT REST

Julia Maria Scott
Died:03/27/1927   Age: 7m
Certificate No. 0015,0329
Parents: Leroy Scott & Tresa Bost

OK-NO MARKER
INFANT
Informant: Emma Austin
Bpl.: Salisbury, NC

Noble & Kelsey: 115

Mary Barber Scott
Died:03/02/1944   Age: 55
Certificate No.0029,0466
Parents: James Barber & Emma Harley

BN-870-M MISSING
Housewife
Informant: James D. Scott
Bpl.: Rowan Co., NC

Noble & Kelsey

Mason Scott
Died:05/12/1979   Age: 81
Certificate No. 0059,0391
Parents: John & Jenette Scott

NO MARKER
Funeral Director
Informant: Lucille Scott, Wife
Bpl.: Mecklenburg Co., NC

Mitchell & Fair

Neal Scott
Died:09/19/1909   Age: 42 yrs

NO MARKER

Summersett
Funeral Home Record

Rose Mary Scott
Died:01/20/1985   Age: 85 Certificate Not Found
Teacher

OK-O NEW MARKER

Retired Elementary School

ROSE MARY
SCOTT
MAY 5, 1900
JAN. 20, 1985

Vance Scott
Died:07/11/1959   Age: 74
Certificate No. 0040,0038
Parents: UNKNOWN

NO MARKER
Retired from Southern Railroad
Informant: Mrs. Willie M. Smith
Bpl.: Rowan Co., NC

Noble & Kelsey: 66

Donald Sellers
Died: 10/16/1992   Age: 51
Certificate No. 0072,0828
Parents: Thurman Sellers & Bisfie Marshall

UH-627-G MISSING
Cement Finisher @ Construction Co.
Informant: Elnora J. Sellers
Bpl.: Chesterfield, SC

Noble & Kelsey

Dorothy Ann Sellers
Died:07/20/1985   Age: 19
Certificate No. 0065,0624
Parents: Donald Sellers & Elnora Johnson

NO MARKER
Unemployed
Informant: Elnora J. Sellers, Mother
Bpl.: Rowan Co., NC

Mitchell & Fair

BURIALS

Marion Setzer OK-119-N Ellis, Mangum, & Fair
Died: 06/18/1961   Age: 21 Nursing
Certificate No. 0027,1433 **Informant** Maude McKain
Parents: Alonzo Setzer & Maude McKain Bpl.: Salisbury, NC

MARION SETZER
BORN NOV. 20 1920
DIED
JUNE 18 1941

Maud E. McCain Setzer NO MARKER Ellis, Mangum, & Fair
Died: 11/07/1947   Age: 43 Domestic
Certificate No. 0030,0982 **Informant**: Alonza Setzer, Husband
Parents: John Mclean & Cora House

Mary Lee Sharp OK-362 -I/J Chesire & Callahan
Died: 12/26/1923   Age: 49 Domestic
Certificate No. 0017,0564 **Informant**: W. A. Sharp, Husband
Parents: John Osborne & Lula Hobson Bpl.: Davie Co., NC

MARY LEE
wife of
REV. W. A. SHARP
SEPT. 15, 1880
DEC. 26, 1929

William Alexander Sharp NO MARKER Ellis, Mangum, & Fair
Died: 10/20/1940   Age: 58 Minister: New Shepard Baptist Church & Macedonia
 Baptist Church
Certificate No. 0027,0795 **Informant**: A. R. Sharpe
Parents: Abraham Sharp & Rosa Chunn? sp Bpl.: Davie Co., NC

Christine B. Sharpe UH-639-G MISSING Certificate Not Found

Cleveland Sharpe UH-NO MARKER Ellis, Mangum, & Fair
Died: 03/09/1938   Age: 26 Machine Helper, Caring Tools
Certificate No. 0026,0085 **Informant**: Alma Linheymer
Parents: Rev. W. A. Sharpe & Marry Lee Fowler Bpl.: Salisbury, NC

Katie Miller Sharpe NO MARKER Ellis, Mangum, & Fair
Died: 10/13/1951   Age: 53 Domestic
Certificate No. 0032,0923 **Informant**: Ella Sherrill
Parents: Fred McDowell & Unknown

Gus Shaw NO MARKER Cheshire & Mangham
Died: 03/31/1927   Age: 44 Laborer
Certificate No. 0015,0327 **Informant**: Sarah Shaw
Parents: Millage Shaw & Lizzie Caretta

Sarah Shaw UH-NO MARKER Ellis, Mangum, & Fair
Died: 07/25/1944   Age: 67 Certificate Not Found

BURIALS

Annie Cenovia Shelton UH-418-H
Died:02/01/1996   Age: 86   Certificate Not Found

ANNIE CENOVIA SHELTON
JULY 2, 1908
FEB. 1, 1996

Georgia Shelton   NO MARKER   Fraternal Funeral Home
Died: 03/29/1930   Age: 24   Teacher
Certificate No. 0018,0195   **Informant:** Jessie Shelton
Parents: George & Jessie Shelton   Bpl.: Salisbury, NC

Estella Sherrill   BN-   Noble & Kelsey
Died:05/28/1951   Age: 63   Housewife
Certificate No. 0032,0774   **Informant:** Rev. W. M. Wyatt
Parents: UNKNOWN

ESTELLA SHERRIL
AUG. 8, 1888
MAY 28, 1951

Jennie Louise Sherrill   OK-035-N   Noble & Kelsey
Died:08/02/51   Age: 14
Certificate No. 0032,0907   **Informant:** Mrs. Josephine Sherrill
Parents: Richard Sherrill & Josephine Price   Bpl.: Salisbury, NC

Josephine Price Sherrill   OK-041-N Price Plot   Noble & Kelsey: 47
Died:02/07/1985   Age: 91   Retired Livingstone College Librarian
Certificate No. 0065,0144   **Informant:** Richard Sherrill Sr.
Parents: Joseph C. & Jennie S. Price   Bpl.: Rowan Co., NC

JOSEPHINE PRICE
SHERRILL
DEC. 28, 1893

Richard Wadsworth Sherrill   OK-042-N Price Plot   Noble & Kelsey: 47
Certificate Not Found   Principal of Aggrey Memorial School in Landis.
NC, Manager of Granite Realty & Insurance Co. of Salisbury, NC   Manager of
A.M.E. Zion Publishing House
Parents: ????   Bpl.: Rowan Co., NC

RICHARD W.
SHERRILL
DEC. 6, 1887

Sutter Sherrill   NO MARKER   Bingham, Cheshire, & Carter
Died: 06/16/1926   Age: 56   Laborer @ Railroad
Certificate No. 0014,0227   **Informant:** Estella Sherrill, Wife
Parents: Unknown   Bpl.: NC

BURIALS

David Shipp
Died: 02/24/1922 Age: 4days
Certificate No. 0010,0492
Parents: George Shipp & M Pryor

OK-NO MARKER
INFANT
Informant: George Shipp
  Bpl.: Rowan

Noble & Kelsy: 266

George W. Shipp
Died: 04/14/1947 Age: 60
Certificate No. 0030,0536
Parents: Wilson & Mamie Shipp

OK-225-K
Farmer
Informant: Mrs. Mamie Shipp, Wife
  Bpl.: Mt. Holly, NC

Noble & Kelsy: 266

SHIPP
GEORGE W.   MAMIE P
DIED APRIL 14, 1947   DIED APRIL 9, 1958

Mamie Pryor Shipp
Died: 04/09/1985 Age: 69
Certificate No. 0039,0037
Parents: Not Known (See George W. Shipp)

OK-226-K
Housewife
Informant: Mrs. Margaret Brotherton

Noble & Kelsy: 266

Tryplemia (sic) Shipp

OK-226-K NO MARKER

Noble & Kelsy: 266

Jennie Ann Shuford
Died: 07/19/1949 Age: 56
Certificate No. 0031,0943
Parents: UNKNOWN

OK-120-N
Domestic
Informant: Winnie Wood, Philadelphia

Ellis, Mangum, & Fair

Angel Lovette Sifford
Died: 06/14/1967 Age: INFANT
  ANGEL LOVETTE
   SIFFORD
  JUNE 14, 1967
  JUNE 14, 1967

OK-344-I/J
Certificate Not Found

Idella Wooly Siler
            Died: 12/17/2002 Age: 91

BN-NEW MARKER (POST 1996 SURVEY)
Certificate Not Found

**IDELLA WOOLEY
   SILER
SEPT. 25, 1911
DEC. 17, 2002 & Plot of
 IDELLA SILER**

Shirley Ann Siler
Died: 08/19/1968 Age: 31

NO MARKER
Certificate Not Found

Mitchell & Fair

Samson Simes
Died: 03/02/1917 Age: ∞19
Certificate No. 0005,0310
Parents: J. S. Simes & Lizzie Poter

NO MARKER
Laborer
Informant: J. S. Simes, Father

Summersettt

BURIALS

A. T. Simmons
Died: 08/28/1940   Age: 75

BN-047-N
Certificate Not Found
Broken Condition on 08/19/2003

Noble & Kelsey 388

A. T. SIMMONS
APR. 15, 1865
(rest broken off)

George Simmons
Died: 10/25/1939   Age: 78
Certificate No. 0027,0538
Parents: William Simmons & Not Known

NO MARKER
Farmer
Informant: Mrs. Cola Hall
Bpl.: ALA.

Noble & Kelsey: 388

Glendora Simmons

NO MARKER

Noble & Kelsey: 388

Malissa Fraley Simmons
Died: 10/05/1929   Age: 73
Certificate No. 0017,0509
Parents: Edmond & Priscilla Fraley

BN-045-N MISSING
Housewife
Informant: Mrs. Willie Ellis
Bpl.: GA

Noble & Kelsey

Mary Hall Simmons
Died: 12/21/1936   Age: 80
Certificate No. 0024,0326
Parents: Phill & Liza Hall

UH-378 -I/J
Housework
Informant: Ruth Rollinson
Bpl.: Lincolnton, GA

Peterson & Mangnum

SIMMONS
MARY HALLS
WIFE OF
WEBB SIMMONS
MAR. 12, 1856
DEC. 21, 1936
AT REST

Mose Simmons
Died: 05/07/1952   Age: 72
Certificate No. 0033,0333
Parents: Webb Simmons & Mary Hall

UH-384-I/J
Storehouse laborer in Spencer Shops
Informant: Ruth Rollinson
Bpl.: Lincolnton, GA.

Ellis, Mangum, & Fair

MOSE SIMMONS
APR. 15, 1880
MAY 7, 1952

Philip Simmons
Died: 04/12/1945   Age: 51
Certificate No. 0029,0627
Parents: Webb Simmons & Mary Hall

NO MARKER
Laborer
Informant: Ruth Rollinson
Bpl.: Lincolnton, GA

Ellis, Mangum, & Fair

Ida Fitzgerald Simon
Died: 12/02/1956   Age: ∞56

UH-516-H

Certificate Not Found

IDA FITZGERALD SIMON
FEB. 3, 1900
DEC. 2, 1956
ASLEEP IN JESUS

BURIALS

Frank Walter Simpson UH-491-H Noble & Kelsey
Died: 01/17/1951   Age: 53   Laborer
Certificate No. 0032,0534   **Informant**: Phoebe Simpson
Parents: Ned & Phoebe Simpson   Bpl.: Chester Co., SC

FRANK WALTER
SIMPSON
1899 – 1951

Julius Simpson UH-NO MARKER Ellis, Mangum, & Fair
Died: 07/09/1952   Age: 43   Trucking: North Carolina Finishing Co.
Certificate No. 0033,0347   **Informant**: Julia Simpson
Parents: Robert Simpson & Lula Grace   Bpl.: Chester Co., SC

Lillian Bingham Evans Simpson OK-188-O Plot Noble & Kelsey: 166
Died: 07/04/1989   Age: ∞ 90
Certificate No. 0069,0659   **Informant**: Theodore Evans Jr., Son
Parents: Lillington H. Bingham & Henrietta Browne   Bpl: Salisbury
 Bingham Plot

George Singleton UH-NO MARKER Ellis, Mangum, & Fair
Died: 05/29/1959   Age: 63   Laborer @ NC Finishing Co.
Certificate No. 0039,0636   **Informant**: Marie Singleton, Wife
Parents: UNKNOWN

A. H. Sloan UH-433-H Plot MISSING Noble & Kelsy: 251
Died: 10/04/1914   Age: 45y9m29d   Preacher
Certificate No. 0001,0818   **Informant**: Willie Sloan
Parents: Frank Sloan & Not Known   Bpl.: Rowan Co., NC

Alphonzo Sloan NO MARKER Ellis, Mangum, & Fair
Died: 02/20/1943   Age: 5 months   INFANT
Certificate No. 0028,0730   **Informant**: Beatrice Setzer, Mother
Parents: Thomas Sloan & Beatrice Setzer   Bpl.: Salisbury, NC

Frank Sloan UH-433-H MISSING Noble & Kelsey:
Died: 07/25/1915   Age: 50   Farmer
Certificate No. 0002,0201   **Informant**: Sallie Sloan
Parents: UNKNOWN   Bpl.: Rowan Co., NC

Jessie Lowe Sloan UH-433-H Plot
Died: 01/08/1972   Age: 76   Certificate Not Found

JESSIE LOWE
SLOAN
OCT. 22, 1896
JAN. 8, 1972

BURIALS

Sallie Sloan OK-227-K Noble & Kelsy: 251
Died: 12/10/1929   Age: 67 Certificate Not Found

SALLIE SLOAN
WIFE OF FRANK SLOAN
JULY 19, 1862
DEC. 10, 1929
AT REST

Sylvia LaJune Sloan UH-NO MARKER Ellis, Mangum, & Fair
Died: 12/31/1945   Age: 7 mos   INFANT
Certificate No. 0030,0191   **Informant:** Beatrice Sloan, Mother
Parents: Thomas Sloan & Beatrice Setzer   Bpl.: Salisbury, NC

William Sloan UH-433-H Plot MISSING Noble & Kelsy: 251
Died:06/10/1922   Age: 3y5m14d CHILD
Certificate No. 0010,0374   **Informant:** William Sloan
Parents: William Sloan & Jessie Partee   Bpl.: Salisbury, NC

William Lonnie Sloan UH-433-H Plot
Died:03/25/1946   Age: 52   Preacher
Parents: Rev. Abraham & Eliza Sloan   Bpl.: Rowan Co., NC

SLOAN
REV. WILLIAM LONNI
SLOAN
APRIL 30, 1894
MARCH 28, 1946
HOLY BIBLE, BOOK DIVINE,
PRECIOUS TREASURE, THOU ARE MINE.

Alexander Smith UH-NO MARKER Ellis, Mangun, & Fair
Died:07/18/1941   Age: 54y10m07d   Farmer
Certificate No. 0027,1456   **Informant:** Elizabeth Smith

Alice Smith OK-109-N Noble & Kelsey: 7
Died:06/30/1937   Age: ∞72   Domestic & Housewife
Certificate No. 0057,0249   **Informant:** William Pierson
(See Henry Smith for marker)

Amanda Smith OK-NO MARKER Noble & Kelsey
Died: 04/06/1913   Age: 19   Domestic
Certificate No. 0001,0279   **Informant:** William Smith, Father
Parents: William Smith & Millie Mosely   Bpl: Cleveland Co., NC

Arabella Smith NO MARKER Noble & Kelsey
Died: 02/05/1926   Age: ∞51   Housewife/Domestic
Certificate No. 0014, 0107   **Informant:** Maggie Hayes
Parents: Delphi Kimball & F. H. Lewis   Bpl.: Salisbury, NC

Brister(sic) **Smith** NO MARKER Noble & Kelsey
Died: 02/14/1924   Age: 57,11,9   Hand Driller @ Rock Quarry
Certificate No. 0012,0307   **Informant:** Arabell Smith, Wife
Parents: Brister & Elizabeth Smith   Bpl.: Fairfield, SC

BURIALS

Elizabeth Smith
Died: 07/25/1952   Age: 66
Certificate No. 0033,0444
Parents: Allen Wright & Emily Maxie

NO MARKER   Ellis, Mangum, & Fair
Domestic
Informant: Viola Wood
   Bpl.: Rayles Georgia

Emma Smith
Died: 01/26/1915   Age: 63
Certificate No. 0002,0088
Parents: Jessie Chambers & Millie Kessler

OK-NO MARKER   Noble & Kelsey: 51
Nurse Midwife
Informant: Lulu Craige
   Bpl.: Davidson Co., NC

Fredrick Smith
Died: 11/21/1923   Age: 1,4,0
Certificate No. 0011,0528
Parents: Roland & Bulah Smith

NO MARKER   Bingham & Carter
Baby
Informant: Bulah Smith, Mother
   Bpl.: Salisbury, NC

Henry Smith
Died: 10/05/1932   Age: 59

OK-110-N   Noble & Kelsey: 7
Employed @ Southern Railroad; Member: Soldiers
   Memorial
Certificate Not Found

HENRY SMITH
DIED OCT. 5, 1932
AGE 59 YEARS
HIS WIFE
ALICE SMITH
DIED JUNE 30, 1937
AGE 72 YEARS

Henry D. Smith
Died: 06/02/1922   Age: 67
Certificate No. 0010,0370
Parents: Not Known

OK-NO MARKER   Noble & Kelsey: 39
Laborer, U. S. Post Office
Informant: Edna Gant

Henry Lee Smith
Died: 11/10/1993   Age: 69
Certificate No. 0073,1054
Parents: Joe Smith & Lou Ella Finger

UH-644-G MISSING   Noble & Kelsey
Brick Mason Helper @ Construction
Informant: Jean C. Jackson
   Bpl.: China Grove, Rowan Co., NC

Hurclese Smith
Died: 05/28/1944   Age: 74
Certificate No. 0029,0160
Parents: Hercules & Christine Smith

OK-64-N   Noble & Kelsey 62
Barber on North Lee Street, Preacher, & Teacher
Informant: Miss Lettie M. Smith
   Bpl.: Eastover, SC

SMITH
REV. HURCLESE   L. SUJETTE HARRIS
JUNE 15, 1870   FEB. 28, 1870
MAY 28, 1944   DEC. 9, 1947

Jakia Synquis Smith
Died: 04/04/1990   Age: INFANT

UH-547-G

Certificate Not Found

JAKIA SYNQUIS
SMITH
OCT. 10, 1989
APR. 4, 1990

BURIALS

James E. Smith
Died:09/24/1918 Age: 37y3m18d
Certificate No. 0006,0501
Parents: Su?ial & Clara Smith

NO MARKER Noble & Kelsy: 388
Tailor, Member of Soldiers Memorial
Informant: Alberta Poag
Bpl.: Salisbury, NC

James Vickers Smith
Died:08/07/1968 Age: 96
Certificate No. 0048,0482
Parents: Anderson Smith & Susie Miller

NO MARKER Mitchell & Fair
Retired None Given
Informant: Mr. John H. Smith
Bpl.: GA

Janie Lucy Smith
Died: 08/26/1927 Age: 58
Certificate No. 0015, 0419
Parents: William Palmer & Annie Atkins

OK Noble & Kelsey
Domestic
Informant: Frank Smith
Bpl.: Stanley Co., NC

John D. Smith
Died: 10/12/1961 Age: 45
Certificate No. 0042,0091
Parents: James Smith & Addie Martin

OK-336 -I/J Ellis, Mangum, & Fair
Freight Caller @ Southern Railroad
Informant: Laura Smith, Wife
Bpl.:Spotts, Ala.

SMITH
JOHN D. SMITH
DEC. 25, 1915
OCT. 12, 1961
GONE BUT NOT FORGOTTEN

John Wiley Smith
Died: 11/05/1994 Age: 87
Certificate No. 0074,1048
Parents: Thomas Smith & Earlene Sanders

BN-680-P Noble & Kelsey
Janitor @ Newspaper
Informant: Dorothy L. Etheredge
Bpl.:Fairfield Co., SC

JOHN WILEY SMITH
SEPT. 10 NOV. 5,
1907 1994

Leonard Smith
Died:02/16/1951 Age: 36
Certificate No. 0032,0559
Parents: John Smith & Susie Copeland

NO MARKER Ellis Mangum, & Fair
Cement Finisher
Informant Susie Smith

Lula Sujette Harris Smith
Died: 12/09/1947 Age: 77
1921 –1927 Member of Moores Chapel A.M.E, Zion Church
Certificate No. 0030,1014
Parents: Harrison & Hazeltine Harris
(See Hurclese Smith for marker)

OK-063-N Noble & Kelsey: 62
Rural Supervisor of Colored Schools in Rowan Co.
Informant: Mrs. Lottie M. Whittington, Daughter
Bpl.: Madison, Ga.

BURIALS

M. B. Smith BN-851-M Noble & Kelsey
Died:01/11/1982   Age: 74   Laborer @ Railway
Certificate No. 0062,0802   **Informant**: Magdaline Smith, Wife
Parents: Raymond Smith & Odella Simmons   Bpl.: Cherokee Co., SC

M. B. SMITH, Sr.
APR. 16, 1908
OCT. 11, 1982
REST IN PEACE

Maria Ellis Smith UH-NO MARKER Ellis, Mangum, & Fair
Died:02/27/1954   Age: 86   Laundry Work
Certificate No. 0035,0166   **Informant**: Mrs. Edna Gantt
Parents: Thomas Ellis & Unknown   Bpl.:Salisbury, NC

Maugaritte Smith NO MARKER Noble & Kelsey
Died: 03/15/1923   Age: 3 mos.   INFANT
Certificate No. 0011,0057   **Informant**: Charles Smith, Father
Parents: Charles Smith & Henrietta Robins   Bpl.: SC

Nora Smith UH-NO MARKER Summersett
Died: 12/29/1907   Age: 24yrs. 4dy.   Funeral Home Records

Patricia Smith NO MARKER Mitchell & Fair
Died:04/05/1968   Age: 49   Funeral Home Record

Robert Lee Smith BN-788-P
Died:05/31/1942   Age: INFANT

[Front]   [Back]
ROBERT LEE   Sleep on sweet babe
SON OF   and take thy rest, God called
W. T. & MINNIE SMITH   thee home He thought it best.
MAY 31, 1942 JUNE 1, 1942

Susie C. Smith NO MARKER Mitchell & Fair
Died:05/04/1968   Age: 67   Housewife
Certificate No. 0048,0277
Parents: Unknown & Lillie Smith

T. C. Smith NO MARKER Ellis, Mangum, & Fair
Died:09/05/1964   Age: 50   Funeral Home Record

Mary Snow NO MARKER Ellis, Mangum, & Fair
Died:02/27/1953   Age: 63   Domestic
Certificate No. 0034,0179   **Informant**: George Rozzell
Parents: Lobe Davenport & Unknown   Bpl.: Gaston Co., NC

John Solom BN-743-M   MISSING
Died: Age: Certificate Not Found

BURIALS

Rev. John A. Spaulding OK-423-H Noble & Kelsey
Died: 04/09/1911   Age: 54y05m27d   Baptist Minister
Certificate No. 0004,0208   **Informant:** Mrs. Lula Spaulding Kelsey
Parents: Benjamin Spaulding &??   Bpl.: Columbus Co., NC

REV. JOHN A. SPAULDING.
BORN
OCT. 12, 1856
DIED
APR. 9, 1911
AGED 54 YRS.
5M'S. 27 D'S
An honest man is the noblest work of God.
SPAULDING

Chris Speights NO MARKER Noble & Kelsey
Died: 05/17/1926   Age: ∞76   Preacher
Certificate No. 0014,0251   **Informant:** William J. Trent   Bpl.: NC

Effie Spencer BN-795-P
Died: 04/26/1980   Age: 55   Certificate Not Found

EFFIE SPENCER
FEB. 7,   APR. 26,
1925   1980

Nancy Hanks Spratt BN-864-M Noble & Kelsey
Died: 02/18/1940   Age: 64   Housewife
Certificate No. 0027,1059   **Informant:** Mrs. Mollie???
Parents: Silas & Maria Black

NANCY
HANKS
SPRATT
1876 - 1940
GONE, BUT NOT
FORGOTTEN.

Johnie Mae Spring BT-297-K Certificate Not Found
Died: 04/27/1964   Age: ∞44

JOHNIE MAE
SPRING
WIFE OF
E. E. LYLES
NOV. 25, 1920
APR. 27, 1964

John E. Springs BN-016-M Military burial
Died: 09/23/1934   Certificate Not Found

JOHN E.
SPRINGS
NORTH CAROLINA
PVT. 351 FIELD ARTY.
92 DIV.
SEPTEMBER 23, 1934

BURIALS

John Henry Springs
Died: 11/09/1958   Age: 47
Certificate No. 0039,0356
Parents: Henry Srings & Bella Massey

NO MARKER
Laborer
Informant: Estelle Garris
Bpl.: SC

Ellis, Mangum, & Fair

John W. Springs
Died: 08/05/1964   Age: 77

NO MARKER

Ellis, Mangum, & Fair
Funeral Home Record

Leaper Springs
Died: 06/07/1916   Age: 37y11m3d
Certificate No. 0003,0219
Parents: Willie Springs & Addie Johnson

NO MARKER
Brickyard worker
Informant: Daisy Springs
Bpl.: Fort Will, SC

Noble & Kelsey

Lemmel Springs
Died: 04/25/1914   Age: 44
Certificate No. 0001,0773
Parents: Granderson Springs & Emily Steward

NO MARKER
Blacksmith helper @ Southern Railway Shops
Informant: Mamie Springs
Bpl.: SC

Noble & Kelsy: 353

Lena Springs
Died: 08/31/1955   Age: 66
Certificate No. 0036,0374
Parents: Wilson Bowens & Matilda Read

NO MARKER
Domestic
Informant: John Springs
Bpl.: York Co., SC

Ellis, Mangum, & Fair

Lucille Springs
Died: 06/26/1933   Age: 18y00m11d
Certificate No. 0021,0212
Parents: Robert Springs & Savannah Torrance

NO MARKER

Informant: Savannah Reid
Bpl.: SC

Noble & Kelsey

Robert Springs
Died: 07/14/1915   Age: 5 days
Certificate No. 0002,0192
Parents: Leaper Springs & Daisy Scott

NO MARKER
INFANT
Informant: Leaper Springs, Father
Bpl.: Salisbury, NC

Noble & Kelsy: 353

Robert Hope Springs
Died: 01/02/1918   Age: 32y5m27d
Certificate No. 0006,0350
Parents: Lemly Springs & Lizzie McCoulah

NO MARKER
Day Laborer
Informant: S. Springs
Bpl.: Rockhill, SC

Noble & Kelsey

Sarah Stafford
Died: 06/28/1941   Age: 44
Certificate No. 0027,1442
Parents: Jim Greer & Unknown

NO MARKER
Housewife
Informant: Samuel Stafford, Husband
Bpl.: Belmont, NC

Ellis, Mangum, & Fair

Annie Standard
Died: 03/05/1911   Age: 15y 06m
Informant: Polly Standard, Mother
Parents: Will Blackmer & Polly Standard
Register of Death, Salisbury, County of Rowan, NC (09/1909-10/11/1911 pg. 29)

NO MARKER
Single

Bpl.: Rowan

Noble & Kelsey

George I. Stanley
Died: 08/31/1959   Age: 70
Certificate No. 0040,0129
Parents: Ben Stanly & Unknown

NO MARKER
Laborer
Informant: Mrs. Frances Chalk
Bpl.: GA

Ellis, Mangum, & Fair

BURIALS

Kevin Eugene Stanley
Died: 03/16/1964   Age: 22 dys.
Certificate No. 0044,0185
Parents: David Walker & Frances Stanley

NO MARKER

Informant: Mrs. Sarah
   Bpl.: Salisbury, NC

Ellis, Mangum, & Fair

Lena Griffin Stanley
Died: 04/07/1950   Age: 62
Certificate No. 0032,0275
Parents: UNKNOWN

NO MARKER
Domestic
Informant: George Stanley

Ellis, Mangum, & Fair

Guilbert Starr
Died: 06/05/1918   Age: 25
Certificate No. 0006,0442
Parents: & Suity (sic) Starr

NO MARKER
Laborer @ Southern Railroad
Informant: Toni Robinson
   Bpl.: Fairfield, SC

Summersettt

Vina Starr
Died: 08/14/1945   Certificate Not Found

NO MARKER

Ellis, Mangum, & Fair
Funeral Home Record

William Steel
Died: 02/02/1908   Age: 49yrs.

NO MARKER

Summersett

Summersett Funeral Home. T. W. Summersett Jr. Proprietor (Watson, June C. Rowan Co. Cemeteries, Vol. I, Salisbury, NC The Genealogical Society of Rowan Co., North Carolina, © 1988)

Gladys A. Roberts Steele
Died: 08/09/1998   Age: 46
Parents: Basle & Vinetta Roberts

UH-xxx New Marker
Certificate Not Found

Noble & Kelsey

GLADYS A. ROBERTS
STEELE
ON EARTH
APR. 9, 1952
IN HEAVEN
AUG. 9, 1998

Lisa Crystal Alicia Steele
Died: 01/02/1994   Age: 24

BN-681-P
Pauline Knitting Co. Laborer @ Cotton Textile Mill
Informant: Judith Merritt, Mother

Mitchell & Fair

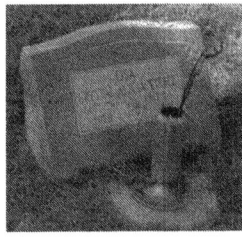

Parents: Judith Steele Merritt, Father Unknown
(Source: Interview: Rosaline Mitchell, Mitchell & Fair Funeral Home, Salisbury, NC: 03/2004)

LISA
CRYSTAL ALICIA STEELE
SEPT. 29, 1970
OCT. 2, 1994

Sarah Hogans Steele
Died: 05/02/1910   Age: 61
Certificate No. 0004,0363
Parents: Dennie Hogans & Mother Unknown

NO MARKER
Cook
Informant: H. J. Anderson

Noble & Kelsey

Viola Steele
Died: 10/15/1975   Age: 79
Certificate No. 0055,0711
Parents: Jacob Miles & Sally Unknown Miles

NO MARKER
Laundry
Informant: Mrs. Nellie Beatty
   Bpl.: SC

Mitchell & Fair

BURIALS

Jimmy Stephens
Died: 08/17/1992   Age: 75
Certificate No. 0072,0685
Parents: John Stephens & Hattie Unknown

UH-617-G MISSING   Noble & Kelsey
Sheet Maker @ Cotton Cloth Mill
Informant: Tammie L. McCullough
   Bpl.: Hamlet, NC

Johnie Stephens
Died: 01/12/1971   Age: 57
Certificate No. 0051,0033
Parents: Wilson Stephens & Lela Huff

NO MARKER   Mitchell & Fair
Retired Railroader
Informant: Mrs. Roberts Stephens
   Bpl.: GA

Angie Stevenson
Died: 12/01/1910   Age: 17
Certificate No. 0004,0319
Parents: Jim Stevenson & Alice Minton

NO MARKER
Not Given
Informant: Eastell Sherrill
   Bpl.: Chester, SC.

Pinkney Alexander Stevenson
Died: 02/04/1911   Age: 54y10m17

Certificate No. 0004, 0137

Parents: Elias Stevenson & Mother Unknown

NO MARKER   Noble & Kelsey
Shoe Maker instructor, Livingstone College Industrial
   Department
Informant: Sallie M. Stevenson, Teacher @ Salisbury
   Graded School 1909
   Bpl.: Iredell Co., NC

Hattie Stewart
Died: 07/25/1957   Age: 74
Certificate No. 0053,0518
Parents: George Cowan & Texanna Shealt

NO MARKER   Ellis, Mangum, & Fair

Informant: Mrs. Georgia Grier, Brooklyn, NY 11206
   Bpl.: SC

Linda Kay Stewart
Died: 0412/1951   Age: 1y06m00d
Certificate No. 0032,0782
Parents: Charlie Stewart & Annie Mae Davis

NO MARKER   Noble & Kelsy: 184
CHILD
Informant: Anna Stewart
   Bpl.: Salisbury, NC

Melvin Stewart
Died: 10/09/1952   Age: 60
Certificate No. 0033,0546
Parents: Thomas Stewart & Mary Heath

NO MARKER   Ellis, Mangun, & Fair
Trucker @ Transit Shed
Informant: Hattie Stewart

Jasper Stinson
Died: 11/05/1993   Age: 51
Certificate No. 0073,1071

UH-643 G MISSING   Noble & Kelsey
Janitor @ Hospital
Informant: Jackie A. Stinson

Gertrude Boozer Stoner
Died: 02/09/1999   Age: 80
Certificate No. 0079,0187
Parents: Forrest Thomas Boozer & Bessie Harris

BN-New (Post 1996 Survey)   Mitchell & Fair
Clerk @ US Pentagon
Informant: Cynthia D. Neely
   Bpl.: Rowan Co., NC

IN LOVING MEMORY OF
GERTRUDE B. STONER
MAY 5, 1919
FEB. 9, 1999

Brenda D. Oglesby Stoval
Died: 06/13/1990   Age: 37
Certificate No. 0070,0534
Parents: Franl Oglesby & Unknown

UH-566-H MISSING   Noble & Kelsey
Presser @ Commercial Laundry
Informant: Albert Stoval
   Bpl.: New York, NY

BURIALS

Agustus Strawder
Died: 02/03/1979   Age: 78
Certificate No. 0059,0124

BT-238-K   Noble & Kelsey
Retired Yadkin Hotel
Informant: George Strawder, Brother
Parents: Robert Strawder & Dolly Rankin   Bpl.: Rowan Co., NC

AGUSTUS STRAWDER
NOV. 7, 1900
FEB. 3, 1979

Robert Strawder Jr.
Died: 03/26/1977   Age: 53

BT-240-K
Certificate Not Found

ROBERT STRAWDER JR.
JULY 4, 1924
MAR. 26, 1977

John Strong
Died, 01/24/1929   Age: 34
Certificate No. 0017,0331
Parents: James & Marie Strong

UH-NO MARKER   Cheshire & Mangum
Laborer
Informant: Mary Moore
   Bpl.: Chester, SC

Leon Sumner Strother

Died: 05/05/1970   Age: ∞68   Certificate Not Found

UH-503 H

(CRIP)
LEON SUMNER
AUG. 24, 1902
MAY 5, 1970

Mary Sumner Strother
Died: 05/29/1986   Age: 89
Certificate No. 0066,0489

UH-502-H   Noble & Kelsey
Nurse @ Hospital
Informant: Mary J. Smith, Granddaughter
Parents: W. C. Sumner & Jennie Harris   Bpl.: Rowan Co., NC

MARY SUMNER
STROTHER
DEC. 16, 1897
MAY 29, 1986

Will Strother   UH-504-H MISSING

Essie Mitchell Sturdivant   UH-508

Died: 11/07/1955   Age: ∞49   Certificate Not Found

ESSIE MITCHELL
STURDIVANT
APR. 29, 1906
NOV. 7, 1955

Teresa Marie Sturdivant
Died: 12/13/1968   Age: 7
Certificate No. 0048,0725

BT-302-K   Noble & Kelsey
CHILD
Informant: Clayton Sturdivant, Father
Parents: Clayton Sturdivant & Magdalene Hobson Bpl NC

TERESA "TESS" STURDIVANT
JAN. 12, 1961
DEC. 13, 1968

BURIALS

Corinthia Burton Summers
Died: 06/21/1937   Age: ∞65
Certificate No. 0025,0179
Parents: William Burton & Louisa Branner
SEE WEB SUMMERS

OK-052-N
Housewife
Informant: Gladys Raggan
 Bpl.: Ellenton, GA

Noble & Kelsey

Destini A. Summers

UH-536 H MISSING

Webb Summers
Died: 05/27/1926   Age: ∞56
Certificate No. 0014,0221
Parents: Nathanial & Mary Summers

OK-051-52-N
Machinist Helper @ Southern Rail Road
Informant: Mrs. Summers, Wife
 Bpl.: NC

Noble & Kelsey: 83

WEBB SUMMERS
DIED 1926
AGE
ABOUT 56 Yrs.
HIS WIFE
CORINTHIA
SUMMERS
DIED
JUNE 14, 1937
AGE
ABOUT 86 Yrs.

James D. Sumner
Died: 05/06/1960   Age: 42
Certificate No. 0040, 0568
Parents: John Sumner & Florence Setzer

NO MARKER
Machinist Helper
Informant: Otelia Sumner

Ellis, Mangum, & Fair

Jennie Harris Sumner
Died: 02/25/1973   Age: 96 (82-bcrt.)
Certificate No. 0053,0185
Parents: Wilson Harris & Mary Holtsclaw

UH-505-H
Housewife
Informant: Mrs. Jennie Jones
 Bpl.: NC

Noble & Kelsey

MOTHER
JENNIE HARRIS
SUMNER
MAY 1, 1877
FEB. 25, 1973

John Sumner
Died: 04/04/1952   Age: 67
Certificate No. 0032,0785
Parents: UNKNOWN

OK-NO MARKER
Laborer, Southern Railway
Informant: James Sumner

Noble & Kelsy: 122

Nancy Sumner
Died: 11/18/1938   Age: 55
Certificate No. 0026,0256
Parents: Charles & Elmira Phoroneberger

OK-371-I/J
Maid, Dr. Shaffer's office
Informant: Elmira Bruce
 Bpl.: Cleveland, NC

Noble & Kelsey

NANCY SUMNER
DIED
NOV. 18, 1938

Thelmore Summer
Died: 04/30/1938   Age: 30

NO MARKER

Ellis Mangum, & Fair

BURIALS

Will Charlie Sumner
Died: 06/23/1952 Age: 65
Certificate No. 0033,0340
Parents: Ruben Summer & Emerline Lowery

UH-
Laborer @ Duke Power Co.
Informant: Jennie Summer
  Bpl.: Rowan Co., NC

Noble & Kelsey

FATHER
WILL SUMNER
JAN. 15, 1887
JUNE 23, 1952

Earlie Swift
Died: 11/23/1991 Age: 68
Certificate No. 0071,1062
Parents: Jessie Swift & Rilla Johnson Bpl.: Philadelphia, PA

UH-607-G
Cleaning Person @ Construction Co.
Informant: Dwight R. Wilheim

Noble & Kelsey

EARLIE SWIFT
FEB. 28, 1923
NOV. 23, 1991

Jessie Swift
Died: 03/12/1952 Age: 69
Parents: Jesse Swift & Unknown

NO MARKER
Laborer

Ellis, Mangum, & Fair
Funeral Home Record

Rilla Swift
Died: 07/09/1952 no birth date given
Certificate No. 0033,0341
Parents: Harris Johnson & Lizzie Davis

NO MARKER
House Keeper
Informant: Katie Wright
  Bpl.: Cannon, GA

Ellis, Mangun, & Fair

Emma Clinkscales Taggart
Died: 07/27/1962 Age: 82
Certificate No. 0042,0584
Parents: Tom Clinkscales & Unknown

UH-407-H
Housewife
Informant: Mrs. Clinton Cowan
  Bpl.: Abbeville SC

Noble & Kelsey

TAGGART
EMMA CLINKSCALE
WIFE OF
PROF. R. C. TAGGART
AUG. 29, 1880
JULY 27, 1962
MAY SHE REST IN PEACE

Reece Conrad Taggart
Died: 03/01/1957 Age: 78
See Emma Clinkscales Taggart.

UH-407-H
Teacher

Ellis, Mangum, & Fair
Funeral Home Record

TAGGART
PROF. R. C. TAGGART
OCT. 14, 1871
MAR. 1, 1957

Sharitale Tasha Talford
Died: 07/07/1994 Age: 3 CHILD

BN-690-P

Certificate Not Found

SHARITALE TASHA
TALFORD
DEC. 22, 1989
JULY 7, 1994

BURIALS

Ella Louise Harden Tate
Died: 05/05/1949   Age: 25
Certificate No. 0031,0865

UH-482-H
Housewife
Informant: Willie Tate
Parents: Durke Dunlap & Hope Harden

Noble & Kelsey

DUNLAP –	TATE
HOPE DUNLAP	ELLA LOUISE TATE
DEC. 26, 1899	AUG. 28, 1923
JULY 31, 1974	MAY 5, 1949

Berdie Brown Taylor
Died: 08/30/1955   Age: no bd given
Certificate No. 0036,0421
Parents: Albert Brown & Linda Hacket

UH-NO MARKER
Domestic
Informant: Eunice Taylor
Bpl.: Salisbury, NC

Ellis, Mangum, & Fair

Rev. Samuel Arthur Taylor
Died: 01/08/1953   Age: 66
Parents: Jeremiah Taylor & Unknown

UH-488-H
Minister

Ellis, Mangum, & Fair

REV. SAMUEL A. TAYLOR
NOV. 15, 188
JAN. 8, 1953

Roxie Hairston Taylor
Died: 07/11/1969   Age: 70
Certificate No. 0049,0443
Parents: George Hairston & Not Given

BT-257-K
Housewife
Informant: Mrs. Katie M. Barger
Bpl.: NC

Noble & Kelsey

LOVING MOTHER & GRANDMOTHER
ROXIE HAIRSTON TAYLOR
OCT. 4, 1895
JULY 10, 1969

Willett Irene Taylor
Died: 09/20/1952   Age: 18d
Certificate No. 0033,0445
Parents: Not Given & Caldonia Taylor

NO MARKER
INFANT
Informant: Caldonia Taylor
Bpl.: Salisbury, NC

Ellis, Mangum, & Fair

Doc Teaseley
Died: 11/21/1952   Age: 65
Parents: William Teasley & ??

NO MARKER
Laborer

Ellis, Mangum, & Fair
Funeral Home Record

Helen Marie Teasley
Died: 03/13/1968   Age: 43
Certificate No. 0048,0176
Parents: Dock Teasley & Carrie Barber

NO MARKER
Presser

Mitchell & Fair

BURIALS

John Teasley
Died:03/08/1969
Parents: Dock Teasley & Carrie Barber

NO MARKER

Mitchell & Fair
Funeral Home Record

Lula May Teasley
Died:02/28/1920 Age: 1y29d
Certificate No. 0008,0138
Parents: Derek Teasley & Carrie Barber

NO MARKER
INFANT
Informant: Carrie Teasley
  Bpl.: Salisbury, NC

Noble & Kelsy: 250

James Templeton
Died: 12/25,1961 Age: 72
  Certificate No. 0042,0182
  Parents: Monroe Templeton & Jane Templeton

OK-231-K
Cook @ Elks Club
Informant: J. M. Campbell
  Bpl.: Iredell Co., NC

Noble & Kelsey: 232

JAMES TEMPLETON
SEPT. 14, 1890
DEC. 25, 1961

John McCrorie Thirdgill
Died: 10/26/1930 Age: ∞56
Certificate No. 0018,0321
Parents: Unknown & Margaret McCrorie
  Plot Contains John Thirdgill, INFANT 10days old, Mary Thirdgill, Warren Carter

OK-NO MARKER.
Cook
Informant: Ellen Thirdgill
  Bpl.: Anson Co.

Noble & Kelsey: 14

Mary Thirdgill
Died: 12/02/1910 Age: 21
Certificate No. 0004,0318
Parents: John Thirdgill & Ellen Wilson

OK-NO MARKER
Laborer
Informant: John Thirdgill, Father
  Bpl.: Salisbury, NC

Noble & Kelsey: 14

Eliza Holmes Goler Thomas
Died:03/25/1912 Age: 97
Certificate No. 0001,0127
  Parents: Jacob Goler & Armelia Travers

OK-071-N Goler Plot in curb
Domestic
Informant: William H. Goler
  Bpl.: Nova Scotia

Noble & Kelsey: 18

ELIZA THOMAS (Certificate & Marker Conflict)
JUNE 5, 1841
APR. 16, 1911

Leroy Thomas
Died: 10/22/1976

NO MARKER
Certificate Not Found

Mitchell & Fair
Funeral Home Record

Winifred Thomas

BN-882-M
Died:06/15/1986 Age: 74

Certificate Not Found

WINFRED THOMAS
AUG 6,   JUNE 15,
1912   1986

Ada Thompson
Died:08/12/1948 Age: 62
Certificate No. 0031,0427
Parents: William & Lizzie Robinson

NO MARKER
Domestic
Informant: Edward Fincher
  Bpl.:Union Co., SC

Ellis, Mangum, & Fair

BURIALS

Annie Mae Little Thompson
Died: 09/12/1950   Age: 47
Certificate No. 0032,0413
Parents: Lee Walker & Mary Bruce

NO MARKER
Domestic
Informant: Annie Rabb
db. 11/13/1880

Ellis, Mangum, & Fair

Cora Vina Hunt Thompson
Died: 10/13/1952   Age: ∞58 Certificate Not Found

UH-480-H

THOMPSON
CORA VINA HUNT
WIFE OF
JERRY A. THOMPSON
DIED OCT. 13, 1952
AGED ABOUT 58 YEARS
THY TRIALS ENDED THY REST IS WON.

Nannie Besota King Thompson
Died: 10/29/1969   Age: 79
Certificate No. 0049,0671

UH-452-H

Informant: Jerry A. Thompson, Husband

Mitchell & Fair

THOMPSON
NANNIE BESOTA KING
BRYANT
WIFE OF
JERRY A. THOMPSON
OCT. 11, 1890
OCT. 29, 1969
MY TRUST IS IN GOD.

Will Thompson
Died: 03/05/1959   Age: 63
Certificate No. 0039,0546
Parents: Squire Thompson & Maggie Roninsin

UH-NO MARKER
Laborer
Informant: Mrs. Bell McCluney
Bpl.: SC

Ellis, Mangum, & Fair

Maudaree Talford Threadgill
Died: 04/12/1994   Age: 63
Certificate No. 0074,0453
Parents: Albert Talford & Maudaree Canty

BN-689-P
Spinning room Worker @ Textile Mill
Informant: Andrew Threadgill
Bpl.: Chester, SC

Noble & Kelsey

BLEST BE THE
TIE THAT BINDS
OUR HEARTS IN CHRISTIAN LOVE
MAUDAREE TALFORD
THREADGILL
APR. 23, 1931
APR. 12, 1994

James Robert Tillman
Died: 09/16/1961   Age: 3
Certificate No. 0032,0899
Parents: James D. Tillman & Hattie Walker

BN-875-M MISSING
CHILD
Informant: Mrs. Hattie Tillman, Mother
Bpl.: Salisbury, NC

Noble & Kelsey

Shirley Ann Tillman
Died: 09/16/1961   Age: 4
Certificate No. 0032,0900
Parents: James D. Tillman & Hattie Walker

BN-876-M MISSING
CHILD
Informant: Mrs. Hattie Tillman, Mother
Bpl.: Salisbury

Noble & Kelsey

BURIALS

Emma Timmons — UH-NO MARKER — Ellis, Mangum & Fair
Died: 12/06/1952   Age: 48
Domestic
Certificate No. 0033,0576
Informant: J. G. Timmons
Parents: George Gaston & Mattie Rhinehardt
Bpl.: Shelby, NC

Willie James Tomblin Jr. — BN-04-M — Noble & Kelsey
Died: 09/18/1992   Age: 41
Dyer, Textile
Certificate No. 0072,0741
Informant: Ruby Shuford Tomblin
Parents: Willie James Tomblin, Sr. & Ruby Shuford
Bpl.: Salisbury, NC

WILLIE J. TOMBLIN JR.
DEC. 2   SEPT. 18,
1951   1992

Willie James Tomblin Sr. — BN-05-M — Noble & Kelsey
Died: 12/04/1987   Age: 64
Janitor, Cotton Cloth Mill
Certificate No. 0067,1016
Informant: Ruby J. Tomblin
Parents: John Arthur Tomblin & Margaret Carr

WILLIE J. TOMBLIN, SR
OCT 12   DEC. 4
1923   1987

Anthony L. Torrence — UH-657-G MISSING

Dallas Torrence — NO MARKER — Noble & Kelsey
Died: 12/17/1918   Age: 62
Generator & Day Laborer
Certificate No. 0006,0599
Informant: James Tarce[sic]
Parents: Ephram Torence & Venious Clarke
Bpl.: Davidson Co., NC

James Curtis Torrence — BN-844-M — Noble & Kelsey
Died: 04/07/1988   Age: 39
Truck Driver @ Brick Manufacturer
Certificate No. 0068,0391
Informant: Terry Diane Torrence, Wife
Parents: Gilley Odell Torrence Sr. & Louvenia Brown
Bpl.: Rowan Co., NC

J. C. TORRENCE
FEB. 7, 1949
APR. 7, 1988
ALWAYS LOVED, J.C.

Sha Cole Torrence — UH-538-H MISSING

Bessie Trice — NO MARKER — Cheshire & Callahan
Died: 06/09/1929   Age: 36
Domestic
Certificate No. 0017,0427
Informant: Sylvester James Smith
Parents: Henry Williams & Alice Goldsmith
Bpl.: Anderson, SC

Benjamine Trott — OK-NO MARKER — Noble & Kelsey: 200
Died: 11/23/1942   Age: 55
Janitor @ Wachovia Bank & Trust Company
Certificate No. 0028,0424
Informant: Dora Clingenan
Parents: London Trott & Sallie Barber
Bpl.: Franklin Co., NC

Bessie Trott — OK-NO MARKER — Noble & Kelsey: 220

BURIALS

Chlora E. Trott
Died: 12/16/1939   Age: ∞73
Certificate No. 0027,0300
Parents: NOT KNOWN

BN-832-M   Noble & Kelsey
Domestic
Informant: Garfield Trott
    Bpl.: Rowan Co., NC

MOTHER
CHLORA E. TROTT
1866 - 1939

Effalena Speas Trott
Died: 10/14/1927   Age: 36
Certificate No. 0015,0441
Parents: John Speas & Ida Matthews

OK- NO MARKER   Noble & Kelsy: 200
Housewife, Domestic
Informant: Mrs. M.A. Houser
    Bpl.: Bithynia Twp. Forsyth Co., NC

James Garfield Trott
Died: 10/20/1974   Age: 75

BN-833-M
Certificate Not Found

TROTT
JAMES	MARGUERITE
GARFIELD	SUMNER
MAR. 21, 1899	MAY 10, 1914
OCT. 20, 1974	OCT 20, 1974

Marguerite Sumner Trott
Died: 10/20/1974   Age: 60
Certificate No. 0054,0714
Parents: Unknown & Mary L. Sumner
(See James Garfield Trott)

BN-834-M   Noble & Kelsey
Housewife
Informant: Ruth Perkins
    Bpl.:NC

Ella Farmer Trueblood
Died:08/08/1921   Age: 22
Certificate No. 0008,0520
Parents: J. F. Farmer &?????

UH-   Summersett
None Given
Informant: J. F. Farmer, Father
    Bpl.: Rowan Co., NC

Ella Mae Trueblood
Died:07/19/1961   Age: 30

UH-NO MARKER   Ellis, Mangum, & Fair
    Funeral Home Record

Esther Boyd Trueblood
Died: 11/25/1952   Age: 43
Certificate No. 0033,0537
Parents: James C. Boyd & Christine Peterson

UH-NO MARKER   Ellis, Mangum, & Fair
Domestic
Informant: Mrs. Jessie B. Kelly
    Bpl.: Fairfield Co., SC

William Pierce Truesdale
Died:01/21/1939   Age: 39
Certificate No. 0027,0047
Parents: William Truesdale & Margaret Truesdale

BN-836-M   Noble & Kelsey
Caller @ Southern Railroad transfer shed
Informant: Mrs. Mildred Truesdale
    Bpl.: Kerr Co., SC

WILLIAM P.
TRUESDALE
MAY 25, 1900
JAN. 21, 1939

BURIALS

Willie Truesdale UH-605-G
Died:08/06/1991   Age: ∞94   Certificate Not Found

WILLIE TRUESDALE
DEC. 14, 1897

AUG. 6, 1991

Juanita Davis Tucker   BN-NEW MARKER   Noble & Kelsey
Died:03/24/2002   Age: 64   Hemmer @ Cotton Mill (Textiles)
Certificate No. 0082,0313   **Informant:** Frederick D. Tucker Sr., Husband
Parents: Jesse Davis & Mattie Woods   Bpl.: Rowan Co., NC

FREDERICK D. Jr.	TO	JUANITA DAVIS
JUNE 2, 1934	GOD'S	MAR. 14, 1938
	CARE	MAR. 24, 2002
	TUCKER	

Lawrence Tucker   BN-665-P
Died:03/31/1938   Age: 49   Certificate Not Found

LAWRENCE TUCKER
MAR. 31, 193
OCT. 30. 1987

Lucille Reese Tucker   UH-594-G   Noble & Kelsey
Died:03/05/1994   Age: 83   Domestic Worker @ Hotel
Certificate No. 0074,0269   **Informant:** Christene Ellis
Parents: Jerry Reese & Lucinda Scott   Bpl.:Atlanta, GA

LUCILLE S. TUCKER
APR. 10, 1910
MAR. 5, 1994

Delia Christian Tugman   BN-801-M   Noble & Kelsey
Died:01/07/1982   Age: 84   Homemaker
Certificate No. 0062,0047   **Informant:** Joe B. Tugman

DELIA C. TUGMAN
FEB. 4, 1897
JAN. 7, 1982

Joseph James Turner   UH-531-H   MISSING

Lamar Covington Turner   UH- NO MARKER   Ellis, Mangum, & Fair
Died:09/13/1959   Age: 54   Funeral Home Record

Lelia A. Turner   NO MARKER   Mitchell & Fair
Died:08/25/1971   Age: 19   Youth Corp. & Housewife
Certificate No. 0051,0578   **Informant:** Mr. Olin A. Turner, Husband
Parents: Henry Perry & Margaret   Bpl.:NY

Nora Turner   OK-N NO MARKER   Noble & Kelsey: 69
   Kelsey Map & Funeral Home Record

BURIALS

Samuel Turner　　　　　　　　　　OK-NO MARKER　　　　Noble & Kelsey: 69
　　　　　　　　　　　　　　　　　　　　　　Kelsey Map & Funeral Home Record

Tamer N. Turner　(FEMALE)　　　BT-340-K
Died:09/17/1959　　Age: 54　　　　Cook @ Livingstone College
Certificate No. 0040,0134　　　　　**Informant:** Louise Turner
Parents: Amos Covington & Lula Mae Richardson　　Bpl.: GA

TAMER N. TURNER
APR. 5, 1905
SEPT. 17, 1959
IN MEMORY OF OUR DARLING MOTHER

Thomas P. Turner　　　　　　　　NO MARKER　　　　　　Ellis, Mangum, & Fair
Died:01/04/1944　　Age: 54y06m25d　Minister
Certificate No. 0029,0071　　　　　**Informant:** Tamer N. Turner, Wife
Parents: Augustus Turner & Saraf Allen　　Bpl.: Norwood, NC

Mary Bell Tyson　　　　　　　　　UH-NO MARKER　　　　Ellis, Mangum, & Fair
Died: 10/28/1949　　Age: 75　　　　Domestic
Certificate No. 0031,1014　　　　　**Informant:** Bessie Elizabeth Best
Parents: Levy Tyson & Elizabeth Luck　　Bpl.: Carthage, NC

Emma A. Unthank　　　　　　　　OK-073-N　　　　　　　Noble & Kelsey: 18
Died:00/26/1907　　Age: ∞40　　　Housewife
Parents: Harman Unthank & Mariah Stedman　　Bpl.: Morehead, Guilford Co., NC
(Stonecutter made error. She was born ∞1867 according to 1870 U.S. Census.)

EMMA A. UNTHANK
WIFE OF
REV. W. H. GOLER
MAR. 27, 1889
SEPT. 26, 1907

James M. Vinson　　　　　　　　　UH-NO MARKER　　　　Ellis, Mangum, & Fair
Died:09/10/1938　　Age: 11　　　　School Boy
Certificate No. 0026,0206　　　　　**Informant:** Will Vinson, Father
Parents: Will Vinson & Nelie Weldon Moss　　Bpl.: Salisbury, NC

Lando Vinson　　　　　　　　　　UH-NO MARKER　　　　Mitchell & Fair
Died:08/24/1965　　Age: 33　　　　Roofer
Certificate No. 0045,0485　　　　　**Informant:** Margaret Vinson, Wife
Parents: Odis Vinson & Donnie UK　　Bpl.: Rowan Co., NC

Mr. Sandy Alexander (B) Vutner　NO MARKER　　　　　　Noble & Kelsey
Died:02/06/1915　　Age: 87　　　　Farmer
Certificate No. 0002,0503　　　　　**Informant:** Charles P. Butner
Parents: Unknown & Melisha Butner　　Bpl.: Rowan Co., NC

Robert W. Wade　　　　　　　　　NO MARKER　　　　　　Noble & Kelsey
Died: 06/17/1925　　Age: 55　　　　Preacher
Certificate No. 0013,0375　　　　　**Informant:** Willie Wade
Parents: Unknown　　　　　　　　　Bpl.: SC

Samuel Monroe Wakefield Jr.　　UH-NO MARKER　　　　Ellis, Mangum, & Fair
Died:04/14/1949　　Age: hrs.　　　INFANT　　　　　　　　Funeral Home Record
Parents: Wakefield Sr.

BURIALS

Clarence Hardin Walker　　　　　　UH-NO MARKER　　　　　　Mitchell & Fair
Died:04/04/1966　　　　　　　　　　　　　　　　　　　　　　　Funeral Home Record

Harold Lee Walker　　　　　　　　　BT-304-K　　　　　　　　Noble & Kelsey
Died: 12/30/1986　　Age: 57　　　　Mechanic @ Cone Textile Mill
Certificate No. 0066,1162　　　　　　**Informant:** Johnny S. Walker, Brother
　　　　　Parents: Scottie Walker & Lizzie Haynie　　　Bpl.: Rowan Co., NC

　　　　　HAROLD LEE WALKER
　　　　　　MAR. 22, 1929
　　　　　　DEC. 30, 1986

Jacqueline Walker　　　　　　　　　BT-305-K
　　　　Died: 11/15/1986　　Age: 49　Certificate Not Found

　　　　　JACQUELINE WALKER
　　　　　　AUG. 10, 1937
　　　　　　NOV. 15, 1986

Janie Lee Walker　　　　　　　　　BT-306-K　　　　　　　　Noble & Kelsey
Died:07/22/1961　　Age: 6　　　　　CHILD
Certificate No. 0041,0661　　　　　　**Informant:** Harold Lee Walker, Father
Parents: Harold Lee Walker & Juanita Smith　　Bpl.: Salisbury, NC

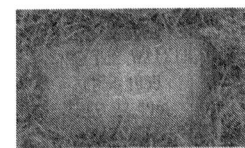

　　　　　JANIE LEE WALKER
　　　　　　FEB. 4, 1955
　　　　　　JULY 22, 1961

Jesse H. Walker　　　　　　　　　　BN-822-M　　　　　　　Noble & Kelsey
　　　　Died:03/29/1922　　Age: 46　　Veteran of WW I
　　　　Certificate No. 0010,0334　　　**Informant:** Lee R. Walker
　　　　Parents: Lee Richard Walker & Chaney E. N.　　Bpl.: Davidson, Co., NC

　　　　　JESSE H.
　　　　　WALKER
　　　　NORTH CAROLINA
　　　　　　SGT.
　　　312 SERV. BN QMC
　　　　MARCH 29, 1921

Lee Walker　　　　　　　　　　　　UH 433-H MISSING　　　　Noble & Kelsy: 252
Died:09/13/1916　　Age: 48y3m11d　　Day Laborer
Certificate No. 0003,0274　　　　　　**Informant:** Mary Walker
Parents: Abe Walker & Maria?　　　　　Bpl.: Chester, SC

Lizzie Haynes Walker　　　　　　　BT-307-K　　　　　　　　Noble & Kelsey
Died:02/15/1976　　Age: 81　　　　　Housewife
　　　　　　Certificate No. 0056,0135　　**Informant:** Mrs.Theresa J. Walker, Balt. MD
　　　　　　Parents: John Walker & Lizzie Gaines　　　Bpl.: SC

　　　　　LIZZIE H. WALKER
　　　　　　MAY 29, 1894
　　　　　　FEB. 16, 1976

BURIALS

Ora Walker
Died: 07/08/1929   Age: 34
Certificate No. 0017,0458
Parents: William Croford (sic) & Hanner Saunders

NO MARKER
Domestic
Informant: Dale Walker
Bpl.: SC

Cheshire & Callahan

Scottie Walker
Died: 07/14/1958   Age: 67
Certificate No. 0039,0187
Parents: Frank Walker & Unknown

BT-308 -K
Laborer @ Salisbury Ice & Fuel
Informant: Mrs. Gene Edwards
Bpl.: SC

Noble & Kelsey

SCOTTIE WALKER
FEB. 11, 1889
JULY 14, 1958

Winnie Walker
Died: 01/24/1900   Age: 74

BT-241-K

Certificate Not Found

WINNIE WALKER
JAN. 24, 1900
JAN. 23, 1974

Lucy S. Wallace
Died: 05/15/1967   Age: 58
Certificate No. 0047,0367
Parents: Wilson Stephens & Lela Huff

NO MARKER
Domestic
Informant: Weldon Stephens
Bpl.: Wilkes Co., GA

Mitchell & Fair

Wakefield Walters
Died: 09/26/1910   Age: 31y01m17
Certificate No. 0004,0258
Parents: Allen Walters & Mary Davis

NO MARKER
General Laborer
Informant: Bessie Walters of Salisbury
Bpl.: Rowan Co., NC

Noble & Kelsey

Febby Walton
Died: 10/01/1922   Age.: 63

OK-165 -O
Concrete Headstone

Noble & KelsEy: 110

FEBBY WALTON
APR. 17, 1859
OCT. 1, 1922
AT REST

John Walton

OK-165-O NO MARKER

Noble & Kelsey: 110

Emiley Ward
Died: 06/21/1952   Age: 51
Parents: Charles Rose & Alice Gaither

NO MARKER
House Keeper

Ellis, Mangum, & Fair

BURIALS

Lillie Mae Gaddy Ward
Died: 01/30/1990   Age: 81

BT-316-K
Certificate Not Found

AN INSPIRATION TO
ALL WHO KNEW HER
OUR DEAREST AUNT
LILLIE MAE GADDY WARD
SEPT. 12, 1909
JAN. 30, 1990

Edgar L. Ware
Died: 11/16/2001   Age: 83
Certificate No. 0081,1112
Parents: Harrison Ware & Rachel Burch

BN-Brand New   Noble & Kelsey
Machine Operator @ Cotton Mill
Informant: Shunta L. Ware
Bpl.: Coosa Co., Ala.

OUR LOVING FATHER
EDGAR L. WARE
APR. 9, 1918
NOV. 16, 2001
A man amongst men.

Elizabeth Hart Warren
Died: 04/10/1990   Age: 88
Certificate No. 0070,0352
Parents: Otha Hart & Hannah Torrence

UH-563-H   MISSING   Noble & Kelsey
Worked @ Aluminum Mfg. Co.
Informant: Charles Withers
Bpl.: Mecklenburg Co., NC

Amie Washington
Died: 04/13/1983   Age: 97
Certificate No. 0063,0310
Parents: Aaron & Matilda Register

BN-847-M   Noble & Kelsey
Homemaker
Informant: Richard Washington, Son
Bpl.: Winston Co., AL

AMIE WASHINGTON
OCT. 11, 1886
APR. 13, 1983

Frank Washington
Died: 06/21/1953   Age: 63
Certificate No. 0034,0277
Parents: George Washington & Unknown

UH-403-I/J   Ellis, Mangum, & Fair
Laborer for Piedmont Gas. Company
Informant: Mattie Washington
Bpl.: Rowan Co., NC

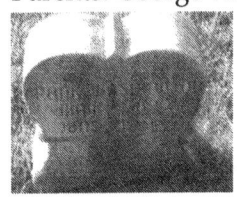

FRANK WASHINGTON
MAR. 2, 1890
JUNE 21, 1953

Gertrude Washington
Died: 07/23/1941   Age: 50
Certificate No. 0027,01457
Parents: UNKNOWN

NO MARKER   Ellis, Mangum, & Fair

Informant: Frank Washington, Husband
Bpl.: Catawba Co., NC

BURIALS

Rose Washington
Died: 04/13/1918 ∞75
Certificate No. 0006, 0407
Parents: UNKNOWN

NO MARKER Summersettt
Domestic
Informant: George Anna X Chambers
 Bpl.: Florida

Ella Youngblood Watkins
Died: 09/30/1993 Age: 86
Certificate No. 0073,0897
Parents: UNKNOWN

UH-632-G MISSING Noble & Kelsey
Housemaid @ Private Homes
Informant: Alma R. McKenzie

Tom Watkins
Died: 11/16/1909 Age: 56
Certificate No. 0004,0453

NO MARKER
Mechanic
Parents: Henry Watkins & Mary Gibson: Bpl.?

Connia Henry Watson Sr.
Died: 05/26, 1994 Age: 90
Certificate No. 0074,0594
Parents: Andrew Watson & Rachel Livingstone

OK- Noble & Kelsey
Insurance Agent
Informant: Connia H. Watson, Jr.
Bpl.: Charlotte, NC

IN LOVING MEMORY
WATSON
MABEL E. SCOTT   CONNIA HENRY, SR.
SEPT. 10, 1904   C. H.
APR. 3, 1999   DEC. 14, 1904
MAY, 26, 1994

Mabel E. Scott Watson
Died: 04/03/1999 Age: 95

OK
(See Connia Henry Watson Sr.)

Lula Johnson Watts
Died: 04/03/1949 Age: 55

UH-435-H Noble & Kelsey
Housewife
Certificate No. 0031,0832 **Informant:** Ernest Querry, Yonkers, NY
Parents: Tom Johnson & Unknown Bpl.: Cabarrus Co., NC

LULA JOHNSON WATTS
DEC. 25, 1880
APR. 3, 1949

James Andrew Waugh
Died: 10/28/1927 Age: 70
Certificate No. 0015,0454
Parents: James Andrew & Rachel Waugh

OK-NO MARKER Cheshire & Mangum
Brick Layer
Informant: Helen Waugh
 Bpl.: Salisbury, NC

Kenneth Wayne
Died: 06/22/1982 Age: 1dy

BN- 7??
INFANT Certificate Not Found
Parents: Bernadette C. Brown, mother

KENNETH WAYNE
JUN. 21, 1982   JUN. 22, 1982
SON OF
SP 4 BERNADETTE C. BROWN
USA

Effie Kelly Webb
Died: 02/28/1969 Age: 63
Certificate No. 0049,0157
Parents: Celen Kelly & Darcus Goodman

BT-273 K MISSING Noble & Kelsey
Housewife
Informant: Mrs. Mildred Johnson
 Bpl.: Rowan Co., NC

BURIALS

Oscar Webster
Died: 12/21/1929   Age: 43
Certificate No. 0017,0557
Parents: Page Webster & Martha Price

NO MARKER
Day Laborer
Informant: Lula Webster, Wife
   Bpl.: Jackson Co., GA

Cheshire & Callahan

Wilson Weeks
Died: 04/22/1974   Age: 55
   Certificate No. 0054,0291
   Parents: Thomas Oneal Weeks & Naomia Hunter   Bpl.: NC

BT-244-K
Retired: Taylor Clay Co., NC
Informant: Mrs. Jannie Weeks

Noble & Kelsey

WILSON WEEKS
MAY 26 1918
APR. 22, 1974

Clark Welborne
Died: 05/25/1953   Age: 86
Certificate No. 0034,0280
Parents: Unknown & Harriet Leach

NO MARKER
Laborer

Ellis, Mangum, & Fair

Ms. Eura Henderson Welborne
Died: 11/02/1976   Age: 81
Certificate No. 0056,0801
   Parents: John & Fannie Henderson   Bpl.: NC

BN-802-P
Housewife
   Informant: Mrs. Fannye W. Kelsey

Noble & Kelsey

EURA HENDERSON   **SCOTT TERRY**
DEC. 14, 1892   **OCT. 26, 1878**
NOV. 2, 1976   **MAR. 18, 1942**
WELBORNE

Scott Terry Welborne
Died: 03/18/1942   Age: 53
Certificate No. 0028,0264
Parents: Anthony Welborne & Ann Welborne
  (See Eura Henderson Welborne)

BN-802-P
Principal @ Piedmont Institute- Minister
Informant: Mrs. Eura Welborne
   Bpl.: Randolph Co., NC

Noble & Kelsey

Clarence W. Wells
Died: 02/08/1970   Age: 58
Certificate No. 0050,0104
Parents: John Wells & Mary Roberts Wells

NO MARKER
Parrish Bakery
Informant: Mrs. Anna Bell Wells
   Bpl.: Gaston Co., NC

Mitchell & Fair

Annie Richardson Westberry
Died: 03/27/1978   Age: 97

OK-077-N
Certificate Not Found

Noble & Kelsey: 19

WESTBERRY
ANNIE RICHARDSON
WESTBURY
DEC. 8, 1881
MAR. 27, 1978
SHE WAS A KIND AND AFFECTIONATE WIFE,
A FOND MOTHER AND A FRIEND TO ALL.

BURIALS

Rev. John Elliot Westberry OK-078-N Noble & Kelsey: 19
Died: 10/25/1941   Age: 66   Minister
Certificate No. 0027,1531   **Informant**: Annie Westbury, Wife
Parents: Rufus & Penda V. Westbery   Bpl.: Lee Co., SC

WESTBERRY
REV. JOHN E. WESTBERRY
NOV. 16, 1875
OCT. 25, 1941
SERVANT OF GOD WELL DONE (UNREADABLE)

Edward Elmore Wheeler, Jr.   NO MARKER
Died: 11/27/1955   Age: 67   Laborer
Certificate No. 0036,0557   **Informant**: Mollie Brown
Parents: Edward Wheeler Sr. & Unknown

Theodore Wardell Whisonant   BN-652-P MISSING   Mitchell & Fair
Died: 11/01/1994   Age: 75   General Laborer @ Construction
Certificate No. 0074,1054   **Informant**: Sadie Welborne Whisonant
Parents: Raymond Whisonant & Alveno Moore   Bpl.: Shelby, NC

Daniel Maurice Whitaker   BN-686-P MISSING   Noble & Kelsey
Died: 04/27/1994   Age: 27   Wrought iron assembler @ Outdoor Furniture Mfg.
Certificate No. 0074,0456   **Informant**: Johnnie Blakeney Whitaker
Parents: Not Given & Gloria Dean Gaston   Bpl.: Washington, DC

Johnnie Mae Whitaker   BN-682-P MISSING

Bessie Clark White   OK-203-L   Noble & Kelsy: 190
Died: 10/01/1985   Age: 83   Homemaker
Certificate No. 0065,0883   **Informant**: Milton White, Husband
Parents: Will Clark & Alice Moss

WHITE
MILTON   BESSIE CLARK
SEPT. 10, 1898   DEC. 6, 1902
OCT. 1, 1985

Charlie White   NO MARKER   Noble & Kelsy: 345
Died: 10/07/1914   Age: 1y9m9d   CHILD
Certificate No. 0001,0497   **Informant**: J. H. White
Parents: J. Harman White & Anna Marant   Bpl.: Salisbury, NC

Cora Lee Knox White   NO MARKER   Ellis, Mangum, & Fair
Died: 10/03/1948   Age: 47   Teacher   Funeral Home Record
Parents: Henry Knox & Emma Steele

George W White   NO MARKER   Noble & Kelsy: 139
Died: 02/03/1924   Age: ∞50   Day Laborer
Certificate No. 0012,0297   **Informant**: Mrs. Effie White
Parents: John & Nancy White   Bpl.: Moore Co.

INFANT Of John White   NO MARKER   Summersett
Died: 01/04/1910   INFANT
Certificate Not Found

BURIALS

Joe White
Died: 06/25/1929   Age:
Certificate No. 0017,0433
Parents: Joseph White & Edna Woodruff

NO MARKER   Noble & Kelsey
School Boy
Informant: Willie Stewart
  Bpl.: Winston Salem, NC

Lola Bell White
Died: 05/19/1926   Age: 8mos 7days
Certificate No. 0014,0200
Parents: Dawson White & Rocksy ????

NO MARKER   Noble & Kelsy: 222
INFANT
Informant: Dawson White
  Bpl.: Salisbury, NC

Milton White
Died: 04/26/1991
(See Bessie Clark)

OK-203-L   Noble & Kelsey: 190
Certificate Not Found

Octavia White
Died: 05/27/1924   Age: 56
Certificate No. 0012,0376
Parents:

NO MARKER   Bingham & Carter
Housewife
Informant: Cymore[sic] White, Son
  Bpl.: Cabarrus Co., NC

Robert White
Died: 12/28/1920   Age: 5y9m17d
Certificate No. 0008,0275
Parents: Houston White & Mary B. Miller

NO MARKER   Noble & Kelsey: 154
CHILD
Informant: Houston White
  Bpl.: Iredell Co., NC

Ruby Smile White
Died: 03/21/1930   Age: 2y9m22d
Certificate No. 0018,0189
Parents: Houston White & Mabel Miller

NO MARKER   Noble & Kelsey: 154
CHILD
Informant: Houston White
  Bpl.: Salisbury, NC

Will White
Died: 01/22/1910   Age: 30
Certificate No. 0004,0474
Parents: Green White Mother Unknown

OK-unmark.   Noble & Kelsey: 300
Blacksmith Helper
Informant: Green White
  B.pl.: Cabarrus Co., NC

Margie Whitener
Died: 09/10/1927   Age: ∞27
Certificate No. 0015,0426
Parents: Norris Edwards & Lena Brock

NO MARKER   Noble & Kelsey
Housewife/Domestic
Informant: James Whitner, Husband
  Bpl.: Townsville, SC

Andrew Robinson Whittington
Died: 06/18/1960   Age: 58
Certificate No. 0040,0610
Parents: Allen Whittington & Unknown

UH-500-H   Noble & Kelsey
Janitor @ Salisbury Post Office
Informant: Lottie Mae Whittington, Wife
  Bpl.: Wildwood, NC

Lottie Mae Whittington
Died: 06/01/1986   Age: 76
Footstone Missing (See Andrew Robinson Whittington)

UH-499-H   Noble & Kelsey
Retired elementary school teacher

WHITTINGTON	
LOTTIE MAE	ANDREW R.
FEB. 6, 1910	NOV. 28, 1902
JUNE 1, 1986	JUNE 18, 1960

Bettie E. Whoozer
Died: 05/23/1939   Age: ∞63
Certificate No. 0027,0134
Parents: Mr. Whoozer & Elizabeth Whozer

NO MARKER   Noble & Kelsey: 17
Cook
Informant: Ada Poach
  Bpl.: Rowan Co., NC

BURIALS

Elizabeth Whoozer   OK-337-I/J   Noble & Kelsey: 16
Died:05/24/1961   Age: 48   Certificate Not Found

MARY ELIZABETH BOST
JAN. 10, 1913
MAY 24, 1961

Elizabeth Boyden Whoozer   NO MARKER   Noble & Kelsey 16
Died: 10/13/1914   Age: 80   Cook, General Housework
Certificate No. 0001,0500   **Informant:** Bettie Boozer, Daughter
Parents: Isaac & Elizabeth Boyden   Bpl.: Surry Co., NC

Hattie Douglas Whyte   OK-030-N   Ellis, Mangum, & Fair
Died:06/20/1954   Age: 64   Teacher
Certificate No. 0035,0283   **Informant:** Mrs. Rose Douglas Aggrey, sister
     Parents: Walter Douglas & Martha Bell   Bpl.: Portsmouth, VA

WHYTE
HATTIE DOUGLAS
WIFE OF
HARRY A. WHYTE
JULY 22, 1880
JUNE 20, 1954
BELOVED SISTER AND AUNT

Deshaun M. Wilder   UH-542-H

Lila Wilder   NO MARKER   Ellis, Mangum, & Fair
Died: 10/23/1957   Age: 57   Nurse& Dressmaker
Certificate No.: 038,0316   Informant: Wesley Wilder, Husband
Parents: Jim Mayfield & Unknown   Bpl.: GA

Lila Mae Connor Wilder   NO MARKER
Died: 10/23/1957   Age: 62   Domestic Worker
Certificate No. 0052,0504   **Informant:** Mrs. Nellie Ellerbe
Parents: Robert Thomas & Elizabeth Unknown

Mattie Barber Wilder   UH-620-H MISSING   Noble & Kelsey
Died:06/27/1992   Age: 83   Homemaker @ Own Home
Certificate No. 0072,0509   **Informant:** Hilary Wilder
Parents: Frank Barber & Agnes Unknown   Bpl.: Rowan Co., NC

Elliott B. Wilkes   OK-333-I/J
Died:08/23/1968   Age: 56

WILKES
ELLIOTT B.
WILKES
AUG. 5, 1912
AUG. 23, 1968

Diamond Carr Wilkins   UH-408- I/J
Died:03/26/1957   Age: ∞47   Certificate Not Found

DIAMOND C. WILKINS
1910 ---- 1957

BURIALS

Floyd Wilkins OK-159-O MISSING Noble & Kelsy: 145
Died: 2000   Age 99
Certificate No. 0080,0629
Parents: James Wilkins & Mamie Mack

James Wilkins OK-159-O Noble & Kelsy: 145
Died:01/17/1924   Age: 4 CHILD
Certificate No. 0012,0285 **Informant:** Floyd Wilkins
Parents: Paul Wilkins & Annie Ganett Bpl.: Cowpens, SC

JAMES
WILKINS
1920 - 1924
PAULINE
WILKINS
1822-1923
AT REST

Jim Wilkins OK-NO MARKER Noble & Kelsy: 387
Died:09/28/1938   Age: ∞67 Machinist Helper @ Southern Railway Shops
Certificate No. 0026,0228 **Informant:** Mr. Floyd Wilkins
Parents: Henry Wilkins & Mary Makeson Bpl.: Cowpens, SC

Pauline Wilkins OK-159-O Noble & Kelsy: 145
Died: 12.22/1923   Age: 1y06m21d CHILD
Certificate No. 0011,0305 **Informant:** Floyd Wilkins, Father
Parents: Floyd Wilkins & Anna Garrett
(See James Wilkins)

George Wilks NO MARKER Ellis, Mangum, & Fair
Died: 10/14/1952   Age: 66 Laborer
Certificate No. 0033,0538 **Informant:** Agnes Wilks
Parents: Thomas Wilks & Unknown Bpl.: Chester Co., SC

Louvenia Eller Wilks BN-710 -P Noble & Kelsey
Died:08/08/1977   Age: 43 None Given
Certificate No. 0057,0629 **Informant:** Valiean Mcconneaughey
Parents: Richard Eller & Irana Alexander Bpl.: NC

LOUVENIA ELLER
WILKS
JULY 2, 1934
AUG. 8, 1977

Major Wilks UH-519-H

Died:04/22/1957   Age: 58   Certificate Not Found

MAJOR WILKS
OCT. 16, 1899
APR. 22, 1957

Jannett Willett NO MARKER
Died: 10/15/1959   Age: 92 Housewife
Certificate No. 0040,0235 **Informant:** Charles C. Willett
Parents: Thomas Warrick & Carrie Lewis Bpl.: Missouri

BURIALS

Clestus Williams NO MARKER Summersett
Died: 02/08/1909   Age: 22 yrs.

Edward Williams NO MARKER Ellis, Magnum, & Fair
Died: 02/15/1943   Age: 32 Barber @ cotton Mill
Certificate No. 0028,0731 **Informant:** Not Given
Parents: Moses & Vina Williams   Bpl.: Greenville, SC

Estelle Partee Williams **NO MARKER** **Noble & Kelsey**
Died: 08/22/1957 Housewife
Certificate No. 0038,0202 Informant: Mrs. Nonnie Johnson
Parents: Levi Partee & Maria Bost   Bpl.: NC

Florence Lorraine Williams BN-692-P MISSING Noble & Kelsey
Died: 03/14/1989   Age: 19 Never Worked
Certificate No. 0069,0277 **Informant:** Louise Neal Williams, Mother
Parents: McKinley Williams & Louise Neal   Bpl.: Brooklyn, NY

James Williams OK-
          Died: 07/09/1941   Age: Certificate Not Found   Veteran

JAMES
WILLIAMS
NORTH CAROLINA
PVT. 371 INF. 93 DIV.
JULY 9, 1941 P/H

Janie Lee Williams NO MARKER Fraternal Funeral Home
Died: 03/07/1930   Age: 55 Housewife
Certificate No. 0018,0183 **Informant:** Ambrose Williams, Husband
Parents: George Mills

Johnsie Williams OK-072-N NO MARKER Noble & Kelsey: 18
Certificate No. Certificate Not Found Kelsey Map In <u>Goler Plot</u> Parents:

Mabel Elaine Williams OK-072-N Goler Plot Noble & Kelsey: 18
Died: 05/24/1912   Age: 20 Student
Certificate No. 0001,0145 **Informant:** Alice V. U. Williams, Mother
Parents: John Robert Williams & Alice Virginia Unthank   Bpl.: Gilford Co., NC

MABEL ELAINE WILLIAMS
SEPT. 29, 1892
APR. 30, 1912

Malik Almud Williams UH-648-G Noble & Kelsey
Died: 01/05/1994   Age: 21 Bagger @ Grocery Store
Certificate No. 0074,0113 **Informant:** Louise N. Williams, Mother
Parents: McKinley Williams & Louise Neal   Bpl.: Brooklyn, NY

Pettigrew Williams Jr. NO MARKER Ellis, Mangum, & Fair
Died: 05/15/1953   Age: 22 Laborer
Certificate No. 0034,0293 **Informant:** Mrs. Rosa Lee Williams, Oakley, SC
Parents: Pettigrew Williams Sr. & Rosa Bell Williams   Bpl.: Oakley, SC

BURIALS

Victoria Williams
Died: 01/03/1923   Age: ∞42
Certificate No. 0011,0363

NO MARKER
Tenant Farming
Informant: G. C. Dyer
   Bpl.: SC

Noble & Kelsey

Winema Campbell Williams
Died: 09/16/1943   Age: 32
Certificate No. 0028,0867

NO MARKER
Teacher
Informant: Minnie Campbell

Ellis, Mangum, & Fair

Nannie Mae Willoughby
Died: 03/15/1970   Age: 80

BT-263-K
Certificate Not Found

NANNIE MAE WILLOUGHBY
WIFE OF
JOE DAVIS
JULY 1, 1890
MAR. 15, 1970

Adam Lee Wilson
Died: 02/02/1960   Age: 74
Certificate No. 0040,0416
Parents: Frank Wilson & Sallie Hogan

NO MARKER
Preacher
Informant: Prof. Booker T. Wilson
   Bpl.: NC

Annie Mae Wilson
Died: 07/12/1991   Age: 50
Certificate No. 0071,0663
Parents: Ross Wilson & Elsie Smith

UH-600-G MISSING
Presser for Denim Mfg.
Informant: Ross Wilson
   Bpl.: Rowan Co., NC

Noble & Kelsey

Billie Jean Wilson
Died: 04/06/1963   Age: 33
Certificate No. 0043,0242
Parents: Pete Summer & Lula Partee

NO MARKER
Domestic
Informant: Ollie Henderson
   Bpl.: Salisbury, NC

David J. Wilson
Died: 11/22/1909   Age: 03m. 14d
Certificate No. 0004,0481
Parents: John Wilson & Halosie J. Foot:

NO MARKER.
INFANT
Informant: John Wilson
   Bpl.: Iredell Co., NC

Noble & Kelsey

Ella Robinson Wilson
Died: 02/08/1927   Age: 70
Certificate No. 0015,0296
Parents: Jacob & Dolly Robinson

OK-084-N
Housewife, Domestic
Informant: Mrs. M. C. Ferron
   Bpl.: Fair Castle, VA

Noble & Kelsey:

WILSON
HUSBAND   WIFE
WILLIAM WILSON   ELLA WILSON
NOV. 10, 1850   JAN. 20, 1857
AUG. 15, 1911   FEB. 8, 1927
GONE BUT NOT FORGOTTEN

Franklin Wilson
Died: 01/22/1914   Age: 3y18d
Certificate No. 0001,0750
Parents: John Wilson & Malessia L. Foot

OK-NO MARKER
CHILD
Informant: John Wilson
   Bpl.: Weva Co., West VA

Noble & Kelsey: 32

BURIALS

Harrison Wilson   UH-330-I/J   Noble & Kelsey
Died: 02/03/1958   Age: 69   Retired, Wilson Construction Company
Certificate No. 0038,0492   **Informant:** W.W. Wilson; Brooklyn, NY
Parents: Green Wilson & Annie Smith   Bpl.: NC

HARRISON WILSON
AUG. 13, 1888
FEB. 3, 1958

Hezekiah E. Wilson   UH-448-H
Died: 02/14/1951   Age: 63   Certificate Not Found

WILSON
HEZEKIAH E.   LILLIAN C.
MAR. 15, 1888   SEPT. 12, 1894
FEB. 14, 1951   JAN. 29, 1962

James Wilson   OK-360-I/J   MISSING   Certificate Not Found

Malissa Foot Wilson   OK-NO MARKER   Noble & Kelsey: 32
Died: 01/15/1914   Age: 23y09m21d   Domestic
Certificate No. 0001,0745   **Informant:** John Wilson
Parents: Emery Foot & Della Gaither   Bpl.: Iredell Co., NC

Rose Kelly Wilson   BN-NEW MARKER
Died: 10/03/2000   Age: 73   Certificate Not Found

ROSA KELLY
WILSON
JUNE 23, 1923
OCT. 3, 2000

Saunders "Pete" Wilson   UH-529-H   Noble & Kelsey
Died: 02/09/1975   Age: 67   Retired Laborer @ Livingstone College
Certificate No. 0055,0111   **Informant:** Elizabeth R. Wilson
Parents: Luther Wilson & Rena Partee   Bpl.: NC

WILSON
SAUNDERS PETE WILSON
JAN. 1, 1906
FEB. 9, 1975

Terry Lee Wilson   UH-603-G   Noble & Kelsey
Died: 08/02/1991   Age: 18   Material Handler @ Industrial Thread Mfg.
Certificate No. 0071,0739   **Informant:** Johnnie M. Parker
Parents: Terry Lee Alexander & Johnie Parker   Bpl.: Salisbury, NC

A LOVING SON
TERRY LEE
WILSON
1973 -- 1991

William Wilson   OK-083 N   Noble & Kelsey: 56
Died: 08/15/1911   Age: 61   Funeral Home Record   (See Ella R. Wilson)

BURIALS

Willie Wilson
Died: 10/30/1950 Age: 48
Certificate No. 0032,0453
Parents: Rufus Wilson & Esther Harris

NO MARKER
Laborer
Informant: Mrs. Esther Harris
Bpl.: Rowan Co., NC

Noble & Kelsey

Leonard L. Winford
Died: 06/23/1924 Age: 10
Certificate No. 0012,0394
Parents: Leroy Winford & Marry Simmons

OK-222-L
School Boy
Informant: Leroy Winford
Bpl.: Salisbury, NC

Noble & Kelsy: 282

LEONARD
WINFORD
OCT. 16, 1914
JUN. 23, 1924
AT REST

Bertie Winfry
Died: 11/02/1908 Age: 4 yrs

NO MARKER

Summersett
Funeral Home Record

Betty Bingham Wingate
Certificate Not Found
Parents: Lillington H. Bingham & Henrietta Browne

OK-188-O Bingham Plot

Bpl: Salisbury

BETTY BINGHAM
WINGATE

Annie E. Wiseman
Died: 12/16/1947 Age: 89
Certificate No. 0031,0233
Parents: William Ferron & Mariah Bullon
(Plot also Contains Robert Wiseman & Mary Propst)

OK-096-N Curb NO MARKER
Housewife
Informant: Robert Wiseman
Bpl.: Salisbury, NC

Noble & Kelsey: 1

Estella Wiseman
Died: 08/27/1954 Age: 51
Certificate Not Found
Parents: Robert Wiseman & Bettie Etchson

UH-394-I/J
Domestic

WISEMAN
ESTELLA WISEMAN
AUG. 4, 1903
AUG. 27, 1954   (E.W.) footstone

Lewis Connor Wiseman
Died: 01/18/1966 Age: 53
Certificate No. 0046,0041
Parents: Robert Wiseman & Betty Etchinson

NO MARKER
Laborer
Informant: Miss Mary Wiseman
Bpl.: Davie Co., NC

Mitchell & Fair

Mary Wiseman
Died: 06/21/1988 Age: 84
Certificate No. 0068,0581
Parents: Robert Wiseman & Betty Etchison

UH-393-I/J
Domestic Work in private homes
Informant: Noah L. Wiseman, III
Bpl.: Mocksville, NC

Mitchell & Fair

MARY WISEMAN
MAR. 22, 1904
JUNE 21, 1988

BURIALS

Ollie Gainey Wiseman
Died: 01/17/1968   Age: 60
Certificate No. 0048,0037
Parents: Isom Gainey & Amanda Thompson

OK-N MISSING
Housewife
Informant: Walter Lee Wiseman: Husband

Mitchell & Fair
Funeral Home Record

Robert L. Wiseman
Died: 06/29/1932   Age: ∞59
Certificate No. 0020,0247
Parents: John Wiseman
Plot also Contains Annie Wiseman & Mary Propst According to Kelsey map.

OK-096-N Curb Cheshire & Lynn @ Noble & Kelsey: 2
Employed by Southern Railway
Informant: Ollie Wiseman, Wife
   Bpl.: Rowan Co., NC

Sherman Wiseman
Died: 01/03/1968   Age: 64
Certificate No. 0048,0036
Parents: Benjamin Wiseman & Elizabeth Sloan

NO MARKER Noble & Kelsey
Laborer/ Self Employed
Informant: Edith Childress

Christine Jones Witherspoon
Died: 05/06/1969   Age: 56
Certificate No. 0049,0303
Parents: Rufus Jones & Unknown

BT-269-K MISSING
Housewife
Informant: Roosevelt Witherspoon, Husband
   Bpl.: VA

Noble & Kelsey

John Witherspoon
Died: 01/18/1912   Age: 35 yrs.
Parents: Bob Witherspoon

NO MARKER

Summersett
Funeral Home Record

Roosevelt Witherspoon
Died: 06/01/1986   Age: 79 - 75dc

Certificate No. 0066,0499
Parents: Richard Witherspoon & Mattie Lewis

BN-023-N
Graf-Davis-Collet Co. Rubber Manufacturer Machine
   operator
Informant: Roxie Archie, Sister
   Bpl.: Wilkes. NC

Noble & Kelsey

ROSEVELT WITHERSPOON
FEB. 12, 1907
JUNE 1, 1986

Columbus J. Wood
Died: 07/25/1939   Age: 65

NO MARKER

Ellis, Mangum, & Fair
Funeral Home Record

Daisy B. Wood
Died: 04/12/1957   Age: 51
Certificate No. 0037,0589
Parents: John Scott & Not Known

MISSING MARKER
Domestic
Informant: Watt Wood, Husband
   Bpl.: Mecklenburg Co., NC

Ellis, Mangum, & Fair

Ella Hannah Wood
Died: 04/03/1948   Age: 73
Parents: Scott Carr & Charlotte Thomas

NO MARKER
Teacher

Ellis, Magnum, & Fair
Funeral Home Record
bd. 04/29/1875

Joann Wood
Died: 05/23/1953   Age: 1m.
Parents: James Wright & Bessie Wood

NO MARKER
INFANT

Ellis, Mangum, & Fair
Funeral Home Record

BURIALS

McDilla Woodard — OK-210-O — Noble & Kelsey
Died: 08/07/1977 Age: 76
Housewife
Certificate No. 0057,0673 **Informant:** Lewis
Parents: Richard McKeown & Maggie McKeown Bpl.: SC

1901   MCDILLA WOODARD   1977

Emma Moore Woodburn — UH-MITplt. — Noble & Kelsey
Died: 06/29/1947 Age: 44
Domestic
Certificate No. 0030,0879 **Informant:** James Woodburn, Husband
Parents: George Moore & Ida Sumner Bpl.: Rowan Co., NC

EMMA MOORE
PETER J. WOODBURN
AUG. 15, 1902
JUNE 29, 1947
THEN THE JUST
WILL SHINE FORTH. MATTHEW III; 4, 3

ET. Louis Woodruff — OK-NO MARKER — Noble & Kelsy: 150
Died: Age: 24,4,29
Cook for Private Families
Certificate No. 0015, 0425 **Informant:** William Woodruff
Parents: William Woodruff & Ada Foster Bpl.: Mocksville, NC

Josie Woodruff — NO MARKER — Noble & Kelsy: 360

Sarah Scott Woodruff — NO MARKER — Ellis, Mangum, & Fair
Died: 04/17/1952 Age: 74
Domestic
Certificate No. 0033,0213 **Informant:** Joe Woodruff
Parents: Dan Scott

William Woodruff — OK-200-O — Noble & Kelsy: 150
Died: 06/14/1943 Age: 65 - 62dc
Day Laborer, Salisbury Laundry
Certificate No. 0028,0814 **Informant:** Ada Woodruff
Parents: Henry Woodruff & Claremont Foster Bpl.: Davie Co., NC

WILLIAM WOODRUFF
AUG. 6, 1878
JUNE 14, 1943:
(Top line of bottom inscription broken off)
Be given that we may meet in heaven
(condition on 08/19/2003)

William Henry Woodruff — OK-200-O MISSING — Noble & Kelsy: 150
Died: 08/22/1951 Age: 75 Laborer
Certificate No. 0032,0905 **Informant:** Minnie Woodruff, Cooleemee, NC
Parents: Unknown & Annie Woodruff Bpl.: Davie Co., NC

Carrie Woods — NO MARKER — Mitchell & Fair
Died: 12/08/1968 Age: 73
Laundry
Certificate No. 0048,0762 **Informant:** Mrs. Eva Koontz

BURIALS

Millie Woodside
Died: 04/03/1914   Age: 114
Certificate No. 0001,0419
Parents: UNKNOWN

NO MARKER
None
Informant: William Woodside
  Bpl.: Iredell Co., NC

Noble & Kelsy: 338

Ezell Woodson

Died: 04/29/1956   Age: 32

UH-455-H

Certificate Not Found

EZELL WOODSON
BORN 9. 3. 1914
DIED: 4.29.1956

John Woodson

UH-454-H MISSING

Marie Authur Woodson
Died: 09/06/1960   Age: 64
Certificate No. 0041,0104
Parents: Peter Authur & Lizzie Oalmer
Condition on 09/07/03

UH-???
  Housewife @ Home
Informant: Willie Mae C. Hargraves
  Bpl.: SC

Noble & Kelsey

MRS. MARIE WOODSON
BORN. OCT. 22 1896
DIED: SEPT. 6, 1960

Elbert Wooley
Died: 02/01/1929
Certificate No. 0017, 0332
Parents: George Wooley & Ella Richardson

OK-NO MARKER
Laborer & School Boy
Informant: Georgianna Wooley
  Bpl.: Albemarle, NC

Cheshire & Mangum

George Washington Wooley
Died: 01/03/1953   Age: 75
Certificate No. 0034,0085
Parents: UNKNOWN

OK-184-O Wooley Plot
Southern Railroad Retiree
Informant: Gladys Wright, New York, NY
  Bpl.: Stanley Co., NC

Noble & Kelsy: 187

WHOOLEY

Georgianna Wooley

GEORGIANA
GRANDPARENTS

Grandparents Wooley

Mary Wooley

Died: 1956   Age: ∞ 72
(Name & dates on metal insert in stone marker)
Mrs. Mary Wooley
1894   1956

UH-H

BURIALS

Paul S. Worthy Jr.
Died:01/27/1922   Age: 09m24d
Certificate No. 0010,0308
Parents: James W. Wortha & Hanna Woods

NO MARKER
INFANT
Informant: Jim Worthy
 Bpl.: Salisbury, NC

Noble & Kelsey: 81

Sadie Ruth Worthy
Died:04/23/1927   Age: 09m08d
Certificate No. 0015,0351
Parents: J. W. Worthy & Hanna Woods

NO MARKER
INFANT
Informant: J. W. Worthy
 Bpl.: SC

Noble & Kelsey: 81

Willie Davis Worthy
Died: 05/31/1927   Age: 9
Certificate No. 0015,0367
Parents: James W. Worthy & Hanna Woods

NO MARKER
School Girl
Informant: J. W. Worthy, Father
 Bpl.: Salisbury, NC

Noble & Kelsey

Anna Sloan Wright
Died:01/24/1959   Age: 74
Certificate No. 0039,0457
Parents: Martin Sloan & Lina McKorkle

NO MARKER
Hair Culture
Informant: Lina W. Stewart
 Bpl.: NC

Noble & Kelsey 094

Ethel Wright
Died: 12/18/1923   Age: 16
Certificate No. 0011,0550
Parents: Wesley & Phoenicia Wright

OK-NO MARKER
School Girl
Informant: J. L. Moore
 Bpl.: Rutherfordton

Noble & Kelsy: 145

Gladys W. Wright

OK-185-O MISSING

Noble & Kelsy: 187

S. P. Wright
Died:03/01/1924   Age: 56
Certificate Not Found
Parents: Derrick & Anna Wright

OK -? N
Resident physician @ Livingstone College1893
Informant: Anna Wright
 Bpl.: Bladen, Co., NC

Noble & Kelsey: 94

DR. S. P. WRIGHT
DIED
MARCH 1 1924
WE WILL MEET AGAIN

Velva Wright
Died:03/19/1949   Age: 01m20d
Certificate No. 0031,0812
Parents: Johnie Wright & Katie Lue Swift

NO MARKER
INFANT
Informant: Jessie Swift
 Bpl.: Salisbury, NC

Will & INFANT Wright   OK-NO MARKER   Noble & Kelsey: 15
INFANT Certificate Not Found   Plot Contains Will Wright and INFANT 7 weeks old

Anita Blackwell Yongue
Died: 12/05/1971   Age: 68
Certificate No. 0051,0748
Parents: William & Ollie Kent

OK-087-O MISSING
Housewife
Informant: Miss Margie Blackwell
 Bpl.: PA

Noble & Kelsey

Alexander Young
Died: 10/01/1939   Age: 2y 10m
Certificate No. 0027,1520
Parents: William Young & Julia Mashare

NO MARKER
CHILD
Informant: Julis Young, mother
 Bpl.: Salisbury, NC

BURIALS

Irene Bevins Young
Died: 10/29/1929   Age: 20
Certificate No. 0017,0515
Parents: John Burns & Ella Zeal

NO MARKER
Housewife
Informant: Will Young, Husband
   Bpl.: Belton, SC

Fraternal Funeral Home

James Wells Younge
Died: 01/01/1940   Age: 50

OK-065-N
Brick mason, Treasurer of Livingstone College, &
   Financial Secretary of the A.. M. E. Zion Church
   Bpl: Cleveland Co., NC

Noble & Kelsey: 63

```
                    YOUNGE
   JAMES WELLS          PEARL SHINES
   MAR. 25, 1890        FEB. 12, 1881
   JAN. 1, 1940         APR. 12, 1972
      THEY DIED AS THEY LIVED CHRISTIANS
```

John William Younge
Died, 07/28/1927   Age: 62,3,13
Certificate No. 0015,0407
Parents: James & Malinda Young

NO MARKER
Janitor @ Cotton Mill
Informant: Minnie Younge, Wife
   Bpl.: SC

Noble & Kelsey

Madison McCrary Younge
Died: 05/27/1969   Age: 86
Parents: Younge M. McCrary & Unknown

NO MARKER
Coal Miner

Ellis, Mangum, & Fair
Funeral Home Record

Mary Elizabeth Younge
Died: 07/13/1918   Age: 11d
Certificate No. 0006,0465
Parents: Arthur Young & Mary Partee

NO MARKER
INFANT
Informant: Arthur Young
   Bpl.: Salisbury, NC

Noble & Kelsy: 346

Pearl Shines Younge
Died: 04/12/1972   Age: 91
(See James Wells Younge)

OK-066-N
Certificate Not Found

Noble & Kelsey: 63
Librarian Rowan Public Library

Johnnie Mae Lineburger Zimmerman
Died: 04/15/1995   Age: 57
Certificate No. 0075,0359
Parents: Odell McCluney & Alma Sharp

BN-664-P
Housemaid @ Private Homes
Informant: Cleveland Jameson
   Bpl.: Rowan Co., NC

Noble & Kelsey

```
   JOHNNIE MAE LINEBERGER
           ZIMMERMAN
      JUNE 6      APR. 15
       1937        1995
```

BURIALS
PART TWO
END NOTES

---

1 **Edwin W. Smith.** *"Aggrey of Africa. a study in black and white."* (London; Student Christian Movement, ©1929, p. xii, 279)

2 Dorothy Sharp Johnson & Lula Co.sby Williams. *"Pioneering Women of the African Methodist EpisCo.pal Zion Church."*. (Charlotte NC: A.M.E. Zion Publishing House, © 1997, pg. 41)

APPENDIX A

CAUSES OF DEATH RECORDED IN AVAILABLE DOCUMENTS FUNERAL HOME RECORDS ROWAN COUNTY DEATH CERTIFICATES BIOGRAPHICAL INFORMATION	Number
ACCIDENTS [Struck by Auto / Train] [Auto Wreck] [Explosion / Fire [Drowning] [Exposure]	047
ALCOHOLISM	015
ALZHEIMER'S DISEASE	009
ASTHMA	008
CANCER [Breast / Uterine / Prostate / Colon / Lung / Liver]	109
CIRRHOSIS	005
DIABETES [Type 1 & Type 2]	033
HEART DISEASE [Congestive / Infarction / Carditis / Artery Disease / Rheumatic]	228
HIV	003
HOMICIDE [Gunshot / Stabbing]	011
INFLUENZA / PNEUMONIA	094
INTESTINAL OBSTRUCTION	004
MALARIA	004
NEPHRITIS, BRIGHTS KIDNEY DISEASE, NEPHROSIS	078
PEDIATRIC DISEASE [i.e. Colic / Measles / Whooping Cough]	041
PELLAGRA	017
PULMONARY EMBOLISM	005
RABIES	001
SEPTICEMIA [Blood Infection, Blood Disease, Gangrene]	013
SICKLE CELL	003
STD	002
STILLBIRTH	113
STROKE / CEREBROVASCULAR DISEASES / MENINGITIS / PALSEY / APOPLEXY	155
SUICIDE	002
TUBERCULOSIS	050
UNKNOWN	021
TOTAL NUMBER OF RECORDS LISTING CAUSE OF DEATH	1,071

APPENDIX B

ANNUAL OAKDALE / UNION HILL CEMETERY BURIALS
1905 TO 2005

Year	No.	Year	No.	Year	No.	Year	No.	Year	No.
1905	2	1926	26	1947	33	1968	18	1989	13
1906	0	1927	29	1948	12	1969	22	1990	20
1907	4	1928	12	1949	22	1970	14	1991	17
1908	14	1929	31	1950	13	1971	12	1992	15
1909	17	1930	20	1951	22	1972	13	1993	19
1910	44	1931	9	1952	42	1973	5	1994	24
1911	30	1932	7	1953	17	1974	10	1995	4
1912	12	1933	5	1954	16	1975	7	1996	8
1913	9	1934	9	1955	22	1976	11	1997	3
1914	15	1935	3	1956	21	1977	13	1998	5
1915	27	1936	3	1957	28	1978	9	1999	3
1916	15	1937	13	1958	17	1979	10	2000	3
1917	9	1938	17	1959	23	1980	16	2001	2
1918	34	1939	23	1960	20	1981	18	2002	5
1919	8	1940	15	1961	33	1982	16	2003	13
1920	15	1941	14	1962	8	1983	9	2004	2
1921	7	1942	19	1963	13	1984	3	2005	0
1922	22	1943	21	1964	21	1985	19		
1923	38	1944	23	1965	10	1986	16		
1924	27	1945	11	1966	15	1987	8		
1925	24	1946	12	1967	13	1988	15		

Total   1536

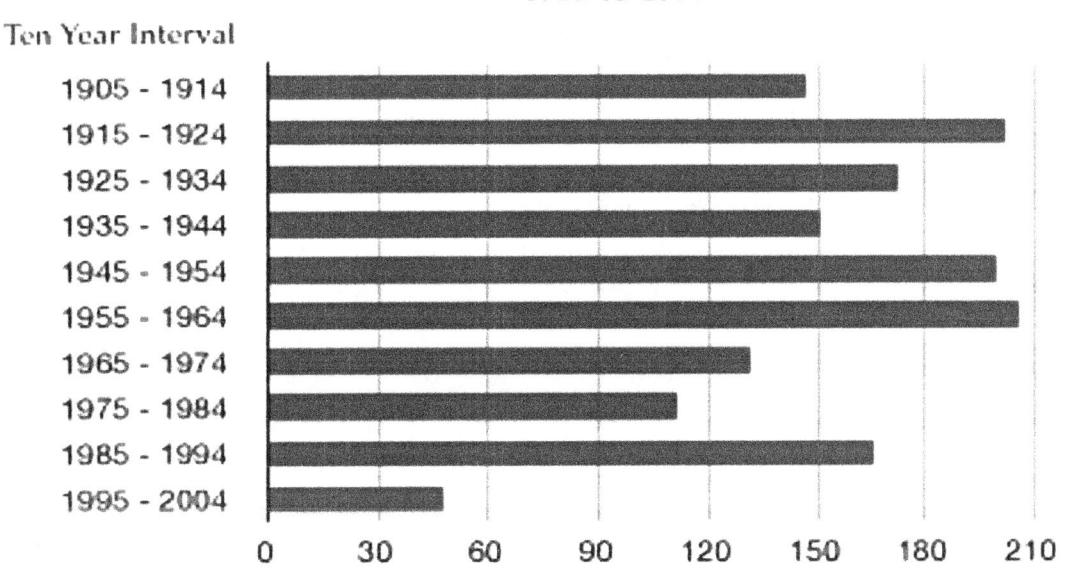

APPENDIX C

FUNERAL HOMES ACCOUNTABLE FOR BURIALS AND BURIAL SOCIETIES

Funeral Homes currently in business are in bold print. All businesses had Salisbury, North Carolina addresses.

Summersett T. Walker   **Summersett,** Est. 1907
                                  315 N. Jackson St.
                                  315 West Innes Street

George W. Wright   George W. Wright
                                  415 W. Fulton

Noble & Kelsey   **Stephen Noble & William F. Kelsey,** Est. 1903
                                  225 E. Fisher Street
                                  223 E. Fisher Street

Chesire & Mangum   Leroy R. Cheshire & Travis R. Mangum
                                  120 N. Lee Street

Bingham & Carter   Richard Bingham & Marshall Carter
                                  126 N. Lee Street

Cheshire & Callahan   Leroy R. Cheshire & Callahan
                                  N. Lee Street

Fraternal Funeral Home   Proprietors & Address Unknown

Bingham, Carter, & Cheshire   Richard Bingham, Marshall Carter, & Leroy Cheshire
                                  120 N. Lee Street

Peoples Undertaking Co.   Bingham, Carter, & Cheshire
                                  N. Lee Street

Ellis, Mangum, & Fair   Charles Ellis, Travis V. Mangum, and James C. Fair
                                  701 West Horah Street

Mitchell & Fair   **Allen L. Mitchell & Rosalind Mitchell**
                                  418 South Craige Street

The Florence Progressive Mutual Burial Association of Mitchell and Fair
(Ellis, Mangum, and Fair)

The Kelsey Mutual Burial Association of Noble and Kelsey

APPENDIX D
MAPS

FACING THE RISING SUN

The following photograph and map represents the southern part of the Circle Subsection located in the Oakdale Section facing east from the John Holt family plot. The prefix for the subsection is OK and its map suffix is N. The northern part of the Bingham / S. E. Duncan, Sr. Subsection on map O is in the photograph with the Kelsey family plot and the freedman reburial site in the distance.

SECTION / SUBSECTION MAP

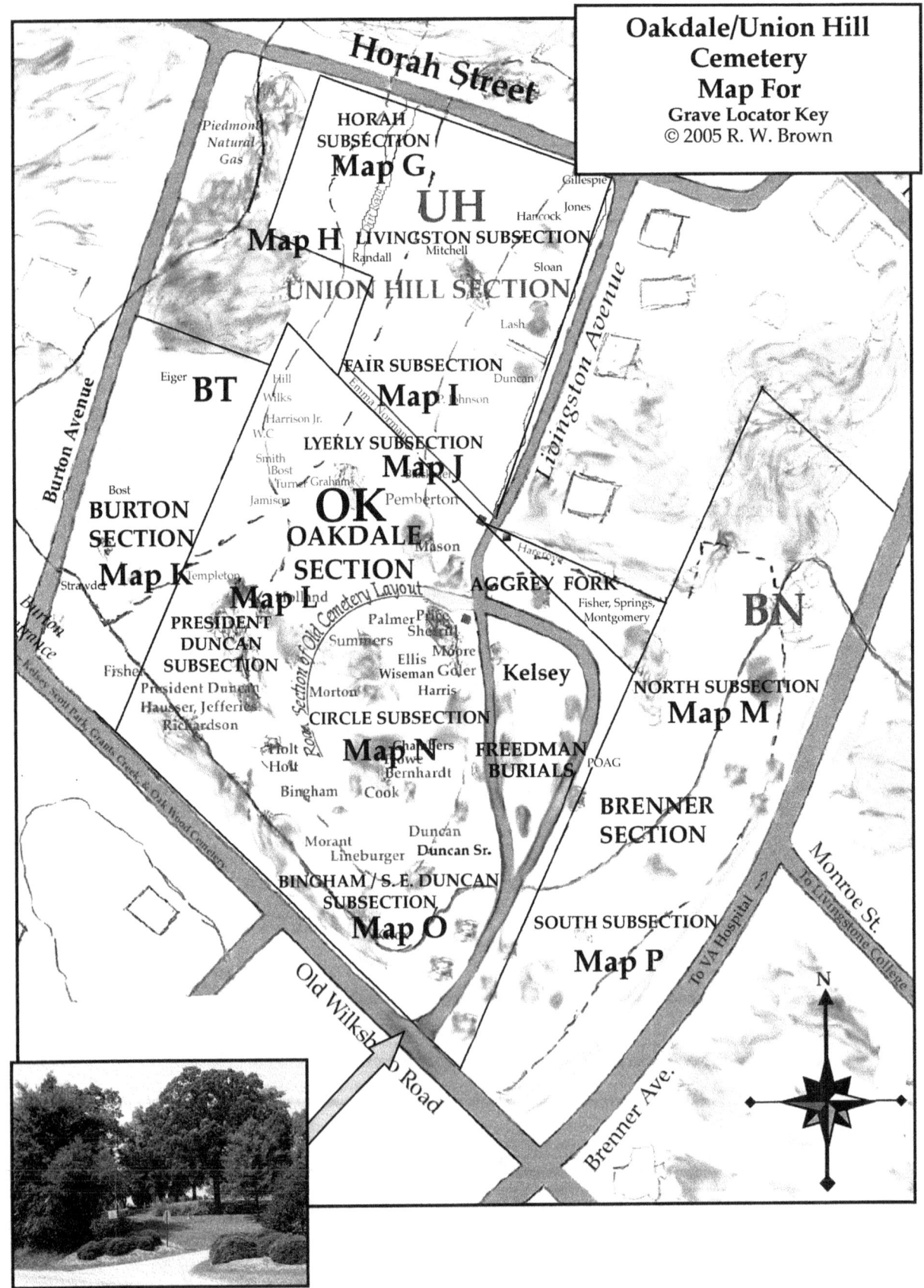

251

Map G
HORAH SUBSECTION

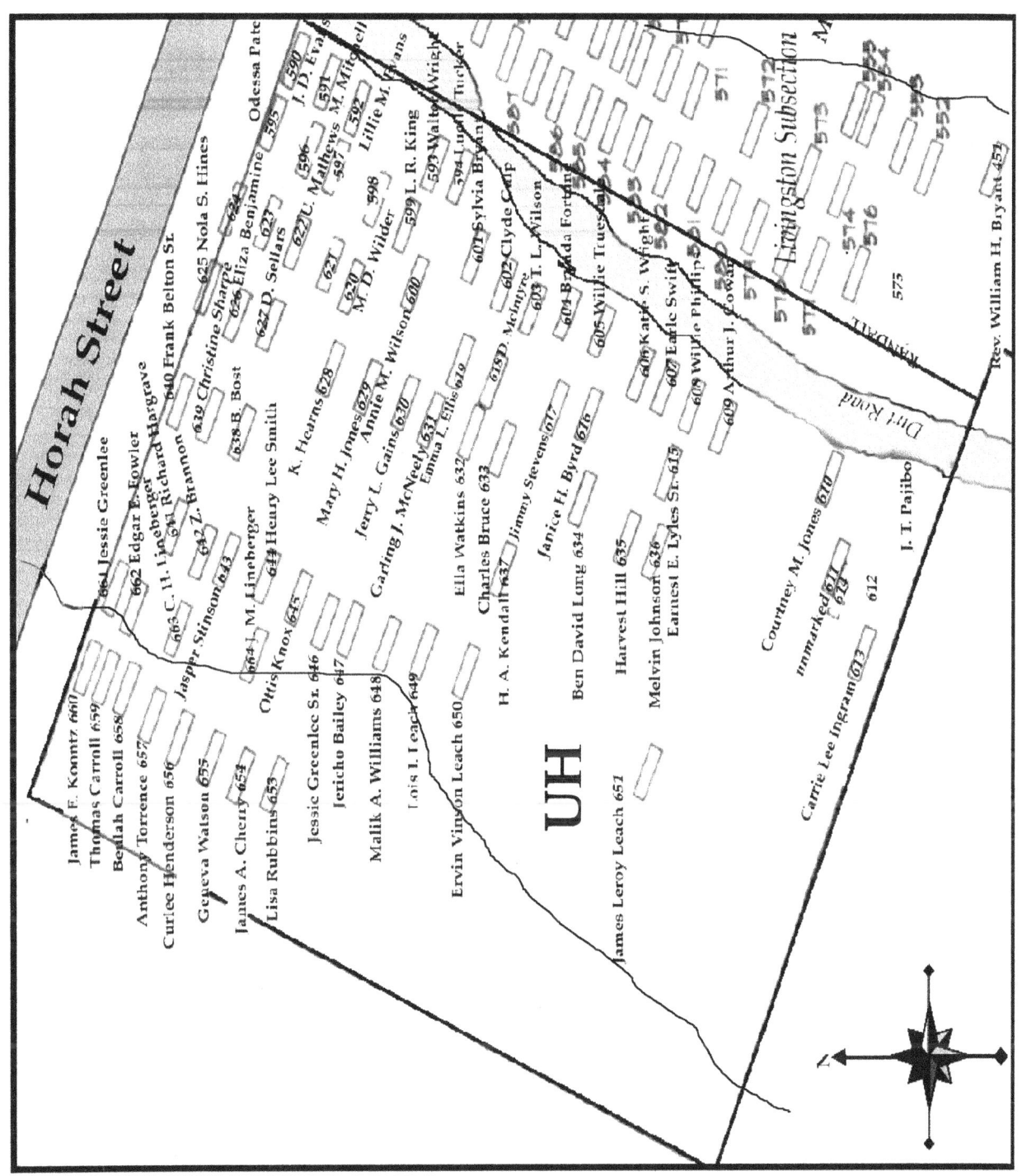

Map H
LIVINGSTON SUBSECTION

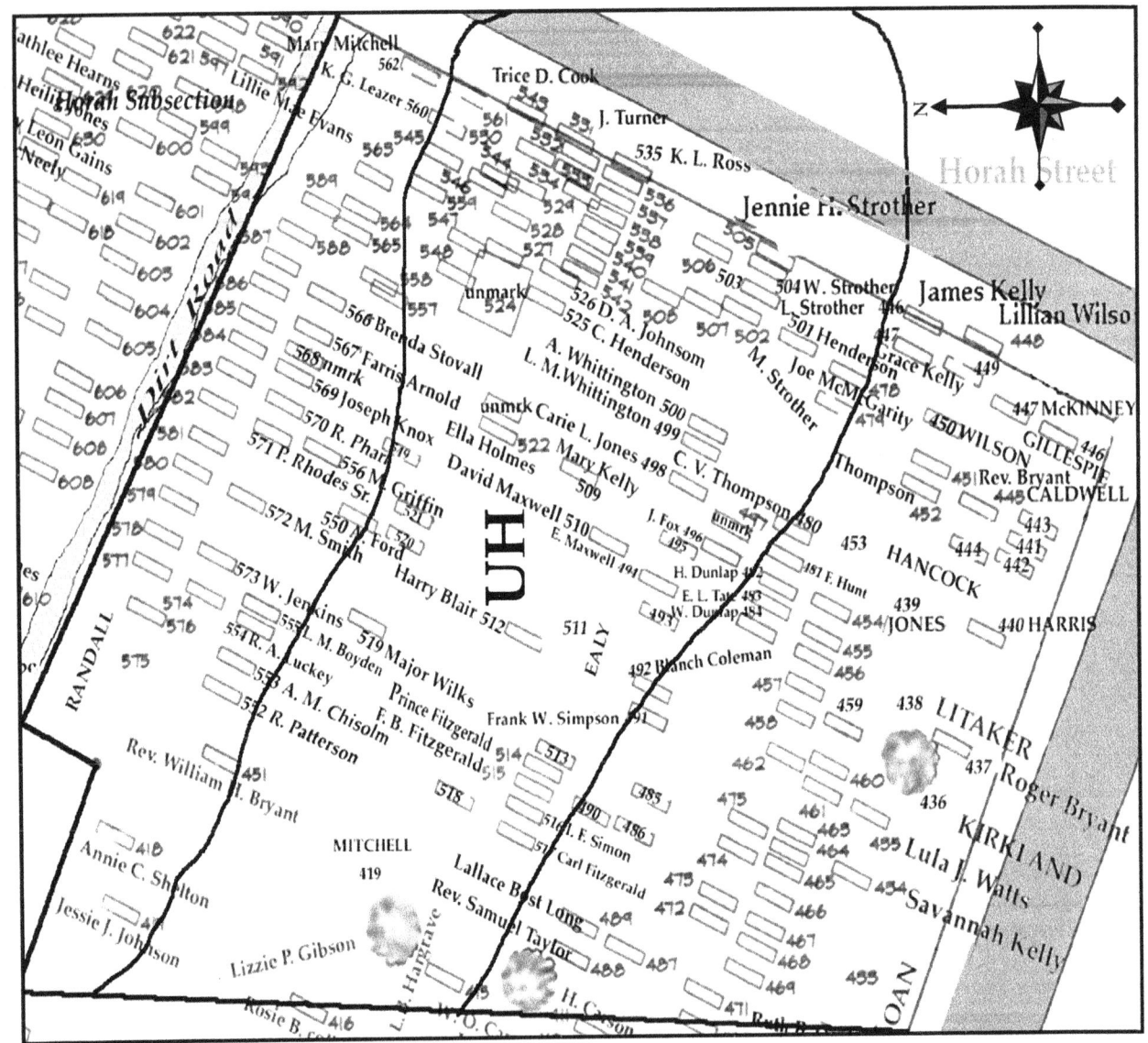

Map I / J
FAIR / LYERLY SUBSECTIONS

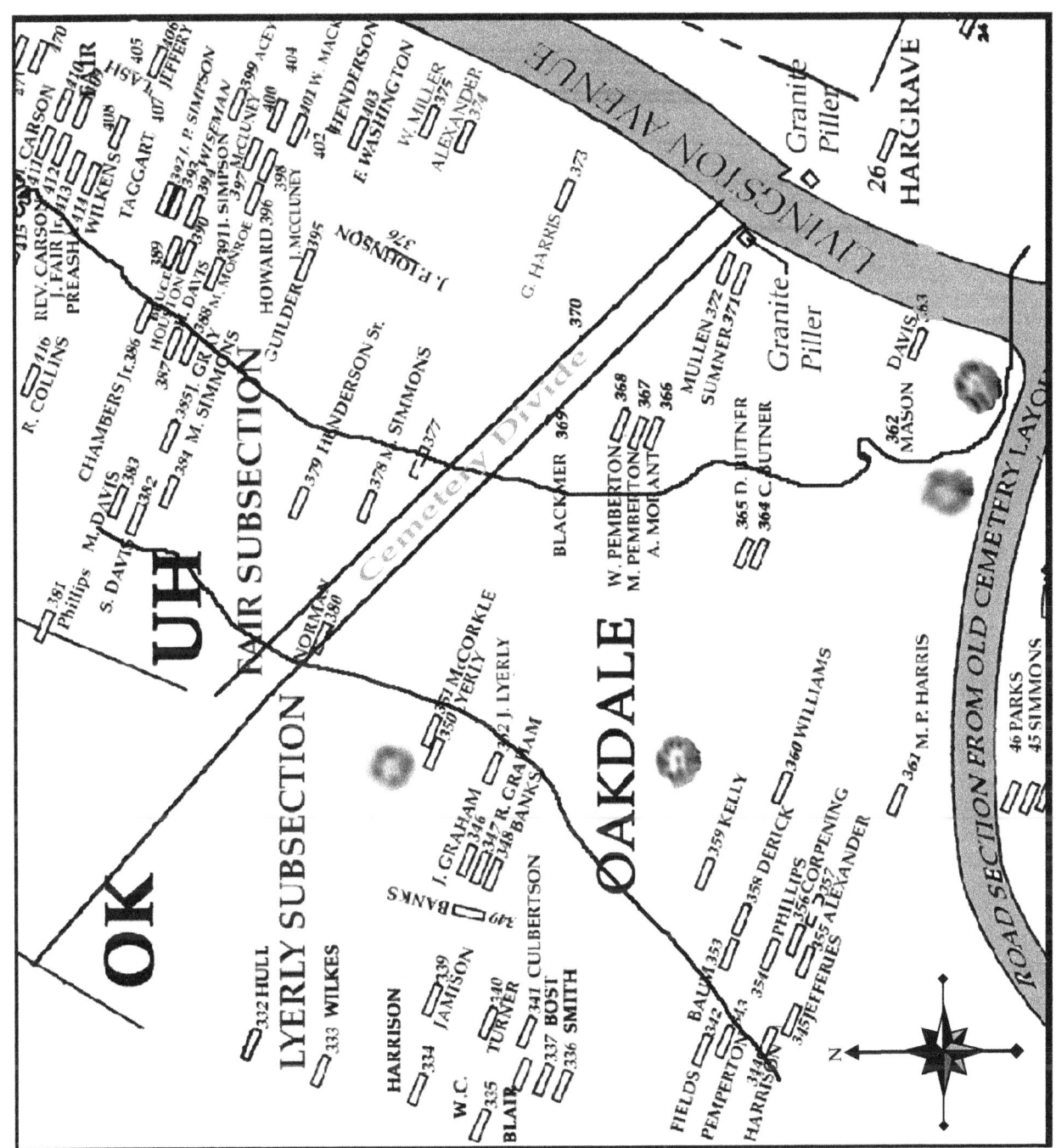

Map K
BURTON SECTION
OAKDALE WESTERN SECTION

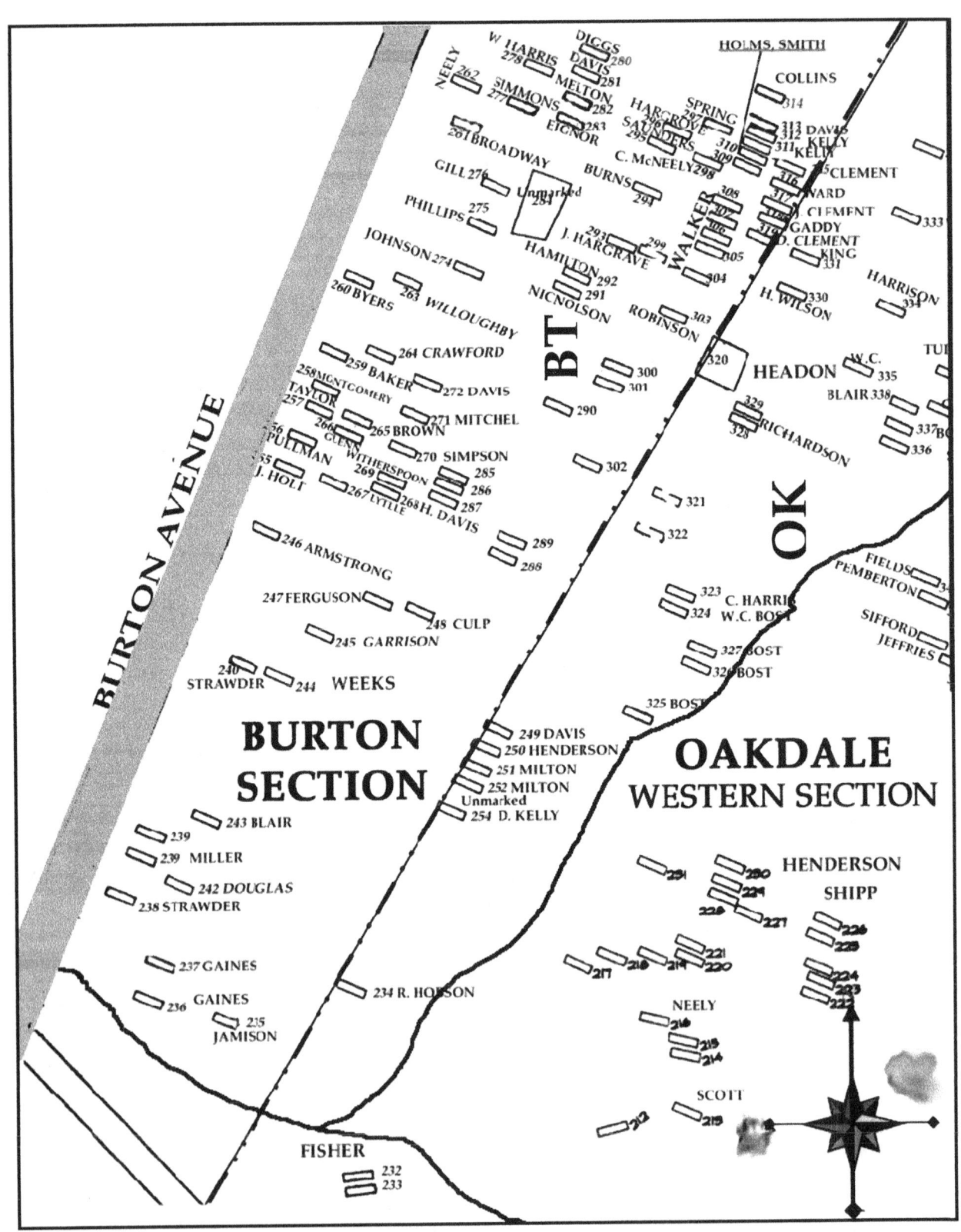

Map L
PRESIDENT DUNCAN SUBSECTION

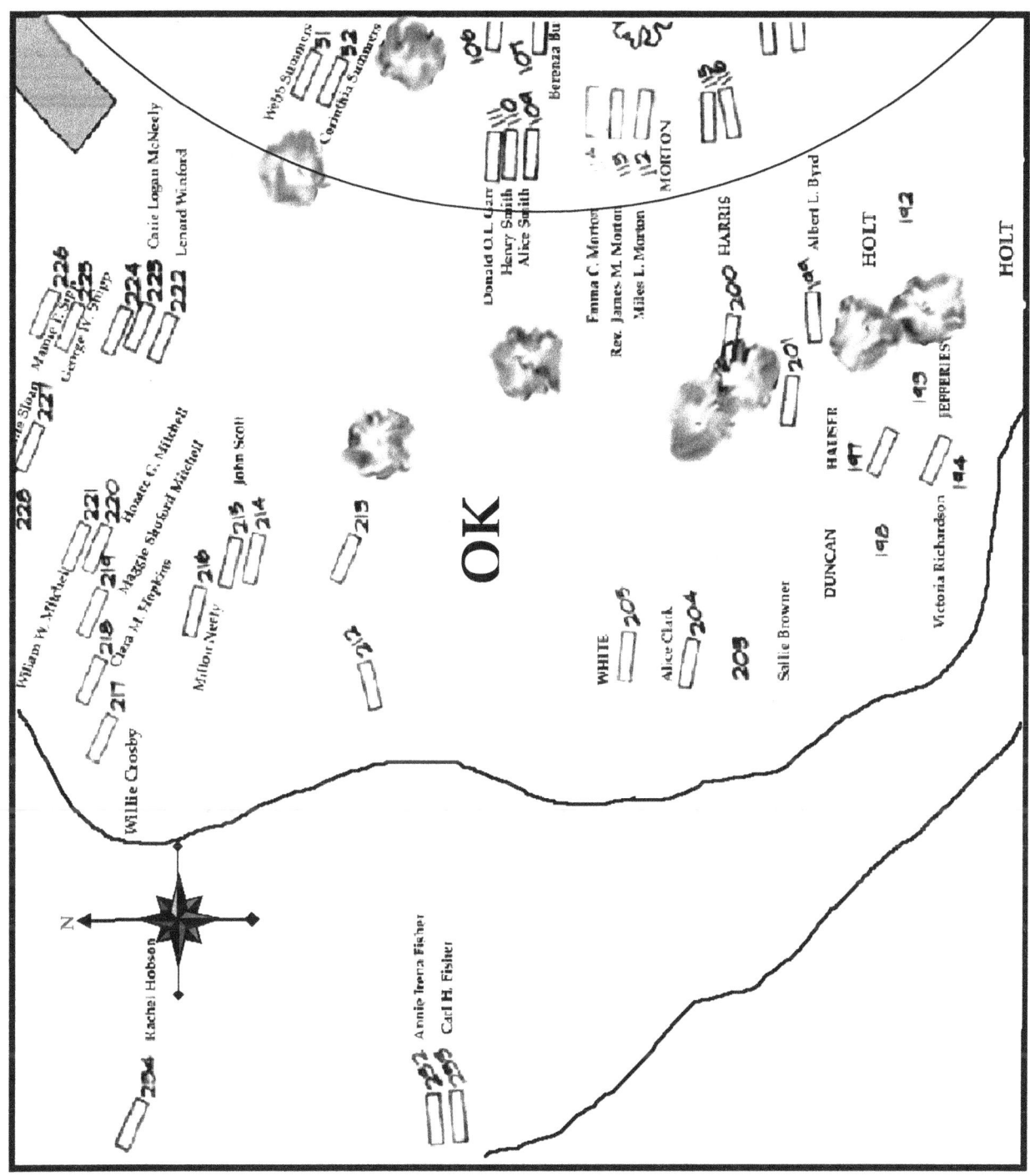

Map M
BRENNER NORTH SUBSECTION

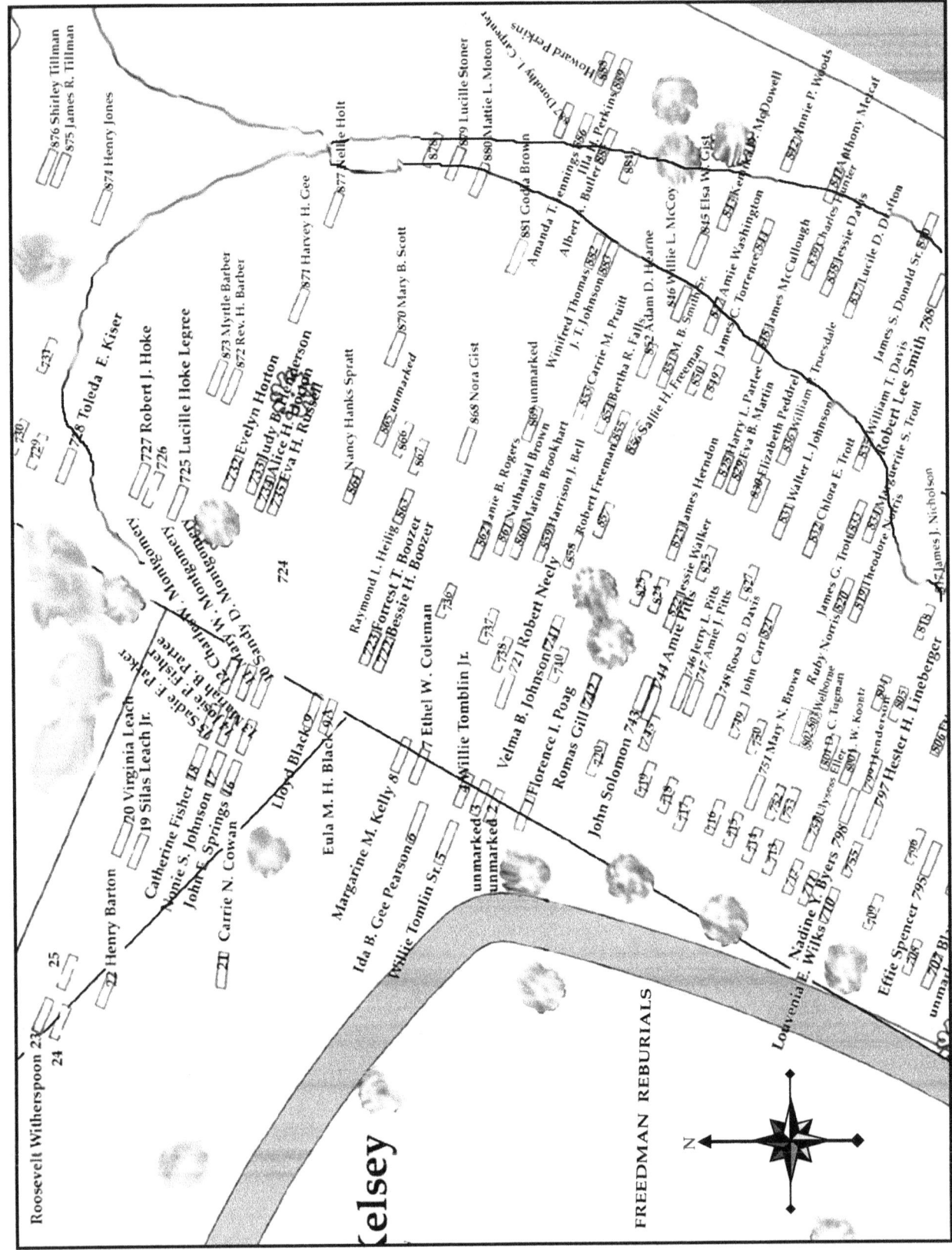

Map N
CIRCLE SUBSECTION

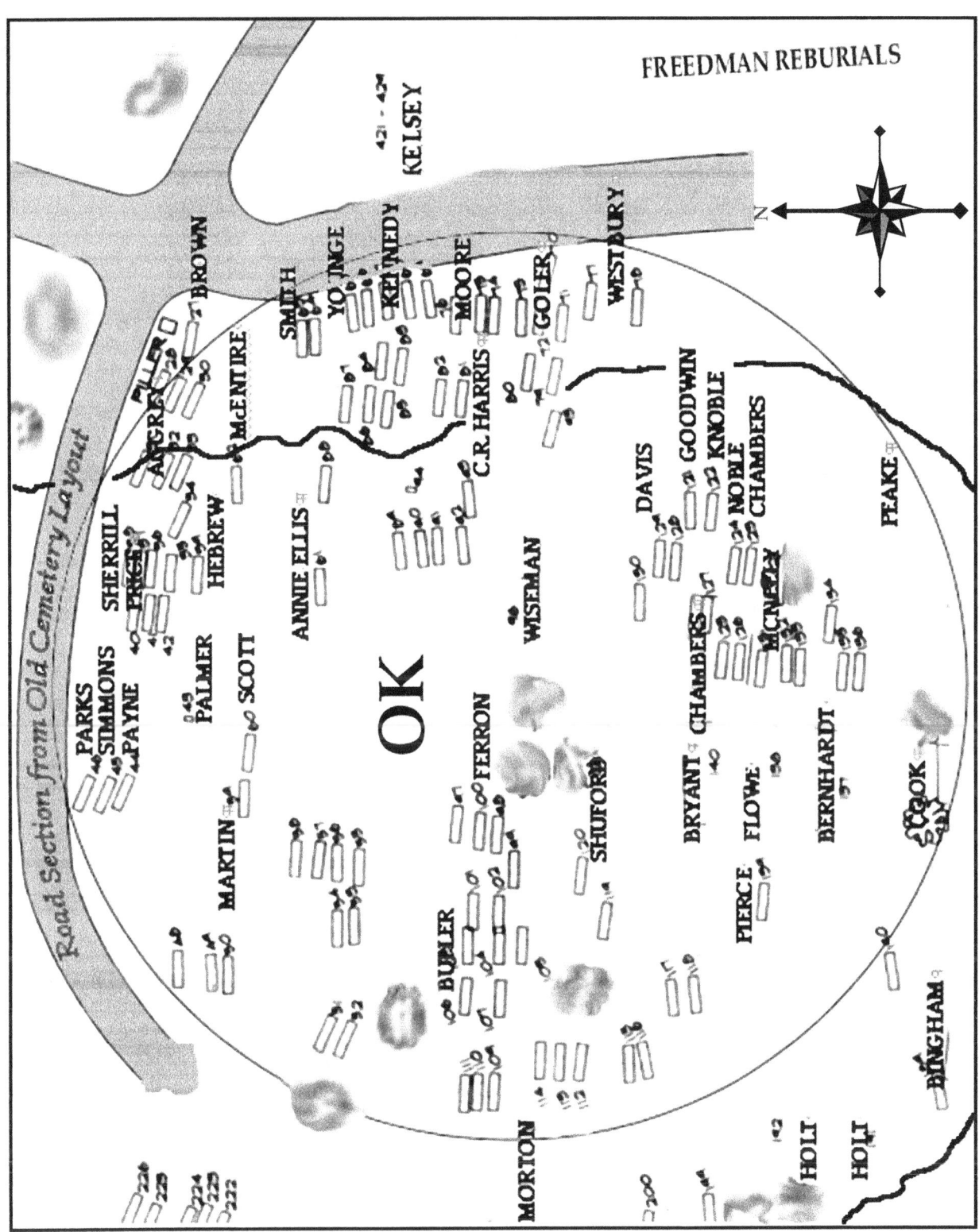

Map O
BINGHAM / S. E. DUNCAN SR. SUBSECTION

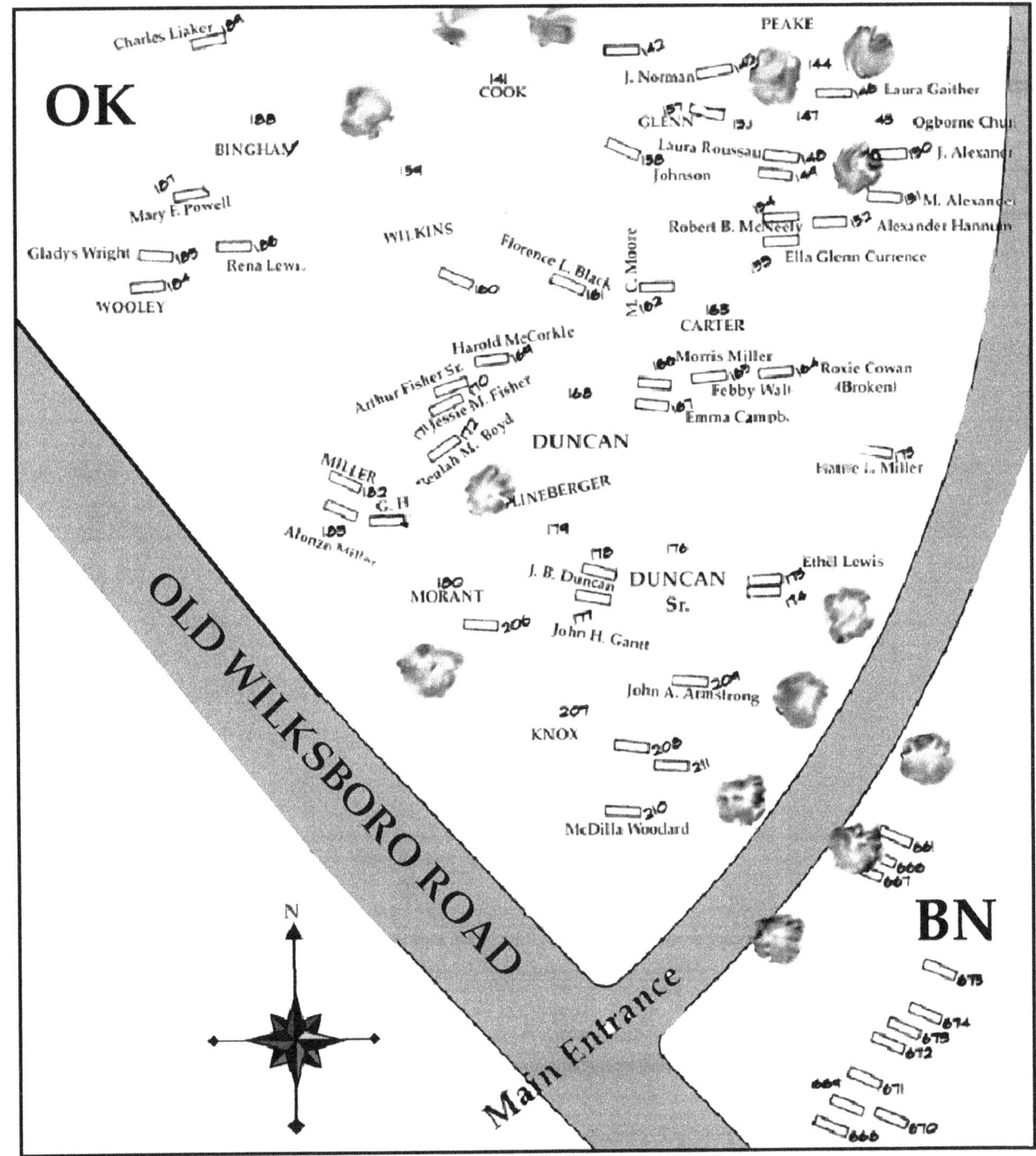

Map P
BRENNER SOUTH SUBSECTION

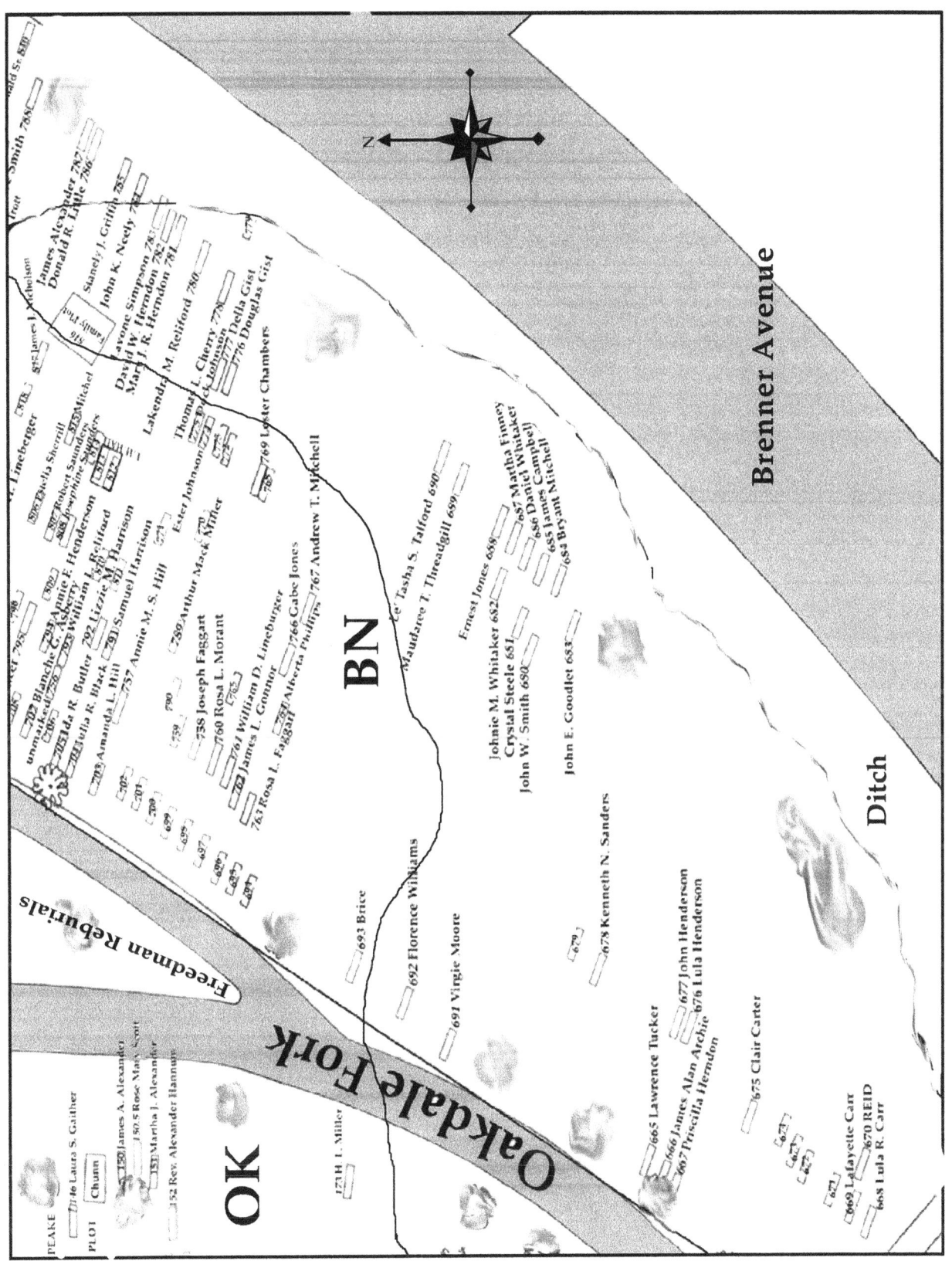

SOURCES

ARTICLES

Anonymous. "Auction Sale of Homes for Colored People." *Salisbury Evening Post*. Thursday, June 27, 1907.

Anonymous. "Liberty Street, Work of Opening Block Commenced This Morning." *Salisbury Evening Post*. July 22. 1910, Vol. 6, No. 56:8.

Bingham, Arthur Brown. "Some Light Shed On Old Cemetery." *Salisbury Post*. Editorial October 10, 1975.

Brawley, James. "The Outpost" *Salisbury Evening Post*, June 3, 1956.

Brownlee, Ann, "Stoneman's Raid: Salisbury and the Yadkin Bridge." http://www.tradingford.com/stoneman.html (accessed December 4, 2007).

McCorkle, J. M. "Salisbury Yesteryears." *Salisbury Post*, May 7, 1950 .

Post, Rose. "Unmarked Graves Located" *Salisbury Post*. November 19, 1998.

Raynor, George. "Milford Hills, Developed as a huge plantation by John and Thomas Frohock, area has a unique and colorful history of power riches." *Salisbury Sunday Post*. May 15, 1983.

BOOKS

Brawley, James. *Rowan County, a Brief History*. Raleigh, North Carolina: Department of Cultural Resources, Division of Archives and History, 1974.

Brooks, George. Alexander Sr. *Peerless Layman in the African Methodist Episcopal Zion Church, Vol. 1*. State College Pennsylvania: a. M. E. Zion Church, 1974..

Edwards, Murray, Pastor. *The People of Soldiers: Our Heritage & Our Vision*. Salisbury, North Carolina: Auli Printing & Copy Plus, Inc., 2002..

Henderson, Archibald. *Washington's Southern Tour. 1791*. Boston & New York: Houghton Mifflin Company, 1923.

Hughes, Roberta Wright. *Lay Down Body: Living History in African-American Cemeteries*. Detroit: Visible Ink Press, 1996..

Johnson, Dorothy Sharp & Williams, Lula Goosby. *Pioneering Women of the African Methodist Episcopal Zion Church.*. Charlotte NC: A.M.E. Zion Publishing House, 1997.

Petruceli, K. S., ed. *The Heritage of Rowan County Vol. I*. Rowan County, North Carolina, Genealogical Society of Rowan County Inc., 1991.

Rountree, Louise Marie, ed. *A Brief Chronological History of Black Salisbury- Rowan*. Livingstone College: Salisbury, North Carolina, 1976 .
_____. *Livingstone College, Salisbury, North Carolina 1979 – 80, Administrative Profiles for the Centennial Celebration.*. Livingstone College Centennial Publication, Salisbury, North Carolina, 1980.

Rumple, Jethro,. *A History of Rowan County North Carolina, Containing Sketches of Prominent Families and Distinguished Men.*. Baltimore: Regional Publishing Co., 1974.

Sell, Kenneth D. *Guide to the Cemeteries of Rowan County, North, Carolina.*. Salisbury, North Carolina: Unpublished, 1988.
_____.*Obscure Cemeteries of Rowan County, North Carolina.*" Salisbury, North Carolina: Unpublished, 1988..

Smith, Edwin W. *Aggrey of Africa. a study in black and white*. London: Student Christian Movement, 1929

Walls, William J. *Joseph Charles Price Educator and Race Leader*. Boston: The Christopher Publishing House, 1943

Wheeler, B. F. *Cullings From Zion's Poets*. Place of Publication Unknown: A.M.E. Zion Church, 1907.

SOURCES

COLLEGE CATALOGS

Livingstone College, *"Catalog of Livingstone College 1887-88."* Concord, North Carolina: Livingstone College Press, 1894 – 95.

_____ *"Catalogue of Livingstone College 1901, 1902-1904, 1905."* Salisbury, North Carolina: Livingstone College Press, 1901, 1904, 1905.

_____ *"Catalogue of Livingstone College 1911 – 12."* Salisbury, North Carolina & Lynchburg, Virginia: Livingstone College, 1911 – 12.

Zion Wesley College. *"Catalogue of Zion Wesley College 1884-85."* Salisbury, North Carolina.

CEMETERY MARKERS (URBAN)

North Carolina, Rowan County, Oakdale/Union Hill Cemetery, Salisbury. Photographs and tombstone data by Reginald W. Brown

CENSUS

North Carolina, Rowan County U.S. Census 1870, 1880, 1900 – 1920, population schedule, county level copy. Edith Clark History Room, Rowan Public Library, Salisbury, North Carolina

DIRECTORIES

"Directory of Salisbury, North Carolina, Vol. I." Chicago & New York: Interstate Directory Company, 1901.

Miller, Ernest H. ed. *"Salisbury – Spencer, North Carolina, City Directory, Vol. II."* Ashville, North Carolina, Piedmont Directory Co., Inc. 1910..

_____ *"Salisbury – Spencer, North Carolina, City Directory, Vol. VI."* Ashville, North Carolina, Commercial Service Co., Inc, 1910 – 1920.

_____ *"Salisbury – Spencer, North Carolina, City Directory, Vol. VI."* Ashville, North Carolina, Piedmont Directory Co., Inc., 1922 – 23.

DOCUMENTS

Charter, City of Salisbury, North Carolina, 1903, Chapter 366, Sec. 1 – 3. Ratified March 9, 1903

Clarke, Dorothy, Submitter *"Rowan County, North Carolina - Will: Thomas Frohock - 1794"*, dated February 26, 1794 US Gen Web Archives http://ftp.rootsweb.com/pub/usgenweb/nc/rowan/wills/f6200002.txt (accessed December 15, 2007)

Brown, Dave. Survey and Planning Branch, Archaeology and Historic Preservation, June 1980, North Carolina Division of Archives and History, Raleigh, North Carolina.

Brown, Dave, Consultant. National Register of Historic Places, Inventory – Nomination Form: United States Department of the Interior, Heritage Conservation and Recreation Service.

Frohock, John Jr. Last Will And Testament. Rowan County, North Carolina dated 1768..
http://www.rootsweb.com/~ncrowan/rowan_wills.htm25 (accessed November 25, 2004)

McCubbins, Mamie. Collection, Frohock file, Dead Book 6: 66, Edith M. Clark History Room, Rowan Public Library and Rowan County Register of Deeds, Salisbury, North Carolina.

_____ Collection, Frohock file, Dead Book 13: 412 - 413. Rowan Public Library and Rowan County Register of Deeds

McCubbins, J. F., Clerk of Superior Court, Rowan County, North Carolina. Deed Book 156, 271.

McCubbins, J. F., Clerk of Superior Court, Minnie Lord Henderson, Executive of Stephen F. Lord, Decedent. Statement of Real Property, Rowan County, North Carolina, March 24, 1921

SOURCES

Minutes: The City Council of Salisbury, North Carolina, November 21, 1995 4:00 p.m. OAKDALE/UNION HILL CEMETERY Page 267.

Rowan County Register of Deeds	Deed Book 47, 368	
	Deed book 98:: 184 - 185.	October 6, 1903 Registered October 13,1903
	Deed Book 145, 167	December 6, 1913
	Deed Book 145,166	January 7, 1914
	Deed Book 148, 142	March 17, 1913
	Deed Book 156, 271	May 9, 1919
	Deed Book 183,6	June 26, 1924
	Deed Book 986: 222.	September 3, 2003 (Quick Claim)

FUNERAL PROGRAMS

Duncan, John Bonner, Funeral Service Program, 1994, Hoggard Papers, Heritage Hall, Livingstone College, Salisbury, North Carolina

Kelsey, Lula S., Funeral Services for Lula Spaulding Kelsey, April 13, 1947, Noble and Kelsey Funeral Home, Salisbury, North Carolina

Kelsey, William F., Funeral Services for W. F. Kelsey, Sr. February 20, 1944, Noble and Kelsey Funeral Home, Salisbury, North Carolina

Smith, Lula Sujette Harris, Funeral Service Program, 1947, Hoggard Papers, Heritage Hall, Livingstone College, Salisbury, North Carolina

INTERVIEWS

Evans, Fred and Raemi L. A series of informal interviews with author concerning Raemi's grandparents, parents, aunt, and great aunt during the Summer of 2004 at the Aggrey family home in Salisbury, North Carolina

Hairston, Tommy, Noble and Kelsey Funeral Home, Salisbury, NC. Informal interview and tour of Oakdale Circle Section with author on April 3, 2003. at the Oakdale/Union Hill Cemetery, Salisbury, North Carolina

Mitchell, Allen L., Mitchell & Fair Funeral Services, Salisbury, NC. Personal interview and tour of Oakdale/Union Hill Cemetery, especially the Lyerly – Fair subsections given to the author in March 2003.

Mitchell, Rosalind, Mitchell & Fair Funeral Service, Salisbury, NC. Informal interview with the Author in August 2003.

Sherrill, Charles and Blanche. A series of informal interviews concerning his grandparents, parents, and uncles with the author during the summer of 2004 at the J. C. Price family home, Salisbury, North Carolina

Verly, Arletta Bingham. An informal interview with the author concerning her grandparents, parents, aunts, and other family members buried in the Oakdale/Union Hill Cemetery

MAPS

Hunnicutt & Associates. *Tax Map No. 5, City and Township of Salisbury, Rowan County*. Scale not given. Petersburg, Florida: 1907.

Jacob & George Chace, Engineers and O. W. Gray & Son. *Grays New Map of Salisbury, Rowan County, North Carolina 1882*, Philadelphia: O. W. Gray & Son Geographers and Publishers of Maps and Atlases (Reprinted by Edward H. Clement, 1973)

Kelsey, William F. & Lula S. *Union Hill Cemetery*. Scale not given. Salisbury, North Carolina: Noble and Kelsey Funeral Home (Unpublished canvas map circa 1920)

Kluttz, James W. *Early Landowners of Rowan County map sheet 3/6*. Scale not given. Landis, North Carolina, Kluttz ©1994

"Livingston Park", *Salisbury Evening Post*, June 27, 1907, p. 7.

SOURCES

Moore, Donald J. *Survey Plat of Union Hill Cemetery, Brenner Avenue, Salisbury Township, Rowan County, North Carolina.* Salisbury, North Carolina 1996

U. S. Geological Survey. Salisbury Quadrangle, North Carolina [map] Photorevised 1962. 1:24,000. 7.5 Minute Series. Washington 25, D. C. : United States Department of the Interior, USGS, 1962.

PART ONE INDEX

Aggrey, 19
   Abna, 21
   James E. K., 9, 16, xi
   James Emman K., 21
   Rose D., 1
   Rose Rudolph (Douglass), 21
   Rosebud, 9
   Rosebud D., 21
   Rosebud Douglass, xi
Ballard, Joe, 1, xii
Bingham
   Arthur Brown, 22
   Arthur Browne, xi
   Henrietta Browne, xi
   Lillington H., xi
   Lucile (Bitting), 22
   Mabel Myers, xi
Bitting, Lucile, 22
Braithwaite, Alma (Price), 21
Brawley, James S., 2
Brown
   Dr. Frank Reginald, v
   Mrs. Fletcher Jones, v
Carroll, Richard, 6
Clark, Edith M., 12
Corpening, Bessie, 21
Crittenden
   Lizzie, 22
   William Bentley, 22, xi
Curry, Adline, 22
Dale, Ellen, 1
Davie, William R., 4
Davis, Sadie, 20
Dodge
   Annie B., 14, 20
   Cecelia (Giles), 20
   Grace Marie, 20
   Mary A. (Gray), 20
   Wiley E. Jr., 1, 14, 20
   Wiley E. Sr., 14, 20
Douglass, Rose Rudolph, 21
Duncan
   Elizabeth, 20
   Ida Hauser, xi
   John Bonner, 20, xi
   Joseph C., 20
   Julia Belle, 16, 20, xi
   Lena Belle Jordan, xi, 20
   Samuel E., 16
   Samuel Edward Jr., 20
   Samuel Edward Sr., 20
Ellis
   Annie B. (Dodge), 14, 20
   Charles A., 20
Evans
   Fred, xi
   Raemi, xi

Fair
   Delbert Sepheria, 20
   James C. Sr., 20
   Mrs, James C., 1
   Rev. James C., 1
   Robert W., 20
   Sadie (Davis), 20
Ferron
   Maria, 20
   William A., 20
   William O., 20
Fowler, Mary Jane, xii
Frohoch, xiv
Frohock, xiv
   Alexander, 4
   John Jr., 4
   Thomas, 4, 6–8, 14
   William, 4
Galloway, Phyllis, xi
Getsinger, B. W., 6
Giles, Cecelia, 20
Gion, Mariah E., 21
Goler
   Emma Unthank, xi, 15, 21
   W. H., 9
   William Harvey, 16, 19, 21, xi
Graves
   Mable Harris, xi, 21
Gray, Mary A., 20
Grundy, Mayzonetta, 20
Hairston
   T. H. Sr., xii
   Tommy, 2
Hall
   Bessie (Corpening), 21
   Edmonia (Kent), 20
   Louicio Hamilton, 21
   Oliver Cleveland, 20
Hannum, William Henry, 22, xi
Harris
   C. R., 9
   Cicero Richardson, 21, xi
   Lula Sujette, 22
   Mabel, 21
   Mariah E. (Gion), 21
   Mariah Elizabeth G., xi
Hauser, Mary Anna Speas, xi
Henderson
   Ellen, 7
   Minnie Lord, xii
   Thomas, 7
Hunt
   Annie, 5
   Charles, 4
Jackson
   Andrew, 4
   Israel Joseph, 22

Johnson
   James H., 20
   Julius P., 21
   Rev. Julius P., 1
   Wiley Hezikiah, 20
Jones
   Adeline C., 1
   Adline (Curry), xi
   Bishop Raymond Luther, 11
   Carrie Lena (Smith), 22
   Julius Jackson, 22
   Mabel Miller, 11, 22
   Raymond L., 22
Jordan, Lena Belle, 20
Kelsey
   Alex, 9
   Lula, 1–2, 9
   Lula Spaulding, 6, xii
   William, 1
   William Francis, xii
   William Frank, 6
Kent, Edmonia, 20
Kluttz, James W., 2
Koontz, Elizabeth Duncan, 16, xi
Lancaster
   Abna Aggrey, xi, 21
   Spencer W., 21, xi
Lash
   Mayzonetta Grundy, 1, 20
   Rev. Wiley Hezekiah, 1
Long, John, 4
Lord
   Annie Cremonia (Macay), 5
   Stephen F., xii
   Stephen Ferrand, 5–7
   William, 5
MaCay, xiv
Macay
   Alfred, 5
   Annie Cremonia, 5
   Annie (Hunt), 5
   Judge Spruce, 4–5, xiv
   William Spruce, 5
MaCoy, xiv
Macoy, xiv
MaKay, xiv
Mason
   Mrs. Fisher R., 1
   Rev. Fisher R., 1
Massey, Arletta Bingham, xi
McCubbins
   F., xii
   F. N., 6
   N. C., 4
McNeeley, Robert Burton, 7
Miller, Isaac H. Sr., 11

PART ONE INDEX

Mitchell
  A. L., 2, 11
  Allen L., xii
  Rosalind, 2
  Rosaline, xii
Moore
  Donald, 9
  Donald J., 10
  Dr. Edward Sr., 9
  Edward Jr., 9, 21
  Edward Sr., xi
  Louise (Price), 21
  Mrs. Edward Sr., 9
  Serena L., 21
Morton, James M., 9
Noble, Frank, 21
Partee, Frank, 6
Poag, J. Edgar, 6
Price
  Alma, 21
  Emma Louise, 21
  Jennie Smallwood, xi, 9, 21
  Joseph C., xi
  Joseph Charles, 11, 16, 21, xi
  Josephine, 16, 21
  Louise, 21
  William Dodge, 21, xi
Propst, Mary, 9
Randall
  Kathleen, 1
  Thomas, 1
Raynor, George, 6
Richardson
  Mabel Harris Graves, 22
  Victoria, 16, 21–22, xi
Rountree, Dr. Louise Marie, v
Sell, Dr. Kenneth D., 12
Sherrill
  Charles Price, xi
  Jennie Louise, 21

Sherrill (continued)
  Josephine Price, xi, 16, 21
  Richard W., 21
  Richard Wadsworth, xi
Shines, Pearl, 20
Simpson, Lillian Bingham Evans, xi
Slave
  Abraham, 4
  Abram, 4
  Absolom, 4
  Bett, 4
  Bill, 4
  Bill Jr., 4
  Billy, 4
  Bristo, 4
  Clary, 4
  Darcy, 4
  Dick, 4
  Dinah, 4
  Frank, 4
  George, 4
  Grace, 4
  Jack, 4
  Mary Ann, 4
  Nanse, 4
  Nick, 4
  Patrick, 4
  Pegg, 4
  Peter, 4
  Phil, 4
  Poll, 4
  Sall, 4
  Sam, 4
  Sarah, 4
  Sharper, 4
  Such, 4
  Suck, 4
  Till, 4
  Vice, 4

Smallwood, Jennie, 21
Smith
  Carrie Lena, 22
  Herclese, 16
  Hurclese, 22
  Lottie Mae, 22
  Lula Sujette (Harris), 22
  Rev. Herclese, 1
  Thomas Jefferson Randall, 22
Spencer, Betty Dan, xii
Stevenson, Pinkney A., 1, 21
Stoneman, Gen. George, 5
Suggs, Daniel Cato, 11
Sumner, Marguerite, 20
Thomas, Eliza Holms Goler, 21
Trent
  William J., 20
  William Johnson, 11, 22
Trott
  James Garfield, 20
  Marguerite (Sumner), 20
Unthank, Emma, 21
Washington, Booker T., 6
Whittington
  Andrew, 20
  Andrew Robinson, 22
  Lottie Mae (Smith), 22
Whyte, Hattie Douglass, 21, xi
Williams
  Johnsie, 21
  Mabel Elaine, 21
Wiseman
  Annie, 9
  Robert, 9
Younge
  James Wells, 20
  Pearl (Shines), 20

Hidden Name Index, Part Two

(Names other than the main entry name, including parents, informants, names on the same tombstone, etc.)

Acey
  Amos, 41
  Jessie, 41
Adams
  Carrie, 107
  Frances, 111
  Julia, 60
  Melinda, 41
  Nat, 41
Adkins
  C. A., 41
  Henry, 187
  Ruth, 41
Aggrey
  James Emman Kwegyir, 154
  Kodwo Kwegyir, 42
  Rose Douglas, 234
  Rose Rudolph Douglas, 154
  Rosebud, 154
Agnew
  Luella, 43
  Rosa L., 43
  W. E., 42–43
  Willie, 43
Aldrich, Lilly, 54
Alexander
  Adam, 43, 165
  Alex, 43, 165
  Alexander, 44
  Charlie, 59
  Cyrous, 81
  Ella J., 55
  Ernestine, 43
  Irana, 235
  Irma, 95
  Leon, 43
  Maggie Bookhart, 78
  Mark, 94
  Martha, 43
  Terry Lee, 238
Allen
  Gertrude, 44
  Richard, 44
  Saraf, 226
Allison
  Mary A., 73
  Peter, 197
Amie, Lula, 143
Anderson
  Alexena, 186
  Annie, 112
  Ephron, 111

Anderson (continued)
  H. J., 215
  Lena, 177
  Lewis, 46
  Mary Jane, 193
  Sarah, 192
Andrew, Bessie, 179
Andrews
  Fate, 45
  Lisha, 131
  Lishia, 137
  Mary, 45
  Sophia, 94
Andua, Abna, 42
Angle, Nola, 72
Archer, Anna, 191
Archie
  Ada, 45
  Margaret K., 153
  Roxie, 240
Armstrong, Ella, 45
Arnold, Alene, 131
Asberry, Rev. E. T., 45
Ashwood
  Arthur, 46
  Florence, 46
Atkins, Annie, 211
Aubry, George, 179
Austin, Emma, 203
Authur, Peter, 242
Bailey
  Annie, 107
  James, 46
  Joe, 106
  Lula, 75
  Mattie, 201
  Willeth, 46
  Willett, 46
Baker, Susan, 127
Baldwin
  Maria, 100
  Ruth, 131
Ballard
  Joe Jr., 47
  Margaret, 47
Bameket, Clyde, 60
Banger, Mary, 95
Banks
  James B., 47
  Margie, 116
  Mary G., 47
  Moses, 149
  Peter, 47

Barber
  Bishop, 133
  Carrie, 220–221
  Francis, 161
  Frank, 234
  Henry, 48
  James, 203
  Katie, 48
  Linnie, 47
  Lucinda, 86, 132, 151
  Mollie, 48
  Ronald, 195
  Sallie, 223
  Sarah, 47
  William, 48
Barger
  Ben, 140
  Clara Mahore, 73
  Katie M., 220
Barker, Maria, 188
Barksdale, Tranham, 163
Barnhardt, Eva, 136
Barnhart, Mamie, 51
Barns, Sarah, 154
Barrett, William, 48
Barringer, Henry, 132
Barton
  Carrie T., 48
  Charleston, 172
Bates, Charlie, 89
Battle, Peter, 48
Beattie, Rev. M. C., 48
Beatty
  Donald Ray Sr., 48
  John, 80
  Nellie, 215
Beau, Alexena, 186
Bell
  Betty Holmes, 123
  Harrison, 49
  Harrison Sr., 123
  Martha, 234
Belle
  Martha Anne, 42
  Millie, 97
Belton
  Clarence, 49
  Frank, 49
  Geraldine J., 49
  Margaret, 111
  Sarah, 49
Benet, Martha, 48

Hidden Name Index, Part Two

Benjamin, W. F., 49
Bennett
  Helen C., 82
  Jack, 197
  Rachel, 197
Benson, Ella, 183
Berngardt, James Isaac, 201
Bernhardt
  James Isaac, 71
  Mattie, 103
Bernhart, Mattie, 71
Berry, Mary, 49
Berton, Prince, 138
Best, Bessie Elizabeth, 226
Bethea, John, 49
Bickson, Sandy, 187
Biggers
  Andy, 83
  James H., 50
  Marry, 50
Bingham, 96
  Arthur B., 51
  Arthur Brown, 51
  Charles, 51
  Grace, 51
  Harvey, 51
  Henry H., 51
  Lillington H., 50, 208, 239
  Mrs. Ollie, 77
Bitting
  Lucille, 50
  Robert L., 51
Black
  Bette E., 94
  Eula M., 125
  Eula Mae Heilig, 52
  Eva, 52
  James, 52
  Jim, 198, 200
  John, 52
  Lloyd, 125
  Lulu, 52
  Maria, 213
  Silas, 213
  Thomas, 52
Blackman
  Aurora D., 48
  Isabel, 52
  White, 41
Blackmer, Will, 214
Blackmon
  Charles, 52
  Lula, 52
Blackwell
  Bill, 127
  Hattie, 179

Blackwell (continued)
  Margie, 243
  Sam B., 84
Blair
  Allen, 77
  Harry, 53
  Mary, 53
  Mildred, 53
  Robert, 53
  William, 98
Blake
  Adam, 169
  Henry, 109
  Pearl, 169
Blunt
  Homer, 53
  Will, 53
Bobbitt, Gertrude, 49
Boger
  Ben, 54–55
  Clara, 106
  Elizabeth, 67
  Elsie, 55
  Henry, 54
  Janie, 54
  Lydia, 54
  Nancy, 54
  Richard, 54
  Rosa, 161
  William, 54
Boler
  Liza, 68
  Martha, 174
  Willie, 197
Bonner, Lewis, 86
Booker, George, 54
Bookhart, Jessie Davis, 54
Boozer
  Betty, 234
  Forest, 54
  Forrest T., 54
  Forrest Thomas, 216
  Susie, 54
Bost
  Ephraim, 55, 67
  John A., 55
  Lizzie, 55
  M. E., 53
  Maria, 236
  Mary Elizabeth, 234
  Odessa N., 55
  Tresa, 203
Bowens, Wilson, 214
Boyd
  Arch, 56
  Henry, 55

Boyd (continued)
  J. N., 56
  James C., 224
  Janie, 191
  Lavonia, 167
  Leliah, 175
  Lena, 153
  Mrs. Archibald, 55
Boyden
  Elizabeth, 234
  Henry, 70
  Isaac, 234
  Lauren, 56
  Sarah, 97
Bradford, Carrie, 180
Braithwaite, Alma Price, 194–195
Branch, Will, 144
Branner
  Louisa, 218
  Mary, 63
Brice
  Cedric, 162
  Mary, 44
Bridge, Ollie, 184
Bridges
  Jessie, 201
  Nancy, 136
Broadenax, Nancy, 107
Broadway
  Elizabeth, 57
  John, 57
  Juanita, 162
Brock, Lena, 233
Brooker
  Michael, 57
  Pearl, 57
Brookhart, Marion, 49
Brooks
  Cora, 68
  Isabelle, 97
Brotherton
  Margaret, 206
  Wilmer, 43
Brown
  Adline, 184
  Albert, 220
  Alberta, 196
  Alex Jr., 60
  Alexander, 60
  Amos T., 58
  Annie, 189
  Arnienta, 78, 83
  Bernadette C., 230
  Bertha Mae, 59
  Calvin, 58
  Dave, 191

Hidden Name Index, Part Two

Brown (continued)
  Debris P., 58
  Derick, 59
  Elex, 57
  Elnora, 58
  Emma, 163
  Eva, 58
  Florence, 93
  Gable, 58
  Georgia, 53
  Giles, 44
  Goldia, 59
  Jack, 74
  Lawrence T., 59
  Lilly, 58
  Louvenia, 223
  Lula, 184
  Margaret, 50, 200
  Matilda, 184
  Mattie Alexander, 58
  Mollie, 232
  Mrs. Johnie E., 90
  Ola, 108
  Phillis, 74
  Robert V., 60
  Tom, 163
  W. M., 58
  William, 50
Browne, Henrietta, 50, 208, 239
Browner, B., 60
Bruce
  Elmira, 218
  Jim, 60
  Mary, 222
Brunson, Mary Lou, 114
Bryant
  Addie, 152
  Carrie G., 110
  Emma, 61
  Nannie K., 61
  Rev. William Henry, 61
  W. H., 123
  Will, 61
  William H., 73
  William Henry, 61
Buford
  Arthur, 62
  Simon, 61, 189
Bullon, Mariah, 239
Bunyon, John, 62
Burch
  Carl, 62
  Rachel, 229
Burgin, Sylvia, 125
Burley, George, 62
Burnett, William, 163

Burns
  Dudley, 81
  Elijah, 62
  John, 244
  Ola Mae, 62
Burris, Samuel, 177
Burton
  George G., 63
  Jim, 63
  R. M., 62
  W. J., 63
  William, 218
Bush
  Josephine, 49, 123
  Juanita, 115
  Lashonda Lee, 85
Butler
  Berenza, 62
  Lewis, 63
  Usher, 62, 168
  Will Bell, 62
Butner
  Charles, 64
  Charles P., 64, 226
  Lillia Elis, 172
  Mary, 192
  Melisha, 226
  Melishie, 64
  Sandy, 64
  Victoria, 64
Byers
  Edna Ruth, 65
  Fannie, 80
  Fannie H., 104, 134–135
  George, 65
  John, 65
  John W., 65
  Mrs. Tiney, 190
  Torrance, 65
Byrd, Ernest, 65
Caldwell
  Adolphus, 66
  Catherine Waiters, 66
  Charity, 193
  Clara, 66
  Clara Mahore, 66
  Fannie, 66, 111
  Herman, 65
  John Lee, 66
  Lewis, 111
  Lewis James, 65–66
  Mary J., 190
  Melvin Archie, 74
  Rena, 66
  Richard, 67
  Sarah, 73

Caldwell (continued)
  Thelma, 74
Camp, Odell Jr., 113
Campbell
  Calvin, 135
  Della, 67
  Isaac, 67
  J. M., 221
  Josephine, 52
  Minnie, 237
  Minnie A., 55
  Rachel, 135
  Ruth Davis, 85
Cannon
  Bertha, 67
  George, 67
Canty, Maudaree, 222
Caretta, Lizzie, 204
Carlton, Dock, 198
Carol, Betsy, 65
Carough
  Archie, 147
  Mattie, 147
Carpenter
  Lonnie Ray, 200
  Lonzo, 68
  Merry L., 68
Carr
  Amanda, 68
  Carolina, 155
  Dorothy S., 69
  Jim, 68
  Lottie Mae, 100
  Margaret, 223
  Minnie, 68
  Scott, 240
  Sirler, 68
Carrington, William O., 69
Carroll
  James, 69
  Kenneth T., 69
Carson
  Bonnie, 69
  Charles, 69
  Rachel E., 158, 182
  Will, 69
Carter
  Arthur, 145
  Frank, 60
  Henry, 71
  John A., 70
  John W., 70
  Josephine, 71
  M. J., 71
  Samuel, 133
  Warren, 221

269

Hidden Name Index, Part Two

Cartha, Eliza, 95
Caruth
    Adam, 49, 103
    Mattie, 70
Catholic, Laura, 193
Chalk
    Annie Ruth, 71
    Frances, 214
Chambers
    George Anna, 230
    Herbert C. Sr., 72
    Jessie, 210
    Lester, 192
    Margie Leola, 137
    Moses, 156
Chandler, George, 118
Chapel, Mary, 112
Charles, Joseph, 57
Charleston
    Annie, 75
    Jonah, 75
Chattman, Lucy, 69
Chavis, Avara, 160
Cherry
    Fannie, 147, 192
    James W., 73
    Laura, 73
    Ruth Miller, 172
Cheshire
    Alvin H., 73
    Annie, 73
    Clarence, 73
    Leroy R., 73
Childress, Edith, 240
Chinbard, Amery, 179
Christian
    Andrew, 74
    Cicero, 74
    James, 74
    Julia, 74
    Millie, 188
    Rachel, 74
    Wiley, 74
Chun, Lula, 184
Chunn
    Neal, 69
    Rosa, 204
Clark
    Alma, 178
    Amanda, 150
    Brenda, 51
    Caroline, 143
    Daniel, 75
    James L., 74
    Maggie, 126
    Margaret, 181

Clark (continued)
    Mrs. Byron, 59
    Samuel, 75
    Will, 74, 232
Clarke, Veious, 223
Clehorne, Sarah, 179
Clement
    Jane, 162
    Jess, 75
    John, 162
    Lula, 104
    May, 138
    Merette, 47
    Zion, 47
Clemmons, Maggie, 170
Click, Adam, 114
Clingenan, Dora, 223
Clinkscales, Tom, 219
Clinton, Henry, 54
Clodfelter
    Amanda, 119
    Frank, 119
    Mary, 148
Coil
    Alexander, 76
    Willie, 76
Colbert, Dorothy, 127
Coleman
    Arthur, 186
    F. H., 77
    Francis A., 76
    Jerry, 154
Collins, Hilliard, 77
Colman
    Frank, 76
    Odessa, 134
Colston
    Fred, 77
    Gooding, 77
    Sara, 77
Condiff, Emma, 179
Connelly, Ike, 170
Connors
    John, 200
    Olden, 190
    Willie, 106
Cook
    Alberta, 128
    Clyde Innis Cook Sr., 158
    Clyde Innis Sr., 182
    Mitt, 78
    Sarah B., 117
Cooke, May Troy, 78
Copeland, Susie, 211
Coplen, Bird, 143
Cornelia, Susie, 168

Corpening, Murphy, 78
Covington, Amos, 226
Cowan
    Adam, 78
    Alex, 68
    Calmeus, 172
    Charlie, 105
    Esther Rosetta, 78
    George, 216
    Lula M., 189
    Mrs. Clinton, 219
    Neal, 72
    Roxie, 78
Crafford, Sarah, 172
Craig
    Anna, 79
    Laura, 79
    Matt, 79
Craige
    Adeline, 79
    Frank, 79
    Jefferson, 79
    Lulu, 210
Crasford, Robert, 184
Craven, Katie, 135
Craver
    Cartha H., 65
    Roy B., 80
Cravern, Mattie, 113
Crawford
    Claude, 80
    George, 80
    Isaac, 69
    Katie, 85
Crisp, Cora, 133
Crittenden
    Lizzie, 80
    Vera, 80
    William, 80
Crockett, Willie, 52, 141
Croford, William, 228
Croom, Mary Ellen, 141
Crosby
    Berry, 81
    John, 81
    Julia, 81
    Thomas, 81
Crowell
    Charlotte, 141
    William, 81
Cruze, Carrie, 185
Cundiff, Alexander, 179
Currence, Frank M., 82
Curry, Laura, 145
Cuthbertson, Katie, 72
Cuthrell, Rosa Mae, 126

Hidden Name Index, Part Two

Daniel
  Ellie, 82
  Selene, 82
Daniels, Pinky S., 163
Danley, C. L., 198
Dans, Sallie, 156
Darden, Mayola, 131
Davenport, Lobe, 212
Daves, Hattie, 84
David, Elious, 176
Davidson
  Alfred, 82
  Ellen, 82
  Essie, 82
  Frances, 144
Davis
  Alice Nicholson, 147
  Annie Mae, 216
  Bobber, 84
  Charlie, 132
  Dennis Lamont, 85
  Dora, 53
  Ezekiel, 84
  Fred, 62
  George, 84
  Georgia, 84
  Janie, 167
  Jennie Mae, 195
  Jesse, 225
  Jessie Mae, 83
  Jim, 84
  Joe, 237
  John, 83
  Josephine, 187
  Lee, 83, 85–86
  Leon, 148
  Lillie M. Mason, 163
  Linda, 55
  Lizzie, 219
  Lucy, 126
  Luther, 83
  Maggie, 83
  Marie, 86
  Mary, 84–85, 228
  Mattie L. Wood, 84
  Maude, 83
  Nannie M., 84
  Nelson, 128
  Rally, 83
  Ray, 83
  Robert, 83
  Robert E., 85–86
  Roxy, 84
  Sadie, 98, 132
  Sallie, 98
  Sam, 65

Davis (continued)
  Sandra Lyes, 86
  Susan, 143
  Tammy, 147
  Vivian Ray, 85, 148
  Wench, 83
  Wennie, 84
  Wilson, 86–87, 98
  Zilpha, 98
  Zilphia, 86
Dawkins, Susan, 87
Delmore, Mary, 76
Diggs, Hosea, 138
Dikes, Luvenia, 60
Dirk, David, 57
Dixon, William, 88
Dodge
  A., 87
  Grace, 95
  Mary, 95
  W. E., 87
  Wiley, 87
  Wiley E., 87
  Wiley E. Jr., 87, 95
  Wiley E. Sr., 87, 95, 169
Donald, Lyonell C., 88
Donaldson
  Della, 88
  Enoch, 88
  Henderson, 88
  Meryl, 88
  Nannie, 88
Douglas
  Josephine, 88
  William, 85
Douglass
  Doris, 135
  Katie, 191
  Lorene, 165
  Rose, 42
  Walter, 234
  Walter E., 42
Dowans, Anna, 177
Dowel, Mollie, 138
Dowley, Marie, 48
Drain, Geronia, 148
Dublin, Gladys, 72
Dudley
  Alex, 89
  Charles, 89
  Connie, 89
  Marie, 89
Dukes, Luvenia, 60
Duncan, 132
  Aileen Wade, 91
  Carl T., 153

Duncan (continued)
  Catherine, 90
  Fred Jr, 89
  Joseph C., 89
  Joseph Sr., 91
  L. Jr., 90
  L. Sr., 91
  Lena, 144
  Mrs. Samuel E., 123
  Samuel E., 90–91
  Samuel Edward Sr., 91–92
  Samuel E. Sr., 153
  William, 90
  William J., 93
Dunlap
  Bob, 84
  Durke, 220
Dunlop, Bob, 84
Dunn
  Sim, 180
  Sinnis, 114
Dyer, G. C., 237
Eagle, M., 88
Ealy
  Emmanuel, 93
  Florence, 93
Earl, Nettie, 131
Earnhardt, Robert, 152
Edwards
  Esther, 78
  Mrs. Gene, 228
  Norris, 233
Eigner, David, 94
Eisenhower, Charles, 60
Elder
  Jean Carol, 94
  Ruby Lee, 94
Eller
  Amanda, 118
  Dennis R., 95
  Edgar, 94
  Richard, 95, 235
Ellerbe, Nellie, 234
Elliot, Luke, 139
Ellis
  Annie B. Dodge, 87
  Charles A., 95
  Christene, 225
  David, 64, 125
  Elfrances, 190
  Emma, 117
  Emma Lee, 95
  Leroy, 73
  Letitia, 125
  Maggie Bookhart, 75
  Maria, 107

Hidden Name Index, Part Two

Ellis (continued)
  Melinda, 95
  Mollie, 76
  Mrs. Willie, 207
  Thomas, 212
Elmore, Jake, 48
Ephram, Peter, 152
Etchinson, Betty, 239
Etchison, Betty, 239
Etchson, Bettie, 239
Etheredge, Dorothy L., 211
Eury
  Johnson, 95
  Noah, 95
Evans
  Freddie M., 96
  Harry, 97
  Lillian, 50
  Lillian B., 96
  Lillie, 97
  Margaret Shinpool, 97
  Owens, 182
  Rachel, 182
  Raemi Lancaster, 154
  Robert, 96
  Robert L., 96
  Theodore, 96
  Theodore Jr., 208
  Wayne S., 96
  Willie, 96
Eveligh, Nora, 117
Everhardt
  Bradley, 97
  Martha, 97
Exum, Ida, 170
Fagatt, John, 97
Faggart
  Archie, 97
  Josephine, 97
  Katie, 189
  Phifer B., 97
  Rosa, 97
  Sadie, 97
Faggott, Annie, 179
Fair
  J. C., 98
  Rev. James, 194
  Sadie Davis, 194
Farmer
  J. F., 224
  Jennie, 187
Faulkner, Sallie, 77
Feamster
  A., 99
  Right, 99

Feaster
  Hattie, 99
  Helen C., 99
  Hough, 99
  Jean, 99
  Primas, 99
Ferbee
  Ida, 99
  John, 99
  Rebecker, 99
Ferguson
  Edwards, 99
  Gertrude, 81
  Lula, 99
  Mary Elizabeth, 84
  Plumie, 81
Ferrar, Annie, 118
Ferriber, Callie, 99
Ferron
  Annie, 119
  Mrs. M. C., 237
  William, 100, 239
Fields, Charles II, 101
Fincher, Edward, 221
Finger
  Lou Ella, 210
  Wilma, 133
Fisher
  Don, 171
  Gladys, 101
  H. Carl, 101
  H. L., 102
  Helen C., 166
  Henry, 199
  James, 101
  Janet, 175
  John, 56, 144, 185
  Josie Partee, 185
  Kerr, 102
  Maggie, 101, 103
  Norah, 101
  Rena, 101, 108
  Stokes, 101
  William, 101
Fitzgerald
  Dionne, 59
  John, 103
  Liddell, 95
Flack
  Flora, 201
  P. R., 104
Fleck, Flora, 71
Fleming
  C. J., 134
  Clarence J., 65, 104
  Herma K., 65

Flowe, Rev. C. L., 104
Flowers, Adelaide, 162
Floyd
  Bettie, 121
  Eliza, 104
  Sarah, 104
Foil
  E. L., 183
  Lawson, 105
Foot
  Emery, 238
  Halosie, 237
  Malessia L., 237
Ford
  Catherine, 105
  Martha, 138
Foster
  Ada, 241
  Claremont, 241
  George, 133
Foust, Tom, 87
Fowler
  Jasper, 110
  Laura, 71
  Marry Lee, 204
Fox
  Billy Sr, 106
  Wesley, 103
Fraley
  Edmond, 207
  Priscilla, 207
Frazier, Lottie Mae, 164
Frohock, John Sr., 106
Frost
  Valerie Lavern, 106
  William A., 186
Fuetez, Marita, 170
Gable
  Eaph, 45
  Nellie, 114
  Nellie C., 52
Gaddy, Joseph, 75
Gadson, Maggie, 78
Gaines
  George W., 74
  Lizzie, 227
  Odessa, 107
  Victoria, 106
Gainey, Isom, 240
Gaither
  Alice, 102, 228
  Della, 238
  Leon, 107
Galloway
  Annie, 107, 196
  Charlie, 107

Hidden Name Index, Part Two

Ganett, Annie, 235
Ganies, Tisha, 138
Gant, Edna, 210
Gantt, Edna, 212
Garner
    Beulah Mae, 108
    Elijah, 108
    Len, 167
Garrett, Anna, 235
Garris, Missouri, 173
Garrison
    Annie Walker, 108
    Estelle, 214
Garwood
    Annie Irena, 102
    Berry, 108
    Green Berry, 108
    Leola, 108
    Rena, 102
Gaston
    George, 223
    Gloria Dean, 232
Gay, Eliza, 117
Gee
    Kemper, 187
    Lewis, 110
George, Martha, 141
Gibson
    David, 109
    F., 174
    Frontis, 109
    Joshua, 109
    Laura, 109
    Lizzie, 174
    Mary, 87, 230
Gibson, Alex, 114
    Bob, 128
Gilchrist, Julia, 51
Giles
    Allen, 87
    Cecelia, 87, 169
Gill
    James, 109
    Loraine, 109
    Mary, 109
Gillespie, Delia, 110
Gilmore, Annie B., 110
Gilyard, Janie, 131
Gist
    Della, 110
    Lizzie, 110
    Rev. W. W., 110
    William, 60, 110
Glasca, R. G., 111
Glasco
    R. G., 110

Glasco (continued)
    Rufus, 111
Gleen
    John, 111
    Lubertha, 111
Glenn
    Clayton, 111
    Clayton L., 112
    Ella, 82
    Emanuel, 111
    Frank, 82, 111
    Lubertha, 190
    Mrs. Willie, 111
    R. F., 170
Goinnes, Mae Helen, 170
Goins, Peter, 105
Goldsmith, Alice, 223
Goler, 236
    Emma U. Unthank, 112
    Jacob, 221
    Rev. W. H., 226
    William H., 221
Gooding, Virginia, 86
Goodlett
    David, 112
    John H., 112
    Roy. L., 112
Goodman
    Darcus, 230
    Peggy, 113
Goosby, Georgiana, 202
Goosebee, Mildred, 114
Grace, Lula, 208
Graham
    Brodie, 113
    Cora, 175
    Eliza, 126
    Etta, 113
    John L. Sr., 47
    Jossie, 175
    Julius, 113
    Malinda, 192
    Margaret L., 113
    Margaret Lyerly, 47
    Mary, 47
    Rose, 113
Granford, Marie, 78
Grasty, Sam, 113
Graves
    Luella J., 144
    May, 198
Gray
    Bertha W., 114
    Cahill, 180
    Charles, 87
    Daniel, 114

Gray (continued)
    Ester, 120
    Jane, 87
    June, 142
    Mary, 87
    Sallie, 180
    Sylvia, 114
Greed, Laura, 83
Green
    Charlotte, 115
    Della, 111
    Ellen, 114
    Jessie, 114
    John, 114
Greene
    Flora, 118
    Hill, 121
Greenlee
    Julius, 114
    Nellie, 52, 141
Greer
    Jim, 214
    Stewart, 126
Gregg, Daisey, 152
Gregory
    Broadus, 173
    Jack, 173
Grey
    Ester, 134
    Mary, 95
Grier, Georgia, 216
Griffin
    Curtis E. Sr., 115
    Fannie, 165
    Mary Miller, 115
Guest
    Annie, 84
    Carrie, 187
Guider, Eugene, 115
Hacket, Linda, 220
Hairston
    Fannie, 115
    George, 220
    Henry, 96, 115
    J. W., 72
    Louise, 198
    Mrs. Pennix Jr., 115
    Nancy, 76
    Nellie, 115
    Pearl, 94
    Pennix, 115
    Sara, 82
Hall
    Abraham, 116
    Alice, 105
    Amanda, 116

Hidden Name Index, Part Two

Hall (continued)
  Angeline, 188
  Cecelia, 127
  Fannie, 95
  Gun, 116
  Harriet, 116
  Hester, 157
  Ida Bell, 149
  John, 116
  Jule, 126
  L. H., 97, 115
  Lewis, 95
  Liza, 207
  Loretta, 111
  Mack, 116
  Mary, 59, 128, 207
  Mrs. Cola, 207
  O. C., 116
  Phill, 207
  Phoebe, 68
  Robert, 158
  Samuel, 82, 116
  Willis M., 116
Halloway, Gertrude, 150
Hamilton
  Benjamin, 131
  Willie, 117
Hampton
  Major, 128
  Margerett, 176
Hancock
  Adam, 117
  Darrell, 154
  Richard E., 154
Hanna, Jessie, 62
Hannum, Samuel, 117
Harbison
  Florence, 117
  Meg, 117
  Neete, 117
Hardback, Jackson, 118
Harden
  Hope, 220
  Louise, 91
Hargrave
  Abe, 118
  Betty W., 119
  Henry, 118–119
  Janet, 115
  Jennie E., 155
  John Lewis, 115
  Lewis, 148
  Lillie Mae, 118
  Lindsey, 118
  Mary, 118
  Theodore, 119

Hargraves
  Hodges, 96
  John, 46
  Lillie Mae, 96
  Richard, 49
  Willie Mae C., 242
Harley
  Emma, 203
  Martha, 119
  Mattie, 119
  Paul, 119
  Walter, 119
Harris
  Ben, 107
  Benjamine Church, 120
  Bertha, 121
  Bessie, 216
  Bishop C. R., 122
  Charles, 119
  Charlotte, 120
  Cicero R., 53, 114, 122
  Dan, 54
  Edward, 122
  Edwards, 120
  Esther, 239
  Fannie, 195
  Fannie S., 119
  George, 136, 145
  Grace, 54
  Harrison, 44, 211
  Haseltine, 196
  Hazeltine, 211
  Henry, 121, 178
  Jacob, 120
  Jennie, 217
  John, 119
  L. Sujette, 210
  Lena, 166
  Lona, 178
  Lucille, 123
  Lula, 175
  Malinda, 121
  Mariah E., 53, 114, 120
  Martha A., 122
  Mary, 44
  Mattie, 54
  Nellie, 121–122
  Pauline, 121
  Robert, 121
  Sarah, 198
  Sujette, 145
  Westley, 121
  William, 121
  William C., 120
  William Charles, 121
  Wilson, 120–122, 169, 218

Harrison
  Earldena, 53
  Emory, 123
  Lizzie Mae, 123
Harshane, Dowell, 56
Hartley
  Mrs. Laurence, 129
  Otha, 229
  Thomas, 138
Hartman, Elex, 124
Haughton, Persila, 191
Hauser
  Columbus, 124
  Mary Anna Speas, 124
  Sanford, 90
  Sanford Henry, 123
Hawkins, Ollie, 187
Hayden
  Amanda, 115
  Ben, 105
Hayes
  Isaral, 124
  Maggie, 209
Haynes, Rankin F., 100
Haynie, Lizzie, 227
Hays, Gladys, 162
Headen
  Lula, 135
  Taylor, 135
Hearne
  Birdie Guthledge, 124
  Jake, 124
Heath
  Lorene, 137
  Lorene H., 131
  Mary, 216
  Sidney, 136
Heggins
  Jessie, 115
  John, 189
Heileg, Mollie, 164
Heilig
  Arch, 147
  David, 136
  Eliza, 136
  Eula, 125
  Larin, 51
  Mammie, 200
Hemphill, Elijah, 125
Henderson
  Abraham, 127
  Alex, 125
  Alice, 64
  Alice Ellis, 126
  Annie, 162
  Archie L., 125

Hidden Name Index, Part Two

Henderson (continued)
  Caslem, 127
  Charlotte, 180
  Clanton, 125
  Crafford, 164
  Dorothy A., 127
  Douglass, 125
  Eddie Leon, 128
  Eddie Leon Sr., 61
  Elijah, 129
  Elizabeth, 126, 128
  Ellen, 125
  Eveline, 201
  Everline, 71
  Fannie, 231
  George, 128
  Henry, 127, 129
  James, 127
  James P., 65, 128
  Joe, 126
  John, 180, 231
  John Alexander, 128
  Johnson, 126
  Leo, 127
  Lucy, 126
  Luella, 43
  Lula C., 127
  Mary, 70
  Ollie, 237
  Phifer, 126
  Sallie, 44
  Shontell Monique, 125
  Susan, 125
  Thomas, 126
  William, 127
  Winslo, 165
Henry
  George, 129
  Will, 129
Herd, Amanda, 41
Herndon
  James, 129
  Jean, 129
  Jim, 129
  Mary Jean, 129
  Mary Jean Ross, 129
  William, 130
Hester
  Fannie, 94
  Viola, 55
Hicklin, Bessie, 70
Hickman
  George, 130
  Joseph, 130
  Sallie, 130
  Susie, 130

Hickman (continued)
  William, 130
Hickumbotton, Henry, 178
Hide, Samson, 140
Hill
  Laura, 131
  Lula, 73
  Matthew J., 202
  Walter, 131
Hilton, Walter, 94
Hinson, Ned, 156
Hinton, Susan, 144
Hipps
  Eddie, 131
  Georgia, 82
  Nettie, 131
Hobson
  Adam, 86, 132, 151
  Annie, 132
  Arthur, 132
  Delia, 46
  Edwards, 132
  Lula, 204
  Magdalene, 217
  Magritte, 184
  Martha, 46, 132
  Sudie, 83, 85
  Warrick, 132
  Zoo, 132
Hodges, Lizzie, 94
Hoffman, Will, 133
Hogans
  Dennie, 215
  Margrett, 64
  Sallie, 237
Holland
  John, 80
  Johnnie, 133
Holly, Isom, 95
Holman, Lizzie, 157
Holmes
  Bettie, 108
  Betty, 49
  Lester, 133
  Louis, 108
  Tommie, 134
  William, 121
Holt
  A., 135
  Addie, 65
  Annie, 171
  Beatrice, 165
  Betty L., 161
  Edward, 134
  Francis, 135
  Francis H., 134

Holt (continued)
  John, 52, 80, 104, 134
  Julia, 171
  Julia F., 65
  Mamie, 104
  Mrs. Wilson, 135
  Robert Lee, 104
  Sarah, 134
  Susan, 134
Holtsclaw, Mary, 218
Hoover
  Pink, 135
  William Pinkney, 154
Hopkins
  Arthur, 182
  James, 136
Horley, Sarah, 139
Hornes, Willie Mae, 79
Horton
  Alice, 127
  Jesse, 136
Hosch, Linda, 128
Hoshe, Rosa, 51
Hoskins, Harriett, 124
Hostery, Annie, 179
House
  Cora, 204
  Judge, 136
Houser, Mrs. M. A., 171, 224
Houston
  Elmina Bruce, 60
  Louis, 136
Howard
  Aurther, 137
  Fannie Chambers, 72
  Julia, 63
  Prince, 180
Howell
  Brenza, 168
  James, 63
  Minnie, 80
Howie, Ellison, 164
Hudson, Eveline, 105
Huff
  Essie Mae, 109
  Lela, 216, 228
  Roy, 64
  Sallie, 64
  Victoria, 64
Hugans, Malinda, 121
Huggan, Marie, 129
Hunt
  Jane, 141
  Lottie Mae, 138
  Robert, 138
  T. O., 56

Hidden Name Index, Part Two

Hunter
  Alice, 138
  Mary, 200
  Naomia, 231
  Rev. Jimmy, 138
Hurley, Minnie, 198
Hyde, Cilices, 113
Hyler, Josephine, 197
Ingram
  Gentle, 59
  Milden, 115
  Timothy, 115
Isenhour
  Martha, 60
  Nettie, 60
Izzard, Elizabeth, 44
Izzards, Adline, 199
Jackson
  Desie Mae, 138
  Henry, 138
  Ida, 75
  Jean C., 210
  Mae B., 158
  Ned, 138
  Patricia, 114
James
  Annie, 44, 139, 146
  Geneva, 88
  Virginia, 185–186
Jameson, Cleveland, 244
Jamison
  A., 53
  John, 117
  Judge, 139
  Wade, 139
Jefferies
  Ambrose, 140
  Ermine, 82
  Hattie, 140
  J. D., 82
Jeffers, George, 202
Jefferson, Hallie, 140
Jeffries, Hattie C., 95
Jenkins
  Cale, 141
  E. H., 140
  E. K., 140
  Laura, 140
  Nellie, 126, 128
  Pattie Ann, 141
Jennings, Harry, 141
Jeter, Dave, 176
Johnson
  Andy, 143
  Annie, 56
  Annie J, 144

Johnson (continued)
  Caleb, 120, 134
  Charlie, 124
  Charlotte, 127
  Clarence, 82
  Didelia B., 142
  Dupree, 143
  Edna, 141
  Elnora, 203
  Emmanuel, 175
  Estella, 119
  Evelyn, 154
  Florence, 119
  Florence S., 120
  Frank, 144
  Gad, 117
  George, 71, 117
  Grace L., 88
  Harris, 219
  Hattie, 154
  Henry, 136, 144
  Isaiah, 195
  J. P., 144
  James, 80
  Jannie, 144
  Jennie, 59
  Jesse, 142
  John McCall, 143
  Lula F., 82
  Martha, 44
  Mary, 141
  Mary A., 64, 192
  Mary Jane, 124
  Mildred, 230
  Minnie, 52
  Naomi P., 142
  Nonie, 185
  Nonie F., 143
  Nonnie, 236
  Nonnie F., 102
  Oscar E., 119
  Peter P., 143
  Postelle, 142
  Rev. Julius P., 122
  Richard, 143
  Rilla, 219
  Robert, 141
  Susie, 143
  Tom, 230
  Walter L., 188
  Willie, 119
  Willie M., 94
  Willie Mae, 118
  Wyatt, 144

Jones
  Adline, 147, 199
  Alice, 146
  Alice H., 145
  Amanda, 170
  Anna, 160
  Beulah, 57
  Bishop R. L., 145
  Carolina, 173
  Doris, 139
  Edwards, 146
  Fannie, 117
  Felix, 147
  Gladys, 105
  Hattie, 58
  Hortense, 146
  Humphrey, 159
  Ida, 56
  Jannie, 43
  Jennie, 42–43, 218
  Julia B., 147
  Larry, 147
  Lee Clarence, 145
  Lula, 144
  Marie, 172–173
  Marion V., 146
  Rufus, 240
  Umphrey, 145
  Willie C., 146
Jordan
  Joseph, 144
  Lena, 90
  Lena B., 91, 153
  Lena Belle, 92
  Rosette, 196
Judge
  Donald, 192
  Quary, 147
  Quay, 192
Kelley, Laura S., 129
Kelly
  A. G., 147
  Alice, 156
  Arthur, 148
  Bertha, 149
  Celen, 230
  Early, 149
  Grace, 119
  James, 149
  James Sr., 148
  Louis, 148
  Mrs. Jessie B., 224
  Nathaniel, 147
  Pattie, 198
  S. L., 128

Hidden Name Index, Part Two

Kelsey
    A. R., 64, 145
    Alexander, 150
    Alexander Sr., 150
    Fannye W., 231
    Lula Spaulding, 213
    Mary, 178
    W. F., 45, 80, 105, 147, 149–150, 166
    William F. Jr., 183
Kendall, Mary, 77
Kendrick
    Jannie, 201
    Joshua, 112
Kennedy
    John, 151
    Lula, 105
Kent
    Caroline, 151
    Ollie, 243
    Tom, 116
    William, 151, 243
Kerns
    Adam, 151
    Brutus, 151
    James, 47
Kerr, Lucy, 79
Kermerly, H. S., 124
Kessler, Millie, 210
Key
    Annie Ruth, 71
    Charles, 58
Keyes, Peggie, 177
Kinball, Delphi, 209
King, James, 114
Kirk, Samantha, 184
Kirkland, Calvin, 47
Kirkley, Tammy, 147
Kiser, James N., 152
Kitchen
    Classie, 88
    Frank, 88
Knoble
    James, 158, 182
    Minnie G., 158
    Stephen, 158, 182
Knox
    Creola, 152
    Della, 153
    George S., 153
    Henry, 232
    James, 153
    Lewis, 153
    Lie Ella, 96
    Mary, 160

Koontz
    Elizabeth Duncan, 91
    Eva, 241
    George, 153
Krider, Mrs. Napoleon, 161
Lancaster
    Abna A., 42, 154
    Spencer Wellington, 154
Land, Charles, 154
Laney
    Annie, 77
    Emma, 117
Lash
    Adrienne, 140
    Elaine, 140
    Hezikiah, 155
    Jacob, 155
    Mary, 107
    Mayzonetta Grundy, 155
Lassiter
    Celestine, 155
    Thomas, 198
Lawrence
    Annie B., 126
    L. B., 126
Leach
    Harriet, 231
    Josephine, 68
    Lois I. Hinson, 155
    Margaret, 73
    Martha, 109
    Merry, 68
    Sallie, 156
    Silas, 156
Leak
    A. D., 198
    Pattie, 198
Leake, Annie, 156
Leazer, Dave, 156
Lee
    Cora, 161
    E. Spurgeon, 157
    Henry, 161
    John W., 156
    John Wesley, 157
    Willie, 131
Lenner, Linwood, 46
Leonard, Margerett, 176
Lewis
    Carrie, 235
    F. H., 209
    Mattie, 240
    Ned, 143
    William, 198
Lincoln, Mary O., 152
Linden, James, 89

Linder, Patty, 77
Lindsay
    Alice, 145, 157
    Julius, 157
Lineberger
    Hester, 158
    J. D., 158
    J. H., 158
    James, 157
    John Henry, 157
Linheymer, Alma, 204
Lipscombe, Harriet, 143
Litaker
    Alta Mills, 159
    Angeline, 182
    Blanch, 159
    Daniel, 158
    John, 159
    Julia, 158
    Julius, 158
    William, 159
Little
    Annie Mae, 162
    Isabel Belton, 159
    James R., 159
    Janie Daughters, 159
    John Robert, 159
    Zettie R., 159
Littlejohn
    Grace, 125
    J. H., 72
    Pettie, 148
Livingstone, Rachel, 230
Lloyd, Julia, 101
Lockett, Ernest J., 146
Lockhart
    Jessie, 160
    Rosa, 97
    Thomas, 97
Logan
    Carrie, 169
    William, 169
Long
    Amanda, 79
    Avery, 160
    Bud, 160
    George, 160
    Jesse, 160
    King, 159
    Leroy, 160
    Marcie, 160
Love, Louise, 157
Lowery, Emerline, 219
Luck, Elizabeth, 226

Hidden Name Index, Part Two

Luckey
  Daisey, 160
  Enoch, 160
  Laura, 44
  Nelia, 160
Lucky, Viola Wilkerson, 160
Luke
  Lewis, 159
  Sallie, 159
Lyerly
  Alfred, 161
  George, 161
  Harrison, 161
  John, 166
  John Henry, 161
  Lena, 108
  Margaret, 47, 113
  Ralph, 108
  Thaddeus, 161
Lyes, Sandra, 86
Lyles
  E. E., 213
  John, 161
  Laura, 161
Lyttle, Nelson, 161
Mack
  Daughter, 152
  Gussie, 162
  Isaac, 162
  Mamie, 235
  Oscar, 55
  Paul, 162
Macula, Hester, 58
Makeson, Mary, 235
Malone
  Julius, 104, 162
  Love, 162
  Lula, 104
  Mary, 162
Mango, Katie, 75
Mangum, T. V., 151
Manuel, Theodore, 162
Marant, Anna, 232
Maroney, Elizabeth, 73
Marrow, Mary Frances, 89
Marsh
  Dr. Frank B., 138
  Estella, 162
  Harry, 162
Marshall, Bisfie, 203
Martin
  Addie, 211
  Fred, 143
  G. W., 163
  Jake, 163
  Mary Dulin, 163

Martin (continued)
  Zema, 163
Mashare, Julia, 243
Mason
  Everette H., 85, 163
  Fannie B., 85, 163
  Fisher R., 163
  Rev. Fisher R., 85
  Thomas, 94
Massey
  Bella, 214
  Elmon, 164
  George H., 164
  William, 197
  Willie M., 164
Massy
  Henry, 164
  Julia, 164
  Sam, 164
Mathes, Annette Morant, 178
Matthews
  Ida, 123, 224
  John, 123
Maxie, Emily, 210
Maxwell, George, 164
Mayfield, Jim, 234
Mays, Eva, 119
McCain
  John, 164
  Mary, 168
McCauley, Mattie, 188
McClain, Alma, 49
McCluney
  Mrs. Bell, 222
  Odell, 244
McConalley, Martha, 188
McConnaughey
  Bertha, 165
  Lydia, 159
  Mitchell, 165
McConneaughey, Valiean, 235
McCorkle
  Aaron, 166
  Candace, 166
  Frances, 43
  J. A., 166
  James, 166
  Jessie, 56
  Laura, 166
  Lina, 103, 107
  Magritte, 165
  Margritte, 165
  Miller, 193
  Mira, 200
  P. A., 166
  Rev. P. A., 165

McCorkle (continued)
  Walter, 165
McCortell, Henry, 41
McCoskey, Diana, 165
McCoulah, Lizzie, 214
McCoy, Effie, 166
McCrary
  Young M., 166
  Younge M., 244
McCrorie, Margaret, 221
McCubbins, Silvous, 166
McCullough
  Eliza, 80
  John Junior, 167
  Lovenia, 167
  Maria, 164
  Marie, 164
  Phoebe, 200
  Sally, 109
  Tammie L., 216
McDaniel, Willie Mae, 147
McDonald
  Cresie, 80
  Roxie, 177
  Silas, 143
McDowel, Ella, 170
McDowell, Fred, 204
McElvin, Mrs. Francis, 183
McFadden, Betsy Ann, 157
McGarity
  Ambress, 167
  Wilson A., 167
McGill, Thelma, 167
McIllwain, Mary, 168
McIlwain, Mary, 168
McKain, Maude, 204
McKelley, Della, 111
McKennzie
  Ceaser, 168
  Susie, 168
McKenzie
  Alma R., 230
  Daisy, 121
McKeown
  Maggie, 241
  Richard, 241
McKinney
  Ava D., 63
  Avara, 168
  Isaac, 168
  Katie, 168
  Laura, 168
  Serlena, 168
McKinzie, Cleo, 180
McKorkle, Lina, 243
McLaughlin, Clark, 168

Hidden Name Index, Part Two

Mclean, John, 204
McLilly, Pauline, 196
McMoris, Maude, 169
McMullen, Samuel, 70
McNair, Syie, 69
McNeely
    Charlie, 169
    Nancy, 169
    Will, 169
McNinch, Lessie, 99
Medlin, Ernest, 50
Meeks
    Louis, 82
    Louise, 111
    Mamie, 111
    Samuel, 111
Melchor, Amos, 66
Melton
    Bernice M., 170
    Carl, 170
Meniers, J. A., 170
Merritt
    Elizah, 170
    Judith, 215
Metz, John, 170
Miles
    Henry, 170
    Jacob, 215
    Sally, 215
Miller
    Alexander, 172
    Alice, 88
    Alonzo, 119, 172–173
    Cora, 52
    Edward, 73, 171
    Eliza, 171
    Emma, 135
    Ethel, 163
    Frank C., 113
    George, 173
    Ida, 48, 167
    Jamie, 171
    Jean R., 161
    John, 171
    Julia, 134
    Julia F., 80
    Karen, 106
    Leola, 180
    Lizzie, 190
    Lonnie B., 173
    Mabel, 233
    Marcy A., 197
    Margrett, 171
    Maria, 171
    Marie, 119, 171
    Mary, 54, 115

Miller (continued)
    Mary B., 233
    P. R., 172
    Ruby L., 173
    Ruby Lee, 119
    Sam, 135
    Susie, 211
    Will, 171
    William, 172
Mills
    Alta, 159
    Eliza, 172
    George, 236
    Sebastien, 172
Minton, Alice, 216
Mitchell
    Annie June, 174
    Frank, 174
    Harry, 174
    John Hamilton, 174
    Josephine, 52
    Laura G., 174
    Laura Gibson, 174
    Lula, 175
    Martha, 174
    Neal, 175
    Otis, 174
    Rosaline, 215
    Silver, 174
    Trot, 175
    Willie, 174
Mobly
    William, 175
    William Anderson, 175
Moffitt, Willis, 73
Monroe
    Avis Fair Wilkins, 194
    Avis F. Wilkins, 98
    Julia Ann, 191
Montgomery
    Ava, 185
    Dora, 192–193
    Erhane, 176
    Francis, 81
    George, 176
    Marie Callie, 176
    Sara, 176
Mooney, Henry, 117
Moore
    Alveno, 232
    Annie L., 151
    Benjamin, 74
    Dr. Edward, 178
    E. H., 151
    Ed Sr., 176
    Edward, 177

Moore (continued)
    Edward MD, 140
    Etta, 175
    Eva, 177
    George, 241
    J. L., 243
    James, 177
    Julia, 80
    Kirk, 176–177
    Mary, 178, 217
    Sam, 84
    Serena, 177
    Vera M., 70
    Walter, 178
Morant
    Arminta, 188
    Charlie, 178
    Harvey Alexander, 178
    Mary, 178
    Rena, 121
    Rena Harris, 178
    Rosa, 178
    William Fred, 178
Morgan
    Fannie, 64
    Jessie, 179
Morise, Ed, 179
Morris
    Arron, 97
    Edwards, 179
    Martha, 132
    Sedie, 179
Morrison, Ionia, 138
Mors, Frances, 85
Morton
    Emma C., 179
    Eugene, 179
    Ida May, 73
    J. M., 179
    James M., 179
    William, 179
Mosely, Millie, 209
Moss
    Alice, 232
    Nelie Weldon, 226
    Susie, 76
Moton
    Joe B., 180
    Lucille, 180
Mourrey, Odessa, 125
Mullen, Jack, 180
Murdock, C. Z., 180
Murphy
    Elvie, 142
    Will, 102

Hidden Name Index, Part Two

Murry
   Montana, 46
   Odessa, 125
Musgrave, Rev. T. G., 180
Muskelley, James, 157
Neal
   Hattie, 104
   Louise, 236
Neely
   Albert, 177
   Angeline, 122
   Cynthia D., 216
   Elizabeth, 181
   Elizabeth Worthey, 181
   Frank Sr., 181
   Ivory, 181
   James, 159
   Janie B., 81
   Laura, 128
   Leonard Albert, 181
   Maggie, 158
   Margaret, 182
   Mary, 83
   Mickie, 70
   Nellie, 177
   Richard, 182
   Robert, 181
   Walter S., 55
Nichols
   Charlotte, 200
   Giles, 200
Nicholson, Joshua, 41
Nobel, Bill, 45
Noble
   Angeline, 183
   Annie, 182
   Frank, 182
   Stephen, 79, 105, 182
   Steven, 163
Norman
   Columbus, 183
   John W., 183
   Mrs. Jessie, 183
   Rosa Lee, 183
   Vivian, 156
   Vivian A., 155
Norris
   Edward, 72
   Emily, 61
   John, 184
   Mary, 72
   Ruby Louise Wilks, 183
   T. R., 183
   Theodore R. Jr., 184
   William, 123
Oalmer, Lizzie, 242

Oates, Maggie, 124
Oglesby
   Eliza, 155
   Frank, 216
   Sarah, 175
   Viola, 86
Opostal, John, 65
Ormand, Jessie, 184
Osborne
   Alex, 184
   Alice, 184
   Freeman, 184
   Henry, 74
   John, 204
Owens, Joyce, 55
Palmer
   Hattie, 141
   William, 211
Parham, James, 53, 185
Paris, Mrs. Willie, 100
Parker
   Dixie, 59
   Elsie, 71
   Johnie, 238
   Johnnie M., 238
   Johnson, 49
   Peter, 59
   William, 185
Parks
   Elsie L., 185
   John Henry, 185
Partee
   Charlotte, 172
   Jessie, 209
   Josie, 144
   Levi, 236
   Livi, 102
   Lula, 237
   M. H., 186
   Mary, 244
   Rena, 238
   Robert, 186
   William, 185–186
Paterson, Rosa Lee, 73
Patterson
   Arrilee, 107
   Jannie, 171
   Maggie Bookhart, 54
   Robert, 108
   William, 175
Payne
   Alonzo, 132, 186
   Catherine, 90, 93
   Catherine P., 93
   George, 132
   Mary, 41

Payne (continued)
   Nancy, 175
Peake
   Franklyn, 187
   Lela Josephine, 187
   Myrth, 187
Peaks, Leliah, 187
Pearson
   Daniel, 56
   Elizabeth, 101
   Fannie, 202
   Ida Bell, 187
   Jack, 187
   Jesse, 187
   Joseph, 187
   Nancy, 187
   Nicholas, 199
   Pollie, 143
Peck
   Adline, 66
   Anderson, 121
   Emeline, 121
   Martha, 108
Pedrick, Rebecca, 133
Peeler, Thomas, 96
Pemberton
   Alice, 188
   Herbert, 188
   Hubert, 188
   Rinthie, 188
   Sandy, 188
   William, 188, 196
   William P., 178
   Willie, 153
Penn, Jiminia, 170
Pennington
   Jacob, 188
   Jane, 188
   Lottie, 188
People, Mary Lizzie, 185
Perkins
   Howard, 189
   John, 189
   Laura, 188
   Lillian, 189
   Lillian B., 61
   Marie, 43
   Rosa, 96
   Ruth, 224
   William, 189
Perry
   Henry, 225
   Margaret, 225
   Maria, 127
   Mariah, 129
   Mary Ann, 127

Hidden Name Index, Part Two

Peterson, Christine, 224
Pethral, Eliza, 114
Pharr
  Louise, 128
  Miss A. B., 116
  Walter, 190
Phifer, William, 190
Phillips
  Melvin, 191
  Sallie, 65
  Willie Jr., 191
Phoroneberger
  Charles, 218
  Elmira, 218
Pierce
  Daisy, 159, 191
  Dan, 191
  Daniel, 145
  John, 191
  Julius, 191
  Mowery, 201
  Robert, 191
  Sarah, 191
Pierson, William, 209
Pike, Luvenia, 57
Pikes, Luvenia, 60
Pilgram, Wade, 191
Pinkston
  Dave, 192
  Emma, 139
  Laura, 171
  Martin, 171
  Ray, 102
  Walter, 192
Pitts
  Amie H. Judge, 193
  Annie, 147
  Frank, 193
  Gerolene, 193
  Jerry Lee, 192
  Lewis, 176, 192
  Lewis F., 192
  Lewis Frank III, 193
  Lewis Frank Sr., 193
  Richard, 192
  Sophia, 193
Poach, Ada, 233
Poag
  Alberta, 211
  James G., 193
  John, 193
Poe
  Fate, 58
  Richard, 137
Pope
  Charles, 193

Pope (continued)
  Dewilla, 166
Porterfield, Charles, 100
Poter, Lizzie, 206
Powell
  Josephine, 194
  Marie, 127
  Oliver, 194
  Prince, 194
Pratt, Ned, 164
Price
  Emma Louise, 57
  J. C., 120
  Jennie S., 205
  Jennie Smallwood, 57, 194–195
  Joseph C., 194–195, 205
  Joseph Charles, 194
  Josephine, 205
  Luther, 195
  Martha, 231
  Robert, 194
  Rufus, 195
  Ruth H., 56
  William Diedge, 57
  William Dodge, 194
Propst
  Mary, 239–240
  Robert, 195
Provoid
  Edna Ruth, 65, 128
  Mildred, 69
Provough, Annie, 98
Pryor
  Frank, 107
  M., 206
Quattlebaum
  Edward, 195
  JJ, 195
Querry, Ernest, 230
Rabb, Mary, 222
Ramseur
  Jane, 193
  Lewis, 193
  Ray, 160
  Rosa, 137
Ramseure, Tom, 41
Ramsey
  Julia, 132
  P. R., 132
Randall, Thomas, 195–196
Rankin
  Delia, 82
  Dolly, 217
  Jim, 82
  Sallie, 76

Rankins
  Delia, 134
  Fannye, 132
  John, 134
  Julia, 69
Ratsford, Bertha, 200
Read, Matilda, 214
Reese, Jerry, 225
Reeves
  Frank, 188
  Herman, 196
  Lethis, 196
  Mary, 41
  Sara, 145
  Sarah, 56
Register
  Aaron, 229
  Matilda, 229
Reid
  Ed, 197
  James, 196
  Janie, 81
  Joseph, 196
  Noah, 85
  Sallie, 156, 193
  Savannah, 214
  Willie, 196
Reliford
  Henry, 197
  Mae H., 197
Reudle, Fannie, 108
Reynolds, Harriett, 191
Rhinehardt, Mattie, 223
Rhodes
  Henry, 200
  Josephine Cowan, 200
Rice
  Harvey L., 163
  James, 68
Richardson
  Cicero, 198
  Ella, 242
  Frank, 197
  Frank N., 197
  James E., 197
  Lula Mae, 226
  Rossalie M., 197
Ricks, Carrie Bell, 141
Rippy
  Dulcie, 64
  Wilbur, 64
Rivers
  Eddie, 88
  Reuben Benjamin, 152
Robbins, Eliza, 176

Hidden Name Index, Part Two

Roberson
  David, 199
  Henrietta, 198
  Lizzie, 60
  Tom, 198
Roberts
  Alice, 137
  Basle, 215
  Doris, 171
  Doris M., 149
  John, 195
  Please, 199
  Vinetta, 215
Robins, Ola M., 45
Robinson
  Alberta, 146
  Beatrice M., 199
  Charity, 199
  Clarence, 199
  Dolly, 237
  E. D., 200
  Fannie, 199–200
  Henrietta, 212
  Jacob, 200, 237
  John, 145
  Lee, 200
  Lizzie, 221
  Loretta, 199
  Mary, 200
  Mott, 199
  Pierce, 200
  Tom, 199
  Toni, 215
  William, 221
Rodgers, Jeff, 54
Roland, Lizzie, 180
Rolland, Rev. G. W., 57
Rollinson, Ruth, 207
Roninsin, Maggie, 222
Rose
  Alice, 199
  Charles, 199, 228
  Charlie, 102
  Maggie, 101
Roseboro, Robert, 200
Rosebough, Lucinda, 149
Ross
  Durlie, 62
  Irene, 129
  Mary Jean, 129
  Maudine Mardella, 200
  William, 129
Roundtree, James, 160
Rousseau, W. G., 200
Row, Jim, 201

Rowe
  Eva, 45
  Gilder, 200
  John, 165
Rowland, Jack, 57
Rozzell, George, 212
Rush, Melvin J., 103
Russell, Eva, 201
Russill, R. P., 81
Rustin, Ruth Anna, 89
Samuel, Dorothy, 162
Sanders
  Charles E., 201
  Earlene, 211
  Henry, 201
  John, 201
  Josyline, 202
  Mary, 201
  Mrs I. J., 201
  Ruth, 201
  Sarah, 201
Sanford
  Burl, 191
  James, 191
Saunders
  E. D., 158, 182
  Hanner, 228
  Janie, 202
  Jordan, 202
  Westlong, 201
Savage
  Allace, 202
  Harriett, 202
  Willis, 202
Saver, Levi, 155
Scarborough, Doretha W., 153
Scott
  Adeline, 88
  Arthur, 202
  Bessie, 202
  Carrie, 164
  Daisy, 214
  Dan, 241
  Eliza, 173
  James D., 203
  James E., 68
  Jenette, 203
  John, 202–203, 240
  John Henry, 68
  Leroy, 203
  Lucille, 203
  Lucinda, 225
  Mabel E., 230
  Mason, 112
  Maude, 154
  Maudy, 135

Scott (continued)
  Mrs. John, 203
  Odell Jr., 202
  Vance, 202
Segal, Hattie, 139
Sellers
  Donald, 49, 203
  Elnora J., 203
  Paul, 41
  Thurman, 203
Setzer
  Alonzo, 204
  Beatrice, 208–209
  Florence, 72, 218
Shamrock, Henry, 96
Shanks, Geneva, 69
Sharp
  Abraham, 204
  Alma, 244
  W. A., 204
Sharpe
  A. R., 204
  Rev. W. A., 204
Shaver, Henry, 44, 139, 146
Shaw
  Millage, 204
  Sarah, 204
Shay, A. R., 132
Shealt, Texanna, 216
Shelton
  George, 205
  Jessie, 205
Sherrill
  Eastell, 216
  Ella, 204
  Estella, 205
  Josephine, 205
  Richard, 205
  Richard Sr., 205
Shields, Dinah, 116
Shimpoch, Henry, 96
Shimpock, Henry, 96
Shimpop, Henry, 96
Shines, Pearl, 244
Shipp
  George, 206
  George W., 206
  Gertrude, 190
  Mamie P., 206
  Wilson, 206
Shores, Mary, 124
Shuford, Ruby Lee, 223
Shuman, Leanna, 72
Simes, J. S., 206
Simmonds, Mabel E., 69

Hidden Name Index, Part Two

Simmons
  Marry, 239
  Odella, 212
  Webb, 207
  William, 207
Simpson
  Julia, 208
  Ned, 200, 208
  Phoebe, 208
  Robert, 208
  Sarah, 201
Sims, Hattie, 153
Singleton, Marie, 208
Sire, Henry, 105
Sloan
  Beulah, 73
  Eliza, 209
  Elizabeth, 240
  Frank, 208–209
  Martin, 103, 107, 243
  Rev. Abraham, 209
  Sallie, 108, 208
  Thomas, 208–209
  Will, 67
  William, 209
  Willie, 208
Small, Peter, 180
Smarr, Sarah, 184
Smith
  Albert, 110
  Alexander, 105
  Alice, 210
  Ambrose, 159
  Anderson, 211
  Andy, 55
  Annie, 238
  Arabell, 209
  Bobby, 125
  Brister, 209
  Bulah, 210
  Charles, 212
  Christine, 210
  Clara, 88, 211
  Doris, 135
  Elizabeth, 209
  Ellen, 76
  Frank, 211
  Henry, 107, 130, 209
  Hercules, 145, 210
  James, 131, 137, 211
  Joe, 210
  John, 211
  John Frank, 58
  John H., 211
  Juanita, 227

Smith (continued)
  Laura, 79, 211
  Lececilia, 64
  Lettie M., 210
  Lillie, 212
  Lizzie, 159
  Louis, 73
  Mae Bell, 174
  Magdalene, 212
  Margaret, 57
  Maria, 105
  Mary J., 217
  Minnie, 212
  Mrs. Willie M., 203
  Obadiah, 79
  Polly, 129
  Raymond, 212
  Richard, 202
  Robert L., 43
  Roland, 210
  S., 44
  Souie, 88
  Sujette, 195
  Susie, 211
  Susie C., 143
  Sylvester James, 223
  Thomas, 211
  W. T., 212
  William, 209
  Wlsie, 237
Spaulding
  Andrew, 201
  Benjamin, 213
  John, 150
  Lucy, 201
  Lucy Ann, 150
  Lula, 150
Spease
  Anna, 90
  John, 224
Spencer, Virginia, 88
Springs
  Granderson, 214
  Henry, 214
  John, 214
  Leaper, 214
  Lemly, 214
  Mamie, 214
  Robert, 214
  S., 214
Stacey, Harriet, 89
Stafford, Samuel, 214
Staley, James, 69
Standard
  Pollie, 152
  Polly, 214

Stanley
  Frances, 215
  George, 215
Stanly, Ben, 214
Starrs
  Alice, 49
  Suity, 215
Stedman, Mariah, 226
Steel, Annie, 152
Steele, Emma, 232
Stephens
  John, 216
  Mrs. Roberts, 216
  Weldon, 228
  Wilson, 216, 228
Steps, Lula, 125
Sterling
  Charlotte, 162
  John, 145
  Mary, 145
Stevenson
  Elias, 216
  Jim, 216
  Sallie M., 216
  Steve, 193
Steward, Emily, 214
Stewart
  Anna, 216
  Charlie, 216
  Hattie, 216
  Lina W., 243
  Thomas, 216
  Willie, 233
Stinson, Jackie A., 216
Stirewalt, Carrie, 186
Stith, Nancy, 130
Stockton, Lillie Mae, 165
Stokes, Margaret, 76–77
Stoner, Gertrude, 54
Stout, Mrs. Willie E., 166
Stoval, Albert, 216
Stowe, Elizabeth, 80
Stowers, George, 130
Strawder
  George, 217
  Robert, 217
Strickland, Minnie, 123
Strong
  James, 217
  Marie, 217
  Mary, 178
Sturdivant, Clayton L., 217
Suber
  Bettie, 58
  Glen, 58
Suggs, Serena L., 140

Hidden Name Index, Part Two

Summer
    Emma, 202
    Jennie, 219
    John, 72
    Otelia, 156
    Peter, 237
    Ruben, 219
    Salina, 172
Summers
    Henrietta, 143
    Margrett, 186
    Mary, 218
    Nathanial, 218
    Rachel, 182
    Web, 218
Summons, Webb, 59
Sumner
    Ida, 241
    James, 218
    John, 218
    Julius, 136
    Marguerite, 224
    Mary, 140
    Mary L., 224
    Mervin S., 49
    Otelia, 218
    W. C., 217
Sutton
    Sallie, 62
    William, 62
Swift
    Jessie, 219, 243
    Katie Lue, 243
Tabor, Mary, 142
Taggart, Prof. R. C., 219
Talford, Albert, 222
Tarce, James, 223
Tate
    Amos, 187
    Ella Louise, 93
    Emma, 187
    Julia, 114
    Willie, 220
Taylor
    Caldonia, 220
    Eunice, 220
    Jeremiah, 220
    Rhoda, 179
Teasley
    Carrie, 48, 221
    Derek, 221
    Dock, 220–221
    William, 220
Templeton
    Jane, 221
    Monroe, 221

Thirdgill
    Ellen, 221
    John, 221
    Mary, 221
Thomas
    Carol D., 167
    Charlotte, 240
    Ed, 78
    Hosetine, 44
    Janie, 153
    Robert, 234
Thompson
    Amanda, 240
    Charlotte, 69
    Eliza, 169
    Hattie, 197
    Jerry A., 222
    Mary R., 152
    Squire, 222
Thorpe, Sarah, 81
Threadgill, Andrew, 222
Thunderburk, Lizzie, 160
Tillman
    Hattie, 222
    James D., 222
Timmons, J. G., 223
Tinnen, Hortense, 146
Todd
    Addie, 148
    Laura E., 166
Tomblin
    John Arthur, 223
    Ruby J., 223
    Ruby Shuford, 223
    Willie James, 223
Tomlin, Ella, 189
Tomlinson, Walter, 190
Torence, Ephram, 223
Torrance
    Eunice, 192
    Savannah, 214
Torrence
    Gilley Odell, 223
    Hannah, 229
    Lottie, 172
    Terry Diane, 129, 223
Tott, William, 159
Travers, Armelia, 221
Trent, William J., 213
Trillon, Lula, 147
Trott
    Garfield, 224
    James Garfield, 224
    Lon, 67
    London, 223
Troutman, Mary, 48

Truesdale
    Margaret, 224
    Mildred, 224
    William, 224
Trusdel, Martha, 196
Tucker
    Fred, 141
    Frederick D., 225
    George, 140
    Johnie, 141
    Juanita D., 85
Tugman
    Delia, 53
    Joe B., 225
Turner
    Augustus, 226
    Louise, 226
    Olin A., 225
    Tamer N., 226
Turnipseed, James, 115
Tutt, Jack, 51
Tutterow, Minnie, 102
Twitty
    Eva Mae, 199
    Samuel, 199
Tyler, Marry, 63
Tyson
    Levi, 49
    Levy, 226
Unthank
    Alice Virginia, 236
    Harman, 226
Urquhart, Elizabeth, 60
Valentine, Elijah, 151
Verley, Dr. Aletta M., 50
Vinson
    Laura, 188
    Margaret, 226
    Odis, 226
    Will, 226
Wade
    Horace, 89
    Willie, 226
Waiters
    Catherine, 66
    Nevolia, 67
Walker
    Abe, 227
    Ben, 53
    Cresie, 80
    Dale, 228
    Davidson, 215
    Frank, 228
    Harold Lee, 227
    Harriet, 53
    Hattie, 222

Hidden Name Index, Part Two

Walker (continued)
  Jack, 53, 79
  Janette, 53
  Janie, 81
  John, 80, 227
  Johnnie S., 227
  Laura, 79
  Lee, 44, 222
  Lee Richard, 227
  Margaret, 180
  Mary, 227
  Sam, 196
  Scottie, 227
  Theresa J., 227
Wallace, Sam, 138
Walters
  Allen, 228
  Bessie, 140, 228
Warden, Mary Jane, 179
Ware
  Harrison, 229
  Shunta L., 229
Warner
  Andrew Jackson, 76
  Bishop A. J., 122
  Ethel, 186
Warrick, Thomas, 235
Washington
  Alice, 197
  Frank, 229
  George, 197, 229
  Mattie, 229
  Richard, 229
Watkins
  Garrison, 108
  Henry, 230
  Julia, 108
  Lula, 87
Watson
  Andrew, 230
  Connia H. Jr., 230
  Lizzie, 48
  Rena, 162
  W. W., 124
Watts, O. B., 48
Waugh
  Helen, 230
  James Andrew, 230
  Rachel, 230
Webb, J., 60
Webster
  Lula, 231
  Page, 231
  Sam, 194
Weeks
  Jannie, 231

Weeks (continued)
  Mary, 131
  Thomas Oneal, 231
Welborne
  Ann, 231
  Anthony, 231
  Eura, 231
  Eura Henderson, 231
Welch, Mary, 178
Wells
  Anna Bell, 231
  John, 156, 231
  Mary Roberts, 231
Wennmon, Lydia, 103
Westbery
  Penda V., 232
  Rufus, 232
Westbury, Annie, 232
Westlong, Mrs. J. E., 117
Wheeler, Edward Sr., 232
Whisonant
  Raymond, 232
  Sadie Welborne, 232
Whitaker
  Johnnie Blakeney, 232
  Lewis, 182
White
  Alice, 105
  Cymore, 233
  Dawson, 233
  Effie, 232
  Emma, 52
  Green, 156, 233
  Houston, 233
  J. H., 232
  J. Harman, 232
  John, 232
  Joseph, 233
  Locke, 161
  Milton, 232
  Nancy, 232
  Nina, 174
Whitner, James, 233
Whittington
  Allen, 233
  Andrew Robinson, 233
  Lottie M., 211
  Lottie Mae, 233
Whoozer
  Elizabeth, 69, 233
  Mr., 233
Whyte
  Harry A., 234
  Hattie, 154
Wilborne, Eura, 182

Wilder
  Hilary, 234
  Wesley, 234
Wilheim, Dwight R., 219
Wilkerson, John, 83
Wilkins
  Floyd, 235
  Henry, 235
  James, 235
  Paul, 235
  Pauline, 235
Wilks
  Agnes, 235
  John, 183
  Thomas, 235
Willett, Charles C., 235
Williams
  Alice, 193
  Alice V. U., 236
  Ambrose, 236
  Frank, 193
  Henry, 101, 223
  John Robert, 236
  Julia, 46
  Louise Neal, 236
  Maggie, 53
  Malik, 46
  McKinley, 236
  Moses, 236
  Pettigrew Sr., 236
  Ray, 139
  Rosa Bell, 236
  Rosa Lee, 236
  Rosco, 193
  Vina, 236
  Willie, 162
Williamson, Fannie, 88
Wilson
  Angelie, 158
  Angeline, 159
  Booker T., 237
  Caroline, 182
  Elizabeth R., 238
  Ella R., 238
  Ellen, 221
  Frank, 237
  Green, 238
  Harriet, 67
  Jake, 158
  James, 171
  John, 237–238
  Lizzie, 111
  Luther, 238
  Robert, 103
  Ross, 237
  Rufus, 239

Hidden Name Index, Part Two

Wilson (continued)
  W. W., 238
  Wilhelmina, 41
  William, 237
Winford, Leroy, 239
Wise
  Florence, 153
  Lizzie, 122
  Willie, 122
Wiseman
  Amanda, 162
  Annie, 195, 240
  Benjamin, 240
  John, 240
  Linda, 128
  Malinda, 120
  Mary, 239
  Melinda, 122
  Mrs. R. L., 119
  Noah L. III, 239
  Ollie, 240
  R. L., 118
  Robbert, 195
  Robert, 239
  Walter Lee, 240
Witherspoon
  Bob, 240
  Charles, 229
  Elveree, 77
  N., 112
  Richard, 240
  Roosevelt, 240
  Sarah, 166

Wood
  Bessie, 240
  Henry, 85
  Mattie, 85
  Watt, 240
  Winnie, 206
Woodard, Mary, 187
Woodburn
  James, 241
  Peter J., 241
Woodruff
  Ada, 241
  Annie, 241
  Edna, 233
  Henry, 241
  Joe, 241
  Minnie, 241
  William, 241
Woods
  Hanna, 243
  Mattie, 225
  Sandy, 193
Woodside
  Mary, 61, 189
  Millie, 61
  Son, 78
  Viola, 210
  William, 242
Woodson, Annie Mae, 45
Wooley
  George, 242
  Georgianna, 242
Wortha, James W., 243

Worther, Della, 110
Worthy
  Fannie, 110
  J. W., 243
  Jim, 243
Wright
  Allen, 210
  Anna, 103, 243
  Anna S., 107
  Derrick, 243
  Gladys, 242
  Hattie, 153
  James, 240
  Johnie, 243
  Katie, 219
  Phoenicia, 243
  Wesley, 243
  Will, 243
Wyatt, Rev. W. M., 205
Young
  Arthur, 244
  James, 244
  Julis, 243
  Malinda, 244
  Pearl, 47
  Will, 244
  William, 243
Younge
  James Wells, 244
  Minnie, 244
Zeal, Ella, 244

ERRATA
BURIALS

Ada Foster Woodruff
Died: 12/12/1953   Age: 72
Certificate No. 0034,0542
Parents: John Foster & ?

OK-200-O NO MARKER   Noble & Kelsey
Buried Next to Husband   Housewife
Informant: Mrs. Maggie Jackson
   Bpl.: Davie Co., NC

Lauresa Woodruff
Died: 02/23/1932   Age: 31
Certificate No. 0020,0149
Parents: James Woodruff & Rachel Summers

NO MARKER   Noble & Kelsey
Hotel Maid
Informant: Mrs. Willie Stewart
   Bpl.: Salisbury, NC

Lizora Woodruff
Died: 02/10/1946   Age: 60
Certificate No. 0030,0215
Parents: Frank Kelly

NO MARKER   Noble & Kelsey
Housewife
Informant: Eva Charles Woodruff
Bpl: Unknown

www.ingramcontent.com/pod-product-compliance
Lightning Source LLC
Chambersburg PA
CBHW081347230426
43667CB00017B/2748